D1432967

CIVILIANS IN A WORLD AT WAR, 1914–1918

CIVILIANS IN A WORLD AT WAR, 1914–1918

Tammy M. Proctor

NEW YORK UNIVERSITY PRESS
New York and London

NEW YORK UNIVERSITY PRESS
New York and London
www.nyupress.org

© 2010 by New York University
All rights reserved

Library of Congress Cataloging-in-Publication Data

Proctor, Tammy M., 1968–
Civilians in a world at war, 1914–1918 / Tammy M. Proctor.
p. cm.
Includes bibliographical references and index.
ISBN-13: 978–0–8147–6715–3 (cl : alk. paper)
ISBN-10: 0–8147–6715–x (cl : alk. paper)
ISBN-13: 978–0–8147–6780–1 (ebook)
ISBN-10: 0–8147–6780–x (ebook)
1. Civilians in war. 2. World War, 1914–1918—Social aspects. I. Title.
D524.6.P76   2010
940.3'1—dc22   2010008283

Manufactured in the United States of America
10 9 8 7 6 5 4 3 2 1

Dedicated to
Eleanor M. G. Proctor
a civilian munitions worker
and
to the memory of
Archie E. Proctor
(May 29, 1920–October 10, 1985)
a citizen-soldier in a later war

Contents

Illustrations

TABLES

Acknowledgments

The idea for this book emerged slowly as a result of two quite disparate experiences in 2001. First, a conference in Lyon, France, sponsored by the newly formed International Society for First World War Studies, challenged me to consider transnational experiences of war. Jenny Macleod and Pierre Purseigle made this conference a truly international event, for which I am most grateful. I returned from the conference on September 9, 2001, and had barely recovered from the flight when the second event occurred, the attacks of 9-11. Over the next two years, as war in Afghanistan and Iraq dominated U.S. headlines, these two experiences came together in the idea that became this book. I began to wonder where our contemporary notions of warfare and civilians had developed. Why were civilian contractors carrying out the work of war in Iraq, and why were so many Afghan and Iraqi people considered "collateral damage" in the conflict? How did volunteer armies on multiple tours of duty deal with the strain of war and how did they bridge the gap to their civilian lives? I decided to delve into these questions and others by examining the civilian experience in the First World War, which was a formative moment in the modern history of warfare.

While many of my fellow historians have questioned my sanity in taking on such a broad topic, I wanted a book that the undergraduates in my sophomore seminar could read—something that forced them to make connections and ask big questions. Given that intended audience, my first debt is to the students at Wittenberg University who have asked questions that sent me scurrying to the archives and libraries for answers. In particular, my gratitude goes to the two faculty aides who have helped me with research, Jessie Zawacki and Brian DeSantis. John Flora, who is really more of a coteacher than a student, has been a stalwart friend who always passes on his book lists and ideas about history and our contemporary world. Special thanks also to Seth Bitter for undertaking some bibliographic work. In addition to the students, my colleagues at the university have inquired after the work, read chapters, and listened to my woes. Particular thanks go to Dar Brooks Hedstrom, Margaret Goodman, Jim Huffman, Amy Livingstone, Nancy McHugh, Joe O'Connor, Chris Raffensperger, and Molly Wood, all of whom read and commented on parts of the work. Margaret Debuty has been unfailingly cheerful, and I appreciate her friendship and daily help.

Most useful in starting the project was a 2004–2005 Fulbright U.S. Scholars grant to Belgium that allowed me to spend time at the Katholieke Universiteit Leuven consulting with other scholars and using Belgian archives and libraries. In Leuven, so many people were generous with their time and ideas, including Leen Engelen, Idesbald Goddeeris, Chloe Heermans, Emiel Lambert, Patrick Pasture, Jan Rogiers, Leen Van Molle, Vincent Viaene, Louis Vos, Andries Welkentruysen, and Kaat Wils. Special thanks to Flor Buttiëns for patiently teaching me Flemish and to our friends in Leuven, especially Lance Rips and Mikhail and Liudmila Kriselev. The Fulbright scholar and alumni community in Belgium/Luxembourg is outstanding; they really make the experience meaningful and rich. Maggie Nicholson and Eddy and Elena Van Bouwel-Salles were exceptionally welcoming as we made the move to Belgium.

This project has necessitated travel to several archives, and I am grateful for funding from the Franklin Research Grant program at the American Philosophical Society and the Herbert Hoover Presidential Library Travel Grant. Wittenberg has also been generous with its financial support through sabbatical leaves and research grants over the past several years. I have also depended upon the generosity of many archivists and librarians; thanks to Alan Franklin (Manx National Library), Dominiek Dendooven (In Flanders Fields), Martine de Reu (Gent), Mark Derez (KUL), Carol Leadenham (Hoover Institution), Matt Schaefer (Herbert Hoover Presidential Library), Lucy Shelton Caswell (Cartoon Research Library), Mitch Yockelson (NARA), Jonathan Casey (National World

War I Museum), Margaret Courtney (Girlguiding UK), Paul Moynihan and Pat Styles (Scout Association), Lori Judy and Suzanne Smailes (Thomas Library), and countless staff members at the Archives Générales du Royaume, Australian War Memorial, British Library, Churchill College Archives–Cambridge, Imperial War Museum, Library of Congress, Mitchell Library (Sydney), National Archives of Australia, National Library of Ireland, National Archives UK, the Society of Friends Library–London, and the Stadsarchief Leuven.

Friends and colleagues have offered advice, criticism, resources, and good conversation. The fabulous VICKIs—Carol Engelhardt Herringer, Chris Oldstone-Moore, Rick Incorvati, Barry Milligan, and Laura Vorachek—continue to be a source of inspiration and good counsel; I will definitely be buying the beer for the group when this book appears. John Gillis, a generous advisor for almost two decades, has followed this project and offered encouragement and comment. My sincere gratitude to those who have made the time to read or discuss various aspects of the manuscript, especially Dave Barry, Jim Beach, Deborah Buffton, Emmanuel Debruyne, Vince DiGirolamo, Leen Engelen, Sue Grayzel, Nicoletta Gullace, Beatrix Hoffman, Ben Lammers, April Masten, Pat McDevitt, Tim Parsons, Tony Peffer, Rainer Pöppinghege, Susanne Terwey, Sophie de Schaepdrijver, and Larry Zuckerman. The book is much richer for the conferences, conversations, and resources developed by the International Society for First World War Studies and the global community of scholars who share their time and talents. New York University Press has been patient and helpful throughout the writing of the book; I would like to thank Eric Zinner, Emily Park, and Ciara McLaughlin as well as the anonymous reviewers.

Friends who have helped me see beyond the project and have "a real life" in the midst of work include Miguel Martinez-Saenz and Julie Holland, Patrick Braham, Nancy McHugh, Molly Wood, Darren Heilman, Martha and John Schott, and Sheryl Maisenhelder. Thanks to the Possums for keeping the music coming: Margaret Goodman, Doug Andrews, Rick Incorvati, Susan Finster, and Brenda Bertrand. My large extended family provides support and encouragement for all I do. I am grateful to the Shirley clan for putting up with me all these years: Johnnie, Brenda, Terry, Karen, Rachael, Jonathan, Lisa, and Patrick. My love and gratitude to my mother, Eleanor Proctor, and to Rex and Carole McGuire; Matt and Kim McGuire; Mindi, Kyle, and Kirstyn Crane; Gayla, Rob, Joanie, Marcie, and Jason Rich; Dennis, Anne, Katie, Lacy, and Devin Proctor; and Don, Suzy, Rachael, Savannah, and Spencer Proctor. Finally, to Todd Shirley, thanks for spending Christmas at Verdun; however, I am still ahead of you in spotting the World War I memorials.

Introduction

In war, civilians are cheap things at best.
——Ellen LaMotte, *The Backwash of War*

"I would make a good soldier," twelve-year-old Elfriede "Piete" Kuhr confided to her war diary on August 4, 1914, in her East Prussian town of Schneidemühl.[1] That same month on the other side of the developing battle lines, ten-year-old Yves Congar was playing with his toy soldiers when the Germans marched into his home town of Sedan, France.[2] Across the Channel in England, a teenaged Girl Guide packed a special bag with provisions, which she tied around her waist at night in order to "be prepared" for the call to active service in the war.[3] Meanwhile her fellow Girl Guides in Poland faced invasion of their country and banning of their organizations, while Russian Jewish children found themselves on train cars, deported to an unknown future. All these children were civilians in a world at war, faced with the sudden mobilization and militarization of their lives.

Like their adult counterparts, children found themselves caught up in a wartime world that was transforming before their eyes, forcing them to find a place in this transformed world. The actions that ordinary people decided to take in the face of war help frame the central question of this book: what does it mean to be a civilian?

This seemingly simple query delves into the heart of our modern notions of war, morality, heroism, and sacrifice. In recent wars, most

[1]

This French family is equipped for the dangers of industrial warfare with gas masks. *U.S. Signal Corps, National Archives and Records Administration.*

notably in the United States' war in Iraq begun in 2003, the generic term "civilian" almost always refers to Iraqi civilians, living in the war zones. While technically American citizens were also civilians in this war, they are rarely referred to as such. In fact, the experiences of Iraqi civilians and American civilians are nothing alike. Showing abstract "support for our troops" has little in common with the threat of roadside bombs, rolling power outages, or the presence of armed soldiers in the streets. Even U.S. civilian contractors live removed from the Iraqi civilians, under the protection and control of the American military, yet still defined as separate from soldiers, both by their pay and by their titles.

For some, war is a present and daily reality. For others, it is a distant echo, perhaps even a vague annoyance. For yet others, war blurs the lines between civilian and military identities, putting ill-prepared citizens into uniforms and calling them soldiers while simultaneously uniforming other personnel and naming them noncombatants. These odd juxtapositions and relocations, the disruptions of war, reshape identities fundamentally, but sometimes only temporarily. A civilian drafted into service as a soldier who is captured in his first battle and put in a prisoner-of-war camp looks little different than a civilian man of military age interned because he could be a soldier in his own country. Both have little experience of war or of killing, but their perceptions of self are somewhat different since one has actually worn a military uniform. Given the significance of military service as a symbol of masculinity in the twentieth century, even being a soldier for a day or a week sets a man apart from one who has never shed his civilian status.

Using World War I, the first modern, global war, as a lens, this book examines the different ways civilians work and function in a war situation. The years between 1914 and 1918 witnessed the invention of the modern "civilian," the first mentions of the "home front," and the advent of a totalizing war strategy that pitted industrial nations and their citizenries against each other. For the generation born in the late nineteenth and early twentieth centuries, civilians' role in warfare became both more and less central. In actual experience, civilians were crucial to maintaining modern industrialized warfare, yet rhetorically, armies defined civilians as separate from battle and in need of protection. World War I heralded a new era of warfare, which consolidated and expanded changes that had been building throughout the previous century, but it also instituted new notions of war. The 1914–1918 conflict witnessed the first aerial bombing of civilian populations, the first widespread concentration camps for the internment of enemy alien civilians, and an unprecedented use of civilian labor and resources for the war effort. Humanitarian relief programs for civilians became a common feature of modern society, while food became as significant as weaponry in the fight to win. Vast displacements of civilian populations shaped the contemporary world in countless ways, redrawing boundaries and creating or reviving lines of ethnic conflict.

Most strange in this new warfare was the split between civilian and soldier that emerged in popular understanding and came to define twentieth-century warfare. After all, what really separated an enlisted civilian male who donned a military uniform and carried a gun from a civilian male who made guns in a war factory under military control? Both contributed to the war effort, both were subject to governmental demands and restrictions on their lives, and both defined themselves as patriots working for the war effort. One of these men lived at the "battle front" and the other at the "home front," but nonetheless the lines between these imagined entities were not entirely clear. Civilians in the First World War were not immune from the violence of war, nor were they uninvolved in sustaining it, despite rhetoric to the contrary.

Historically, notions of what constitutes a civilian and what the civilian's role in war should be have remained almost constantly in flux. Noncombatants have never been clearly distanced from the ravages of wars. As European armies marched off to crusades in the Holy Land, they persecuted heretics and Jews in their paths, burning buildings and humans in their zeal for violence and purification. Ancient and medieval towns suffered the pain of living under siege and saw their crops destroyed by invaders time and again. Certainly destruction of civilian lives and property was a feature of the Mongol expansion across Eurasia, and during the Thirty Years War, noncombatants suffered terribly at the hands of armies living off the land and trading atrocities. Even relatively small-scale conflicts in the seventeenth and eighteenth centuries between professional armies of mercenaries involved the raiding and pillaging of homes and villages in the paths of the forces.

Despite such numerous examples of attacks on unarmed populations in time of war, the term "civilian" suggests a protected category of people who live apart from war. News reports in our world speak with outrage of the "collateral damage" inflicted on civilian lives and property, and pains are taken to distinguish between military and civilian deaths in official statistics. Clearly the word "civilian" has evolved to mean a person protected from war or an innocent victim of war. The gendered imagery of modern war is significant here. While civilians are both men and women, "civilian" assumes a particularly strong feminine connotation as it becomes a sort of shorthand for the phrase "innocent women and children." The term "civilian man" becomes an oxymoron, as states try to mobilize all adult men for service to the state. This stance stigmatizes those needed behind the lines or those unfit for service, but it bolsters the idea that soldiers (men) protect civilians (women and children) in war. These male soldiers live at the front, apart from civil society, while women and children live at home, apart from the war. Civilians in the First World War are central to the maintenance of a sense of moral outrage for populations at war, but that psychological role as justification for battle ("we must protect our women and children") mandates that civilians have nothing to do with war. They must be ideological "bystanders" to the conflict, both incapable of their own defense and divorced from the battle lines themselves. Such dichotomies played well in the propaganda produced during the war, but they failed miserably in accurately capturing the multiple identities and experiences of war that both soldiers and civilians (of both sexes) faced.

This definition of a civilian as a nonmilitary person protected from war is a relatively recent one. In English usage, the term "civilian" has undergone a transformation from the early modern period to the present. The word "civilian" does not appear in codes and laws of war explicitly until after the First World War; instead the monikers used are "unarmed inhabitants, non-combatants, and the enemy or occupied population."[4] Popularly in the late medieval and early modern periods, the word "civilian" meant a practitioner of civil law, as opposed to canon or common law. Later, as Britain's empire expanded, the word was used to describe non-military men in India (members of the East India Company). Only in the nineteenth century do references begin to appear that suggest that a "civilian" is any nonmilitary person, and it is not until the twentieth century that this definition of a civilian as a noncombatant became common parlance. In French, the term moves from its meaning of citizen or civil law to include by the 1830s the notion that *un civil* is a nonmilitary person.

As this etymological transformation was occurring, parallel developments were affecting the meaning of militaries in European societies.[5] Armies were professionalizing and shedding their rough image of the past—simultaneously becoming both more and less civilian. They were becoming more "civilian" in personnel as mandatory conscription led to the incorporation of nonprofessional soldiers into armed forces for short service periods. These citizen-soldiers were increasingly housed in purpose-built barracks rather than billeted with families, and the army emphasized military service as an exceptional period in a man's life, a short interlude of work for the nation. Military service was even used as an argument for denying full citizenship through suffrage to women because they were excluded from this service to the state.

So while ordinary male citizens lost their civilian status with conscription, the civilians who had traditionally supported armies were also purged. It was a common sight in European armies of the past to see noncombatant men selling food or driving wagons, while women guarded baggage, carried water, or sold spirits at battle fronts, and military wives were paid to cook, clean, sew, nurse, and do laundry for regiments from at least the seventeenth century to the late nineteenth century. For example, British army regulations mandated the maximum number of "official" wives allowed to accompany regiments, but many more "unofficial" women also traveled with armies in the field.[6] In fact, the British army legitimized women's presence "on the strength" (meaning that they were recognized by the army as part of the unit) by paying them for their work and subjecting them to military justice. As historian Holly Mayer has noted, "Women were ineligible for military service but not for service to the military."[7]

However, as the military professionalized in Europe in the nineteenth century and began to change its image, wagoners, sutlers (vendors), and "camp followers" were increasingly pushed out of their traditional roles as the armies incorporated such labor directly into formal battalions and services. Barton Hacker describes the process in this way: "As armies became more professional and bureaucratic—they became, in fact, more exclusively military—they also became more exclusively male, as striking parallel to the contemporary masculinization of medicine. . . . By the time of the First World War the once integral place of women in Western armies had faded from memory."[8] Hacker astutely points out that as professional history was emerging as a field in the late nineteenth century, "civilians" had already been purged from many armies, so they were virtually invisible to the military historians chronicling the wars of the past.[9]

Part of the reason for professionalizing armies was to make them more efficient and to provide better central control. Stricter military codes emerged with more standardized regulations, and the men and women civilians who had served in various capacities were excluded. Noncombatant services increasingly fell to male army battalions created for that purpose (e.g., Army Transport Corps or Quartermaster's Services), while medical services developed that funneled men into roles as physicians and women into nursing corps; other women's participation in army life became confined to sexual services in regulated brothels. Those women who were still hired to do domestic work for armies, such as cooking, sewing, and laundry, worked increasingly through offices charged with hiring and managing civilian contractors.[10] These changes in civilian access to war were further shaped by the demands of the war machine between 1914 and 1918, which led to unprecedented needs for civilian service and labor.

Civilians also served an important rhetorical purpose in modern, industrial, total warfare. Nation-states would find it difficult to mobilize troops of noncareer soldiers (ordinary civilians) to fight in an increasingly bloody and protracted war without advertising the necessity for protection of unarmed civilians. Soldiers needed a reason to fight that touched their personal lives. The "home front," in fact, served as a vital complement to the "battle front," and as an important ingredient in governmental propaganda machines. The First World War was not only a battle of strategists, generals, and ordinary soldiers, but it was also a war of bureaucrats, who orchestrated the creation of the civilian/soldier dichotomy to help sell war. The war drew in people from around the world in a variety of supporting roles. Civilians were required to produce the necessary goods for war and to fund the war effort itself, so their lives needed to be managed and monitored, just as those of the citizen-soldiers were managed. Both military and nonmilitary personnel faced rationing, conscription (either for soldiering or for work duties), restrictions on movement, and invasion of privacy (through censorship and identification papers). In short, World War I militarized civilian populations and mobilized people and resources worldwide in a way that changed understandings of warfare.

This book tells the story of the civilian as a counterpoint to the story of the soldier in the Great War, but it also asks questions about the meaning of these roles (civilian and soldier) by teasing out the nuances of the civilian experience of war during the 1914–1918 conflict and letting many of the voices from the period speak for themselves. It aims to be a broad, "global" work that demonstrates that despite differences of political structure, language, age, race, gender, class, and geographical location, civilians in all countries faced many of the same challenges in making sense of the war and their place in it. The First World War was an international conflict that crossed national, religious, and ethnic boundaries, but few historians have attempted to synthesize the various national accounts of the war. Yet this cross-national story is an important one because it captures the messiness of the wartime displacements and upheavals, many of which ignored the boundaries that scholars set for themselves in their studies.

Within this broadly global context, the chapters focus on the variety of meanings of "civilian" in wartime, showing the descriptive limits of the term. Citizen-soldiers of the Great War were rarely well-trained military professionals, and many of them maintained their civilian perspectives and aspirations, despite the interruption of the war. Chapter 1 describes the process of creating soldiers out of civilians in World War I, which involved unprecedented mobilization of resources in this era of mass armies. As the first large-scale and sustained test of the notion of the "nations in arms" since the French Revolution, the First World War demonstrated the difficulty of turning conscripts and volunteers into killers. As John Horne has noted, not only was this a military exercise; it also required a degree of political and cultural mobilization of the masses in order to succeed.[11] In some nations, such mobilization was relatively straightforward and featured the willing participation of citizens in 1914, while other governments relied on more coercive measures to uniform their nations.

Part of the transformation of civilians into soldiers required states to assign to these men special status as "warriors," creating the problem of finding labor for the less thrilling logistical work of war. Some civilian workers also enlisted or were drafted into the war effort, but as a temporary measure designed to demonstrate patriotism and service to nation. Both the soldier conscripts/volunteers and worker conscripts/volunteers coexisted in war zones, staging areas, and behind the lines, and the notion of a pure separation between civilian and military labor was a fantasy. Here, as the second chapter discusses, nations turned to gender, class, and race as lenses for separating "fighters" from "workers." States utilized their colonies, minorities within their nations, and civilians deemed unfit as soldiers (women, children, elderly men) in the support work of war, carefully maintaining the divide between "soldiers" and "noncombatants" in official descriptions. These divisions proved impossible to maintain, especially as armies relied on the labor of prisoners of war and deportees as well, leading to blurring of categories of labor.

While some of this work occurred in war zones and staging areas, much of it happened on what became euphemistically known as the "home front," which implied a domestic noncombatant zone. As a construction, the "home front" encoded the gendered language of modern war, implying a parallel but separate "civilian" effort that supported the "real" front. This home front encompassed diverse territory and experience, from the relatively untouched civilian homes of the United States to the families in France that went to bed each night to the sound of guns and the fear of invasion. Chapter 3 probes this concept of home fronts in more depth. The dual idea of home/battle front implied a neat divide between two easily defined zones, obscuring not only the overlaps between the two but also the movements between them. Civilians visited battle fronts, soldiers went on leave. Many psychological and real connections existed between the two, yet the home front had a cultural power in popular imagination in the immediate postwar period and continues to dominate understandings of the place of civilians in the First World War today.

The home/battle front divide also renders invisible the people who inhabit neither zone, those caught between the fronts or between the lines of conflict. The fourth chapter exposes these shadowy figures by examining those civilians living in occupied or operations zones. Many of these men and women found their services conscripted, as armies required food, lodging, entertainment, and work. Whether in war zones, occupied territories, or staging areas, civilians living with the daily reminders of war suffered the indignities of requisitions, billeted soldiers, forced labor, and, in some cases, terror. Their resistance to and/or collaboration with the militaries nearby put them in a different category of civilian experience than those living at home fronts that were more removed from the fighting.

In addition to those caught between the lines, there was a large group of people who moved from battle front to staging area to home front, from military to civilian and back in the course of the war: those involved in medical services. Chapter 5 examines ambulance drivers, doctors, nurses, and other medical personnel, who traversed the various theaters and fronts of the war, enjoying official "protected" status but often sharing the dangers and discipline of military life. Some were officially classified as civilians, others were pseudomilitary auxiliaries, and still others were military personnel, but their frequent crossing of civil/military boundaries and their uncertain status within the armed services made identifying their role difficult. Given their mission to save lives rather than to end them, medical personnel were often marked by the media as civilians rather than soldiers. Closely affiliated with and often coordinating with medical workers were those involved in other forms of aid and comfort during wartime, such as humanitarian workers, providers of food and clothing relief, intellectuals, scientists, clergy, and "experts" in a variety of fields. These volunteers and paid professionals physically and emotionally supported soldiers and civilians in wartime, repairing the tattered lives of those caught in the crossfire. Chapter 6 examines this shadow army of experts and volunteers who managed the war. Together, these categories of neutral humanitarian workers, experts, and medical personnel often found themselves to be civilians living among soldiers, under military oversight and negotiating the complex world of civil-military relations.

Perhaps the civilians with the most ambiguous status were those confined to internment camps around the world during the war. Imprisoned as "enemy aliens" or "undesirables," these individuals were targeted by governments concerned with policing the nation and its inhabitants, an increasingly significant role for states in World War I. Chapter 7 examines the global experience of internment from 1914 to 1920, which became a precursor for other modes of internment, detention, and concentration of civilians. The surveillance state cracked down not only on foreign elements but on internal subversion, which by the end of the war had exploded into civil unrest, labor union activity, and even revolution in various countries. The last chapter delineates some of the pressures and tensions of war that helped shape such civil disturbances. The years of 1918–1920 witnessed a rash of civil wars, revolutions, strikes, and political realignments, many of which were tied to wartime shifts. Even in areas where civil unrest did not reshape the postwar realities, conflict simmered. World War I redefined civil commemoration of war service, leading to state compensation initiatives for soldiers and widows, memorials to the dead, and a cult of memory centering on warriors and a few civil martyrs. Yet, civilians in all their variety and with their ambiguous status fit uneasily into the memory of the glorious war dead, and their postwar experiences were as likely to center on recrimination and denunciation as they were to result in a medal for war service.

On the central question of the book—what does it mean to be a civilian in wartime?—the scope of the problem should be clear. By defining civilians by what they were not—namely, not members of the armed forces—military and civil leaders left much room for ambiguity and interpretation. As Hugo Slim has persuasively argued, civilian identity "does not turn on a distinction between people as being armed or unarmed but on more complex notions of involvement and participation, including the subtle attributes of sympathy, incitement, encouragement, support, potential, coercion and choice."[12] These questions of identity raise the specter of responsibility for sustaining war, and they can easily undermine civilian status and identity, turning the notion of civilian protection into one of civilians as targets. If the whole nation is "in arms," then the whole nation must be targeted in a modern total war situation.[13] Cutting off food supplies, bombing cities, taking hostages, forcing labor—all these become not only acceptable means of making war but even indispensable requirements of the waging of war. As this book demonstrates, few remained unaffected by war despite rhetoric to the contrary. Civilians managed, funded, supplied, and derided the war effort from their vantage points at the home front and at the battle front and in between, so their importance in the state's ability to wage war cannot be underestimated.

In the First World War, perhaps the only people who rejected the war entirely were absolute pacifists who refused to labor in any way for the war effort. John Brocklesby, a religious conscientious objector in Britain, recounted his realization that the penal servitude to which he had been condemned, breaking stones, was actually a war activity. The stone, he found out, had been used to repair and build a road to a new naval aerodrome. From that point on he refused work, citing his sense of betrayal over having been tricked into working for the war. Finally, he was put to work in the prison laundry.[14] American conscientious objector Ernest Meyer tried to reason through this same question in his postwar memoir:

I object to the whole game of war, and not the mere business of shooting guns. There is no essential difference between being a soldier and patching up other men in hospitals to go out and continue the slaughter . . . to be consistent, I should commit suicide. I suppose in wartime almost all of our actions aid war in some measure. . . . [All] I can do is die, or draw a line somewhere. I've drawn a line.[15]

As Meyer notes, complicity is a tricky thing, and it seems hard to believe that war could function without the ideological and actual conscription of civilians. After all, can anyone really opt out of a modern war? Ellen LaMotte might see civilian lives as "cheap" in wartime, but nonetheless, history demonstrates that those lives are necessary to war's maintenance and success in the modern world.[16]

[1]

Citizens in Uniform

We are all conscripts.
—Christabel Pankhurst, interview in *The Egoist*

On a cold November day in 1914, Edward Casey interrupted his walk along the Barking Road in East London to enter the army recruiting office. Born of Irish parents and living in the slums of Britain's capital, sixteen-year-old Casey thought of war service as a novelty that would enliven his dreary life. Casey lied about his age to get past the first hurdle, then went for the medical inspection with "posh looking men" in white coats who asked him,

> "Have you ever had measles, scarlet fever, sore throats?" and [a] lot of other names I had never heard of. I said "no" to all the questions. Requesting that I lay on a leather couch, he put a long thing in his ears, and with a long rubber tube with a thing on the end, tested my chest, back and belly, tapping with his fingers. "Take deep breaths" examining my eyes, nose, ears, throat, and telling me to "stand up and bend over." [I heard him] saying: "I want to look up your rear." It was very embarrassing having somebody you don't know looking at, and sticking his finger up, my bum. Then he took hold of my balls, mumbling something. . . . Patting me on the shoulder, he said, "You have passed the exam."

After this somewhat harrowing and confusing medical, Casey was sent to take an oath of allegiance, assigned to the Royal Dublin Fusiliers (infantry), and told to report at Euston Station in two days' time. Casey, a

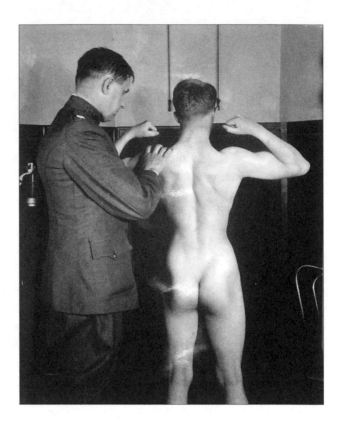

A prospective
citizen-soldier
undergoes
his medical
examination.
*U.S. Signal Corps,
National Archives
and Records
Administration.*

skinny teenager with no real job or purpose in life that November morning, was now a soldier in the British army bound for active service.[1]

Like Edward Casey, most of those enlisting or conscripted into service
for the state as soldiers, volunteers, or war workers knew little of military
life or rules. They were civilians in uniform, called to serve their nations
either through government conscription or through a sense of patriotic
responsibility. These civilians had to be taught war and its rules, and this
education extended not just to the raw recruit in the army or navy but
to the entire populace of nations at war. Civilians were called to service
in a variety of ways, and their service was reinforced through state legislation and funding, propaganda, and community mores. Success in war
depended upon a nation's ability to make all citizens willing conscripts
for war service, either through a government-sponsored draft or through

emotional or financial pressure to volunteer.[2] While some civilians required coercion to offer their services to the state, others essentially "self-mobilized" in 1914 out of a sense of moral, political, or cultural obligation.[3]

What emerged in World War I was a complicated continuum, with trained professional soldiers at one end and civilians far from the battle lines at the other end. All along this trajectory were people who fell somewhere between these extremes—citizen-soldiers eager to retain their civilian identities, prisoners of war in a state of limbo between civil and military life, civilians militarized by foreign occupation or total war. In short, the First World War made it difficult to distinguish between soldiers and civilians, between home and front, between military and civil. Nations at war called on all citizens, whether male or female, to serve the wartime state. As British suffragette Christabel Pankhurst proclaimed, "Everything which militates against the British Empire becoming a military camp until victory is assured is treason. . . . We are all conscripts."[4] This chapter explores the ways in which civilians were conscripted by the wartime states as soldiers, but also as support staff for a massive mobilization of resources. Victory in war necessitated the transformation of nations into military camps.

The Civil-Military Divide

Although the nineteenth century had brought major changes in the waging of war, the meaning of state conscription, and the notion of "civilians," it was not until the First World War that many of these ideas were tested under fire on a sustained and large-scale basis. Prior to the late eighteenth century, states had compelled men to join armed forces, but usually through occasional drafts that were far from universal or fair. For example, in Prussia, the eighteenth-century "canton" (regional) system recruited soldiers mostly from rural areas through a quota system, while in Britain recruiting drives often used coercion to target the poor and dispossessed.[5] European fighting men lived lives of violence and brutality, and common soldiers were marginalized in civil societies. Perhaps the fact that eighteenth-century armies featured more foreign-born mercenaries than "citizens" helped set armies apart from the noncombatants they encountered.[6] Most importantly, many army conscripts or volunteers in the 1700s served at least five years, and often much longer; in Russia, soldier conscripts served twenty-five years, and in Britain, their service terms averaged twenty-one years.[7] The use of mercenaries and long enlistment periods contributed to the creation of armies that had a wide range of ages, experience levels, languages, and nationalities in their camps.

This older system of military life began to transform in the late 1700s. The notion of universal military service for men—citizen armies—was largely a creation of the French Revolution with its insistence on active citizenship in the nation through the 1793 *levée en masse* (mass draft) and Conscription Law. The revolutionary government called up all unmarried men aged eighteen to twenty-five "without exception or substitution," which led to an army of almost 750,000 men by late 1794.[8] This mass draft of male citizens was predicated on the idea that nationalism required active participation from its people, not only in the form of political engagement but also in the form of national defense. France's revolutionary army, so the reasoning went, would fight harder and more passionately because it was composed of citizens fighting for an ideal, the nation. Putting the whole nation in arms meant also militarizing the so-called passive citizens as well, leading to the involvement of women, children, and the elderly in defense of the nation through logistical and economic support. This mobilization of all citizenry raised the stakes for France's opponents and led inexorably to the 1793 blockade of France, which treated the whole French populace as "a besieged town."[9] From this moment on, the civil-military divide was less clear in European wars.

The French mobilization of its nation under revolutionary leaders and during the Napoleonic period also transformed military conscription in Europe over the course of the century that followed.[10] Ordinary civilians rose to resist occupation and the presence of troops on their home turf, especially after brutal pillaging, physical harm, and requisition of basic necessities.[11] To fight the French, popular resistance movements arose in various parts of Europe, most notably in Spain and the German regions, which constituted another kind of citizen-soldiery—guerillas. These two forms of the "people in arms"—conscripted soldiers of the state and guerilla fighters—led to a broader vision of the possibilities in arming and mobilizing the masses for defense of nations and ideas.[12] The rise of popular revolutionary waves in the first half of the nineteenth century helped solidify these changes as citizens joined barricades to defend their nations.

With such ideas percolating throughout Europe early in the 1800s, Prussia passed a comprehensive conscription law in 1814, which institutionalized a draft for all men born in the nation and a permanent standing army composed of citizens. By the late nineteenth century, other European nations such as France, Romania, Italy, and Russia also began eliminating mercenaries from their ranks and creating peacetime conscription systems.[13] Armies of conscripts reshaped the way war was waged, with the increased need for "mobilizing and motivating [the whole] population through the use of propaganda."[14] These changes meant that warfare looked different to soldiers and civilians alike by the turn of the twentieth century.

By 1914, universal male conscription for military service had become a norm in both peace and wartime situations, with Britain being the only European power relying still on a small professional army and volunteer military training. Even Britain, however, had a revived Volunteer Force (1860) and by the early twentieth century, a multitude of military "preparedness" organizations, including the Officer Training Corps (1908) and the Territorial Force (1908) for men, while women could join Voluntary Aid Detachments (1909) or the First Aid Nursing Yeomanry (1907).[15] These "part-time" soldiers and nurses retained their civilian lives, jobs, and perspectives, while constituting a trained reserve force. For the middle-class men and women who "joined up" for such volunteer experiences, the "novelty of camp," the uniforms, the social life, and the prestige meant more than any practical understanding of real war preparation.[16]

In addition, Europe's frequent late nineteenth-century imperial wars created a popular enthusiasm for the idea of war, particularly since these conflicts were fought far from home using mostly colonial troops.[17] Colonial wars aimed at pacification of whole populations, making it difficult to know what victory looked like; battles were not discrete events with a clear beginning and ending but often protracted and violent conflicts that lasted years. The difference "between civilians and combatants . . . was a fluid concept," and European soldiers found themselves redefining their understandings of the enemy in the face of colonial "guerilla" resistance.[18]

Yet, few in the metropoles experienced the imperial wars as more than stories in the newspapers, just as few of the conscripts understood the real nature of war from their mandatory service. The heroic descriptions of boys' fiction did not align with the realities of the warfare that emerged in the late nineteenth and early twentieth centuries. Benito Mussolini, a conscript in World War I and later the fascist dictator of Italy, described this realization in his diary: "A dreary war.... All the picturesque attributes of the old-fashioned war have disappeared."[19] For a generation raised on tales of dashing cavalry charges in the Napoleonic Wars and exotic colonial escapades, the realities of war service came as a shock in 1914.

As war preparedness and service became a reality of life for many Europeans, notions of "civilians" changed as well with the elaboration of laws of war and the first international conventions on peace, both of which sought to codify the experience and limits of war.[20] While civilians were typically defined in opposition to military conscripts, military planners envisioned using civilian labor to fight a modern war and planned to some extent for protections of noncombatants during war. Polish banker and financier Ivan Bloch predicted the changes war would bring to European societies in his book *The Future of War* but was largely ignored by military planners as an amateur. Bloch argued in the late 1890s that the civil populations would be important in making modern war possible because "armies no longer consist of professional soldiers, but of peace-loving citizens who have no desire to expose themselves to danger."[21] Bloch cited the revolutions and colonial wars of the nineteenth century as well as conflicts such as the U.S. Civil War (1861–1865), Russo-Turkish War (1877–1878), and Franco-Prussian War (1870–1871) as his evidence that a modern European war would not be short, would not feature heroic frontal assaults, and would have a high cost in both lives and funds.[22]

While Bloch's work was read widely, pacifists rather than military planners seemed to find it most persuasive. Bloch was invited to attend the gathering of European powers in 1899 for the first Hague peace conference, convened by Tsar Nicholas II. In calling for a multinational peace convention, the tsar instructed his representatives to convene a meeting that would "by means of international discussion, [seek] the most effective means of ensuring to all peoples the benefits of a real and lasting peace."[23] At the Hague, diplomats sought guaranteed protections for soldiers and civilians during war, based upon the moral assumption that noncombatants were "men and women with rights . . . [who] cannot be used for some military purpose, even if it is a legitimate purpose."[24] A second convention in 1907 sought to extend and consolidate the rules agreed upon in 1899. These conventions were innovative, the first of their kind, and they constituted attempts to create "multilateral international" meetings that would "set out agreed rules of law."[25] However, as Nicoletta Gullace notes in her work, international conventions often relied on the arcane language of diplomat-speak, which did not capture the public imagination in the years prior to and during the war.[26] Also, the Hague conventions failed to anticipate many of the scenarios that soldiers and civilians would face in World War I, including aerial bombing and civilian internment. Other Hague rules were vaguely worded, allowing for future loopholes in interpretation.

Perhaps most importantly, despite attempts at the Hague conventions to write "rules" for war, many military leaders discounted these meetings and their outcomes, especially because there was no enforcement mechanism in place. In Germany, for instance, military treatment of enemy civilians actually became more harsh by the end of the nineteenth century, with fewer protections in law for noncombatants. In her study of military culture in Germany, Isabel Hull found not only that German officers largely ignored international law and conventions in the prewar period but also that soldier-recruits received virtually "no instruction in the laws of war."[27] Hull argues that military planners were skeptical of international agreements, and instead inculcated in their men the notion that damages to civilians and their property were "unfortunate, but in any case necessary, expedients in wartime."[28]

Even for those nations that embraced international law, the First World War almost immediately challenged many of these flimsy statutes decreed at the turn of the century and demonstrated the failures of scope in the conventions, particularly in regard to treatment of noncombatants. Understandings of "safety" in wartime changed, and World War I witnessed the birth of elaborate schemes (air raid shelters, civil defense plans, defensive structures) to shield citizens from the ravages of war, despite deliberate military tactics to target civilians through aerial bombing, blockade of food supply, and other means. Most importantly, the attempt to define a clear front with "soldiers" engaged in war and "civilians" engaged in "support" failed in many respects. As Alan Kramer has demonstrated, "the erosion of the distinction between combatants and civilians . . . between combatants and non-combatants, became more and more visible."[29] In short, the whole question of "what is war?" was being problematized.

Few of the lines were clear cut, and understandings of "civil" and "military" varied widely from nation to nation, depending on conscription rules and labor policies.[30] The presence of large numbers of poorly trained civilian-soldiers often undermined the military discipline and specialization that professional soldiers sought to inculcate. Some soldier-recruits broke the rules, were insubordinate, and often retained their civilian identities, never entirely defining themselves as soldiers. Meanwhile, civilians in uniforms of the Red Cross, ambulance corps, medical facilities, or auxiliary forces also saw themselves as soldiers for the greater cause. They prized their uniforms and the sense that they were militarized for war service. In some cases the civilian uniformed workers exhibited better discipline and understanding of army procedures than did the citizen-soldiers, further blurring distinctions between warriors and noncombatants.

With the outbreak of war and mobilization of soldiers, civilians not actively involved in the mobilization often found themselves bystanders to the drama. Historian Margaret Darrow described this strange limbo for noncombatants in the first days of the war in France: "the prescribed role was inaction—waiting, hoping—with all attention fixed upon the battlefield."[31] As the casualty lists rolled in, civilians waited anxiously for news of their soldier loved ones; Henriette Charasson expressed the despair of such waiting in a poem: "day after day the women who stayed at home must / Listen trembling to the ring of the postman's step on the threshold."[32] Yet, the war also brought activity to belie the civilian role of passive waiting that was written into the wartime script—families changed the rhythm of their lives in order to fill the gaps left with the departure of soldiers, finding replacement workers for family farms, checking casualty lists and war news, watching for spies. Others volunteered immediately for service rolling bandages, serving departing soldiers refreshments, becoming nurses or auxiliary workers. In effect, civilians had their own mobilization period that paralleled that of the soldiers.

As the war proceeded, civilians supported military establishments in a variety of ways, providing supplies, funds, and volunteer labor. Red Cross societies mobilized their membership, setting up canteens, package distribution centers, hospitals, and letter-writing agencies. Many volunteers entertained the wounded or spent time reading to soldiers, writing letters for them, or just chatting. For instance, Ethel Cooper, an Australian in Leipzig (Germany), played piano concerts at hospitals for severely wounded soldiers despite her sense of despair at seeing this destruction of the promise of youth.[33] Other civilians performed vital transport services as ambulance drivers or stretcher carriers. For example, in L'viv (Ukraine), Dr. Harry Sniveley described the innovative patient transport "on street cars specially prepared for carrying stretchers. They are carried on stretchers an eighth of a mile perhaps, from the car line to the hospital. It is an interesting sight to see the peasant women carrying those stretchers. They volunteer for the work."[34] Such casual war labor and activity was rarely recorded in contemporary media or postwar histories, but it speaks to the mobilization of civil society in wartime.

While civilians mobilized their homes and minds for war, conscripts and volunteers were facing a similar shift in worldview as they headed to fronts or to training camps. Clearly the conscripts and volunteers of the mass armies of World War I did not have homogenous life experiences, and often these men never developed strong identities as soldiers or warriors. For most, this was a necessary but temporary interlude in their real lives. Plus, the experiential divide among soldiers themselves could sometimes be great, depending on their nation's policies toward recruitment. In some nations, certain men were assigned duties far from dangerous fronts or in regiments devoted to service and supply, rather than combat. In other cases, men were rushed to the front regardless of their military preparedness or their possession of usable weapons and munitions. Medical policies regarding minimum height, weight, and fitness varied across states, leading to different levels of mobilization of male populations. Finally, political considerations and military conscription laws shaped the ways nations approached the problem of mobilizing, fielding, and supplying armies.

Table 1.1[35] presents a snapshot of some of the different national mobilization practices, demonstrating the shift to citizen armies by World War I,

TABLE 1.1.

National differences in mobilization ranges of select nations, 1914–1918[*]

Nation	Minimum Age	Maximum Age	Comments
Austria-Hungary	21	43	Volunteers taken from age 18 up to 50s
Australia	18	45	Volunteer Army, conscription referendums failed; upper age changed from 35 to 45 in 1915
Belgium[**]	20	46	Conscription. German occupation (1914–1918) disrupted Belgian system. Volunteers allowed at 16.
Brazil	21	44	Only males 21–30 called up for war service in 1917
Bulgaria	21	46	Conscription
Canada	18	45	Volunteer army until 1917
England, Scotland, Wales[**]	17	56	Volunteer army until 1916
France[**]	19	48	Conscription
Germany[**]	17	45	Conscription
Ireland	17	45	Volunteer army; 1918 conscription provoked major opposition
Italy	17	45	Draft evasion rates high
Japan	17	40	Conscription
New Zealand	20	45	Volunteer army until 1916
Ottoman Empire	18	45	Many non-Muslims in labor battalions, but subject to conscription
Romania	21	46	
Russian Empire	19	43	Draft age started at 21, but lowered to 19 in 1915
Serbia & Montenegro	21	46	
South Africa	17	60	Volunteers only—decided not to conscript after 1914 rebellion
United States	21	45	31 upper age to begin, then 45 by September 1918

[*] Note that age requirements changed throughout the war, as did enlistment requirements for height and health, but this chart reflects the broadest age range of the war for each country. Additionally, enforcement of conscription guidelines varied widely with local manipulation of the system in some regions. Lastly, such statistics only go so far in telling us about manpower availability.

[**] Policies in the European empires varied considerably, often because of local political realities, European assumptions about the "martial" nature of their colonized citizens, and the costs of implementing conscription. For instance, France recruited mainly soldiers from Senegal but laborers from Indochina; Britain deployed its Indian armies throughout the theaters of operation but used Fijian men in labor battalions.

while also illustrating the broad variety of national policies and the adjustments made as the needs of war led to demand for more men.

As the table clearly demonstrates, each national mobilization varied considerably, often based on different cultural or political atmospheres for military service, historical military traditions, and national need. However, all nations at war between 1914 and 1918 faced the difficulty of turning nonsoldiers, civilian men, into killers. Training entailed technical knowledge about how to use military equipment (rifles, bayonets, artillery pieces), but it also meant instilling "military traits as well, including toughness, alertness, loyalty and discipline."[36] Civilians had to learn to think and react like soldiers and to follow their officers' orders. Educational levels differed, as did occupational background, age, social class, and political loyalty, and questions of ethnic, racial, religious, and linguistic diversity further complicated matters. Older reservists "went to the front lines not from barracks, like regular troops, but from their homes, with virtually no period of adaptation, and their immersion in violence was immediate."[37] For many soldiers, young and old alike, there was no adjustment period, and these men were just barely in uniform when they plunged into conflict.

Mobilizing Citizens

Wars must begin at the local level with mobilization of men, and the First World War witnessed the largest mobilization in history in 1914. Officials at all levels of government turned the wheels of the war machine in July and August 1914, and for such local leaders, mobilization orders meant immediate activity to create the structures and policies of the wartime nation. B. E. Sargeaunt, who worked for the Government Office on the Isle of Man, tried to list all of his wartime duties in his postwar memoir. In addition to those most local authorities faced, such as food control, military service act enforcement, administration of national legislation, and collection of income tax, Sargeaunt also became responsible in fall 1914 for the "erection, maintenance, equipment, and civil administration of camps" for enemy aliens.[38] Retired schoolteacher Dugald Matheson found himself in August 1914 supervising enemy aliens as well, at an abandoned quarantine station on Somes Island off the coast of New Zealand.[39]

In occupation zones, the stakes were particularly high for local officials who felt responsible for guiding their citizenries in a time of widespread fear. In Leuven, Belgium, Mayor Léon Colins published almost daily assurances and calls to action beginning on August 1, 1914, and continuing until his arrest as a hostage by the German military authorities one month later. His first poster (August 1) called for calm and "sangfroid," while later in the same week, Colins announced a state of siege in the town and invited all citizens to turn in their weapons to the local constabulary. By the middle of August, as invasion of the town looked likely, Colins again urged calm and asked the citizenry not to attack the enemy forces, hoping to avoid retaliation. Colins's last official posting, on August 26, 1914, was a list of forbidden activities passed to him by the German occupying authorities. By this time, his attempts to protect the city from the invading armies had failed. For two days beginning on August 25, much of Leuven was ablaze from fires set by the German forces. At the end of the violence, more than one thousand buildings were burned, the university's medieval library was destroyed, and more than two hundred civilians had been murdered. With Colins's arrest, temporary mayor Alfred Nerincx spent much of his time dealing with unemployment, housing shortages, and an emerging black market.[40] For local officials such as Colins and Nerincx, their war featured a different front than that of their fellow citizens.

Mobilization also called for the action of a "host of semi-official and private agencies" to create the socioeconomic changes necessary.[41] In Berlin and Paris, unemployment spiked during the first weeks of the conflict, sending labor inspectors and unemployment offices into a flurry of activity.[42] Financial leaders around the world scrambled to manage stock markets and banking needs, especially as nervous investors worried about their savings. On July 30, 1914, for example, the officials at J. P. Morgan & Co. in New York called for an emergency conference of financiers to discuss informally such issues as stock prices, credit, and currency reserves.[43] In Argentina, the government suspended all commerce and banking for a "week's holiday" on August 3, 1914, while financial institutions throughout Latin America assessed the impact of the war on trade.[44]

Diplomatic communities also were thrown into disarray as they struggled to meet the needs of their citizens and to evacuate from war zones while they still could. Local dignitaries, civil servants, and foreign consuls alike were thrust into action in August 1914, even those who were not at the actual battle fronts. In neutral Denmark, officials had to walk a careful line between British and German demands in August 1914, agreeing to a German policy of mining the sea between Denmark and Germany but fighting a proposed stoppage of Danish exports to Britain. The sympathetic German envoy in Copenhagen, Ulrich Count von Brockdorff-Rantzau, used his local connections and his ties with German leaders to support Danish actions in maintaining their neutrality.[45] In Tokyo, the German ambassador spent the first few days of the war in correspondence with the Japanese foreign minister trying to determine whether Japan would be neutral, while the British ambassador requested Japanese assistance in fighting Germany.[46] Intelligence offices, like their diplomatic colleagues, planned for action in summer 1914 as well. Many of these offices were expected to round up suspected spies and to expand immediately their register of known espionage activity. Britain's counterespionage branch (named MI5 in 1916) arrested more than twenty suspected spies on August 3, 1914, the day before Britain declared war on Germany. They began watching hundreds of others, arresting more suspects as August progressed.[47]

Most nations had war plans in place that called for nationalization of certain industries and for special wartime legislation, so within the first week of the war national assemblies were busy as were local burgomasters and police. In the rural French Dordogne, for example, a telegram from the prefect to all mayors instructed them to alert residents of possible requisitions of farm animals and motorcars on July 31, while exercising "the greatest possible discretion." Two days later the Dordogne mayors publicized the mobilization decree to their citizenry.[48] City and regional officials responsible for posting notices also had to spring into action immediately. Nations with conscription often relied upon local authorities to convey call-up orders and organize men and resources for mobilization. In Serbia, peasant soldiers began descending upon towns and cities after the mobilization call went out on July 27. One eyewitness description gave a glimpse into the task local officials faced in housing and organizing new arrivals: "Convoys of peasants arrive from nearby villages and proceed to report to their district command offices. Their fathers, wives and children follow, carrying food in colourful bags. . . . War veterans . . . pass in front of us in peasant garb and footwear, wearing military caps from last year's war."[49] Labor had to be mobilized quickly as well, especially for war-related occupations. In British East Africa, provincial commissioners had to devise ways of recruiting African porters to carry goods and munitions for the expected East African campaign.[50]

With mobilization often came unrest or resistance, and local officials were expected to handle such problems. In rural Russia, one officer described a village assembly where the elder broke the news of the call-up of able-bodied men to his neighbors and friends.[51] Such local official announcements were the first harbingers of what was to come, and these officials were on the front lines of dealing with local reaction. While some reservists reported quietly for duty, others rioted or otherwise resisted in 1914. For instance, in the Tomsk province of the Russian Empire, mobs rioted to protest requisitioning of horses, closing of liquor stores, and lack of provisions for those called up for service. In another Russian city, Birsk, officials had to deal with a group of conscripts destroying their induction center.[52] When the Turkish army announced mobilization on August 3, 1914, some areas of the Ottoman Empire had to act quickly to quell unrest. For example, in Baghdad on August 6, "the Local Vali proclaimed martial law in this city as a result of objections of the local populace to being impressed into service."[53]

More serious organized disturbances threatened national solidarity as well. In South Africa, more than eleven thousand Afrikaner men who refused to be called up for service in what they considered a British cause rose in rebellion in autumn 1914. Although other factors played a role, the 1912 Defence Act and its proposed call-up of men of military age in 1914 constituted a major reason for the rebellion.[54] The 1912 legislation had also mandated a khaki uniform, which had hateful associations for Afrikaners, for whom it represented their erstwhile enemy in the Anglo-Boer War (1899–1902). Between October 1914 and the rebels' surrender in January 1915, South Africa faced the problem of simultaneously fighting an internal insurrection and raising an army for foreign service.[55]

Mobilization also strained the resources of families, especially in regions such as Aleppo (Syria), where men could either leave their families and answer the draft or try to pay for exemption. The British consul in Aleppo described this "misery and distress" in a 1914 dispatch:

Authorities made no secret that they merely aimed at wringing exemption money from such of the Christians as could pay. . . . [M]erchants and shopkeepers whose resources are paralysed by the moratorium and whose merchandise is requisitioned by the military commission have to scrape together beg or borrow sufficient cash to pay exemption money for themselves, their sons or their employees. . . . The country is being devoured by human locusts.[56]

Such demands on the population by the military rulers of what would become Syria and Lebanon helped contribute to local distress and to deepening divisions of class, religion, and ethnicity.

The Russian Empire provides an excellent example of the challenges facing military planners. When war broke out in 1914, government officials mobilized just under four million men, composed of the peacetime standing army and reserves plus the first wave of conscripts. Every few months, the government mobilized more classes, effectively lowering the draft age in 1915 to nineteen, eliminating exemptions for certain family situations/occupations, and eventually, in 1916, drafting "exempted" ethnic minorities into the army as laborers. Troubles accompanied every stage of the process, with mobilization riots in many areas in July and August 1914; with an estimated five hundred thousand desertions in the first year of the war alone; riots and strikes after the government announced the 1915 lowering of the draft age; and the outbreak of major civil disturbances in Central Asia with the labor drafts of 1916.[57] Mayhem accompanied some of these changes. For example, when the government tried to draft the Kirgiz, a Central Asian ethnic group, they had "no birth records or registration lists" so had to rely on "clan elders to submit lists of men, along with their ages. Private scores within Kirgiz society were correspondingly settled."[58] Eventually the Russian government had to divert a special force to the steppe to deal with the uprising caused by attempted mobilization. The Russian experience of mobilization led to millions of men joining the army for war service, but it also led to significant resistance, desertion, and, over time, dissatisfaction. Few of the conscripts developed a notion of themselves as anything other than civilians temporarily called to the colors. The tsar's last draft occurred on February 3, 1917, and a month later Russia erupted in revolution. The next draft of Russian people did not come until 1918, with the first Soviet "forced levy," accompanied by the inevitable resistance.[59]

As the Russian experience demonstrates, conscripting millions of men into armies was neither straightforward nor easy, and it called for repeated coercion, propaganda campaigns, and contingency plans. Despite the patriotism that fired many men's enthusiasm in 1914, for most, conscription meant abandoning jobs and families, separation from home, and a period of worry over the impact of war on all that they held dear. Those from rural backgrounds knew that mobilization meant abandoning their farms right at the crucial moment of harvest in many parts of Europe, ensuring a certain measure of economic hardship or even ruin for their families. Benjamin Ziemann found in his study of Bavaria that widespread pessimism followed the announcement of German mobilization on the community public notice board. In an account of one Bavarian parish, people were described as "highly agitated and dismayed."[60] Fear, depression, and misery were not uncommon reactions to the outbreak of war, despite accounts that suggested popular elation among certain populations.

When men entered the army, they did not leave their civilian lives behind; they took with them their fears and prejudices, their hopes and ideals. Some rejoiced at their good fortune, welcoming the excitement of war service. Jeroom Leuridan, a twenty-year-old Belgian student, recorded his joy in his diary in June 1915: "Finally! The bonds are broken. I have taken my oath. . . . I go!"[61] Other men experienced homesickness and separation anxiety. Arthur Hubbard wrote home from France in the early summer of 1916 that war was "a proper hell" and said he imagined the family "enjoying a good breakfast and me miles away in this miserable place."[62] These imaginative connections with home both sustained civilian soldiers and upset them. Yet another group of soldiers had to steel themselves for the ordeal they saw before them. David Oppenheim, a 33-year-old Jewish teacher living in Vienna, read the memoirs of Marcus Aurelius, whom he saw as "a man who was also a soldier without having the inclination for it." Never really suited for soldiering, Oppenheim nonetheless felt part of something bigger than himself and envisioned himself as "a member of an important whole that is united down to the last stride." Sent to Galicia in August 1914, Oppenheim was wounded in

October, returning to Galicia in March 1915 to serve another year in the Austro-Hungarian army.[63]

Men who resisted the call to arms or expressed reservations about the war could find themselves imprisoned or attacked by the general population. One of the most egregious social crimes in belligerent nations was "shirking" duty. Nations called their citizenry to action with the understanding that there would be a shared sacrifice. When populations perceived that sacrifice was not being evenly divided or that some were actually profiting from the war, morale broke down and civil society lost its cohesion. The war effort could be sustained only when states could convince their citizens that the cause was worthwhile, that the future was at stake, and that all were sharing in hardships.[64] Therefore, in cases where men refused to enlist or evaded conscription, civilians perceived that such men had not been sufficiently schooled in the ways of war and the needs of the nation, and they were "selfishly" undermining the war effort by not embracing their role as soldiers or patriots in a national cause.

The script denouncing shirkers was particularly pronounced in nations that did not conscript men or that conscripted soldiers only late in the war, such as Britain and Australia. Olaf Stapledon, a British pacifist writing to his Australian fiancée, summed up the popular position of 1915: "To be a pacifist and stay at home quietly needs great courage: to be a pacifist and do Red Cross work is satisfying: to be a pacifist and yet fight must be torture: to approve of war and stay at home quietly is unthinkable."[65] With such public pressure to enlist or serve, men who wanted to retain their civilian lives faced great pressure to "join up." In Britain, recruitment campaigns of 1914–1916 even featured women giving white feathers to men not wearing uniforms, signifying their cowardice and their status as "shirkers."[66] The government in New Zealand finally issued badges to convalescing men to identify them as nonshirkers and protect them from a militant public.[67]

For volunteer soldiers, the sense of obligation toward the nation could be strong, but it was often accompanied by an uneasy sense that a mistake had been made. Roland Philipps, a young man working as a Boy Scout organizer in Britain, spent considerable energy corresponding with Scouts and speaking at secondary schools, telling "yarns from the front." Despite a cheery public persona in Scout journals and in public lectures about the joys of soldiering, Philipps privately confided his misgivings and fears. To Arthur Gaddum, an intimate Scout friend in Manchester, he recorded a bit of despair:

> Last week the Chief [Robert Baden-Powell] sent me a copy of a scheme, which would, if carried through, have the effect of changing the whole basis of the Scout movement. He asked for my outspoken criticisms, and, although I was at the time in a dug-out under intermittent shellfire, yet I felt the matter so deeply. . . . I do ask you to bring every force to bear to preserve the simplicity and purity of scouting, while we are out here carrying out another year of this cruel and wasteful warfare.[68]

Earlier, Philipps had comforted Gaddum, who was not serving at the front, saying both "I loathed joining the Army, but, having done so, made up my mind to give my best to the work" and "it needs a braver man to stay out of the army than to go into it."[69] Likewise, to his friend and fellow Scout-soldier, Stanley Ince, Philipps confided in a letter his feeling that "[s]couting is more noble in its aims and more permanent in its results than soldiering."[70] Philipps died in combat at the Somme in July 1916 at age twenty-six.[71]

Ambivalent feelings about army service were not confined to the civilian-soldiers who volunteered or were drafted into national war service. Many male civilians not in military uniform had to contend with their own feelings of guilt as well as the societal pressures around them to enlist, even if they were not drafted. Well-known writer Vera Brittain, a Voluntary Aid Detachment volunteer in Malta at the time, remembered her 36-year-old uncle's anguish about his continued civilian status, which he confided to her in a 1917 letter:

> I am getting more and more ashamed of my civilian togs . . . and I shrink from meeting or speaking to soldiers or soldiers' relatives, and to take an ordinary walk on a Sunday is abominable. I cannot do anything to alter matters, for even if I walked out of the bank and joined up, I should in all probability be fetched back at once, as the Government are now making entirely their own decision as to which of us go and which stay, but the net result is real misery and the contemplation of the future if one has to confess never to have fought at all is altogether impossible.[72]

In recalling her uncle's letter, Brittain railed against a government that did not think to provide uniforms for those in "necessary" civilian posts. As her story indicates, uniforms signified membership in the nation, and for men, real masculinity. For Brittain, her uncle was also a war casualty, hounded into an early death by his civilian status.

Managing the Civil-Military Divide

The state clearly expected families to support and encourage men to answer draft calls, to enlist, and to fight, but many family members also experienced an ambivalence about the war. They wanted to be proud of their men, yet they feared the results. Fear for their loved ones' lives and health accompanied concerns for their own welfare, especially when the household depended on the soldier's wages for its maintenance. Gogo Dorothy Liwewe, a woman from Malawi, told an interviewer years later that when the men were taken to war, many of the women worried, "How were we to survive?"[73] The mass mobilization of men required that governments explain the need for male war service not only to the men themselves but also to their wives, parents, sweethearts, employers, and neighbors. Raising national citizen armies was a community endeavor, and while only male citizens were sent into combat, all citizens had to be convinced to support the war. As Dennis Showalter has explained it, "Modern conscript armies are held together by a complex interface between front and home, military and civil society, incorporating varying combinations of compulsion, patriotism and ideology. Underlying all of them, however, is an implied contract between the soldier and the system."[74] One could expand that definition to include the contract between civilians and the system as well. Sacrifices were required, and women's duties were clear: encourage men to war service, wait patiently, and support the war emotionally, physically, and materially.

Managing the connections between soldiers at the front and their friends and families became tricky as the war progressed. Some men felt the need to desert during harvest in order to insure that their families could eat, while women living close enough to the fronts desperately tried to circumvent rules in order to visit or follow their spouses and lovers. Marie Pireaud, a young French peasant married only a few months, sidestepped regulations prohibiting wives in the military zone and visited her husband at the front at least three times during the first year of the war.[75] Russian Countess O. V. Bennigsen accompanied her husband in July 1914 to his mobilization area before she began work as a nurse; they met frequently during the three years they both served.[76] When a Malawian woman, Abitisindo, found out that her husband had been called up to fight with the King's African Rifles in East Africa, she accompanied him to war in order "to eat."[77]

For those who could not see their families and friends, letters, packages, and newspapers served as vital connections between soldiers and their civilian lives. Parcels became a major way for families to support soldiers, and as Michael Roper argues for Britain, "In effect, families formed an adjunct to the army, helping to ensure that the soldier stayed clothed, well-fed and healthy."[78] This was especially true for soldiers and civilians in POW camps, where the parcels provided important sustenance as well as a morale boost. For soldiers or prisoners, the parcels meant home, and many of them were marked with sentiments that reinforced that idea; in Belgium, official parcels sent to prisoners were labeled with the phrase "a remembrance from your country."[79] Those receiving the gifts knew that they had not been forgotten.

In some cases, soldiers tried to recreate home at the front. In Vaux, France, the Liverpool Rifles named the landmarks after buildings and streets in their home city: "The officers you will find billeted in the Angel and they look out on a very doubtful Exchange Flags. Then there is Dale Street leading to Abercromby Square and a manure heap that would make the original blush."[80] In prisoner of war camps, soldiers and officers also named barracks after familiar places and created social spaces for recreating home. Belgian Paul Fredericq described the cafe at Gütersloh camp that reminded him of home; it specialized in foods from home such as mussels and featured a hand-lettered sign modeled after Belgian cafe entrances.[81] At Ruhleben camp, British civilian prisoners could do their shopping on "Bond Street" or gather in "Trafalgar Square," both named after famous London landmarks.[82] In addition, entertainments in prisoners' native languages helped pass the time; prisoner theaters flourished in many of the camps, which featured well-known plays and a festive atmosphere of a "night on the town" for men missing their civilian lives.[83]

American citizen-soldiers revert to their home pastimes on leave in France.
U.S. Signal Corps, National Archives and Records Administration.

For soldiers in occupation zones it was sometimes possible to befriend locals, especially those with whom they had regular contact in billeted homes, cafés, or shops. Soldiers surrounded themselves with reminders of home and identity where they could; when they interacted with civilians in villages it was not unusual for soldiers to play games with local children, perhaps thinking of their own kids at home. Furloughs, when they could get them, were opportunities for soldiers to reclaim their civilian lives, however briefly, but they also meant reenacting the pain of separation again when it was time to return to the front.[84]

Certainly soldiers also engaged in intimate relationships with civilians—friendships, casual sexual liaisons, and long-term relationships. Throughout the battle and occupation zones, sexual relationships provided a primary connection between military personnel and civilians. In an example from March 1918, an Australian hospital treated a French woman brought there by a British soldier. The woman, who was six months pregnant, had hemorrhaged and the soldier, unable to find a doctor, had brought her to the Australian military hospital. Medical personnel treated and released her, suggesting followup with a French doctor.[85] Russian peasant families took in prisoners of war on farms, and in some cases, these prisoners had relationships with Russian civilians as sexual partners or as surrogate siblings or children.[86] Turkish prisoner of war Mehmet Arif Ölcen lived in Varnavino (Russia) for part of the war, and he became friendly with the family in charge of his care and with their sixteen-year-old daughter, upon whom he had a crush.[87] In northern France, a village hid British soldiers for much of the war, and one of the men, Robert Digby, had a daughter with a woman in the village before he was caught by the Germans and executed.[88] Stories such as Olcen's and Digby's played out across the theaters of war, with some relationships turning into marriages after the war, while others fizzled over the course of almost five years of conflict.

As part of the contract between nations and their fighting forces, military officials tried to stave off soldiers' homesickness and loneliness by providing entertainments and distractions, often through the cooperation of religious institutions or charitable organizations. The United States, for example, utilized a wide network of YMCA canteens and recreational huts to entertain soldiers with games, concerts, tea and cookies, and conversation. Other organizations that ministered to soldiers' souls and morale included religiously affiliated groups such as the Salvation Army and Knights of Columbus, or international societies like the Red Cross. Popular variety shows (estrada) from Russian cities made their way to the front as morale boosters for soldiers. For example, in open-air amphitheaters, performers-turned-soldiers provided entertainment for fellow soldiers at the fronts. Performances included music, magic and conjuring tricks, clown acts, short skits and plays—in short, a whole host of prewar entertainments came together in these shows.[89] Wherever there were soldiers training, resting, or preparing to fight, entertainments were planned for them. Education, sports, theater, films, reading, and games were all encouraged as appropriate ways to spend time.

Armies did what they could to keep homesickness among soldiers at bay, but these entertainments often helped maintain societal and religious distinctions as well. The YMCA, for example, segregated its recreation huts by race, and African-American soldiers had nowhere near the same access to facilities as white American soldiers.[90] Addie Hunton and Kathryn Johnson, African-American women hired to work with black soldiers in YMCA huts in France, recorded the shocking racism both they and the soldiers encountered among other Americans abroad on war service. As Hunton and Johnson note, the first three African-American women to serve in this capacity were assigned to different camps and segregated from other white women. They described the scene: "There might be a dozen Y women in her camps—but she worked absolutely alone, often her hours stretching from 9 in the morning to 9 at night."[91]

Class divides, ethnic hostilities, and religious differences also divided the men in their search for some semblance of the normalcy of home. Sometimes these divisions were practical—many Jews and Muslims had dietary restrictions that required them to have separate cooking facilities where possible. Language, too, divided the audiences of frontline theaters and concerts, and the languages available in mobile libraries at the front often determined who would patronize them. Officers and enlisted men had different establishments that catered to them, and officers' treatment in official army installations and in prisoner of war camps remained much better throughout the course of the war.

Soldiers and prisoners were not the only ones who needed distraction; governments realized the necessity of providing entertainments and hope for civilians at home, especially as casualty lists began appearing, which happened immediately. Posters, films, and plays trumpeting the impor tance of civilian sacrifice and reminding those on home fronts of the trials facing their soldiers at the front helped provide incentive. War postcards found a thriving market, whether they showed atrocities, famous battles, or ruins of war. Governments also sponsored entertainments on the home front that dramatized the battle front, with most nations holding major war expositions. The Vienna War Exposition, for instance, opened on July 1, 1916, to huge crowds. By the end of the summer, more than half a million people had visited its forty display halls, restaurants, theaters, cinemas, and "real" trench replicas. To maintain the memory of the event, civilians could purchase "official war trinkets" to take home with them.[92] Two female visitors to the 1918 Chicago War Exposition wrote separately to a friend in the army, describing their reactions to that spectacle. One enjoyed looking at all the military equipment, writing, "I think the Exposition was wonderful," while the other noted, "We went to the Exposition and the sham battle was great that gives the people an idea of how our boys are fighting for us."[93] The war expositions in other belligerent nations also featured prisoner of war art on display, demonstrations of new technologies of war, and short films showing the "real" war.

The temptation to "see" the war was great for civilians. Reactions to sightings of prisoners of war, zeppelins and planes, war films, or soldiers from other parts of the world suggest considerable curiosity and interest in the workings of the war. Piete Kuhr, a child in Germany, recorded in her diary the excitement in town with the arrival in spring 1915 of "Red Cross dogs" at the station:

> In their full field uniform the dogs look different. They have a collar from which two leather straps hang, left and right. The straps hold a folded cloth, which is rolled across the throat. Behind these hang two leather pouches with the Red Cross sign . . . in the pouches are bandages, medicines and refreshments. The dogs have to seek out the wounded after a battle, so that the medical services can get them into hospital.[94]

For Piete and her friends, the exhibit was particularly poignant because her friend Dora's dog had been requisitioned earlier in the year as a first aid dog. Now they could see first-hand how he was serving his country.

Those civilians who felt that expositions were not enough like the real war could often engage in wartime tourism, especially if they possessed the right connections and passes. Edith O'Shaughnessy, wife of the former U.S. minister to Mexico, was living in Paris in summer 1917 when she decided to go work among the devastated villages of France near Lunéville. When she arrived, however, she did not plunge into work. Instead, she and her friends took a series of automobile trips to visit the sights of the war, including the citadel and battlefield at Verdun, where she picked up shrapnel as a souvenir. They stopped at ruined villages, visited the nuns at a destroyed cloister in Verdun, and motored around to other sites, sometimes with military escort, sometimes without. Later, as they were leaving the war zone for Paris, the women considered going to look at the ruins of Reims cathedral, but one of the women vetoed the notion, saying, "After all, we're not here to go joy-riding in the war zone."[95] Of course, this realization dawned weeks after they had been doing just that!

Another possibility for civilians seeking a connection to the war was viewing of prisoners of war. POWs (both civil and military) traveled through towns in trains and open trucks on their way to work duties or to internment camps, so this travel provided ample opportunity for the civilian population to interact with or just gaze at the spectacle of enemy prisoners. Another venue for interacting with POWs came through visits to internment camps or work sites, where prisoners sometimes helped in community projects. Prisoner camps and work locations were scattered around the globe, from the United States to Japan to Algeria to Australia to East Africa to Chile.[96] As the war progressed, some of the camps sponsored concerts and theatrical entertainments for nearby populations, or they hosted sales of prisoner crafts. In other cases, civilians just took the opportunity to gawk at prisoners behind barbed wire or sometimes to slip them food and supplies. These connections between civilians and prisoners were not entirely benign, and some prisoners reported being verbally or physically assaulted as they traveled through civilian areas to their prison camps. As one British soldier remembered, "Old German women can spit!"[97] Other civilians felt real empathy for prisoners of war and often noted that they wanted to treat these enemy soldiers the way they would want their own captive sons and husbands to be treated.

Whether through emotional bonds forged through letters, furloughs, and visits or through vicarious connections created by wartime expositions, media, or propaganda, civilians and militaries interacted daily. Soldiers and civilians recognized distinctions between their experiences and identities, but they also lived with the ambiguities created by the realities of modern war. In many ways, the soldier-civilian dichotomy that was emphasized in governmental policies was a false divide that ignored the real ways in which civilians made war possible and the ways in which soldiers retained their connection with civilian identities. As Geoffrey Best has noted of the First World War, "the line of material distinction between 'soldier' and 'civilian' became more blurred" than ever.[98]

Conclusion

Armies in the First World War were not only primarily composed of civilians in uniform, but these armies were also selected, shaped, armed, fed, housed, nursed, rehabilitated, transported, entertained, and buried by civilians. A nineteen-year-old conscript in Russia in 1916 could expect to be summoned to war by a municipal official, chosen by a local draft board, equipped with clothing and arms by a civilian factory under martial law, transported by train to a camp, entertained by civilians (with letters, parcels, food, theater, sex), and treated by civilian nurses at hospitals after being wounded. This same soldier, should he die, might be buried by a crew of forced civilian laborers or prisoners of war; then he would be mourned by his civilian family at home. This brief scenario lays bare the real connections between military and civil, battle and home that complicate understandings of civilians' roles in wartime. As Ivan Bloch had predicted two decades earlier, modern war highlighted the "difficulty of providing for immense masses, as a consequence of the diminution in productiveness, the possibility of economic crises, and popular commotions, and, finally, . . . the extreme difficulty of directing armies consisting of millions of men."[99]

The lines between civilian and military management of the war were rarely clear, and as the war dragged on, the civilian contribution to the war effort became ever more crucial, as did the maintenance of civilian morale. With nearly ten million military dead and billions of dollars of war expenditure by 1918, civilian patience was wearing thin. The work of war—feeding troops, supplying munitions, staffing bureaucracies—competed with the work of life in civilian minds. As women struggled to stand in bread lines for hours every day and cleaned their houses without soap, the fissures in the social contract between government and civilian appeared, threatening the war efforts. Like their family members at home, citizen-soldiers began to question the authority of their officers and the meaning of this endeavor. In some nations, governments had to "remobilize" citizens with persuasion and coercion when civilian morale plummeted, while other nations lost the alliance of their citizenry entirely.[100] It is perhaps, then, no surprise that in the German Revolution of 1918 housewives demanding food marched next to industrial laborers, sailors, and conscripted soldiers. And in the festive atmosphere that came with the armistice, civilians and soldiers celebrated together. Edward Casey, the sixteen-year-old volunteer from London, survived to celebrate the war's end on home duty in Grimsby, where civilians "let their hair down and for the troops everything was for [free]. Plenty of beer, spirits, and plenty of ladies' legs opened for the pleasure [of] men and themselves. You name it: the troops got it for free."[101] The enmeshing of civilian lives with that of the enlisted and conscripted soldiers continued beyond the mobilization and the war itself into the period of peace and beyond, speaking to the new societal and political lines drawn by war and militarization. As Stéphane Audoin-Rouzeau and Annette Becker argue, "violence became integrated with disconcerting ease into the daily life of every civilian and every soldier to the point where it became commonplace."[102] Violence and militarization affected noncombatants and combatants, although to varying degrees, but the framework of violence and war became a common lens through which societies sought to peer at the world around them.

[2]

Civilians and the Labor of War

But not for thee the glory and the praise,
The medals or the fat gratuity;
No man shall crown thee with a wreath of bays
Or recommend thee for an OBE;
And thou, methinks, wouldst rather have it so,
Provided that, without undue delay,
They let thee take thy scanty wage and go
Back to thy sunny home in Old Cathay....
—"To a Chinese Coolie," *Punch*, Feb. 19, 1919

In his autobiography, Stimela "Jason" Jingoes spends considerable time describing his service in the First World War, writing fondly of the adventure the war represented for him and his youthful companions:

> We were a mixed bag of recruits.... We were young, scared and excited, and we got up to some amazing high jinks. Whenever we stopped at a station, we simply poured out of the train, and took whatever we wanted from the railside stalls: food, fruit, magazines, anything that took our fancy. When people tried to get us to pay, we told them gleefully to ask the Government, for we were off to war.[1]

This account of young men going to war could be found in many combatant countries in 1914 as scores of recruits left by train for duties as soldiers—except that Jingoes was not a soldier but a uniformed civilian who had to be "employed elsewhere than in the fighting zone."[2] Jingoes, who was born in the British protectorate of Swaziland, had volunteered in 1917 for service in France as part of the South African Native Labour Contingent (SANLC). After the train journey from his home to Cape Town, he traveled by ship for a month and a half to the camp near the French coast where he lived and worked for more than a year.[3] Jingoes was one of more than seventy-four thousand South Africans to work in French and African war theaters, and part of a larger force of noncombatant laborers that numbered in the millions during the war.[4]

Because the work of war requires vast amounts of labor, not only in the areas of ammunition production or arms manufacturing but also in the mundane logistics of supplying, feeding, housing, and moving armies of millions, the provision of labor was a serious requirement for all the nations who entered the First World War. The need for massive amounts of heavy ammunition, as well as the demands of food for armies, civilians, and service animals (horses, in particular), led to a reliance on workers for docks, railheads, and supply depots. These demands were not new as armies had historically relied on plunder, civilian camp followers, and organized military magazines for supplies, but the scope and realities of modern industrial warfare meant a changing relationship between strategy and logistics as well as a transformation of domestic economies. As Martin van Creveld explains in his study of wartime logistics, "Huge quantities of supplies (e.g., one-and-a-half million shells for the single offensive launched by the British on the Somme in 1916) were brought up [to] the front, dumped at the railheads. . . . To a far greater extent than in the eighteenth century, strategy became an appendix of logistics."[5] Moving shells became as important as moving food, and transport workers became a vital military need for nations at war after 1914.

Some of this work was accomplished by fighting forces, but as World War I continued, the need to free up combatant men and to find labor for home and front combined to create an acute need for dedicated workers. Every nation at war faced this need, but each chose its own path in finding workers. The solutions to labor shortages were complex and dependent on many domestic and international factors, but in all cases, governments tried to identify workers who could not, would not, or were not allowed to serve as combatants. Solutions varied by nation, often reflecting ideological notions of "martial" races as well as realities of what labor might reasonably be available. Colonial powers, such as Britain and France, had developed categories of "martial" or "fighting" races from among the ethnic and language groups in their dependencies, and they relied on these categories to sort out warriors from workers.[6] For nations without major overseas colonies, the need for working bodies at a minimal cost led to the use of forced labor, deportation of populations from occupied zones, employment of men, women, and children as civilian contractors, and even utilization of prison labor, conscientious objectors, and prisoners of war.

The need for labor at the fronts, near the fighting, and behind the lines helped blur the lines between "real" soldiers and the civilians working by their sides. Some of the "followers" or "contractors" shared the same billets, the same dangers, and the same sense of patriotism, but they remained mostly invisible in the postwar histories, which emphasized the masculine heroism of the front-line soldier. Armies created a largely artificial distinction between fighters and laborers where possible in order to maintain notions of status, racial superiority, and masculinity. So even those laborers who were attested (given military status) were not considered true citizen-soldiers, and they endured second-class status within the army and in popular perception. As one officer noted in his history of the Indian Mule Corps (classed officially by the British army as followers rather than soldiers), "[The mule driver] shares to the full the hardships of the fighting troops and, as the casualties prove, the dangers too. . . . Let Government take the lead by abolishing once and for all that degrading word 'follower.'"[7] Workers were known by a variety of names (some of them derogatory), depending on their nationality, occupations, and location: "followers," "coolies," "diggers," "pioneers," "carriers," "contractors," "civilians," etc. Some of these workers had official status as "soldiers," others had quasi-military status, some were prisoners or deportees, and many were purely civilians, often under contract to the armies in the field.[8] While total numbers of laborers engaged in supporting the armies at war are hard to calculate, the figures are in the millions.

This chapter examines some of the groups that made up this "army" of international laborers who worked for the military but who were considered by their employers to be "noncombatant." In particular, nations used ethnicity, race, and gender as yardsticks for measuring those capable of being "combat" soldiers and those only fit for "support" work. Gender was a powerful code for determining combat readiness, and not only were women barred from most combat positions based on their perceived weakness but male "others" within society were also feminized in official propaganda as weak material and unfit for the front. This supposed weakness did not, however, translate into inability to work, as women and men stigmatized as "unfit" in one setting were called upon to do their patriotic duty by laboring for the armies. Governments sought to exploit the labor of marginal groups without having to elevate their status or extend real citizenship.[9]

Official assumptions about the loyalty, intelligence, and fitness (both physical and mental) of ethnic and religious minorities shaped policies, as did long-held racist beliefs about colonized peoples. For example, in a postwar account of his service in East Africa, one British writer described the Nigerian personal servants assigned to officers: "For fifteen months many of these youngsters never had a day's rest, and without grumbling served their masters as only a black man knows how to serve, with almost doglike devotion."[10] In a similar way, another British officer described the Chinese laborers under his charge: "They are a race of Peter Pans, never having grown up. Nightly I thank God they are not going to be soldiers."[11] Stereotypes coexisted with long-held national traditions regarding status for minority groups and citizenship standards. In the Russian Empire, where Jews were barred from service as officers in the tsar's army, many Jews, Muslims, and other religious minorities were targeted for coercion, again based on the assumption that they were unfit for soldiering. In Kazakhstan and Turkestan, the Russians tried a policy of "labor conscription" to force men whom they considered unfit for army service to work for the armies instead.[12] The United States also created a labor pool from its minority groups; even though army officials considered African Americans largely unfit for war service, as one officer said in 1918, "In these days of conservation, when every rag and bone and tin can is saved, human beings cannot be wasted."[13]

This, then, was the crux of the problem for military planners—how to use all available human resources for fighting the war while retaining a particular image of the fighting soldier. Nations at war used their prewar assumptions about human ability and personality to shape their calls for workers. In particular, they relied on four different pools: (1) "nonwhite" men from colonies or pseudo-colonies of the European states; (2) forced laborers and deportees from occupied zones, in some cases minorities or refugees in their own countries; (3) prisoners, not only POWs but also criminals on work release and imprisoned conscientious objectors; and (4) female, youth, and elderly auxiliaries. Military and civil officials in the nations at war classified these groups as "noncombatant" or "civilian" yet allowed them to labor for the military, often in uniformed labor corps. All of them were subject in some form to military housing, food, and law. Although some labored in jobs at "home," a large number of these workers were used in the L of C (Lines of Communications behind the front) or *Etappen* (staging areas) zones such as railheads, ports, hospitals, canteens, and service areas. These camp followers were institutionalized in the First World War as pseudo-military units. Despite their essential duties to the waging of war, civilian workers remained apart from the "real" war fought by soldiers in public imagination and postwar commemoration, while increasingly coming under the control and protection of the military.

Race and Labor

With their histories of large colonial empires, Britain and France approached the war labor problem by raising battalions of so-called native peoples. South African, Chinese, and Indochinese laborers worked alongside recruits from the West Indies, Fiji, Egypt, Mauritius, India, Malta, Senegal, Congo, Palestine, Persia, and Syria, to name a few. The circumstances of their recruitment, work, treatment in the war zones, and compensation all varied according to political circumstances, but in general, these workers had strong imperial connections to Britain or France, complicating their uncertain status. For both the British and the French, centralized regulation and control of labor never reached optimum levels, and the experiences of laboring for the armies remained variable, according to nationality, location, and chance. Several examples demonstrate the broad variety of labor experiences for the "native" corps.

The Indian army, for instance, had long-standing formal categories for combatants and noncombatants. Combatants included infantry, artillery, cavalry, sappers (those who built and maintained fortifications), miners, and signalers, while noncombatant services focused on transport, supply, and medicine. When war broke out, there were already more than forty-five thousand noncombatants in the Indian army, and many of these men were sent with their combatant counterparts to France, East Africa, Gallipoli, Salonika, and other war theaters.[14] The Indians were a considerably different force than the hastily raised and temporary units created elsewhere in the European empires because of their long service history in the British Empire. However, their labor was only a small contribution to the war effort, and the British needed to recruit many more workers, so the army began creating diverse labor battalions as the war entered its second year. In order to regulate this hodge-podge of temporary labor battalions, a formal Directorate of Labour was created in January 1917. At its height, the directorate oversaw the labor of nearly four hundred thousand people in various theaters of war and behind the lines.[15] Problems with its functioning led to a new formation, the Labour Control, in February 1918, which was supposed to lead to a more centralized and efficient system for controlling labor.[16] These supervisory structures incorporated workers from multiple backgrounds, including female civilians, colonized labor corps, contractors from China, and prisoner labor.

The laborers in this international workforce often had different motivations and experiences of the war. Jason Jingoes, for example, was excited by his enlistment in the South African Native Labour Contingent (SANLC) and saw the beginning of his journey to war as an adventure. He and his companions had never seen the sea, let alone taken an ocean voyage, and they were astonished at the military camp in Rosebank (South Africa), where "white and Coloured ladies" served them tea and food.[17] His spirits were considerably dampened, however, when in March 1917 his commanding officer informed the men that theirs was to be the first transport ship to follow an SANLC transport ship, the Mendi, which had been sunk by a German submarine in the English Channel, killing hundreds of men, most of them SANLC members. Jingoes recounted this experience as the first that suggested the danger of their undertaking. Later the poor-quality food, air raids, and abysmally wet weather in France took some of the adventure out of the experience for Jingoes and many of the men. Yet Jingoes, like millions of front-line soldiers, remained positive overall about his war experience, writing, "You see, we had liked our stay in France."[18]

Beyond the novelty of life in France, one reason why men such as Jingoes from British protectorates might have wanted to volunteer for war service was that it gave them an opportunity to visibly demonstrate loyalty to the British crown in order to ensure that the relationship would continue or to maintain their status in the colonial order, a motivation that was particularly appealing to African elites. For Basutho men, for instance, in the wake of the discriminatory 1913 Native Land Act in South Africa, the thought of being incorporated into the South African state and losing their independent identity as a special protectorate was a frightening possibility. The Land Act reserved large tracts of prime land for whites only, forcing many African families in South Africa into crowded reserves with poor agricultural prospects. For the Basutho, who were developing a strong sense of a separate national identity apart from South Africa, this sort of deliberate racial policy was something to be avoided. Esiah Maeli, a thirteen-year-old Basutho teen who had gone to do farm work in South Africa in 1918, remembered that the experience "made me feel more strongly that Lesotho should remain separate."[19] Ntate Mohapeioa also said that "the whole nation was against incorporation because we knew how Boers treated blacks."[20] Indeed, recruitment in the British labor battalions was high among African elites in the British protectorates, with several sons and grandsons of chiefs, such as the grandson of Basutho chief Moshoeshoe, signing on to the SANLC.[21] Even with colonial structures increasing the number of volunteers and conscripts, some Africans probably volunteered for many of the same reasons that Australians or Canadians did: imperial patriotism and adventure. As Jingoes noted in his memoir, "When the First World War broke out, I, as a member of the British Commonwealth, felt deeply involved."[22]

Others clearly served only because they were compelled to do so. For example, in East Africa, British authorities required chiefs and headmen to meet manpower quotas for the Carrier Corps until the extension of Britain's Compulsory Service Act to East Africa in March 1917 led to mandatory service for both Europeans and Africans in the colony.[23] In many areas of the continent, compulsion was the order of the day, and in South Africa, payments to chiefs and recruiting officers helped insure that the numbers of laborers remained steady.[24] Some chiefs used conscription as an opportunity to rid their societies of marginalized men or rivals, but they also met British quotas so they could keep their positions in the colonial hierarchy. In Natal (South Africa), "magistrates threatened to arrest and fine headmen who failed to produce a certain number of recruits," and in the nearby Transkei, an observer noted that "natives are made by force to join" as laborers.[25] In East Africa, military authorities seized wives or cattle to stop resistance to compulsory conscription and coercion.[26]

In addition to imperial loyalty or compulsion, the promise of self-government or personal advancement within the colonial system was a powerful inducement for some. Indeed, Richard Smith has argued that for Jamaicans and other "subject races of Empire," the war allowed them to aspire "to the model of the citizen volunteer, hopeful that wartime sacrifice would confer improved standing."[27] The Chinese, who were not formal colonial subjects of the British or French, may have cherished a similar hope. Certainly the elites who proposed a Chinese labor scheme to the European nations saw this as a way to boost national prestige.[28]

For the laborers themselves, steady wages probably played a more important part; the lure of wages and family support could be a powerful inducement to enlist in labor battalions, as this case of a Chinese recruit illustrates. On November 15, 1916, farm laborer Pei-Zee Tseong enrolled in the Chinese Labour Corps. Tseong entered the temporary camp at Weihaiwei, China, and prepared himself for a three-year stint as a worker for the British army in France. The contract he marked with his sign promised free passage to and from China, free food, clothing, housing, fuel, and medical care, a ten-hour work day, and a pay rate of one franc per day with an additional family allotment for his dependents in China (ten Chinese dollars per month).[29]

The uniform he received featured two lightweight cotton suits for summer and a wadding suit (quilted, padded cotton) with woolen drawers, cardigan, and flannel shirt for winter. He wore a felt hat and boots for work in France, and his status was marked by both a metal badge on his suits and a nonremovable bracelet engraved with his identification number and personal information. For Chinese laborers such as Tseong, wages were the most compelling reason for volunteering. The one-franc-per-day rate paid in France was well above what they could receive in the

Chinese laborers for the British army amuse themselves as they travel through a lock of the Canal de la Somme near Corbie, France. *U.S. Signal Corps, National Archives and Records Administration.*

impoverished Shandong province, and the family allotments and death allowance meant the men could ensure help for their families. Those Chinese who were employed as "gangers" or interpreters received even higher wages, and for some, the opportunity outweighed the risks. Eventually, Tseong would be only one of nearly 150,000 Chinese laborers recruited by the British and the French for service in the First World War.[30]

China's scheme, proposed first in 1915 by Chinese financier Liang Shiyi, carefully avoided violation of China's neutrality by proposing "laborers as soldiers (yigong daibing)" hired through private companies.[31] The Chinese workers had to remain away from combat zones and work rather than fight in the war, and even after China's official entry into the war in August 1917, most Chinese laborers remained outside of front-line areas. In January 1916, the French launched their recruiting station in China, the Truptil Mission, to organize the hiring of Chinese laborers for the western front. In addition to Truptil, other smaller French schemes emerged in China, all ostensibly "private" but really thinly veiled military labor recruitment ventures.[32] As the first Chinese laborers under the French scheme arrived in France in August 1916, the British were preparing their own recruitment system in China's Shandong province. The first British-sponsored Chinese laborers left China in January 1917.[33] While the American Expeditionary Force considered their own Chinese-labor recruitment, they abandoned the plan and instead borrowed Chinese workers from the French in 1918.[34]

Chinese laborers employed by the Allied forces traveled around the world before reaching their workplaces, which included France, Belgium, Mesopotamia, Egypt, Palestine, Algeria, and even Russia (as farm workers for the French and British ally).[35] Many of the labor troop ships passed through the Panama Canal or around the Cape of Good Hope, but as the war progressed more of the ships traveled to Vancouver Island (quarantine stop), where Chinese laborers boarded trains to travel across Canada to the Atlantic coast. From Halifax, the laborers traveled in patrolled Atlantic shipping lanes to France. From their first recruitment through their wartime careers, the Chinese found themselves under military control for most of their daily activities, with army rations, military censorship, and officers commanding their units. Yet despite the militarized nature of these labor corps, Chinese workers also interacted with civilians, populating a zone between military and civilian that was difficult to define. The British built labor concentration camps to house Chinese workers and tried to keep their movements under strict control, but this proved to be an impossible task. French standards allowed for more interaction between Chinese laborers and local populations, at least initially, but their later restrictions on foreign laborers still did not end fraternization between locals and the labor units.[36]

Flemish families living near Ypres, Belgium, remembered their interactions with Chinese workers as cautious but mostly positive, as demonstrated by Jeanne Batteu, a child in the town of Poperinge during the war, who recounted her experiences with the so-called Tsings in a 1995 interview. Batteu remembers that when Chinese laborers arrived in 1917, people were not afraid, but rather curious about these new contributors to the war scene around Poperinge. Chinese workers, according to Batteu, mixed rather freely with the local population, playing with children and visiting cafés, where proprietors often took advantage of their supposed "naiveté" by selling them lemonade that they told the Chinese was champagne. Batteu even remembered a few Chinese words, learned from the laborers eighty years earlier, and she described in an animated way her participation in the local celebration of the Chinese New Year in February 1918, which featured acrobatics and singing.[37]

While this Flemish account suggests good relations between Chinese laborers and Belgians in the war zone, many Chinese and other foreign workers suffered racial insults and physical attacks. In France, white male French workers saw the imported laborers as competitors for jobs and women, and racial tension led to individual assaults and collective rioting. While the most targeted group appears to have been North Africans, Chinese and Indochinese workers were also seen as a threat. Historian Tyler Stovall records this letter from Cang Xuong, an Indochinese worker in France, which shows the dangers from French civilians endured by some of the workers:

> The other day, on returning from Renée's, I met a gang of French hoodlums who attacked me. I submitted to their blows and afterwards continued on my way. Last Saturday, sergeants Sung and [?] got into a fight with the French in the Café de la Fouguette. After receiving a few light blows, our sergeants took to their heels. . . . Here relations between the French civilians and the Annamites are very poor.[38]

The position of Chinese and colonial workers was precarious. Although they too were civilians, often working side by side with French or Belgian civilians, they remained outsiders.

Despite their differences from indigenous populations, the Chinese and other foreign workers did share similar dangers with them, as they too were subject to military attack, especially from the air or on the seas. For example, a troop ship carrying Chinese laborers for the French was sunk in the Mediterranean, killing more than five hundred Chinese men, and the Mendi disaster in the English Channel claimed the lives of more than six hundred South African workers.[39] Chinese workers were targeted in the French port cities as well, by aerial bombing and artillery bombardments in 1917–1918.[40] Having been promised in their contracts that "they [would] not be employed in dangerous places," many Chinese workers staged strikes and disturbances after major bombings by the enemy led to hundreds of dead. In the aftermath of serious bombing raids on Dunkerque and Boulogne in September 1917, more than six hundred Chinese went "missing" and were found at the beach and in local villages. As one British official noted in the official War Diary for this zone, "though the Chinese had hitherto kept very steady, in spite of the bad example set by Belgian labourers, it appears that the limit of their endurance had been reached."[41] Beyond their fear from the attacks, some of the workers also felt "the measures taken . . . for their safety" were not sufficient.[42] Like the civilians killed in the bombing raids with them, they were unarmed, but still targeted. In fact, when a newspaper editorial called for an investigation of promises made to the Chinese about a safe working environment, the British Labour Directorate drafted a reply noting that "the one risk to which they are subjected is that of bombing from enemy aircraft, a risk which they share with the people of London, Folkestone and Southend," implying that their lives were no more at risk than those of other civilians.[43]

Yet, while reiterating the civilian-style risks the Chinese encountered, the writer went on to put the Chinese workers back into a military category when he noted that they lived "in enclosures." While sharing the dangers of civilians, then, Chinese shared the fate of many soldiers as well, since they were under military discipline. In short, they were militarized, but they were not soldiers. Upon arrival at recruiting stations, Chinese men underwent a ritual similar to the initiation for soldier recruits: haircut, bath, uniform. British officer Daryl Klein described this process as a "sausage machine," which turned "an ordinary uninviting workaday coolie into a clean, well-clothed and smartly active human being."[44] Chinese laborers could also be court-martialed, and among the British laborers, several were imprisoned or executed because of violations of military behavior codes. Also, military medical services treated Chinese injuries and illnesses, and most Chinese medical casualties ended up at the Chinese hospital at Noyelles-sur-Mer, which was one of several segregated "native" medical facilities.

At Noyelles-sur-Mer, which was headquarters for the Chinese Labour Corps, the hospital served thousands of Chinese during the war. There was at least one Chinese doctor at the hospital, but the majority of medical personnel were British (or from the British Empire) and French, many with missionary backgrounds. Dr. E. J. Stuckey, an Australian, had served as a medical missionary in China before enlisting as a surgeon at the Chinese hospital in France. Stuckey ran the eye section of the hospital, which was one of a handful of major special medical units, including a surgery, a psychiatric ward, and a leper compound. Stuckey was particularly valuable given his knowledge of the Chinese language, and he noted in a letter home, "It was pathetic to see the delight and satisfaction of the patients transferred to this hospital from other hospitals where no one could understand what they had to say. The opportunity to pour the whole story into a sympathetic ear was more help to them than all the medicine in the dispensary."[45] Stuckey's sympathy extended beyond listening to his patients' medical complaints, and he wrote to his family about the hospital's attempts to cater to its patients through the purchase of canaries to entertain the wounded, the building of a model pagoda, and the celebration of Chinese festivals. This aspect of military life clearly benefited the many Chinese workers who needed to visit the hospital during their time in France. Yet even recuperating patients often labored; for instance, Chinese mental patients at the hospital spent their days weaving baskets for military carrier pigeons.[46]

Despite military control, the armies took care to maintain and reinforce the noncombatant status of the Chinese men, assigning British officers, for instance, but asking those officers to travel in civilian clothes so as to "reassure Chinese officials that this was a non-combatant enterprise."[47] Officials tried to separate "native" workers from soldiers in medical facilities, cafés, entertainment huts, and work sites. The French Colonial Labor Organization Service (SOTC) organized labor groups by nationality, then isolated each group into "separate but equal" living arrangements and work situations.[48] Even the cemeteries were segregated where possible, with a major Chinese war cemetery at Noyelles-sur-Mer and smaller Chinese sections of cemeteries in other areas of France.[49] These attempts at separation did not always succeed. Of the more than four thousand Chinese war dead in France, many of them are buried side by side with British and French soldiers in the areas where they died.[50] Separation proved impossible in leisure as well. One account describes the lineup outside "the No. 4 drinking hall and brothel next door to the

Cathedral" in St. Omer, with Canadians, Australians, Brits, West Indians, and Chinese all waiting together for the euphemistically named "holy communion" they hoped to receive.[51]

For officers, keeping the various labor groups separate and getting their daily work done was sometimes a challenge. For example, the Chinese employed by the French were supposed to be kept separate from the Chinese employed by the British, for as British authorities noted, the French did not put their Chinese workers in camps and they paid them more. Officials wanted no comparing of notes by the Chinese workers. Also, the British wanted to keep Chinese laborers separate from the South Africans, and within the South African corps itself, the Zulus and Basutho fought and insulted each other when they worked together, so authorities worked them in separate sectors. All of these non-European male workers theoretically had to be kept out of areas where French civilian women were employed by the armies, by request of the French government.[52] This sampling of restrictions not only suggests European prejudices about the proclivities and temperament of "native" labor but also underscores the inefficiencies and headaches of managing the various work battalions.

Statistics on labor personnel changed monthly for both the British and French armies as casual local laborers moved into and out of service, but also as colonial battalions were moved and replaced when contracts expired. A snapshot of British labor in France in May 1918 suggests the complexity of the picture:

TOTAL STRENGTH: 313,047
Canadian Labour Battalions
Labour Companies (British)
South African Native Labour Corps
Chinese Labour Corps
Non-Combatant Corps (British)
Indian Labour Companies
Prisoner of War Companies
Fijian Labour Company
Cape Coloured Battalion
Area Employment Companies (French, Belgian, British)
Canadian Employment Companies[53]

This list was supplemented a month later with a new Russian labor battalion composed entirely of Russian-born "aliens" living in England. The chart also fails to reflect noncombatant military laborers from India and Egypt.

The French needed voluminous numbers of workers for their war machine as well, but unlike the British, the French encouraged immigration from other European nations for workers, opening their doors to an estimated three hundred thousand European laborers (the majority from neutral Spain).[54] These foreign "guest workers" provided much-needed labor, but only a fraction of what the French required, so like the British, they turned to their colonies. With colonial labor their assumptions about the fitness of colonized men for soldiering helped them develop race-based labor policies that reflected perceived differences in the suitability of certain "races of people" for service. For instance, those from Indochina were considered more even tempered and quick at specialized tasks, so they filled roles as drivers, clerks, and nurses, while men from Senegal were funneled into the infantry rather than into skilled and semi-skilled labor positions.[55] Altogether the French civilian authorities hired more than two hundred thousand colonial laborers from Algeria, Tunisia, Indochina, and Madagascar, and perhaps as many as another hundred thousand foreign workers (many of them from colonies) worked for the French army directly as military laborers.[56] While the French began by allowing colonial workers a large measure of freedom of movement and housing, they moved toward a position resembling the British one by 1917, with the advent of military discipline, organized work gangs, and encadrement (segregated living/working environments).[57] For example, in Le Havre, Moroccan workers were initially allowed to find their own housing, but after a major street brawl erupted in June 1917, the Moroccans were locked into a fort until suitable separate housing compounds could be provided.[58]

The British often segregated their imperial troops by race, as with the New Zealand Expeditionary Force. While Maori men served in combat roles alongside white New Zealanders at first, from 1916 on the Maori worked mostly as pioneers (an engineering unit) in separate battalions dedicated to digging trenches, wiring, and transport.[59] Other Maori served as domestic servants for officers (batmen), in construction work such as tree felling and hauling, or in raiding and wire-repair work in danger zones. Maori "diggers" as they were known (a term later applied to all New Zealand and Australian forces) served in the same theaters as their white New Zealand counterparts—Egypt, Malta, Gallipoli, and France—but as noncombatants. As official histories note, photos from Gallipoli show Maori "clearing the spoil from the mine-workings below Quinn's Post and dragging watertanks up onto the spurs of Plugge's Plateau," under treacherous conditions, while at the Somme, "The [Maori] platoons worked in relays under gas and shell fire that produced a steady trickle of casualties."[60] Clearly this noncombatant work was not for the faint of heart.

Both the French and British also exploited pseudo-colonial connections where possible, and this was certainly the case in areas of the eastern Mediterranean, where Ottoman rule was disintegrating and Britain and France formed temporary imperial occupying forces. The British employed a large force as porters, dockworkers, construction laborers, artisans, and drivers. These workers came from a variety of backgrounds: India, Mauritius, Palestine, Persia, and Egypt, for example. The multinational nature of the Ottoman Empire meant that the Europeans could identify nationalist aspirations and then isolate groups by ethnicity, religion, or nationality for work in the war effort, especially against the Ottoman army. In Mesopotamia, for instance, the army created Arab, Kurdish, and Persian labor contingents. One particularly unusual contingent raised by the British was the Zion Mule Corps, which was composed entirely of Russian Jews from Syria, who saw significant service as water carriers at Gallipoli.[61]

As with contracted labor from formal colonies, Europeans used compulsion and the exploitation of nationalist aspirations as well as cash to recruit laborers in its informal colonies. Egyptians initially volunteered for the Egyptian Labour Corps because of the high wages the British offered in the early years of the war. However, when wages became less competitive with the local market, the British shifted to compulsion in order to recruit labor.[62] In Persia and Mesopotamia, large groups of men, women, and children worked at building roads and encampments, which the British army portrayed as "charitable" work for the unemployed of their occupied zones.[63] Some of these projects were massive undertakings, as with a "stretch of some hundred miles of railway [that] was built from Nushki in Baluchistan, towards the Persian frontier at Seistan. On this work there were thousands of coolies employed, with their gangers and overseers, engineers, masons, carpenters, smiths, fitters, and plate-layers; and about ten thousand camels with their drivers and owners."[64]

When the United States entered the war in 1917, it too had to solve the problem of labor for the armies, and the examples of France and Britain served as models for how the American army would answer the dilemma. As with the laborers for the French and British, some African Americans laboring for armies at the front were civilians under military custody. About five hundred black civilian contractors accompanied the first U.S. convoy to France in summer 1917, and these stevedores were "technically civilians but subject to military rules because their employers were under contract to the army. Although not soldiers, they wore uniforms, some surplus Union Blues from the Civil War, which a quartermaster officer had dug up."[65] These contracted civilian workers later were replaced by the drafted "Services of Supply (S.O.S.)," composed of largely African-American battalions, who worked in ports, in army staging areas, and in advance positions on the front. More than 160,000 African Americans served in S.O.S. labor battalions after being conscripted in 1917–1918. Military planners assumed that black men would make poor soldiers but that they could work and thereby release white men for combatant service. Most of the laborers did stevedore work such as loading and unloading, warehouse stocking, hauling, digging, and cleaning. Camps were set up throughout the U.S. South for these drafted laborers, while other African Americans were sent to the front as members of pioneer battalions. The pioneers had some simple infantry training in weapons use and field fortification, but the army never really wanted to use black pioneers as combat soldiers; rather, they were wanted as support workers in combat zones.[66]

Like the Chinese and other non-European workers for the French and British, the African Americans worked in gangs, with white officers. In many ways they served punitive sentences, often confined to camps, denied passes, and clothed poorly in reclaimed uniforms or blue work fatigues (similar to those worn by prisoners in chain gangs).[67] One African-American soldier in the 445th Reserve Labor Battalion in 1918 wrote to Emmett Scott, advisor to Secretary of War Newton Baker, summarizing his experiences in the army: "i am riten you to Day Becose you Can Do some good We are Fair mitty hard all so we Have a mean lutenden to us He is a Negro hater it is 600 men Just same as slave is now you is not try to Have any slaves in your army. . . ."[68] The analogy to slavery would have been one that laborers for other armies in the First World War would have understood.

Altogether the British, French, and Americans raised "nonwhite" labor battalions that numbered more than a million men, and they based their formula on the racist notion that only white men and a few "martial races" of colonized men could have the necessary discipline, honor, and courage to fight as soldiers in the trenches. The armies of laborers they created were subject to military discipline, army rations, compound living, uniforms, and officers, as with regular fighting forces, but they remained second-class citizens in the minds of both military officers and civilian officials.

Forced Labor

While Britain, France, and the United States relied on "nonwhite" labor, Germany, Austria-Hungary, the Ottoman Empire, and Russia had to find other solutions to their labor needs, since they did not possess the extensive overseas empires of the British or the French. Even though the Germans did have colonies and used colonial labor, they did so mostly to protect their territories in East and Southwest Africa and found other solutions to labor needs in Europe. One of the strategies employed by the big empires of Central Europe was to use civil and refugee populations as workers. In many combat and occupation zones, civil populations were press-ganged or pressured into volunteering for service as laborers, especially from 1916 until the end of the war. These forced labor situations depended on many things: proximity to the fronts, needs of the combatant nations at any given time, and geography of a region. For example, most forced laborers in East Africa were impressed as porters, while in Lithuania, press-gangs worked in agriculture or on road building and repair.

Laborers for the
Central Powers
lay pipe and build
a road in 1915
Palestine. *Library of
Congress.*

Transport was one of the major areas where laborers were utilized throughout the war; increasingly prisoner and forced labor helped build roads, railroads, canals, and ports. In harsh terrain such as the mountainous front between Austria-Hungary and Italy, civilian gangs drafted by the Austro-Hungarian army built "tracks into the mountains" to help soldiers advance.[69] Likewise in the remote Taurus and Amanus mountains, Turkey relied on labor and porter battalions to work on construction of the Hejaz railway and other transport projects throughout the war.[70] The Russian army conscripted men and women alike for construction work in "provinces close to the front."[71] Much of this transport and construction work has gone unrecorded in official histories of the war because the labor drafts often happened spontaneously in a region. Armies would need laborers for a specific project for a few days, so they would round up locals to perform the task, then release them at the conclusion of the work.

One of the most extensive examples of forced labor occurred during the middle years of the war in the Ober Ost (today the Baltic countries of Lithuania, Latvia, and Estonia). In 1916 the German military governor ordered that all adults, male and female, could be called up for work duties. The forced labor battalions that resulted were as large as sixty thousand people in some areas, and they were kept in locked barracks with improper clothing and poor food. Most were put to work in tree felling, harvesting, or road works. By the time the program ended in 1917, hundreds of thousands had been forcibly employed, with pitiable wages and a food allowance of only 250 grams of bread and a liter of soup per day.[72]

In Galicia, a major theater of war between Austria-Hungary and Russia, armies also forced civilians into labor gangs. In the fortress town of Przemyśl, civilians and soldiers faced a siege by Russian troops from autumn 1914 to the end of March 1915. The civilians left in the city, weakened by hunger, were put to work by the Russian army. Helena Seifertóv Jabłońska, a Polish widow in the city, described the labor battalions of spring 1915 in her wartime diary: "[Jews] are being forced to clean the streets and remove the manure. . . . All civility has vanished and terror is raising its head. . . . It is not just our townspeople and Jews who are being made to do forced labor. The peasantry is also set to work now, repairing the roads or burying dead horses. Children as young as eight are dragged out to work."[73] This state of events lasted only a couple of months until the German army invaded Galicia and forced a Russian retreat in June 1915; at that point civilians became subject to German occupying forces and their labor demands. This sharing of labor between opposing armies was not unusual. When the British entered Palestine, they found evidence of forced labor among the populace. The British utilized these same laborers. As one Australian described the scene in Jerusalem, "Turks left great quantities of stone prepared by the roadside all through the hills. . . . Swarms of workers, ELC [Egyptian Labour Corps] and natives—Aged dignified looking old arabs, haggish old women, graceful girls and boys bearing stones on heads. Road rebuilt in a few days."[74]

In the Russian Empire and along its changing fronts, labor shortages were acute in agriculture and industry by 1915. Refugees (some of whom had been forced to migrate to Russia's interior), women, youth, and older men were all recruited for unskilled occupations. By October 1916, more than 350,000 refugees labored in agriculture in Russia. In the eastern parts of the empire, the Russian government hired Chinese and Korean laborers early in the war, and by 1916, they "decreed that indigenous males aged 18 to 43, who had hitherto been exempt from the draft, should register immediately for military service."[75] These men from Central Asia were slated for work details in construction, transport, and supply for the army, but this "labor draft" backfired and led to a widespread anticonscription revolt in 1916 in Turkestan, Uzbekistan, and Kazakhstan.[76]

Other occupied areas also experienced forced labor, sometimes in large-scale sustained drives but also for short-term projects overseen by soldiers. In summer 1915, the town of Mechelen, Belgium, was threatened with harsh measures when workers at the Arsenal and the rail yards went on strike. The German governor-general posted notices indicating that he would revoke all travel privileges, stop food aid, and close the passport bureau for the whole region if sufficient numbers of workers did not report to work. Governor-General Von Bissing went on to warn that "[i]f the economic life of Mechelen and its environs ... suffers gravely from the aforementioned measures, the fault and the responsibility [lie] with the workers."[77] Belgian workers in other industrial centers, mines, and railway hubs also faced compulsion if they tried collective resistance, work stoppages, or strikes. In an interesting twist, the Belgian government's sensivity to the question of forced labor and deportation meant that in its operations in the Belgian Congo and East Africa, its officers refused to create a general policy of compulsion for its African labor needs.[78]

Throughout war zones, occupying forces utilized forced civilian labor when necessary for specific projects or to maintain the working of local industries, transport, and other vital services. In Sedan (northeastern France), teenager Yves Congar described his brothers' (aged seventeen and nineteen) forced labor for the German army in the bitterly cold winter of 1917, noting that at least they had thick boots for working outdoors.[79] In occupied Lille, Roubaix, and Tourcoing (northwest France) in April 1916, about twenty-five thousand young women and teenaged boys were packed into cattle cars and sent to do military and agricultural work for the German army for much of the summer and early autumn.[80] They were organized into groups and "regimented like soldiers," and their accommodations and food were inadequate to the situation. The German occupiers hoped both to lower costs of feeding this population and use their labor, but they had not reckoned on the inability of the city dwellers to do hard agricultural labor or the outcry from the international community. The women under thirty were sent home after only a few months.[81]

In fact, all along the front lines, staging areas, and occupied zones of Europe, men and women were pressed into labor by military authorities as they were needed. If willing volunteers were not forthcoming, then deportation or force was used. Maurice Pate, a young American working for the Commission for Relief in Belgium, described the scene of forced deportations in his diary in October 1916:

> Our biggest question now is the wholesale requisition of civilians for forced military work. None of the towns in the region, when first approached by the military authorities, would furnish the originally small number demanded. The campaign was then started to arrest all "chomeurs" (men without employment) and has now spread until all young men fit for military service—even those with steady work, and married—are being taken. The gendarmes arrest the men on the streets or at their homes— and many sad scenes take place. . . . [Tournai] received this afternoon the affliction of a fine of 200,000 marks for not having given the list of chomeurs (men out of work) to the military authorities. Six days are given in which to pay, with an additional fine of 20,000 marks for each day's delay in giving the list. It is generally believed that the town will refuse to pay, and suffer the consequences no matter how severe. . . . The situation throughout the whole region is very serious. All the villages have refused to give the lists of chomeurs, and if these are not forthcoming, the authorities threaten to requisition all men between 17 and 30.[82]

The deportations and punitive fines Pate described were part of a concerted effort by the German occupying authorities to recruit a Belgian labor force in 1916. When voluntary recruitment largely failed, the German authorities responded first with the creation of civilian work battalions (Zivil-Arbeiter-Bataillone) in operational and staging areas (*Etappen*). About sixty thousand Belgians were forced to work in these groups as civilian prisoners wearing identifying armbands and under military supervisors. Next, deportations began in autumn of 1916 with another sixty thousand laborers (and a large amount of equipment) shipped to German industrial areas to supplement and support the Reich's war efforts. Part of the reason for implementing the policy was to reduce the high numbers of Belgian unemployed while solving some of Germany's labor shortages, but resistance on the part of Belgian deportees led to an end to the policy by summer 1917. Forced labor did continue, however, in Belgium itself. Jens Thiel estimates that Germany recruited approximately 160,000 Belgians for military work by 1918.[83] From other nations, Germany employed between five and six hundred thousand Russian and Polish workers as well as laborers from neutral lands such as the Netherlands and Scandinavia.[84] In nearby occupied France, Isabel Hull argues that the occupied population was working for the Germans by the end of the war, with more than half a million digging trenches and fortifications by fall 1918.[85]

Another brutal forced labor zone was in the East and West African theaters of war, where whole villages were forced to "volunteer" their labor to armies on both sides of the conflict. In some cases military authorities approached village leaders and asked for a quota of workers (the British called this a "semivoluntary" system), but in other cases individual compulsion or even mass levies were utilized. The official British statistics for Africans used as "followers" in the East African campaign alone topped a million people, and this does not include casual or unrecorded labor.[86] Although it is impossible to calculate numbers of people conscripted into service by the European forces at war in Africa, some areas have estimates that are staggering. In Kenya, "the equivalent of half the total male population of the African reserves . . . had been conscripted" by 1918, and in Northern Rhodesia a commissioner estimated that more than a third of adult males had been pressed into service as military porters.[87] In Central Tanzania, first the Germans, then the British recruited Gogo men as askari (soldiers) and porters; numbers probably topped seventy thousand men (out of a population of 150,000), most of them forced into porterage. Thousands more hid or fled the region to avoid conscription.[88]

Most of those recruited were men aged eighteen to thirty (of age to fight as soldiers), and they risked their lives in the fields of battle and supply. Because of difficult terrain and the tsetse fly, pack animals were almost useless, so human porters were vital to maintain army supply lines.[89] Early attempts to use donkeys in parts of East Africa not only led to long delays but in some cases, the human carriers had to double back and carry the donkeys' loads for them.[90] Porters had unusually hard war experiences in which they could expect to carry fifty pounds for up to twelve miles per day, sometimes in terrible terrain. One particularly bad supply line called for porters to "carry nine miles mostly waist-deep in water, much of it on raised duck walks made of undressed poles laid side by side"; with such conditions, it is unsurprising that the main causes of death were dysentery and pneumonia, in addition to diseases transmitted by the ever-present tsetse fly.[91] Carriers had poor rations that, combined with back-breaking work and poor housing, led to terrible rates of disease and death. The mortality estimates, which were probably conservative, suggest that West African carriers died at a rate of two hundred per thousand. The small laboring group from the Seychelles is symptomatic of this larger problem, with 341 dead out of a total of 791.[92]

As with the British, German forces in East Africa also used compulsion to gain African laborers and porters. These porters were responsible for carrying but also were used to requisition food and supplies, since the German army was largely living off the land. European armies saw the humans they encountered as resources to be seized, much in the same way livestock and crops helped sustain armies in the field. One survivor of German "requisitioning" described his experience to British intelligence officers: "The wretched native of the Ikungu had had everything looted from them by the Germans, including cattle, sheep, goats, and chickens; and after being roped together by their necks had been forced to carry these loads of loot for Naumann's [German general] force."[93] Dead and sick laborers were often abandoned and replaced with new recruits as the army moved into fresh zones. German doctor Ludwig Deppe described the treatment of porters in his hospital unit in 1916: "This morning 35 people ran away from the lookout point in Mtingi, so I had to put almost all the other porters 'on the chain' (they all have iron rings round their necks, which are attached to a chain with six to eight others). This is the only way to control the troublesome new recruits."[94] If this harsh treatment did not kill or incapacitate carriers, disease and malnutrition did. Both poor rations and endemic disease were major killers of carriers and porters in the tropical zones. South African laborers sent to East Africa experienced terrible mortality rates in tropical zones in 1917. For instance, in malaria-infested regions, some labor battalions suffered 80 percent casualty rates, and the monthly mortality rate for the South African contingent of eighteen thousand men was 22.2 per thousand by April 1917.[95]

Forced labor of noncombatants was certainly not new in 1914, but the scope of forced labor was. Throughout the theaters of war and behind the lines, compelling civilians to labor for the armies at war or their governments became standard operating procedure. Even the New York State Assembly passed a forced labor measure in April 1918 that gave the governor the power to requisition the labor of men aged eighteen to sixty who were not already gainfully employed.[96] Using the argument that war necessitated such measures, which was similar to arguments for denying civil rights and legal protections to wartime populations, nations institutionalized the practices of forced labor and labor deportation in the First World War.

Prisoner Labor

By the last years of the war, even forced labor did not generate enough manpower for the war effort. Governments sought any means to identify and utilize "unoccupied" males, and manpower for combat and logistical support became a priority across national boundaries. One source of labor that could be utilized was prisoners of war, hundreds of thousands of whom were sitting idle in camps throughout the combatant nations. For military officials, prisoners of war were a perfect labor force—able-bodied men with time on their hands who could be closely controlled and who would work for cheap. All combatant countries sought to use POWs for labor in civilian and military roles during World War I. Technically, these POWs were captured soldiers, but many of them were essentially "civilians in uniform," often having spent little time in combat before their capture. POWs constituted a massive labor pool, particularly on the Eastern Front, where the Russians captured 2.77 million Austro-Hungarian soldiers, or about one-third of men mobilized. In the Russian Empire, where conscription of fifteen million men by 1917 had created severe manpower shortages, especially in agriculture, POW labor was practically a necessity. According to international conventions, rank-and-file soldier prisoners could be used for labor, while officers were given preferential treatment.[97]

Many Austro-Hungarian, Ottoman, and German prisoners worked for the Russian military and civil authorities during the war. Two-thirds of Austria-Hungary's prisoners of war worked outside of camps in small labor units by the end of 1915, while in Germany 90 percent of the POWs there were working in 1916.[98] Britain, France, Russia, Italy, and other belligerents also relied heavily on POW labor by the end of the war. The lucky ones drew work assignments in agricultural areas well removed from the battle fronts, where food and lodging with local peasant families meant a more pleasant and safe environment. Most POWs in Russia worked in civilian settings under the supervision of large landowners, industrial bosses, or peasant farmers.[99] For belligerent governments, this policy was a dangerous one because it put civilians in close contact with the enemy, perhaps undermining notions of the "otherness" of the enemy. The more unlucky prisoners of war landed work assignments in mines, heavy metal industries, or, in the worst possible case, the Murmansk project. About twenty-five thousand POW laborers died in the construction of the Murmansk railway in 1915–1916.[100]

POW workers in other countries were employed behind the lines in agriculture, but also in areas near the front lines, repairing roads, rail lines, and other installments. More than a million Russian POWs worked during harvest to feed those in Austria-Hungary, while their counterparts (German and Austro-Hungarian POWs) in Russia helped maintain the fuel supply with their labor in the coal industry.[101] These workers sometimes toiled side by side with civilian prisoners, deportees, or press gangs of local laborers, and in occupied zones they performed tasks that ranged from forestry and agricultural employment to industrial jobs. In the Ruhr coal mines of Germany, more than seventy thousand POWs were employed, the largest number of whom were Russians.[102] Altogether, about nine hundred thousand POWs were used as laborers in Germany and its occupied areas, and by 1918, nearly half of the British Labour Corps in France was composed of POW workers.[103] POWs were visible in many civilian areas both near to and well behind the fronts. For example, an American observer described POWs in France, who had been organized into POW corps in 1916, as "tall, stalwart men, wearing the round white cap with its band of red—at work on the roads."[104] Others saw groups of prisoners traveling by train or working on rail lines, in fields, or on roads.

In Vienna, the more than seven thousand POWs cleaned streets, loaded coal, and worked in shops, bakeries, dairies, and nurseries—they certainly were a visible presence in the city.[105]

In addition to POW labor, government officials sought to use criminals as laborers. For example, with labor shortages in Mesopotamia by 1916, the British made an appeal to Indian prisons for workers. In return for a shortened sentence, criminals could volunteer for service as porters and sweepers. More than five thousand such prisoners volunteered for the service from the Punjab alone, and prison labor was also utilized in mines and textile factories.[106] Assam, another region of India, supplied a whole convict labor corps of fifteen thousand men.[107] The British initially viewed prison labor as an experiment and targeted "better-class" prisoners. One officer described his Jail Labour Corps in an official history:

> All ranks are attested and enrolled as followers and are dressed and equipped in exactly the same way as members of the free porter and labour corps, but for obvious reasons, the control and discipline will be a little closer than in the case of the free labour corps. . . . There is, of course, no intention of employing them near the fighting line.[108]

If the men worked for two years or the duration of the war, as they attested, without offense, their sentences were remitted. While working in the labor corps, they were provided with food, clothing, and a small amount of pay. Their numbers included gardeners, laundrymen, sweepers, drivers, and grooms; as many as twelve thousand prison laborers worked in Mesopotamia alone between 1916 and 1919.[109]

The British also turned to another form of prison labor by 1916, taking conscientious objectors from prisons to serve in noncombatant labor roles. While Britain and the United States were the only combatant nations to have policies for exclusion of conscientious objectors from combatant service, neither had figured out what to do with C.O.s who would not serve at all, even in noncombatant service, and there was public pressure to separate "real" C.O.s from "cowards" or "shirkers."[110] Some C.O.s in Britain agreed to serve in a Non-Combatant Labour Corps (NCC), but others refused to do the work of war at all, and they were sent to prisons both in France and in the United Kingdom. Among these "absolutists" on the issue of conscientious objection were a number of religious C.O.s, many of whom were Quakers. Some of these young Quakers were sentenced to detention, field punishments, and even death (although that sentence was quickly rescinded) for their reluctance to fight in spring 1916. Eventually, dozens of these men were turned over to civil authorities at prison camps and prisons in Britain, where some engaged in nonmilitary labor.[111] Despite much effort on the part of British tribunals and civil-military authorities, attempts to put the conscientious objectors to work to free up more men for duty at the front were mostly failures.

As with forced labor of noncombatants, the use of prison labor became an accepted standard in World War I. POWs occupied a liminal land between soldier and civilian, and often they lived and worked with civilian prisoners or other noncombatant personnel, further blurring the lines between military and nonmilitary workers. Their presence in civilian homes and villages made the war a reality for many who lived far from the fighting, and it complicated the divisions war created between enemies; often it was hard for civilian "bosses" not to develop some level of relationship with the POW laborers assigned to their farms and businesses.

Gender, Age, and Labor

The last major group to be recruited as laborers for the war efforts in many combatant countries were civilian women, children, and older men, who often worked side by side or nearby the other laboring groups already described. These groups labored at the home fronts (chapter 3), but many also found themselves eligible for service at or near the fronts. Many willingly volunteered for service as early as 1914, and their sense of patriotic loyalty and duty made them logical choices for military and civil planners seeking labor. Gender and age stereotypes meant a delay in the use of these workers for war work in the field. When armies finally utilized female and youth auxiliaries, officials tried to confine them to highly controlled formations that kept age and gender distinctions in place. For instance, Boy Scouts served as coast guards in Britain, but they did so in uniform with the understanding that this work was "patriotic" service, not employment or military service.[112] Women and men older than military age were targeted for particular war work as well, but they were funneled into specially designed auxiliary corps, some uniformed, that emphasized their separate status from military men. In all cases, these nonsoldiers served armies in the field as a "reserve army of labor," deliberately segregated from "combat," "battle front," and "soldiers" whenever possible in order to maintain the ideological divides between soldier and worker, man and woman, adult and child, young and old.[113]

One of the ways in which noncombatants were drawn into duties on or near the fronts was through the members of the various service auxiliary corps created during the First World War. These corps differed in timing, numbers, and scope according to national needs and political realities, but many countries tried some form of women's auxiliary army. Female auxiliaries were usually drawn from working-class and lower-middle-class backgrounds, in opposition to the predominantly middle- and upper-class women in charitable organizations, nursing, and ambulance corps. Such auxiliaries performed a variety of support duties to free men for front-line duty, but most were specifically barred from combat. One notable exception occurred in Russia, where women's corps briefly became fighting units as the war effort's cohesion was shattered by revolution. Altogether at least six thousand women served in combat units in Russia, both in mixed units and in the special sex-segregated battalions.[114] Women volunteered for reasons of patriotism and longing for adventure; one woman requested, in a letter, to be sent to the front, writing, "we, like men, can also take up arms and go to the defense of our motherland with honor and pride."[115] Individuals, such as this woman, received acceptance or rejection on a case-by-case basis, but it was not until May 1917 that the all-women battalions were formed. Of these sixteen battalions with more than five thousand volunteers, four were combat corps, eleven were communications specialists, and one was a naval unit. Only one corps, the Women's Battalion of Death, with more than two thousand female soldiers, actually served in front-line combat.[116] The Russian women's battalions were anomalies in World War I, however.

More common were militarized women's labor battalions that operated as adjuncts to male military units. For instance, more than sixteen thousand American women served overseas as part of the American

Expeditionary Force, but in carefully controlled and sex-segregated environments.[117] In addition, the United States recruited and hired female telephone operators for service at home and abroad, again to free up men for service.[118] As Susan Zeiger found in her study of American women, female workers "hoped to carve out a path of war service roughly equivalent to the war service of young men, but that goal proved elusive. . . . [Often] officials regarded women's auxiliary work as akin to domestic service."[119] Working women were drawn to the relatively good wages and the call to service abroad, but the novelty of these auxiliary corps undoubtedly sparked the imaginations of young women. Some just wanted a change of pace, as with British schoolteachers Doris Mellor and Bertha Brown, both of whom wanted to travel and see the world, as Brown wrote, "before I am too old."[120] However, gender and age stereotypes often contributed to a tendency to put women and children in jobs that reinforced their dependence on men and their separation from battle. Women auxiliaries found themselves serving tea or dancing with convalescent soldiers at canteens in France rather than engaging in the exciting war work they expected.

In Germany, female auxiliary workers replaced male workers in the cities at home in order to free up soldiers for the front, and by 1917, close to ninety thousand women had replaced men within Germany itself, while more than seventeen thousand female auxiliaries (*Etappenhelferinnen*) replaced male soldier-laborers in occupied zones and staging areas by war's end. In fact, it proved easier to recruit women for jobs in the staging zones than men; women made up 64.4 percent of the *Etappen* auxiliaries by September 1918.[121] German women auxiliaries performed a variety of clerical and manual jobs, in laundries, transport and supply depots, offices, and medical stations. Like the prisoner-laborers, women workers were noticeable additions to occupied zones, and many civilians commented on the novelty of seeing women perform "men's jobs." American Maurice Pate described the German female auxiliaries at work in occupied Belgium in 1917:

> In addition to those in uniform civilian bands of Germans are to be seen everywhere in Belgium engaged in military work under the direction of soldiers. Section gangs working on the RR are composed in large part of stout women-workers. In a word the entire German nation is militarised

Members of the British Women's Army Auxiliary Corps (WAAC) line up for morning inspection in Bourges, France. *U.S. Signal Corps, National Archives and Records Administration.*

and working as a unit to obtain their object. This is the explanation of Germany's admirable resistance against nearly the entire world.[122]

Other nations also sought to utilize their female populations for labor. The Australian Women's Service Corps (AWSC) members labored in clerical occupations and general field auxiliary work to free up male combatants.[123] Tens of thousands of women replaced men in Russia, performing work in the home economy (e.g., munitions, transport), but also serving in war-related support occupations such as nursing and refugee relief.[124] Increasingly the Austro-Hungarian government felt the labor crunch by the latter years of the war, and in 1917 created the Women's Auxiliary Labor Force in the Field. Approximately thirty-six thousand to fifty thousand women served in this force between 1917 and 1918; they worked in labs, staffed clerical offices, and ran telegraph/telephone machinery.

As Maureen Healy has noted of these women, "They wore uniforms; they referred to themselves as 'enlisted'; they were relatively well paid; they traveled far from home and worked alongside men."[125] As with other women "auxiliaries," it was sometimes hard to know why these women were not classified as soldiers, given their military housing, uniforms, and pay, as well as the fact that they were replacing male soldiers.

Britain's auxiliaries provide a useful example of the use of women and the challenges involved in militarizing them. Approximately eighty thousand British auxiliaries staffed dispensaries, performed clerical tasks, and worked as cooks, laundresses, and drivers.[126] Many female noncombatant laborers were members of the Women's Army Auxiliary Corps (WAAC), formed in 1917 with the stipulation that it would employ a uniformed force of women aged twenty to forty years.[127] Other uniformed female auxiliaries in Britain included the Women's Royal Naval Service (WRNS) and the Women's Royal Air Force Service (WRAF). Despite their uniformed status and control by the military, a meeting of army and civil leaders made it clear that female auxiliaries "were to be treated as civilians, not soldiers."[128] The authorities also sought to control those who saw foreign service as a way of being near their husbands, and they made women whose husbands were serving abroad ineligible because of fears that women would enlist only in order to be near their men. Women's morals were the focus of great angst among military officials, who feared promiscuous auxiliaries would lure soldiers away from their duties. To address these concerns, the WAACs were housed in hostels in France supervised by "Lady Supervisors" in order to chaperone the women.[129] As a contemporary British observer of these women's auxiliaries noted at the time, "The whole question of the civilian population has taken on a different aspect since the outbreak of the war . . . but the sub division labeled 'Women' has perhaps undergone more revision than any."[130]

In addition to female units, the combatant nations employed youth or older men in corps for labor duties at the fronts. For example, in 1915 the French created a civil work corps known as the État-Civil du Champ de Bataille to dig up the war dead, mark and rebury the bodies, and "map" battlefields once a combat area was cleared of action.[131] Many of the men employed for this work were too old for active combatant service. An American traveler described one of these workers, a 47-year-old, who was thrilled when in 1917 he was released from this macabre battlefield duty to do light gardening work for a military canteen in the Marne region.[132] Like the French, Germans turned to men over sixty and youth as well, but in small numbers of only about six thousand by summer 1917.[133] Austria-Hungary also tried to mobilize young and old male civilians for labor. The Pupils' Volunteer Corps, created in 1914, organized teens into brigades to work in agriculture, transport, and offices. These children wore "black armbands" to designate their status. Adult men who were too old or not eligible for service were drafted for labor duties on the home front or in staging areas for the armies.[134]

In France and Belgium, male and female civilians of all ages could register for civilian contract labor near the front lines. Civilian women were hired in large numbers to run laundry facilities and baths for the troops of all nations, and indeed these civilian women also washed and ironed for members of the labor battalions. For example, Rachel Maelbrancke remembered her mother trying to make ends meet in their village near Ypres (Belgium) by taking in washing and mending for soldiers.[135] This informal work coexisted with formal employment of laundresses by regimental laundries. One Australian laundry in Bailleul (France), for instance, employed around seventy-five French and Belgian women full time, and returns for civilian labor in the British army in France in 1918 record more than sixteen thousand local men and women at work for the army.[136] In all front-line and occupied zones, civilian men, women, and children performed service tasks for the army, billeting soldiers and officers, providing food, drink, and entertainment, and performing day labor or messenger duties.

Conclusion

The war was a voracious consumer of labor, and every state involved in the conflict faced the problem of finding enough bodies to continue their military campaigns. Men, women, and children of all ages found themselves enmeshed in war work—some voluntary, some forced, and some in between these extremes—militarizing whole populations. Labor needs also created strange configurations that threatened to undermine the careful divisions between friend and enemy, home and front, occupier and occupied that nations construct in modern warfare. Polish villagers living near the front might be forced to build a road alongside German (or Russian) soldiers and POWs from places as far removed as the Ottoman Empire. In the First World War, millions of men and women maintained the war, whether they chose to or not, through their labor.

When the war ended in November 1918, many laborers expected to go home soon. In fact, though, demobilization of auxiliaries, labor battalions, and POW camps was slow, and laborers found themselves doing war work long after the war ended. Repatriation of POWs in Russia, for instance, continued into the early 1920s, and the Chinese labor battalions were not formally dissolved until 1920 (Britain) and 1922 (France).[137] Civilians sometimes found themselves reoccupied by their own or Allied armed services, and their work was required again into the early postwar years. Perhaps the worst aspect of the end of the war for most of the labor battalions was not that they remained at work, although they did so alongside millions of soldiers who were not demilitarized until 1919 or 1920, but that they were given the "clean-up" jobs of the aftermath of war. Many nonwhite battalions, such as the Chinese, were assigned to grave registrations, mine clean-up, and body collection.[138]

While some of the workers in various configurations described here received military honors and some sort of payment upon leaving service, few received formal recognition of their service in the form of long-term health care, pensions, or medals. Those honors bestowed on the laborers of the war were unevenly dispersed and politically charged. Some of the laborers (male and female) were included in victory marches such as the large Allied victory parade in Paris, but the U.S. military barred African-American S.O.S. battalions from marching.[139] Symptomatic of this attitude toward laborers, at the Paris Peace Conference, a British official claimed that China's contribution to the war had not led to "the loss of a single life," conveniently forgetting the two thousand Chinese laborers who had died for the British war effort.[140]

South Africa's postwar commemoration of its laborers became particularly political and provides an example of the debates that followed the war regarding the place of laborers in the conflict. The South African government refused Victory Medals for the SANLC because the men were "noncombatant" and then withheld the British War Medal from them. The

Cabinet finally announced its decision in 1924, noting, "The recent government, as a matter of policy, decided not to proceed with the issue of war medals to non-European members of Coloured and Native Labour Contingents."[141] Interestingly, the SANLC members in British protectorates in southern Africa (Basutholand [Lesotho] and Swaziland) did receive medals, and a monument was erected in Maseru, Lesotho, to their service.[142]

Other laborers faced poverty, famine, and discrimination when they returned home. In parts of East Africa, requisitions of men and crops led to devastating famine, and those carriers who lived through the war had to try to rebuild amidst such serious obstacles.[143] For prisoners of war, readjustment to society was often difficult, especially for those whose health (both mental and physical) had suffered from confinement and forced labor. Some prisoners got caught up in the upheaval of revolution or civil unrest, making it difficult for them to survive and return home. Many Ottoman prisoners found that the freedom given to them by the Russian Revolution was offset by the lack of food and transport home; although they were "guests" of the Russian people, it was often easier to stay in the prison camps and find work than try to make it home through an intensifying civil war.[144]

Finally, the promise of political gain that sustained many of those who contracted to work for the various governments engaged in the war did not materialize. The peace negotiations did not recognize the claims of delegations from Egypt, China, and other nations that had sent labor forces to war, and independence for colonies was still a distant dream. The year 1919 was marked by riots and revolts as many felt betrayed by the peace process, and some laborers and POWs found themselves returning home to revolution, civil war, or devastated homes and crops. For a good number, their nations had simply disappeared to be replaced by new nation-states. Likewise for many women who had given their service to the state as workers, nurses, and auxiliary military personnel, their desires for political participation and voice were not always heard. Even in nations where women were granted the vote, such as Great Britain, it was initially granted only to older women—not most of the young women who had served as WAACs. French, Belgian, and Italian women did not gain the vote until the end of the Second World War, despite their significant wartime contribution in 1914–1918.

The First World War demonstrated the need for labor in a modern war situation and solidified the practice, begun in the nineteenth century, of using civilians as a militarized labor force. It also demonstrated the fallacy of the separate and fixed battle front. As historian Peter Gatrell aptly notes, "the image of a fixed front, conceived as a masculine domain, became increasingly difficult to sustain. . . . Changing military fortunes ensured that 'front' could become 'rear' and vice-versa. Occupation by the enemy brought the front into spaces hitherto occupied by civilians."[145] Despite the fluidity of the front and the necessary efforts of combatants and noncombatants alike in maintaining the war, governments continued to insist upon the special and protected status of civilians, even as armies targeted them for attack. Also, the racial and gender assumptions that propped up the notion of a masculinized European battle front remained intact through the war, shaping the labor policies employed by armies and civil authorities.

In 1916, the U.S. government amended the articles of war to state that "in time of war . . . persons accompanying or serving with the armies of the United States in the field" would be liable to military court-martial for offenses, in effect making camp followers (broadly defined) subject to military law.[146] This legal change, which echoed policies in other countries at war between 1914 and 1918, reflected the new approach to followers, contractors, and auxiliaries in the Great War. Military officials created for themselves the best of both possible worlds—a workforce subject to military law and supervision but with nominal civilian status. Civilian contractors were here to stay after 1918, and as one contemporary explained it, "Some wore khaki, some didn't, but all fought, with weapons suited to sex, age, talent and training."[147]

[3]

Constructing Home Fronts

I guess the war will be over soon for this fourth Liberty Loan
will soon get the Kaisers goat if they haven't got it already. I
bought one and I guess dad is going to buy one so that makes
two I think if every family took two the war would soon be over.
—Josie Yeockel (Chicago) to Walter "Arthur" Richter
(Camp Wadsworth, South Carolina), September 30, 1918[1]

On August 1, 1914, twelve-year-old Elfriede "Piete" Kuhr decided
to start a war diary to record the events around her in her East Prussian
hometown of Schneidemühl, Germany. Life changed for her almost
immediately, but in small ways at first. Piete recorded the new school
rules in her diary for August 3, 1914:

At school the teachers say it is our patriotic duty to stop using foreign
words. I didn't know what they meant by this at first, but now I see it—
you must no longer say "adieu" because that is French. It is in order to say
"lebwohl" or "auf wiedersehen," or "Grüss Gott" if you like. I must now call
Mama "Mother"'. . . . We have bought a little tin box in which we'll put five
pfennigs every time we slip up. The contents of the war savings box will go
towards buying knitting wool. We must now knit woollen things for the
soldiers. I said to our Nature Study teacher today, "Am I to write the history
of the Buzzard in my journal [*Diarium*]?" Herr Schiffman answered, "We
have decided to speak in our lovely German language. The word for journal
is 'Kladde.'" I thought Herr Schiffman was joking, and began to laugh. Then
he got cross.[2]

After school, Piete encountered reservists mustering in the streets on her way home, where her house resembled a warehouse. Her grandmother, with whom she and her brother lived, had already begun preparing goods for distribution at railway stations as part of her duties for the German Red Cross. By August 6, Piete was wearing a Red Cross armband and passing out materials to soldiers at the rail station. In less than a week, Piete's surroundings—home, school, streets—had been militarized, and patriotic nationalism had become the rallying cry.[3]

Like Piete, the majority of civilians in World War I were not displaced by the war, nor did they face occupation or the threat of battle lines in their midst. Most lived well behind the lines on "home fronts" mobilized by patriotism and war production. The war was a reality for them, but in much different ways than for civilians in occupied or front zones. Home fronts were not all equal, however, and the chances of facing real hunger, famine, or death depended chiefly on each nation's proximity to the theaters of war and on each state's ability to mobilize and control its civilian populations. Government management of the home front became a key ingredient in sustaining the war. Indeed, states that mobilized resources and peoples ineffectively often saw their war efforts end in revolutions, civil unrest, or economic collapse. Civilians at home fronts, whether they lived thousands of miles from the fronts in New Zealand or near the action in Italy or Russia, provided essential services for the war effort. Without their labor and their political support, the war could not have proceeded. Civilians worked in agriculture, industry, policing, and civil service jobs, but they also tacitly agreed to make sacrifices in their own food and resources. Such sacrifices made requisitioning of essential war materials possible. Often, civilians continued to support governments even as their loved ones faced death in the war zones.

The home front civilians also functioned as important connections with normalcy for soldiers in the field, and the lively correspondence that moved between battle front and homes demonstrated the strong ties that conscripted soldiers and volunteers felt with their civilian families and friends. Civilians at home pressured soldiers to enlist and "make good." Their very presence as symbols of the nation that was to be protected helped ensure the continuation of soldiers' resolve even as resentment built against those perceived to be benefiting from the war (shirkers, profiteers) while young men died. Rhetorically and emotionally, the home front was absolutely essential to the mobilization and continued fighting of millions of men, but practically, too, civilians at home bolstered the war effort through their material contributions of labor, products, and funds.

Policing Home Fronts

For many civilians living at "home fronts," the first signal that war might bring change to their lives was the emergency and wartime legislation most combatant and neutral countries passed. This legislation varied widely according to national needs and political situations, but in all cases, the new laws were designed to broaden governmental control over the lives of citizens. For some countries, this meant martial law or increased military intervention into daily lives, while in other nations the legislation took the form of state surveillance by civil authorities. Examples of this expansion of wartime state power include Australia's War Precautions Act, which provided the governor-general with increased power to act unilaterally through executive orders; Italy's War Powers law, which seized any materials deemed "prejudicial to the supreme national interests"; or the Habsburg Empire's July 1914 laws suspending civil liberties, creating a war surveillance office, and censoring all press, mail, and telegraph/telephone services.[4] Such legal provisions appeared in virtually every combatant country and even in many neutral countries.[5]

Many of these initial laws were subsequently amended as the war continued, and the weight of new legislation increased exponentially as states scrambled to handle the transformations that accompanied "total" war. Britain's Defence of the Realm Act (DORA), enacted in August 1914, began as a few short paragraphs, but it was designed for amendment, and throughout the war, the government added to it when necessary. For example, DORA Regulation 40, which made it illegal to supply soldiers with "intoxicants," was amended four times to include rules regarding cocaine, prescription drugs, and venereal disease. The last of these amendments, DORA Regulation 40D, passed in March 1918, made "it illegal for a woman afflicted with VD to have intercourse with a serviceman" even if the man was her husband and even if she got the disease from him.[6] By the end of the war, there were 190 emergency statutes and 260 regulations under the Defence of the Realm Act in Britain.[7]

Few ordinary people on either side of the conflict challenged the expanded government role in their lives or questioned their loss of civil liberties. Some previously outspoken social critics of the government even changed their positions in order to "behave as good patriots," as Theodor Heine, the editor-in-chief of the German satirical magazine, *Simplicissimus*, proclaimed. Heine and his journal, known earlier for frequent suspensions and arrests for antistate publishing, became part of the German propaganda machine.[8] Marcus Garvey's Universal Negro Improvement Association, headquartered in Jamaica, passed a resolution expressing loyalty to the British Empire in September 1914.[9] Organizations that had been in conflict with their governments suspended their activities for the duration of the war in order to show their patriotic nationalism. The Women's Social and Political Union (WSPU) in Britain, which had waged a campaign of violence in its quest for votes for women, turned its energies to war work. The WSPU and its leader, Emmeline Pankhurst, suspended both militancy and suffrage propaganda campaigns in August 1914.[10] Pankhurst toured the country to recruit for the war effort, imploring men "to do their 'Duty to the Nation.'"[11]

The avalanche of legislation passed in all combatant countries accompanied an unprecedented expansion of state bureaucracies, increased surveillance of civilian populations, restriction of civil liberties, and mobilization of state-sponsored propaganda. Governments received broad powers to intern and imprison enemy aliens but also those suspected of war opposition, treason, or sedition, and the public sacrificed privacy and civil liberty for the promise of security.[12] The Defence of India Act, for instance, led to the arrest of "most of the [Indian revolutionary] leaders" by 1917, after police were given expanded ability to search and arrest suspects.[13] Trial by jury was suspended in many countries, which led to long-term internment and imprisonment for some suspect individuals, often for vague charges such as "defeatism" or speaking against the war. In the Ottoman Empire, civil courts gave way to "summary military courts" for many crimes.[14] Likewise in Russia, the army created a special section to "coordinate policies toward civilians," including requisitioning, deporting or detaining suspects without trial, and sequestering property.[15] Perhaps such policies might be expected in autocratic states such as the Ottoman and Russian empires, but constitutional guarantees in the United States provided no protection either. As John Braeman put it, "the citizen found himself unprotected by traditional guarantees. . . . [T]rial by jury proved a delusion" as Socialists, suspected spies, and enemy aliens, among others, found themselves stripped of their civil liberties.[16]

During the first months of the war, state suspicion of its citizens was compounded by private vigilance and surveillance. John Horne has argued that the war "generated a specifically wartime 'social morality'— or set of reciprocal moral judgements on the contribution of different groups to the national effort."[17] In effect, civilians policed themselves and their neighbors, sometimes with vigilante-style tactics. Spy mania abounded, as did antiforeign sentiment. As with Piete's school regulations, laws controlling "foreign" elements in society led to restrictions on enemy aliens and banning of enemy languages. For instance, Brazil's entry into the war in 1917 led to the banning of German-language publications, the destruction of German businesses and churches, and the disbanding of German clubs.[18] Germany's ban on foreign words likewise led to changes in public spaces, with the painting over of English and French signs and Berlin's Hotel Royal becoming the Hotel Deutscher Kaiser. American diplomat Joseph Grew made fun of these Berlin rules in a 1917 speech: "Not long ago a General commanding in a certain district ordered a candy dealer not to use the word 'bonbon' any more, to which the intrepid candy dealer replied that he would give up the use of the word as soon as the General ceased to call himself 'General,' which was just as much of French origin as 'bonbon.'"[19]

When the United States declared war in 1917, across the country sauerkraut became "Liberty Cabbage" and German composers such as Richard Wagner were "banned from opera house and concert hall."[20] The German language was removed from high school curricula and purged from public buildings, while people of German heritage sought to prove their loyalty by changing their names. In Cincinnati, Ohio, a community with many German-Americans, civic officials changed Berlin and Bremen streets to Woodrow and Republic streets.[21] More ominous and violent acts also accompanied this antiforeign charge; in April 1918 in Collinsville, Illinois, a German-American coal miner was spontaneously lynched as a spy by the local crowd, with police and city officials allowing the vio-lence.[22] Other U.S. cities witnessed tarring and feathering, beating, and public humiliation of German Americans. In Columbus, Ohio, even Ger-man dog breeds were murdered.[23]

Popular violence against spies was a feature of most home fronts dur-ing the war, especially at moments of perceived crisis. As Australian Gil-bert Graham wrote from Berlin in 1914, popular violence in Berlin against those considered to be "spies" erupted spontaneously:

> The excitement very soon became dangerous for any unfortunate indi-viduals who in the eyes of the mob looked like Russians or French. On such an individual being sighted there would be shouts of "Russian" or "Frenchman," "Lay him out." The Russians had a particularly bad time of it and many were severely injured by the mob. One of the largest cafés in Berlin on the Kurfürstendamm was completely wrecked by the mob one night because it was said that there were Russians in the orchestra. It was now very dangerous to converse in public places in any other language than German as one only had to be overheard to have a frenzied bloodthirsty mob at one's heels.[24]

Throughout combatant countries reports flooded into local and national authorities about "spies in our midst," and denunciations were common. In Périgueux in southern France, a crowd numbering almost five thousand destroyed a German shop on August 4, while in St. Peters-burg, Russian arsonists burned the German embassy and ambassador's residence on July 22, 1914, as a crowd estimated in the tens of thousands watched.[25] It took little for spy hysteria to turn to mob violence. English-woman R. A. Neal remembered being chased with sticks by a mob in late July 1914 in Hamburg, where she was performing with a theatrical troupe; she only escaped Germany by claiming to be an American.[26] In London, police "received nearly 9000 reports from the public of suspicious Ger-mans" by mid-September 1914, and nearly all were false alarms.[27]

The sense of paranoia felt by many civilians on the home front that enemies might be among their own communities was heightened by a dearth of accurate information on the war. Widespread censorship of mails and media limited access to news of other nations and of the war.

Censorship of newspapers and film focused on eliminating information that might be useful to enemies, but it also sought to control civilians' access to "unfavorable" news. *Le Figaro,* a newspaper in France, published this disclaimer with a large blank space in its August 14, 1914, issue: "That space was originally occupied by a news item. However, as we were going to press we received a telephone call from the ministry of war notifying us that the press bureau had decided it was inopportune to publish this item. . . . We agreed because it was our duty."[28] In Italy, all publication was barred during the war unless it came from "official sources."[29]

In both Germany and Britain, censorship began immediately with the outbreak of hostilities, but as the war progressed, both countries developed more effective, more aggressive, and much larger censorship and propaganda machines to better manage the home front.[30] Postal censorship took different forms, and typically, military officers censored their soldiers' correspondence while vast censorship bureaucracies at home took care of civil and commercial mail. The task was enormous. In Germany, approximately seventeen million pieces of post moved daily between home and front or vice-versa, and this does not include other forms of civil correspondence. The civil mail censorship in Britain, for example, handled about 375,000 letters, 117,000 newspapers, and 2,400 parcels per day in 1918, and it employed nearly five thousand workers.[31]

The expansion of state propaganda also manipulated public opinion, and atrocity posters were particularly apt to incite riots from ordinary people. Perhaps most notorious were the anti-German demonstrations that accompanied the sinking of the *Lusitania* with civilians on board in May 1915. Rioting emerged spontaneously in various countries after the news broke of the sinking, with strikes, attacks on German businesses and people, and calls for internment. In Moscow popular violence led to a virtual state of siege in the center of the city, while in cities throughout Britain and France, foreigners or people with "foreign names" were targeted.[32] This incident did not end in May 1915, however, as state-sponsored propaganda sought to reincite civilian anger against Germany by using the *Lusitania* as a rallying cry, especially in the United States.

As government propaganda and bureaucracies expanded, so did the state's need for funds to prosecute the war and to manage the civil population. Civilians became vital to the economic health of the war effort, and they were called upon to sacrifice for the nation. Civilians contributed in numerous ways to the war effort by sacrificing foodstuffs, metals, animals, and other "war-related products" but also by purchasing bonds and paying income taxes to help offset the costs of the war. Throughout Germany and Austria, civilians donated money to war relief funds and in return could put a nail into a large wooden knight statue in the center of towns and cities across the region. Piete Kuhr described a local version of such monuments at her school:

> Grandma says we are making her bankrupt with the school collections. We now have a big Iron Cross made of wood hung on the wall at school in which we have to knock 1,000 iron nails. When all the nails have been knocked in it will really be an "iron" cross. Every girl can hammer in as many nails as she likes. The black nails cost 5 Pfennigs each, the silver ones 10 Pfennigs. I have so far knocked in two black nails and one silver. It makes a bit of fun.[33]

Britain used paper rather than iron to signify civilian participation in its "Victory Loan" campaigns, with War Savings Cards that allowed purchasers to fill them up little by little with six-penny stamps. As with Piete, British children were also encouraged to participate in war loans and bonds; George Butling used the birthday money his soldier-father sent him to buy into the War Loan, as his mother told him it was "as good as any way of keeping it."[34] Children were also encouraged to purchase "official" war games, notebooks, and supplies, and in Austria, a special "child bond" was created, which could be financed with a bank loan.[35] In France, schoolchildren learned arithmetic from math exercises that encouraged them to buy war loans.[36]

Other nations mounted elaborate war bond campaigns, often using performers, local officials, and celebrities to explain the necessity of buying bonds. For example, Charlie Chaplin produced commercial films (*Shoulder Arms*, 1918) and short movies for the United States Liberty Loan Appeal (*The Bond*, 1918), which celebrated the importance of civilian patriotism and the problems of the German threat.[37] His fellow actors Douglas Fairbanks and Mary Pickford both pursued showy liberty bond appeals—Fairbanks with a "whirlwind tour" on a special cross-country train and Pickford with a letter-writing campaign to any contributor donating a day's pay.[38] In the United States and other nations at war, posters and advertisements produced by professional artists also provided simple but effective text and graphics illustrating the need for civilians to subscribe to loans and help pay for the war.

Not only were civilians expected to contribute to official war chests, but they were deluged with requests for charitable donations for wounded soldiers, refugees, war orphans, and war victims in other countries. These appeals were often emotional, with photos and images designed to make viewers feel guilty for their own good fortune. The American Committee for Relief in the Near East published flyers with waifs on the cover and headlines designed to tug at the heart strings: "Has this little girl a home in your heart? She has no other."[39] Germany's campaign for funds to help disabled soldiers included not only General Erich Ludendorff's name but also an explicit reminder that it was only money being sacrificed, not the far worse sacrifice of life or limb.[40]

The Food Front

While governments and their populations policed wartime societies, officials also sought to manage resources needed for war, especially food supplies. For some nations, food and price control became an immediate imperative as in the Ottoman Empire, where potato prices rose by 40 percent and sugar by 200 percent in the first week of August 1914, before the Ottomans had even joined the war.[41] In other states, control of food supply came in fits and starts. Germany began rationing bread in summer 1915, and Bulgaria created a food oversight committee in 1915, but Britain did not have a concerted rationing system until spring 1918.[42] The United States never instituted a formal rationing system in World War I, but instead relied upon a system of "voluntary conservation" by consumers and government guidelines for producers. In addition to regulation of certain products, governments coordinated and managed industrial ventures, agriculture, and transport/shipping in unprecedented ways. Great Britain increased its government expenditure to 38.7 percent of gross domestic product by 1917, providing a good indication of the extent of government spending on the war itself but also management of the war

Propaganda posters such as this Italian one by Ugo Finozzi aimed to motivate civilians to do their part by subscribing to war loans and by sending their men to war. *Library of Congress.*

This German poster helps civilians understand why their money and sacrifices are necessary. *Library of Congress.*

economy and society.[43] Although states differed in their development of food policies, the political and emotional importance of food to home fronts was a significant factor. As one historian has noted, this was a "war of bread and potatoes" more than one of steel or munitions.[44]

Food politics divided into several different issues. First, supply of food was a constant worry for many governments, so management of ports, agriculture, and transport was key, especially in Central European regions suffering from the Allied blockade. Second, rationing of food to provide equity and to maintain supplies was a delicate process. Third, prices of food caused upheavals, with both producers and consumers finding fault with state policies at various times. Finally, the growth of black markets, smuggling, and war profiteering complicated state management of food and caused hardships for some producers, but these illicit markets also allowed survival for populations whose governments had not managed the factors of supply, price, and rationing well.

Food supply for armies at war and civilians at home fronts constituted a major policy issue for states. At any given time between 1914 and 1918, governments had to provide massive quantities of foodstuffs for soldiers in a variety of war fronts while ensuring that the needs of civilian populations could still be met. The Allied blockade of Germany, Austria-Hungary, and the Ottoman Empire strained resources in those states, while the German submarine campaign attacked the food supplies of Britain and its allies. In general, however, the Central Powers suffered more from shortages in supply, especially as the war progressed; once the United States entered the war, the blockade tightened with the U.S. General Embargo of July 1917.[45] Even some neutral nations experienced supply problems. Sweden, which had imported much of its grain from Russia and Germany before the war, had to switch its business to the United States and Argentina and institute bread (and sugar) rationing in late 1916.[46] The Netherlands also rationed bread and had to reduce the ration as the war progressed.[47]

Those nations with the capacity to produce major food crops tried to encourage healthy harvests and high yields, but lack of manpower and draft animals as well as shortages of fertilizers led to disappointing harvests in several of the war years. Remaining civilians did what they could, and whole households took responsibility for agricultural work, but they often needed additional outside assistance. In France and Germany, for instance, the labor of older men, women, and children in the fields was supplemented by two state policies: use of prisoner of war labor and short seasonal agricultural furloughs for soldiers.[48] In the Ottoman Empire, a special Agricultural Obligations Law in 1916 gave the government the power to require minimum cultivation areas for each pair of oxen and to conscript "battalions of women . . . organised by the army" for harvesting.[49] However, these policies failed to make up the labor differential, especially for large farms that had depended heavily on family members.

The bulk of agricultural management fell to females during the war, adding to the already heavy workload of rural women. Marie Pireaud wrote to her husband about their harvest in southern France, explaining how it was accomplished: "I went to Coutancie to help Nadal's wife, she was harvesting with 9 men and 21 women ask yourself how that happens. As for us, we had 19 men and 9 women. To get men, you have to go a long way to look for them."[50] Women such as Pireaud added male labor to their normal tasks, which included animal care, housework, child care, and raising of root crops. Journalist Matilde Serao paid tribute to the courage of civilian women who took over their husbands' and fathers' jobs along with their own: "Italian country women in summer and autumn have doubled, tripled their daily work. . . . [T]he women have reaped, threshed, made oil and wine. . . . [F]rom girls aged eight to women of seventy . . . [she] worked the land as if she were a man, at the same time nursing a newborn, or feeding soup to an old grandfather."[51] Women also had to rely more on their children. Germany's children worked in the fields, some as part of the "potato holidays" that gave children time off from school to help with the harvest.[52]

In addition to lack of labor, poor weather and battles that destroyed farm land made it difficult for states to raise the necessary crops to meet dietary needs. Famously, the harsh winter and poor harvests of 1916–1917 led to the so-called turnip winter because of severe shortages of potatoes in much of central Europe. The turnips (actually rutabagas) contained less nutritional value than potatoes, and many complained of their bitterness. Piete Kuhr liked the substitutes: "We in the East call the turnips swedes. Grandma always puts caraway seed on the swedes. I can't help it—I like eating swedes, but I hardly dare admit it. Everybody complains about the turnips."[53] While Piete did not feel terrible hunger, true starvation accompanied this period in many regions, especially in urban areas or in institutions (prisons, asylums) where it was difficult to supplement the meager rations the state provided.[54]

Over the course of the war, many products disappeared entirely from markets, and "ersatz" or substituted foods emerged. War bread varied from country to country, but it typically contained only small quantities of wheat, with other grains (rye, corn, millet) and substitutions (soy, potatoes, turnips, etc.) added to make a dough. In Belgium a hot "coffee-like" drink called *torréaline* was brewed from roasted rye, while in Germany a malted beverage called Kriegsbier (war beer) provided small quantities of alcohol.[55] Many countries banned or restricted access to alcohol during the war. For example, the Russian Empire instituted a vodka prohibition during the war and closed all liquor stores during the mobilization period, which in some areas led to rioting and looting of these establishments.[56] Britain also restricted access to liquor in August 1914 by allowing local officials to close pubs or restrict their hours by request of military authorities.[57] Short supplies of coal, soap, leather, and other important household products also made life difficult for civilians, and the loss of some of these led to a rise in epidemic disease (especially skin diseases such as scabies), exposure cases, and infant mortality.

Shortages in supplies and long lines for every available foodstuff led to short tempers, riots, and complaints to soldiers at the front and to government officials. Austrian Christl Lang wrote to her soldier-fiancé describing such shortages in March 1916: "Various foodstuffs, such as sugar, coffee, milk, bread, flour, among others, can be obtained only upon order. This means that hundreds of people queue up two abreast . . . many hours pass before everyone gets a turn and the last ones usually go home empty-handed."[58] A year later, Ethel Cooper in Leipzig recorded in her diary the severe shortages civilians faced: "Coal has run out. The electric light is cut off in most houses (I have gas, thank Heaven!), the trams are not running . . . neither potatoes or turnips are to be had."[59]

By 1917, civilians in many of the belligerent and occupied nations spent a considerable amount of every day just getting foodstuffs. They were told to "sacrifice" for the men at the front, reminded that their reduction in food would feed the soldiers. A French poster depicting a soldier scolded civilians saying, "we don't ask you to die, just to live economically."[60] In the United States, civilians were reminded by their new food administrator, Herbert Hoover, that "FOOD WILL WIN THE WAR," and they were encouraged to volunteer to "prove your Americanism by eating less." U.S. women enrolled as members of the food campaign in order to "fight by helping the fighters to fight." These culinary soldiers could help win the war by planning two "wheatless" days a week.[61]

Some civilians sacrificed willingly, seeing their dwindling household supplies and their time-consuming waits as patriotic acts, but they endured more and more forcible reductions in their food supply as the war progressed. Many people tried to play by the rules, even as those rules shifted in front of them. Others tried to protect civilians from the greed or need of others. In Luxembourg, which was under German occupation, local Girl Guides made potatoes the focus of their community service by guarding potato carts during distributions:

> Some charitable people used to go round the country buying up potatoes, which were then . . . distributed in cartloads. The delivery was generally made at night through streets which were kept in darkness on account of the danger of air-raids, and the poverty was so great that often whole cartloads of potatoes disappeared en route. The Guides used to go out with the carts, so as to see that the distribution was carried out fairly.[62]

Equity, fairness, and shared sacrifice were all ideals during the war, but government policies often made a mockery of such sentiments, leading to disillusionment. As more and more citizens failed to see governments meeting their basic daily needs, they "turned to the black market and to the theft of food on a massive scale."[63]

Strict requisitioning and rationing policies by states led some producers to resist government mandates by hiding their crops or resorting to bribery of officials, while others smuggled products through emerging black markets.[64] Consumers as well resorted to hoarding and theft, especially in occupied territories, where hatred of enemy occupiers provided further fuel to resentment about food controls. Yves Congar, a ten-year-old French child in 1914, described his family's attempt to save its potatoes from German requisitioning, first by hiding its potato supply in the cellar and then by getting "up at six and go[ing] potato-pinching" in nearby fields.[65] In some regions organized smuggling rings emerged that hoped to circumvent regulations on potato supply. A Belgian intelligence report identified a potato smuggling ring operating around the district of the Palais de Justice in Brussels, which employed "women and young girls who went into the country on foot or by the local railways; by trying to outbid each other at the farms they created high prices in this so-called market. Each successful trip yielded 20 to 30 francs net profit on potatoes and more on flour (1000 francs per sack in Brussels) and on butter." These smugglers bribed German sentries to let them pass, although tightened restrictions eventually led to nocturnal expeditions so as to avoid sentries.[66]

Riots, robberies, and revolutions resulted in many regions, and food scarcities often played a major role in undermining civilian confidence in and support for the war. Long lines of hungry people and uneven supplies created flashpoints for food demonstrations such as the August 1917 riots in Turin (Italy) or this July 1917 riot in Berlin:

> A number of persons who had to leave the market empty-handed exited the market in small groups headed for the city hall and demanded bread and potatoes there. With the indication from the civil servant that they should get bread where they have it to sell, a number of women now pushed down the Gürtel Street and from the shop of the baker Hans Schwarze . . . , against the will of the clerk, they violently took 30 breads without paying. A riot arose over this, involving about 150 people, in which the shop's show window awning was damaged.[67]

Such riots were not uncommon from 1915 until well after the war in a variety of countries. In Russia, food riots that began in fall 1915 throughout the empire escalated over the next three years. When the International Women's Day demonstrations of March 8, 1917, helped spark a broader revolution that toppled the tsar, it reflected the broad sense of shared grievance felt by soldiers' wives, industrial workers, and peasant women. That day, the women in the crowds shouted "Down with hunger" as they protested wartime conditions, long food lines, and shortages of food, fuel, and supplies. As Barbara Engel has argued, the wartime food riots reflect "an informal community, with a shared notion of justice that included the right to consume . . . [and] a shared hostility toward people whose money gave them privileged access."[68]

While populations protested shortages and hunger, real and widespread starvation threatened in some regions. Ottoman policies toward its Armenian population as well as disruptions of harvests and local resistance to Ottoman mandates led to famines in eastern Anatolia, Syria, and Lebanon that resulted in the deaths of as many as 1.5 million civilians.[69] In Persia, as army requisitioning, war profiteering, hoarding, and poor harvests combined to decimate the food supply, famine conditions ravaged the area. Reports from foreign officials in Tehran in 1916 and 1917 note shortages of bread and other essential foods, long lines, and rioting by women. Dr. Samuel Jordan of Tehran's American College began sending telegrams for assistance in winter 1918, which continued into the early summer:

(February 1918) Forty thousand destitute Teheran alone. People eating dead animals. Women abandoning their infants. . . . (May 1918) Famine conditions unexpectedly increasing and are accompanied by a great epidemic typhoid, typhus. Same conditions in other Persian cities. Food stuffs almost unobtainable; prices enormous; people eating grass, dogs, dead animals, even human beings. If possible send additional hundred thousand [dollars].[70]

Eyewitness Mohammed Ali Jamalzedah wrote of similar desperation in Shiraz (Iran): "As no food was to be found, people were forced to eat whatever that could be chewed—objects or animals. Soon not a single cat or dog or crow was to be seen. Even mice and rats were exterminated. Leaves, grass, and plant roots were traded like bread and meat."[71] Famine conditions also prevailed in colonial territories that suffered from severe requisitioning of people, food, and animals by armies in the field. In central Tanzania, a drought exacerbated the impact of German and British requisitions of cattle and food; altogether, perhaps thirty thousand of the area's population of 150,000 died in the famine.[72]

While such dire conditions threatened civilians in some nations, those living far from the conflict experienced a much gentler food situ-

MINISTRY OF FOOD.	TEA 17	TEA 9	TEA 1
Liverpool Local Food Control Committee.			
	Week ending 2'nd June, 1918	Week ending 27th April, 1918	Week ending 2nd March, 1918
TEA.	L'pool Food Control	L'pool Food Control	L'pool Food Control
	TEA 18	TEA 10	TEA 2
Householder's Name	Week ending 29th June, 1918	Week ending 4th May, 1918	Week ending 9th March, 1918
Address	L'pool Food Control	L'pool Food Control	L'pool Food Control
....	TEA 19	TEA 11	TEA 3
.... Persons.	Week ending 6th July, 1918	Week ending 11th May, 1918	Week ending 16th March, 1918
Retailer's Name	L'pool Food Control	L'pool Food Control	L'pool Food Control
Address	TEA 20	TEA *12	TEA 4
....	Week ending 13th July, 1918	Week ending 18th May, 1918	Week ending 23rd March, 1918
The Registered Number of this Card is .... and this number must be quoted in any correspondence relating thereto.	L'pool Food Control	L'pool Food Control	L'pool Food Control
	TEA 21	TEA 13	TEA 5
DIRECTIONS TO THE HOUSEHOLDER.	Week ending 20th July, 1918	Week ending 25th May, 1918	Week ending 30th March, 1918
This Card must be produced to the Retailer of Tea, Butter and/or Margarine whenever you desire to purchase your weekly ration of any of these articles	L'pool Food Control	L'pool Food Control	L'pool Food Control
The Retailer will detach from the Card and retain the appropriate Coupon.	TEA 22	TEA 14	TEA 6
No Coupon is available *before* the commencement of the week shown thereon, but	Week ending 27th July, 1918	Week ending 1st June, 1918	Week ending 6th April, 1918
	L'pool Food Control	L'pool Food Control	L'pool Food Control

Ration books became a part of life for civilians. The tea stamps in this ration book from Liverpool (Britain) provided a weekly portion of the hot drink for the population. *National Archives UK.*

ation. The United States used persuasion and patriotic rhetoric (along with clever advertising) to reduce consumption and waste, while Latin American nations relied on price controls to help handle the difficulties of shipping and supply. Less lucky were those nations that either would not or could not develop effective rationing programs despite a need for them—the Russian Empire, for instance, failed to institute a workable national rationing scheme. Rationing was a simple concept—government regulation of vital products—but difficult to administer. Typically each person or household, depending on the country, had a card for an individual food or other product to which stamps could be affixed.

Most national rationing programs developed piecemeal as certain products became hard to obtain. In Hungary, for instance, ration cards developed in stages, first with milk (November 1915), then bread (January 1916) and soap (March 1917), and, finally, potatoes (April 1917).[73] Germany rationed bread as early as 1915, while other nations only began rationing schemes much later in the war: Italy (1917), Britain (1917–18), France (1918).[74] Most common were ration cards for bread and sugar, but also rationed were fats, coffee, tea, flour, and potatoes, plus items like coal and soap. Piete Kuhr described the bread situation in East Prussia by July 1915:

> In the town bread is no longer sold without so-called "bread-cards," nor any rolls or biscuits. The bread cards are issued every fortnight in different colours and with different numbers and distributed to individual households by the "Municipal Bread Commission." So many heads, so many cards. . . . The loaves look different from those in peacetime. Whereas there used to be white bread made from wheat meal, now there's "war bread" made from rye meal and potatoes. This bread is marked with a large K—Kriegsbrot [war bread] or Kartoffelbrot [potato bread]. In addition every load shows the date on which it was baked. New bread is not allowed to be issued.[75]

As Piete noted, households had controls on their bread purchases, but often bakers themselves were held responsible for correct bread weights, grain mixtures, and quality. Bakeries and local officials had to police the whole rationing system and face angry crowds bent on violence during shortages or periods of perceived unfair distribution. Consumers recognized the threat of violence as an effective weapon and wielded it when necessary. In Russia in summer 1915, for instance, large groups of women descended on a market in Moscow and vocally refused to leave until merchants dropped their prices on potatoes. In a separate Russian incident a year later, women destroyed market stalls, stole goods, and beat a policeman after a price rise.[76] Municipal offices could also be targeted, and in Berlin, Bread Commission offices were repeatedly vandalized and robbed.[77]

In addition to rationed items, governments set price controls and inspected the quality of products when possible. The German government even accepted the help of volunteers for smoothing the mechanisms of food distribution. For example, the Women's National Service enlisted for duty handing out bread rations, teaching cooking classes, and inspecting bakeries.[78] Most nations at war moved toward control economies as well, creating government monopolies with price and distribution limits. At German and Austrian home fronts or occupied zones, these mechanisms were typically known as "Centrals." The setup was simple—"private businesses specializing in a certain good would form a government-sponsored cartel that served as the clearing house for that product."[79] Despite all state attempts to regulate and control food supply, shortages and price gouging continued, leading inevitably to hoarding by rural producers and merchants, the rise of black markets, and smuggling activities. In Hungary by 1917, prices for household products and clothing had increased by 268 percent and 1,230 percent, respectively.[80] Supply also remained unpredictable and difficult to manage for most nations.

The German case is illustrative, with ration cards for most staples and organized central commodities bureaus. Yet, leaders had not entirely reckoned with the stubborn hoarding, price gouging, and tricks employed by producers and consumers alike. Government promises of equity, controlled supply, and quality foodstuffs often fell short of civilian expectations, leading to protests, work disruptions, and strikes. By the end of 1917, as Belinda Davis argues of those in Berlin, Germans placed little faith in their wartime leaders, who were seen at best as inept fools and at worst as profiteers/speculators themselves.[81]

Illegal activities arose in all nations involved in the war, including belligerent and occupied nations, but black markets and smuggling operations also thrived in neutral nations. Black markets in goods such as potatoes and meat helped civilians survive in regions where rationing and price-control policies were ineffective or where transport systems broke down. Normally law-abiding citizens now habitually evaded government regulations, creating an ugly situation for civilian morale. Scholar Avner Offer has described the "moral trauma" this caused, as states failed in their attempts to provide basic foods for their citizenries. In other words, nations such as Germany "forced every citizen into breaking the law."[82] Other historians have also concluded that political mobilization of civilians often broke down by the end of the war, and neither persuasion nor coercion could revive civilian morale.[83]

Governments tried to respond to these pressures. Municipal kitchens and poor relief in many localities helped relieve some food pressures, but they also depended on adequate supply and transport, which often was not available. In Vienna, families had by 1918 reached a breaking point. They forced the Habsburg state "to post regiments to guard potatoes from its own citizens" during the "potato war" of 1918. Such actions culminated in the events of June 28–29, 1918, when an estimated thirty thousand people descended on potato farms around the city, and "gangs swarmed the fields and stole the young potatoes and late potatoes . . . wide stretches of land were plundered and devastated."[84] Such guerilla actions against rural producers point to the real and perceived social and cultural divides that emerged during the war. Food battles demonstrate well the way in which the war undermined communal ties and perpetuated prewar social and cultural divides among populations while also creating new fissure lines.

Women, especially, became soldiers in the food wars being waged with the state, merchants, and producers. They waited in lines, wrote letters to local officials, organized meager household resources, and, when necessary, they smuggled, stole, and illegally purchased the supplies their families needed. Some women became expert in provisioning their families, resulting in the term, "squirrel" or "hamster" in Germany. "Squirrel trains" to the countryside where foraging and stealing took place were common later in the war, and one historian noted that Germany even "included the population's illegal self-provision in its calculations for food rationing."[85] Civilian Ernst Gläser described the situation perfectly when he wrote, "A new front was created. It was held by the women, against an entente of field gendarmes and controllers. Every smuggled pound of butter, every sack of potatoes successfully spirited in by night, was celebrated in their homes with the same enthusiasm as the victories of the armies two years before."[86]

Most civilians experienced at least some difficulty obtaining foodstuffs, but working-class families, for whom bread and potatoes were central to their diet, felt "singled out" for sacrifice in the war effort, as they faced shortages, soaring prices, and long lines. In public protests throughout the middle years of the war, working-class consumers demanded government action to stop what they saw as war profiteering by merchants and rural growers.[87] The shortages, long lines, restricted rations, and psychological strain of war led to public denunciations of "war profiteers" or "war traitors" both during and, especially, after the war. Thus prewar class tensions were exacerbated by the competition for scarce resources. As historian Roger Chickering noted in his study of Freiburg, potato producers and merchants became, in effect, employees of the state: "Willingly or not, producers became public contractors. Retail merchants were transformed from entrepreneurs into office-holders, managers of public distribution outlets, who administered limited quantities of goods at controlled prices in return for reimbursement fees set by public authority."[88] This particularly complicated distribution systems and helped fuel fears that some were becoming rich off their food contracts while others starved.

People who seemed not to be sacrificing or who actually appeared to profit from the war were treated with bitterness and sometimes violence. Many nations prosecuted war profiteers, both for small-scale crimes and for larger enterprises. In Vienna, Emma Kosel, a milk merchant, spent three days in jail and paid a fine for "watering down" milk for customers. Also in Vienna, lists of those convicted of profiteering were published in the newspapers.[89] Peasants were particularly targeted for denunciations as profiteers by those living in urban areas—many who attempted to hoard supplies or to gain higher prices for their goods were verbally and physically attacked. French markets witnessed "scuffles . . . between peasants selling produce and urban women consumers," in which "the police sided with consumers, and were more likely to arrest the peasants for price-gouging."[90] German urban consumers as well identified selfish and greedy producers as the cause of their food woes, and in Austria, attacks centered especially on Hungarian farmers, who were accused of starving Austria for their own gain.[91]

The enmity and fear caused by shortages helped fuel civilian calls in all nations for "equity." Most civilians seem to have accepted that their nations could call on them in times of war to sacrifice, but they rebelled at the thought that some people were sacrificing while others were profiting. As the war progressed and losses wore away at civilian morale, this sense of "equal" service and sacrifice gained support. Civilians looked to punish "shirkers" and "profiteers." The rising sense of injustice among some communities at war coincided with greater national attempts at mobilization of complete societies and economies. Just as governments tried to mobilize more female and youth labor, a series of strikes and labor unrest emerged by 1917–1918. The food battles spilled over into other sectors of the war economy.

Supporting the Home Front

In 1914 governments recruited labor with calls to patriotism and voluntary service. People sought to "do their part" to support the nation and the fighting forces, but more compulsion entered the equation as the war dragged on and volunteers began to wane. Even with militarized labor corps and prisoners doing work for the state, more labor was required. As the conflict continued past the first year, nations began to mobilize noncombatants as workers at home in vital areas of agriculture, transport, civil service, and heavy industry. Few at home could escape some kind of war activity, whether it was contributing to a Red Cross charitable fund, working in a munitions factory, or buying a war bond. The cash and in-kind contributions to war charities were staggering in their scope. Austria's War Relief Office had received more than twenty-six million crowns in cash by 1917 and more than a million pairs of socks.[92] Civilians were more than happy to show their patriotic fervor and support the war effort as long as they still supported the cause.

It was not hard to find volunteers in the first months of the war, and in fact, many females who volunteered their services to militaries or civil administrations were turned away in 1914. These women found their callings in nonprofit and voluntary organizations, often funded through private charities or individuals. When Scottish physician Elsie Inglis volunteered her services to the British War Office, she was sent away. Inglis found a more willing government in France and helped establish a hospital there. She also gained other funding for her Scottish Women's Hospitals, the first of which was established in Serbia in January 1915.[93] Trained French pilot Marie Marvingt offered to fly for the French war effort, but the government rejected her offer and requisitioned her airplane instead.[94] Other women wanted to volunteer but could not afford the start-up costs. Anna Murr wrote to the Bavarian king in 1918 asking for help in paying for the training course to be a Red Cross nurse.[95]

Women throughout the combatant countries enlisted as nurses and nurses' aides in local hospitals, joined charitable and humanitarian organizations, provided services for refugees, wrote letters to soldiers, and lobbied for other roles in the wartime establishment. Organizations in need of labor and funds played on the patriotic ambitions of civilians. The Women's Reserve Ambulance of the Green Cross Society in Britain sent out this call: "Many girls and women whose home ties prevent them from giving their entire days to war work have offered their spare time to various organisations only to find that 'all or nothing' was the demand." The WRA claimed that it made use of spare time, allowing the busy wife or mother to do her patriotic service as well by transporting the wounded, delivering munitions and comforts, running canteens, and doing ambulance duty for zeppelin raids. One such WRA volunteer, "Corporal" Eunice Graham, logged 468 hours of "spare time" work in June and July 1917, or almost fifty-nine hours per week. This was a reduction for her, as she had put in almost ninety hours per week in the late winter of 1916 until her husband, interned in Germany, complained that she was overworking herself.[96]

One unusual program started in 1915 in France led women to become *marraines de guerre* (war godmothers) by adopting soldiers at the front, to whom they could write letters and send packages. Women *marraines* could express their patriotism by providing the comfort of letters for soldiers far from home and, as Margaret Darrow argues, personifying "the France that [men] were defending."[97] Although implying a sort of maternal connection, the godmothers quickly became sexualized in popular imagination, and the supposed anonymity of the system led to fantasies and humorous satires.[98] In *La Baïonnette!* cartoonists depicted a variety of scenarios: a small child godmother with an adult godson; a godmother who finds out her godson is black; and an elderly godmother trying to decide what to send when her soldier asks for a snapshot.[99]

Although the "godmother" scheme in France garnered much press attention, it was not the only organization created to provide soldiers with a sense of connection with home. As part of her Red Cross work, Piete Kuhr sent out Christmas parcels. When she received a thank-you note from Emil, a soldier who had received one of her parcels, she began a correspondence with him and his sister, Minna. The threesome shared information about conditions at home and at the front, with the two women discussing Emil's health after a bayonet wound and his subsequent return to the front. As the war progressed, Piete expanded her letter writing, and she was writing simultaneously to four front-line soldiers and tending (secretly) to a Russian POW cemetery as part of her own "unofficial" war service.[100]

Although many letter-writing schemes were instigated by private charities, civilians also began their own correspondence campaigns to neighbors, acquaintances, friends, and extended family, understanding that their letters were important to the soldiers. Walter Richter's neighbors wrote to him frequently to keep him abreast of the neighborhood gossip in Chicago after he was sent to France. His close friends, such as Josie Yeockel, sent photos and updates on Chicago life. Mrs. Arado and Mrs. Ritter, both young wives who were near neighbors to Walter in Chicago, reported on his parents' health and dispositions, noting when his father went on a drinking binge and when his mother was ill. All the letters consciously tried to give him courage—with Mrs. Ritter telling him, "Your Mother is only praying for your safe return, & she will try to be brave like a soldier's Mother ought to be," while Josie wrote, "Well some day you will come back and we sure will be proud of you, then no one can call you a slacker like some."[101] Such letters back and forth suggest a tight emotional and psychological connection for soldiers at the front and their home communities, forged through multiple channels of correspondence, whether they be anonymous "godmothers" or the neighbors in the upstairs apartment.

In addition to writing letters and working for charitable organizations, many civilians took jobs in unfamiliar occupations in order to help meet the needs of the wartime state. War work took a variety of forms, but in most cases it meant one of two things: becoming a replacement worker for a man of military age or doing direct war work at home or in the areas of operation. The occupations most affected included agriculture, transport, clerical work, manufacturing (especially munitions), medical care, and service jobs. Some of those employed in "war work" shifted from other occupations, while others were new to the work force. Women, children, and men beyond military age were the main pool of workers from which states drew their labor force, but in some cases, refugee labor, POW labor, and "guest workers" from foreign countries were also employed. Rural civilians mostly found themselves drawn into agricultural work, which was a major need. Especially in countries where literacy rates in the countryside were low and rural communities remained somewhat isolated, agriculture was the thing most peasant women and elderly men felt equipped to perform. Urban dwellers, notably in highly industrialized nations, entered into training in first aid, skilled light industry, and clerical work in order to take advantage of wartime openings.

Social class was a major factor here, as many industrial and service jobs went to working-class men and women, while clerical and civil service jobs were reserved for those with good educations and social connections. Many working-class women in Britain, for example, saw the relatively well-paid munitions work as a step up from the drudgery of jobs as domestic servants, laundresses, or shop girls.[102] In fact, with shifts of women from one industry to another, sometimes opportunities appeared for other marginalized workers. Young people who had been increasingly funneled into schooling and away from paid work at young ages found themselves in paid occupations again. Also, in the United States, when white working-class women gave up jobs in the garment industry for better-remunerated positions in munitions and steel, African-American women filled the jobs in the garment industry.[103] Women's interest in well-paid war work, coupled with conscription of men for the front, led to considerable feminization of workforces in some nations and of particular occupations. As Thierry Bonzon has outlined, in the Citroën factory in France women made up more than 90 percent of the shell-assembly workers and 100 percent of some unskilled jobs.[104] Citroën was unusual in its high number of female employees, but throughout the belligerent nations, women's employment in industry expanded, at least for the duration of the war. In Berlin more than half of those employed in metalwork, chemicals, and machine tools were women, and Britain's Woolwich Arsenal had a workforce of thirty thousand women by war's end.[105]

While many jumped at the chance to do war work, either voluntary or paid, and saw it as a patriotic obligation, others had to be compelled to work. In Germany, to meet the labor demands that seemed to increase as the war dragged on, the state passed an Auxiliary Service Law (Hilfsdienstgesetz) in December 1916, which conscripted "men between sev-

Young munitions workers take a lunch break at a German factory. *U.S. Signal Corps, National Archives and Records Administration.*

enteen and sixty to work in war economy." In effect, the state tried to "compel Germany's civilian population to assist the war effort."[106] While women and youth were excluded from this legislation, they were heavily recruited and encouraged to volunteer to become war workers. Nations such as Germany, but also Austria-Hungary and Britain, tried mobilizing existing women's organizations to help coordinate voluntary and paid employment during the war, with a certain amount of success. In Austria, an umbrella organization emerged during the war that combined the forces of several women's groups, including conservative imperial housewives, Social Democratic women, and Catholic women. When the voluntary structures did not provide enough labor, Austrian military officials created a women's auxiliary force, similar to that of Germany's. However, the question of women auxiliaries touched many flashpoints of conflict during the war—women's sense of entitlement as army employees, men's

Polish women toil in the fields in the labor-intensive peasant farming of the period. *Library of Congress.*

fear of being replaced, and societal concern that women were becoming too manly. Despite their reportedly excellent work and their supervised, sex-segregated housing, the women faced accusations of immorality and even prostitution. Women's outspoken glee about their army service did little to calm fears, as with Austrian auxiliaries, for instance, who "wore uniforms; they referred to themselves as 'enlisted'; they were relatively well paid; they traveled far from home and worked alongside men."[107]

Although all belligerent countries tried to utilize women's labor, these countries' officials envisioned a temporary rise in women's employment "for the duration." Most measures were designed to protect male wages for the postwar period, so women, children, and older men often had to settle for poor pay and a precarious stability to their work lives. In addition, governments sought to preserve the family and home by controlling workers' morality through education and propaganda programs, curfews, and limits on alcohol consumption. Civilians were asked to work for the war, maintain their homes and families, and keep up their morale as well as their moral standards. For many noncombatants this was difficult since the impact of the war visited them regularly in the form of lists of dead, missing, and wounded. Civilians had the difficult role of waiting, often not knowing where their loved ones were or how they were doing, despite correspondence. Leaves, stolen meetings near the fronts, and letters kept the civilians' hopes alive. Vera Brittain, working as a nurses aide in the Voluntary Aid Detachment (VAD) in Britain at the time, recorded her long wait for her fiancé's leave in 1915 and her excitement at his anticipated arrival at Christmastime. She wrote to him, "[W]hen I think of the sweet hours that may be ahead—when I shall see once more 'the things I strive to capture in vain'. . . . 'And shall I really see you again, and so soon?'" Vera flew through her work at the hospital, bought new clothes, and made plans for their meeting at his parents' house on Christmas Day. His death at the front on December 23 was not communicated to Vera and his family until December 26, after a long Christmas of waiting for him to appear.[108]

For other families the wait was short, but no less devastating. Käthe Kollwitz's son, Peter, died in October 1914 in Belgium, only a few weeks after joining up. Kollwitz spent the rest of the war planning a monument to him and decorating his room with wreaths that reflected the changing seasons. She often sat in his room writing in her diary or reading. She recorded one such day in her diary (November 4, 1917): "Alone. Sat at his wooden table. Began to read the Bible." By July 1918 a numbness had set in for Kollwitz: "The feelings are over, the pain is over, the longing is over. . . . The pain has left behind fatigue. It is, after all, not only Peter. It is the war that grinds one down."[109] Such psychological traumas as experienced by Kollwitz and Brittain were enacted again and again over the course of the war in civilian households at the home fronts, a reminder that war was not distant, but personal.

The diary of Mary Martin, an Irish widow who had two sons in the British army and a daughter who was working in a Red Cross hospital, illustrates the trajectory that many civilians faced in knowing their loved ones were in danger. As a way of coping with the news that her son, Charlie, was missing in action in December 1915, she began a diary for him that she planned to give him when he returned. The diary, which commenced with New Year's Day, 1916, chronicles her attempts to get news of Charlie's whereabouts. She began with a host of rosaries/prayers and letters to War

Office officials, then tried to piece together bits of news she received from soldiers who had been with him in Salonika. On January 8, she received a Red Cross letter telling her he was wounded and left behind in a retreat, possibly as a prisoner. On January 10, she got a letter from Charlie himself, but it was dated November 1915. Mary continued to check with Prisoners of War Bureaus and the army, recording additional pieces of information in her diary as they appeared. When a letter from an officer in Charlie's unit arrived, she informed her son in her diary,

> [A]lthough it does not give us much more details of how you were we were delighted to have it & read his praise of you & know that your good work & bravery was really appreciated. I am so proud when I think how wonderfully you carried out the arduous & dangerous enterprise you & your brave companions were asked to undertake.[110]

As she agonized over Charlie's fate, her other children both moved to new locations, Marie to Malta and Tommy to near Salonika. She rejoiced in their regular correspondence and sent them parcels and letters to keep up their spirits, but she also enlisted their help in finding Charlie. Marie interviewed men at the hospital at Malta, finding one in March 1916 who had picked up Charlie's identification disc during the December 1915 advance at which he went missing. This soldier reported that Charlie was wounded and taken by the Bulgarians. Another letter at the end of March added to Mary's increasing despair, when a fellow officer reported that Charlie was not in the POW camp with others from the regiment. On April 8 another report came from Marie that a soldier remembered seeing Charlie alive, but wounded. Whether to distract herself or to record important war news for Charlie, in April Mary turned in her diary for Charlie to the events going on around her in Dublin, telling him in great detail about the Easter Rebellion, which became a welcome descriptive interlude for her. The diary ended abruptly on May 8, 1916, with definitive news of Charlie's death. Mary, who had been writing the journal for Charlie, recorded none of her grief after the six months of waiting and hope.[111]

For those living on the "home fronts," the dangers of war also visited them directly in the form of bombardments from ships or airships (zeppelins and airplanes), sinking of passenger ships, and explosions of munitions installations. Certainly most civilians at the "home fronts" were more protected than civilians living and working in the operations or staging areas, or even those in occupied territories, but they were not entirely immune from the violence of war. Air raids, which became a part of the war for some and made the "home front" an explicit target, brought civilians under fire from the air in their homes, at work, and in medical installations. As the German army advanced in Belgium in 1914, cities behind the front were bombed from zeppelins. In Antwerp, for example, a zeppelin raid in August led to strict regulation:

> To make sure of offering no unnecessary chances for Mr. Zeppelin the authorities had ordered all the lights on the streets put out at eight o'clock. It was dark as midnight and there was no use in thinking of venturing out into the town. The Cathedral clock was stopped and the carillon turned off for the first time in heaven only knows how many years. It was a city of the dead.[112]

While the German advance led to bombing of cities in Belgium, the Russian retreat on the eastern front also led to bombed cities, bridges, railheads, and military depots, with zeppelins depositing bombs on cities such as Wilna in fall 1915.[113]

Aerial bombing was still an inexact science in the First World War, but it did manage to inflict casualties. The first German civilian to be killed in an air raid was in Dusseldorf in September 1914, and more than seven hundred German civilians died in aerial bombing raids, with the worst single incident occurring at Karlsruhe in June 1916, when 260 civilians were killed or wounded.[114] During the course of the war, aerial bombing (from zeppelins and airplanes) and artillery bombardment (long-range shells) led to approximately fifteen hundred casualties in Paris alone.[115] Air raids on British cities took place a bit later in the war, with the first major zeppelin attacks occurring in January 1915, although 142 were killed and several hundred injured in the eastern port cities of Scarborough, Whitby, and Hartlepool in December 1914 after German warships shelled the towns, an older form of attack on noncombatant populations.[116] Other fronts also witnessed the bombing of noncombatant populations. In Tsingtao, China, the Japanese launched shells from ships and dropped bombs from planes during the siege of September 1914.[117] In Venice, an air raid from four planes in the middle of the night in September 1916 led to fewer casualties than expected because of defective bombs. For example, the bombs fell on a church, an "old man's refuge," and two private homes, but only two of the bombs actually exploded.[118] Despite the unexploded bombs, almost one thousand Italians died during the war in the more than 340 German and Austrian air raids.[119] Multiple Bulgarian cities as well, such as Xanthi, had to be evacuated of civilians after repeated French bombing by airplanes and warships.[120] By the end of the war, all belligerents were engaged in bombing of civilian targets.

Civilians learned the meaning of blackouts and air raids sirens, while officials sought appropriate shelters for urban populations exposed to the dangers of war from the air. The environment of many cities facing air raids changed as regulations were put into place, as U.S. observer Joseph Green noted in his account of an autumn 1915 visit to London:

> London, by day, wears such a normal aspect that a stranger requires close observation to detect that anything extraordinary is going on. . . . It is at night that London gives evidence of the crisis which the nation is passing through. The city is much darker than Paris was a year ago. Since the last Zeppelin raid of two weeks ago the regulations are exceedingly severe. Few street lamps are lit—about one to a block—two or three for a square as large as Trafalgar. Even those which are lit have the upper part of the globes painted with black paint so that they only shed a small circle of light directly under them. There are no lights in the shop windows and curtains are drawn everywhere. . . . [We] saw three places where Zeppelin bombs had struck in the last raid. One had destroyed the roof and upper story of the building next to the office; one, said to have landed on top of a bus, had blown a big hole in the pavement near Liverpool St. station and had smashed all the nearby windows. The third had partially wrecked a building in Moorgate St. within a couple of blocks of the Bank. In general the damage seemed to be greater than that done by bombs dropped from aeroplanes in Paris last year.[121]

Officials faced these dangers with regulations that ranged from mandatory blackout curtains or painted windows to temporary air raid shelters.

They also tried to educate the public with posters explaining precautions to be taken and also with guides to identifying enemy airships. Some of these regulations were hurried and not always entirely effective. In London, for example, vehicular and pedestrian tunnels under the Thames were used as air raid shelters for London's working poor, despite the fact that they might not be safe if hit directly. As air raids intensified, authorities had to guard the smaller tunnels at Greenwich and Woolwich to make sure they did not become dangerously overcrowded, while at the Rotherhithe tunnel, the thirty thousand people using it during air raids required temporary "decency conveniences" and drinking water. Municipal authorities tried to provide the necessary arrangements without any real budget.[122]

Despite precautions, civilians were often injured or died in air raids. Civilian contractors at port cities in France were particularly at risk, and several raids on Boulogne, Dunkirk, and Le Havre led to the deaths of civilian contract laborers. For example, an air raid on Boulogne and Dunkirk on September 4–5, 1917, killed fifteen and wounded twenty-one Chinese laborers, but it also inadvertently caused the deaths of another twenty-one men, when the army fired on crowds of striking Egyptian laborers who were protesting their exposure to aerial bombing.[123] In the bustling port of Calais, civilians faced aerial bombing from September 1914 to September 1918. This city experienced sixty-one raids by airplanes, six by zeppelin, and one from a warship for a total of sixty-eight different bombing attacks. From these attacks, more than eighteen hundred projectiles fell, killing 108 civilians and wounding more than two hundred others. More than two hundred homes were destroyed and another five thousand houses were damaged.[124]

Civilians often commented in their diaries and memoirs on the strange reactions they felt to aerial bombing, both a sense of fascination and a feeling of dread. Elizabeth Ashe, working in Paris in April 1918, noted how quickly she got used to the alarms of war:

> There are few quiet moments in Paris now. Between air raids by night and cannonading by day we have a very lively time. It is strange how quickly one gets used to such things. When the bombarding first began, people rushed to the street and curiously looked about to see where the shell had burst,

but now, although we know that each report of that gun means death and destruction to innocent, defenceless people, we hardly raise our eyes from our desks.[125]

Others found the bombing of civilians criminal. Helena Farrington threw eggs at a public funeral for a zeppelin crew brought down by the British, telling the press, "I thought of Belgium and France and Serbia . . . then I bought the eggs. I took them to the cemetery, and threw them on the commander's coffin saying, 'I protest against a military funeral for these murderers.'"[126]

In addition to danger from the air, travelers faced additional peril from attacks at sea, as is evident in the accounts of the *Lusitania* disaster. Submarine warfare, especially in the Atlantic Ocean and Mediterranean Sea, claimed the lives of many civilian volunteer workers, merchants, and travelers. For instance, the Russian hospital ship, *The Portugal,* was sunk by an enemy submarine in the Black Sea in April 1916, with the loss of more than one hundred lives, many of them Red Cross nurses and physicians.[127] Likewise, the British reported seven hospital ships sunk in a period from March 1917 to February 1918.[128] Sometimes the sinking of supply ships also had impacts for civilians when shortages resulted. Dangers came not just from submarine attacks but also from underwater mines laid along coastlines and in major waterways and from explosions of volatile chemicals and munitions on ships. In November 1916, many noncombatants were killed in the Russian port of Bakaritza when a munitions ship caught fire and exploded, damaging harbor installations and destroying a coal ship nearby.[129]

Governments often tried to minimize or cover up such disasters, but often their locations made that impossible. Two of the best-known explosions of war materials occurred in Silvertown (UK) in January 1917 and Halifax (Canada) in December 1917. The first was an explosion at a munitions factory in east London, while the second featured the explosion of a munitions ship in Halifax harbor after it collided with a Belgian relief vessel. In Halifax, more than fifteen hundred died, another four thousand were seriously wounded, and an estimated twenty thousand were left homeless as a Canadian winter hit.[130] At Silvertown, the factory explosion killed at least sixty-nine and injured hundreds more, but more frightening was that the resulting fire came perilously close to igniting the massive Woolwich Arsenal across the river.[131] The arsenal itself, as with other munitions works around the world, experienced small explosions, spills, and fires fairly regularly, but workers were expected to keep such incidents to themselves.

Munitions dangers, like air raids, had a psychological impact on civilian morale. One London observer, Mrs. Fernside, described the scene on the day after the explosion in a letter to a friend:

> We have a <u>most terrible</u> explosion at Silvertown. Though it was so far away, the noise was so terrific that I thought the Huns had dropped a surprise packet about 3 doors away, so opened the door to look out and there was nothing to be seen, decided to remain in the kitchen & "wait and see." The doors & windows shook & so did the ground. This morning the sky is very strange, showing it must have disturbed other elements. . . . There are thousands killed, great gaps cracks [sic] in the roads, people 3 miles off, were blown out of their homes & were running about, seeking a place to shelter. All the London hospitals are full, the ambulances have been busy all night. . . . There was a small explosion at White City last week, but this is impossible to exaggerate. . . . England has never experienced anything so terrible. People on the whole kept calm though there was panic in some of the picture palaces. Plenty of rumors as to how it happened, but that will never be solved. They think a German has done it. The report will be modified so as to keep it from Germany. City shops are boarded up, all windows broken & houses within a mile radius all down.[132]

Just more than a week later, Mrs. Fernside turned her attention to other disasters around them with the German bombing of buildings in Covent Garden, Notting Hill, Vauxhall, and Kew Gardens, all neighborhoods in and around London.[133]

Civilians lived near and worked in munitions factories, which led to dangers from toxic poisoning as well as from explosions. For war workers, especially those on night shift, the dangers increased. Munitions workers faced TNT poisoning, burns, fires, and explosions, while civil servants working in government buildings feared air raids. The night shift at MI5 (counterespionage) headquarters in London, for example, had to be suspended in August 1916 because of "the frequent work stoppages from air raid warnings."[134] Anyone working near a military installation, whether it was a medical facility or a munitions plant, feared targeting by the enemy. Given the nature of wartime mobilization and the deliberate targeting of noncombatants as a war tactic, it became increasingly hard for civilians to find safe havens to shelter from the war and its dangers.

Conclusion

Certainly civilians have never been entirely safe from war, and in the First World War, generally civilians were safer than they would be during World War II. What is significant about home fronts in the First World War is their unprecedented militarization and mobilization as "fronts" in the fight for supremacy in the war. Without civilian labor and sacrifice, the war could not have been fought. Civilians "mediated" the war, experiencing fear, violence, and patriotism along with the soldiers but also providing the necessary normalcy of "life at home."[135] Civilians at "home fronts" knew their duty—to serve their nations with patriotic contributions, labor, and fortitude.

Their emotional connection to the war was a reality to which they clung, and despite talk of the separation between home and battle fronts, many civilian diaries and letters suggest that they saw the gap as negligible. Drawn into the war through government surveillance and intervention in their lives but also through war service, both paid and voluntary, the war made an indelible impression on civilian lives.

Civilians did suffer during the First World War, especially of malnutrition and disease, physical attack, psychological trauma, and emotional distress. Roughly, an estimated six million civilians died as a direct result of war, but many more faced loss of health, mind, and property in the course of the conflict. Relief did not come quickly for most civilians, and indeed, the armistice did not mean an end to the militarization of civilian lives at home fronts. As historian Maureen Healy has astutely noted, "At the end of World War I, there was no official demobilization for civilians."[136] They continued to experience separation from loved ones, rationing and price controls, shortages of food and other products, and wartime surveillance. Perhaps no impression was so great as the psycho-

French women work under contract with the U.S. army to solder biscuit tins, ca. 1918. *U.S. Signal Corps, National Archives and Records Administration.*

logical effects of separation from loved ones, breakdowns in communication, and, for many, the inevitability of death or maiming. The emotional trauma of the war is less easy to measure than the economic costs or the social transformations.

The lingering effects of death were only part of the war's long term impact on civilians' lives. Wounded and maimed soldiers needed care, which often fell to families, but also the 1918 influenza epidemic and wartime food shortages had left a seriously weakened populace in many countries. Females, youth, and older male temporary workers were summarily dismissed from their war work, leaving many without means of subsistence or dependent on the state. Postwar settlements and treaties led to population "exchanges" and return of refugees, while social upheaval and revolution continued the war beyond 1918 for some civilians. In short, most civilians were not abundantly wealthy or healthy after the war, and the 1920s became a period of rebuilding for those societies, families, and individuals who were able to rebuild. These noncombatants had to judge for themselves whether their patriotic sacrifices on "home fronts" had been worth it.

[4]

Caught between the Lines

[T]here is no moment when one can escape the actuality of
the horror. When the far off cannon is not booming, as it is
today—it is a fairly clear day—the aeroplanes are flying, and
one thinks every minute of the butchery going on, and of all
the terrible brutality of this thing thrust on a peaceful world.
——Mildred Aldrich to Harriet Levy, February 1916[1]

Virginie Loveling, a well-known novelist living in Ghent (Belgium), faced the prospect of war with resignation in 1914, when she began
a war diary at age seventy-eight. From the time Belgium mobilized to
face the German threat in August until the armistice in 1918, Loveling
kept a secret journal, describing life in the *Etappen* (staging zone for the
German army) of Belgium. While she recorded the occasional fright of
an air raid warning or an encounter with soldiers on the streets of town,
her diary, like many other civilian accounts of war in the front-line and
occupation zones, showed the small stresses of life during wartime that
eroded morale and attacked the fabric of society. Her entry for March 4,
1916, serves as an example of the daily adjustments that became a way of
life for civilians at war:

> Butter is nearly impossible to get, few eggs, unless through a particular
> favor from your shopkeepers. . . . The bread is hardly edible, it has no wheat
> taste at all: 250 grams per day for each. . . . Each week the economic out-
> look worsens. What state can we expect? Famine? In the past week . . . in
> Mons . . . seven men were shot in the head. They were among thirty accused

of espionage. . . . And I dare not write about wartime events for fear [that I'm risking] my life.[2]

The daily food battles listed here give way to the fear of greater privation and to the seemingly arbitrary terrors of war and occupation. What shines through in every word Loveling writes is a sense of uncertainty regarding the future.

As Loveling's diary demonstrates, unlike civilians living at a "home front," with its distance from the actual battle and a certain measure of protection, civilians living at or near the fronts or in occupied zones faced a different experience of war. Civilians living between the lines in the midst of the action were subject to much more violence and upheaval. They not only faced demands upon their time, their work, and their resources, but they also often shared the psychological strain of war with soldiers. Many lived within sound or striking distance of guns, and they suffered from the extreme violence of invasion and retreat. On some fronts, occupied populations suffered from deliberately cruel policies, while in other regions, neglect was the order of the day. All found their lives militarized and their safety threatened. In his study of civilians in wartime, Hugo Slim lists "seven spheres of civilian suffering," including (1) killing, wounding, torturing; (2) sexual violence and rape; (3) spatial suffering (deportation, forced labor); (4) impoverishment; (5) famine and disease; (6) emotional suffering; (7) postwar suffering from bereavement, loss, displacement.[3] Slim uses these categories to point to the broad range of ways in which war impinges on the lives of those classified as noncombatants. In the First World War, civilians living in front-line or occupation zones experienced all seven of these spheres, often in great measure.

Many sought to evade such dangers by fleeing battle and occupation zones or becoming refugees in their own or other countries. Others were forced to evacuate their homes by the movement of armies or by deliberate government policies. Still others reacted to the invasion of their homelands with resistance in a variety of ways, while some of their neighbors chose varying levels of compliance or collaboration with military forces. Whether they lived in exile or under occupation, the war was a visible presence in the daily existence of these ordinary people. For some, the war created opportunity; for others it brought disaster. For the majority of those under foreign occupation or living as refugees, their lives were certainly not separate from the war being fought around them. Their homes had, in effect, become fronts.

Refugees and Displaced Peoples

War creates refugees, and for some civilians in front-line zones, fleeing was the only option, either because of forced relocation by invading armies or because of voluntary migration. While refugees have been present in war in the past, World War I redefined and broadened the refugee experience. A French historian, Philippe Nivet, tried to capture the nature of this difference by suggesting that the change was one of scope, and that "with total war, a new threshold is reached after 1914, because of the military events, then the redrawing of boundaries by the peace treaties and the residual conflicts in Eastern Europe."[4] Millions of people faced some measure of displacement during the First World War. Refugees sometimes were displaced multiple times during the war and its aftermath— by postwar conflicts such as the Greek-Turkish War, by policies of armies or occupiers that led to property destruction, by new armies or invading forces, by revolutions, and finally by peace itself. In Europe alone (not counting the non-European theaters of war), approximately ten million people were displaced by war between 1914 and 1918, with millions more becoming refugees in the postwar civil wars, revolutions, economic crises, and treaties.[5]

Throughout the wartime world, refugees emerged wherever fighting or the threat of it occurred. When the Japanese blockaded the city of Tsingtao (China) in August 1914, "great swarms of Chinamen, with women and children, left their protectorate on donkeys and carts," anticipating the supply shortages and aerial bombing that would come with the clash between Germans and Japanese.[6] French civilians in the northern occupied zones fled to "free" France, and civilians in Galicia sought refuge in cities such as Vienna.[7] Minority populations, such as Kurds in Persia, had trouble finding safe havens when the war forced them to flee their homes.[8] After the disastrous defeat at Caporetto, approximately one-half million Italians left the war zone for the cities. Serbia's entire popula-

This refugee is representative of the 1.8 million Ottoman Armenians forcibly deported to the Syrian desert. An estimated one million died at the hands of the Turkish army or from starvation and exhaustion. *Library of Congress.*

tion faced some displacement during the war, as did many Greeks and all Armenians in the Ottoman Empire.[9] Multiple cities in France and Belgium faced forced evacuation because of army operations; for instance, the entire town of Bony in northern France was evacuated by the German army in October 1916 with only a few hours' notice to make room for part of the Hindenburg Line defenses.[10] In the Ober Ost German occupation zone (mostly in modern Lithuania and Latvia), people fled in 1914 during the Russian advance and retreat, with its subsequent scorched-earth and forced-evacuation campaigns. Vejas Liulevicius estimated that in this region "roughly a third of the prewar population had fled or fallen victim to the war."[11] In Poland, the movements of Russian, Austrian, and German armies also created mass numbers of refugees. By late 1914, more than one hundred thousand refugees had flooded into Warsaw.[12] A Russian soldier tried to capture the sense of panic and fear that accompanied the crush of refugees in Poland in 1915:

> Refugees are walking and driving from all directions. . . . All the villagers have been ordered to evacuate. They are in despair, and protest bitterly. . . . Oh my God, what's happening on the road ahead? It is blocked by carts, full of kids and household stuff. The cows are bellowing, the dogs are barking and yelping. The poor people are going God knows where, anywhere to get away from the fighting. But the old nags don't have the strength to pull the loads; the air is filled with the sound of horses being whipped and the Polish "tso," and still the carts won't move. We don't have the heart just to drive through them. It's such a heartbreaking scene, we drag one cart after another out of the mud, get them onto the main road and then onto the bridge over the river Narew. I pity them all, particularly the little children, sitting in the carts or in their mothers' arms.[13]

Masses of refugees clogged roads and bridges, interfering with military activities, especially in the early months of the war. Mildred Aldrich, an American living in France, described the traffic jams on the Marne River road near her house in September 1914 just as a battle was about to begin. The road was "full of the flying crowd. . . . The procession led in both directions as far as we could see. . . . [T]here was every sort of a vehicle you ever saw, drawn by every sort of beast that can draw, from dogs to oxen, from boys to donkeys."[14] These ragtag armies of refugees often headed toward towns with shelters and other services. Virginie Loveling witnessed the refugees struggling into Ghent in late August 1914 in a mockery of a procession: "Along the Deinze Canal from Schipdonck they came . . . pitiful throngs on foot, some without shoes; or carrying clogs in their hands."[15] She noted with empathy the meager possessions that each clutched tightly, often just a loaf of bread under the arm and a piece of smoked meat wrapped in paper. Within a week of Loveling's first description of the refugees, more than eight thousand were sleeping in the Feestpaleis (Festival Hall) in the City Park at Ghent.[16]

The Belgian case illustrates the range of difficulties that refugees faced. As German armies approached Antwerp in October 1914, civilians fled their homes and sought shelter in other areas of the country, or in nearby

Refugees, such as this French family, often traveled with any transport available, taking only a few meager possessions with them. *U.S. Signal Corps, National Archives and Records Administration.*

nations such as France, the Netherlands, and the United Kingdom. Altogether more than one and a half million Belgians fled, and many refugees found themselves in concentration camps or "billeted" in strangers' homes, dependent on others for food, work, shelter. Whole families relocated, often for the duration of the war, and some of them had to move more than once to escape changing front lines or because of international agreements. Letters, diaries, and oral histories attest to the difficulties those displaced faced in their temporary homes. Routines, diets, and employment had to change. Six-year-old Marguerite Vansteenkiste wrote a letter to Queen Elisabeth of Belgium asking for assistance in December 1914, explaining, "Some little girls of my age told me that St. Nicholas had come from England to La Panne, he didn't come to us because we are refugees, Would You not like to talk to him for me[?]"[17] Parents had different concerns; often just finding work and getting rations could prove difficult.

Depending on where refugees landed in their quest for security, their lives took different turns. In Britain, for instance, the British used "Poor Little Belgium" both as justification for their entry into the war and as propaganda to mobilize citizens to action, so the nation had little choice but to open its doors to Belgian refugees. Yet, Britain dragged its heels initially, and the government had trouble organizing a viable relief effort and a coordinating committee for dealing with the refugees.[18] Added to the organizational confusion, the bulk of the more than two hundred thousand Belgian refugees destined for Britain were Flemish speakers, a linguistic divide that exacerbated the cultural distance refugees felt from their hosts. Difficulties in finding work and host families, plus class-based conflicts, made the situation hard for both the British "philanthropists" and the Belgian refugees.[19] Belgian refugees created new temporary communities in Britain to deal with the dislocation they had suffered, but their status among the larger population was often contentious and sometimes led to hostility as the strains of war fractured any sense of community. As the war progressed, the Belgian and British governments collaborated to create munitions factories staffed by Belgian workers. In a strange twist of fortune, the Belgian government extended conscription to Belgian adult males who were refugees in Britain, and then called them to work in the armaments factories. The refugee men, unlike British munitions workers, "remained soldiers, subject to military discipline." Discipline was maintained by military police and separate tribunals, again demonstrating the permeability of the civil-military divide in wartime.[20]

For towns along the borders of war zones, such as those in the Russian Trans-Caucausus, where more than two hundred thousand Armenians took refuge from Ottoman extermination policies, the flood of refugees was almost too much to contain. Likewise, the town of Roslav'l (in modern Russia) saw its prewar population of twenty-eight thousand balloon to more than eighty thousand by summer 1915 with an influx of refugees from Galicia, while the six million inhabitants of the Netherlands tried to cope with the arrival of a million Belgians in a matter of a few weeks by building internment camps.[21] Sometimes little villages found themselves booming metropolises almost overnight, with no real provisions for housing or feeding such large numbers. The Serbian town of Valjevo, normally about nine thousand inhabitants in 1914, absorbed more than one hundred thousand soldiers and civilians during the war, leading to a massive typhoid outbreak.[22]

Border areas were especially treacherous for those whose loyalty was questioned. Alsatians faced suspicion from both Germans and French, while populations living on the Austro-Hungarian border found themselves deported either to the Austro-Hungarian or the Italian interior, depending upon which side of the border they lived on. Italians and other minority peoples of the region faced a particularly perilous situation on either side of the border. On the Austrian side, they were subject to forced labor and confinement in concentration camps, while Italy had no refugee bureaus or organized camps for those who had been evacuated, leaving them at the mercy of strangers.[23] Likewise, small villages and cities along the Dutch-Belgian border saw their populations double and then triple almost overnight, forcing officials to rely on makeshift shelters. In Middelburg (Netherlands), a Dutch soldier described the conditions at the height of the exodus from the war zone in October 1914:

> The bandstand was crammed with old men, 70–80 years old. I can still see them clearly in my mind, lying on the floor, they all wore low clogs with leather straps nailed on top of them. They lay in a wide circle with their feet inwards and about 70 of them next to each other, and they were all happy to have a safe shelter. We wound great strips of tarpaulin round the bandstand to keep out the cold and the rain. Many were lying on the Marketplace in the open air. My assistant Hanneke took a seven-year-old boy dead from a wheelbarrow, while I helped transport two women to the hospital who brought little newcomers into the world in the midst of this great misery.[24]

Another kind of displacement of populations came in the form of forced deporation or expulsion of civilian populations in occupied or front-line zones. Germany deported unemployed workers from Belgium in 1916 to work in the Ruhr region, while in the urban centers of Lille, Tourcoing, and Roubaix (France), Germans moved more than twenty-five thousand people, many of them adolescents and young women, to areas in need of agricultural labor in the spring of 1916.[25] As American delegates from the Commission for Relief in Belgium described it, the deportations led to moral and physical degradation:

The deportation was carried out in the most brutal manner. Despite the protest of the people, families were broken up; wives were taken from their homes and families; many young girls and young women from 18 to 25 years old were included among the deportees. Young girls from the most respectable families were placed together with the most unsavoury characters of the city and sent off without any supervision and protection, often without any luggage whatsoever and always without any idea of their destination.[26]

These deportations proved terribly traumatic for the deportees and their families. For example, the Lille deportees, many of whom were from middle-class, respectable households, had to submit to gynecological exams, which humiliated them and marked them with the stigma of prostitution.[27] One young woman, Marie X., described to officials the circumstances she faced as a Lille deportee:

The fear of being taken some day by one of these Germans was for us the most appalling threat.... [N]ear our hamlet, one hundred and fifty women are lodged, or rather parked in an attic. They sleep pell-mell in the straw; they are eaten up by vermin. There prostitution is publicly organized.... The poor women leave the hay where they are lodged, and follow the one who calls. In excuse, the Germans claim that these prisoners are all prostitutes. They lie. We know that they carried off without distinction honest women and public women. One of the most painful aspects of my captivity, ... was to feel weighing on me the scornful gaze of those who not knowing me took me for what I am not ... whore of the Boches![28]

Unlike the Lille deportation, in which many women and young people were taken, the focus of the mass deportation in autumn 1916 in Belgium was unemployed male workers. Between the first deportations in October 1916 and the revocation of the policy in spring 1917, an estimated sixty thousand Belgians traveled to Germany as forced laborers, where their poor rations and living conditions led to a high incidence of sickness.[29] The workers, many of whom had refused to volunteer for work with the German occupying forces or in German industry, found themselves part of a systematic sweep of Belgian cities and towns. The German authorities gained access to lists of unemployed from municipal relief rolls, which were extracted from mayors and civic officials. Cities that did not cooperate faced deportation of their leaders, fines, curfews, or other penalties.

A fascinating record of the scenes of deportation comes from the reports of American neutrals serving with the Commission for Relief in Belgium, who witnessed the process. The reports show that some towns cooperated, while others defied authorities despite the consequences. Tournai, for instance, refused to provide its lists of *chômeurs* (unemployed men) and was fined two hundred thousand marks. When, after a week, the town had still not complied, the Germans assessed an additional fine of twenty thousand marks (later twenty-five thousand) per day, established a 5:00 p.m. curfew, and deported several city officials.[30] In Bruges, the elderly mayor and his son were deported for refusing to turn over the lists.[31] In other towns, the deportations went more smoothly, with men being called to central markets for selection. In Court-St.-Etienne,

I found a group of men . . . who were guarded by soldiers. . . . [T]he first group was marched toward a mill where the military authorities were . . . [they] were examined by an officer, a doctor no doubt, who freed those considered too sick . . . the men who were to be taken were sent "to the right" across the mill to a courtyard where later they were directed to a train. The men that were to be freed were sent "to the left."[32]

The orderly scene in Court-St.-Etienne was not always replicated across the country. In some areas, "the deportation of workers provoked . . . a wave of panic," with some men hiding in forests to escape deportation. Furthermore, the fact that families were not given a chance to say goodbye or to provide food and clothing to their departing men caused great distress.[33] Demonstrations and clashes took place in some villages, and pitiful scenes ensued in places where the Germans had not taken the precaution of separating men from their families before the selection.

On the eastern front, Jewish populations were especially vulnerable to deportation, expulsion, and pogroms, and beginning in summer 1914, Russian armies drove Jews from front-line areas forcibly into the interior. Before large battles or after key losses in the war, Jews were targeted for deportations again. For example, in April 1915, after the Russians suffered a devastating loss, more than twenty-six thousand Jews left Kurland (modern Latvia) under deportation orders issued by the Russian army. In May, another 150,000 Jews followed. Several hundred thousand Jews fled Galicia in 1915, many heading for Vienna.[34] Galicia, indeed, proved to be a death trap for Jews caught in the Russian occupation of 1914–1915. Russian authorities treated Jews as a subversive and alien presence in their occupation zone, targeting Jewish property and homes, but also violently attacking men and women of all ages. Some of the violence was orchestrated, but much of it was spontaneous and largely criminal. An example of how fear helped fuel the anti-Jewish attacks on civilians can be found in the city of L'viv in September 1914. Unexplained gunshots in the Jewish quarter led to rumors that Jews had fired on soldiers. After dark, bands of soldiers entered the Jewish quarter and broke into homes, looted, and shot civilians. This single event left more than one hundred wounded and at least two dozen dead.[35]

Bad as the anti-Jewish pogroms of the occupation period were, worse treatment followed as the Russians retreated in spring 1915 before an Austro-German offensive. Again, Jews especially faced destruction of their property, physical violence such as beatings and rape, and, in some cases, death. Polish eyewitness Helena Seifertóv Jabłońska described the treatment of Jews in another Galician town, Przemyśl, in April 1915:

> The Jewish pogrom has been under way since yesterday evening. The Cossacks waited until the Jews set off to the synagogue for their prayers before setting upon them with whips. They were deaf to any pleas for mercy, regardless of age. They were taken away from the synagogues, from the streets and from their doorsteps and driven towards some enormous barracks at Bakończyce. What are they going to do with them? Some of the older, weaker ones who couldn't keep up were whipped. Many, many hundreds were driven along in this way. They say this round-up is to continue until they've caught all of them. There is such lamenting and despair! Some Jews are hiding in cellars, but they'll get to them there too.[36]

The Russian army deported more than seventeen thousand Jews from Przemysl as they retreated, and altogether the Russians forcibly displaced more than 1.6 million people during their retreat from Galicia.[37] Similarly, in Lithuania and Latvia, tens of thousands of men of military age, Jews, and Lutherans, all considered threats to the Russian army, were driven from their homes and evacuated as part of the Russian retreat in September 1915.[38]

These attacks and displacements were hardly a surprise given that non-combatants have always been vulnerable when armies invade or retreat, but in the context of nineteenth-century claims of just and humane warfare, these experiences bear testament to the ferocity that could still be unleashed in times of war. Particular violence accompanied invasions and retreats, including widespread destruction of property and vicious attacks in the form of beatings, rapes, and murders, but even in "calm" times, refugees faced the threat of deprivation, disease, and death.

Violence and Retribution

Rumor sometimes sparked additional violence, with stories of atrocities fueling fear among untrained soldiers and wary civilians alike. Rumors such as those in L'viv often turned deadly for civilians in frontline zones, and this was especially true of the first months of the war when young, nervous soldiers saw snipers and spies everywhere among the civilian populations they were encountering. In eastern Belgium where the German army first began its invasion, civilians were subject to property destruction and death as German armies tried to deter *franc-tireurs* (free-shooters) from sniping at soldiers despite the fact that there was no widespread civilian armed resistance to the German invasion of Belgium.[39] In fact, much of the fear and anxiety that led to soldiers attacking civilians came from rumors and stories that circulated in the heightened atmosphere of excitement and fear that accompanied the first weeks of war. As John Horne and Alan Kramer describe it, the Germans suffered from a "collective delusion" in which the *franc-tireurs* became "a scapegoat for the soldiers' own anxieties and shaky discipline."[40]

While this may indeed have been a myth, it was a dangerous one that led to more than six thousand Belgian and French civilian deaths at the hands of the German invaders. An estimated fifteen to twenty thousand buildings were destroyed as well.[41] Belgium was not alone; in Italy, approximately five thousand civilians were killed in the invasion of that country, while in Serbia, where Austrian and Hungarian soldiers also harbored fears of an armed Serb resistance, more than a thousand Serb civilians were killed during the invasion of 1914.[42] Real and imagined atrocities and the stories that circulated about them played another role as well. Several historians, working in different national contexts, argue that atrocity rumors fueled national propaganda, helping to mobilize and sustain the conflict.

Atrocity stories made excellent propaganda. Historian Katie Pickles provides an interesting example—a "German Crimes" calendar that featured "an enemy atrocity for each month of the year, with the actual date of each 'crime against humanity' circled in red." This British calendar marked May for the sinking of the *Lusitania* and October for the execution of Edith Cavell, a British nurse shot for helping Allied soldiers escape Belgium.[43] With such encouragement from official sources, people supported their own state's violence as retribution for enemy atrocities, but this propaganda was also designed to justify the seemingly unending war in which they were enmeshed.[44] While this is undoubtedly true and propaganda overemphasized violence, it is important to remember that atrocities did take place with documented cases of beatings, torture, rape, and murder.

One of the areas least discussed and regulated by officials was the problem of sexual violence in the war zones, specifically the victims who were raped or forced into prostitution by circumstances. Many rapes occurred during invasions and retreats, but they also occurred during the course of the war in zones close to training camps and fronts and in occupied regions.[45] Women, especially those living alone or in remote rural areas, proved especially vulnerable to the gendered violence of rape in wartime. In some cases, officials condoned or encouraged rape as an act of war, as in Russia, where in September 1914, evidence showed that "army commanders tolerated the participation of soldiers in pogroms, looting, and rape of Jews and other local civilian populations in the front zones."[46] The violence of rape sometimes caused women to become "double victims" who were not only traumatized by rape but also "stigmatized as having dishonored their family and nation in the act of being sexually abused."[47] The stigma of rape and the complication of where to report such crimes during the war led to great historical silences on the issue, and this in turn has made it difficult to estimate how many people were raped or sexually violated during the war. As Alan Kramer has written, "Rape was probably committed by soldiers in every invasion in the Great War," but victims remained largely silent out of shame and fear of denunciation by family or neighbors.[48]

Occupation zones were particularly problematic areas for women, since bored or inebriated soldiers raped women they saw as available. In the Australian occupation of New Guinea, there were reported cases of rape by the occupying forces of girls at mission schools, women in prisons, and girls/women in their own homes. Drunkenness was a terrible problem among Australian soldiers in New Guinea, contributing to attacks on women and girls.[49] In the German and Austro-Hungarian invasions of Italy, more than seven hundred rapes were officially reported, suggesting a far larger number of actual sexual attacks. Rape and sexual coercion followed in the first few months of the occupation, but again most victims remained silent.[50]

In addition to reports of rapes to local authorities in war and occupation zones, the phenomenon of "war babies" brought the issue to public attention, especially as women were forced to defend their honor against claims of "sleeping with the enemy," collaborating, and undermining the war effort.[51] When women sought abortions or practiced infanticide to avoid raising "children of the enemy," prosecutions ignited controversy about what to do with such cases.[52] The blame for "war babies" often fell squarely on women, whose claims of innocence often raised suspicions that the sex had been consensual. The issue of "war babies" captivated the French nation in the well-known infanticide trial in 1917 of twenty-year-old Joséphine Barthélemy. This case, which was widely reported in the media, crystallized much of the debate about the violations of wartime, rape, abortion, and infanticide. Barthélemy's defense lawyer argued that Barthélemy's 1916 killing of her newborn was an "act of war" and therefore justified in a moral sense. Since the baby's father was German and the child was conceived through violence, he argued that Barthélemy was "not culpable for having killed her infant just as a soldier is not culpable for killing the enemy on the field of battle."[53] Barthélemy was acquitted by an all-male jury in January 1917, setting off a public dialogue about the case. However, most cases of war children and rape remained shrouded in silence throughout the war and afterwards.

Physical attacks on civilians were only one feature of armies' control of noncombatant populations. In the face of fear of civilian resistance, military officials in World War I featured another strategy for insuring the good behavior of civilian populations near the fronts and in occupation zones: hostage taking. In the context of the First World War, hostage taking assumed multiple forms. In some cases, municipal authorities were held each day in their hometowns to ensure the cooperation of their constituents. Other hostages found themselves moved behind enemy lines to internment camps or prisons to serve as long-term insurance for good behavior at home. Finally, hostages could sometimes be seized as part of spontaneous reprisals and retaliations that often featured other retribution, such as punitive fines, labor duties, or curfews. As Stéphane Audoin-Rouzeau and Annette Becker argue, "the war against civilians, the civilians' war, was in itself a genuine war, with objectives no different from those of the war waged on the battlefields. We might even say that the civilians in the occupied regions endured a kind of siege."[54] In a sense, occupied populations became hostages for the good behavior of their inhabitants and their allies, subject to reprisal and coercion at any moment. In all cases, hostage-taking emphasized the importance of civilians to the waging and maintenance of war.

There are many examples during World War I of hostage situations. For instance, as the Russian army moved through East Prussia, Galicia, and other operations zones in 1914, it instituted a policy of hostage taking and deportation. By May 1915, the Russian First and Tenth armies alone had taken close to five thousand hostages to try to control the civilian populations they encountered.[55] As with forced expulsion, Jewish communities were particularly subject to hostage taking in Russian-controlled regions. Many of the Galician hostages were deported to Russia, and their property was confiscated.[56] Altogether, Russian civilian and military officials took thousands of hostages throughout the course of the war, holding some for short periods of time and others indefinitely in prisons.[57]

The Russian policy was not isolated, however, as most armies on both sides of the conflict practiced hostage taking to control civilian behavior, in some cases even using hostages as human shields.[58] In an attempt to quell a 1915–1917 rebellion in the Haut-Senegal-Niger region of West Africa, the French military seized women and children as hostages during the uprising.[59] After the invasion and occupation of Romania, many professional men and women (lawyers, doctors) were interned as hostages by the Central Powers.[60] When in 1915 the British were besieged in Kut al Amara (Iraq) by Turkish forces, the British commander took hostages from among the local civilian population to ensure that they did not communicate with the enemy.[61] Throughout German occupation zones, military officials chose hostages from among the ranks of city leaders and business/financial elites. For instance, when the German army entered Leuven, Belgium, in August 1914, officials quickly seized prominent hostages, including the vice-rector of the university, a prominent local doctor, and local politicians and dignitaries.[62]

In Sedan (France), ten-year-old Yves Congar's father became a German hostage. Yves described the experience in his war diary, noting in October 1914, "Dad is a hostage. Instead of doing 12 hours during the day or 12 during the night, he does 4 hours at night and 10 in the day. It's so unfair. Well, if only that was all there was to put up with, it wouldn't be too bad."[63] Sometimes his father was kept overnight, as the hostage schedule remained erratic. However, by January 1918, Yves was describing his father's removal to Germany along with about sixty male and female hostages from Sedan. Yves recorded his joy when the family finally got word from their father: "We have heard from Dad! We are so happy. They travelled for five days and six nights with no rest at all. For meals they had a bowl of German soup (dirty water in other words) in the morning and a cup of coffee in the evening. That's it! Dad is travelling with 600 others. His postcard is not very reassuring."[64]

As with Yves' father's treatment, conditions in front-line and occupation zones changed over the course of the war, often on the basis of the food and labor needs of the armies, but sometimes too because of actions of the civilian population or political transformations. Requisitions of goods and animals by the military often meant the loss of productive capacity for farmers, so their ability to sell to the armies could mean the difference between eating and starving for some. Occupation forces requisitioned a great variety of products; Austrian occupiers seized from Italians livestock, vegetables, nuts, wine, oil, dry forage, manure, fabric, and household linen in a two-month period in early 1918.[65] Romanians in German-occupied territory turned over food and livestock, but also their precious reserves of quinine for German soldiers' use around the world. Romanian civilians, living in a malarial zone, now found themselves subject to a disease easily controlled with the drugs they had just lost.[66] In Brussels, one woman's war diary recorded a litany of requisitioned goods, from cart horses and large dogs to the wool from their mattresses and their metal knobs, hinges, and window fastenings. At one point, she exclaims, "What next??? How lucky are those who don't live under German invasion!!!"[67]

The armies depended upon the labor, products, services, and housing of the civilian populations near the fronts and in the occupied regions, so they could not operate without interacting with civilians. Likewise, the civilians were displaced from regular employment and often became dependent on military authorities for their food supply and lives. Many civilians billeted soldiers and officers, often for the whole term of the war, while others had to serve soldiers in their restaurants, cafés, bars, shops, and offices. This mutual dependence created a host of ambiguous identities and, often, serious conflicts. With such close living conditions and ambiguous relationships, the lines between resistance and collaboration were blurred—was it complicity to earn a wage selling goods or providing services to a soldier? Civilians struggled to make sense of the wartime world, often witnessing a full range of interactions between occupiers and occupied: passive resistance, armed rebellion, clandestine activities, profiteering, and survival.

Collaboration or Resistance? Civilian Wartime Services

Soldiers from "friendly" countries often expected to be welcomed with open arms by local civilian populations, so they were surprised when they were treated with disdain, fear, or rudeness. While occupying enemy armies had fewer illusions about the treatment they would receive, even they often seemed surprised by the difficulties they faced in interacting at first with civilian populations. Assuming that their money would buy them what they wanted in shops and cafés, soldiers instead encountered rudeness, hostility, and refusal of service. For many civilians, billeting or provisioning soldiers was an inconvenience at the least, whether they were enemy soldiers or friends, and they resented their loss of privacy, the drain on their resources, and the presence of sometimes inconsiderate men.

As time passed, civil populations near the fronts and in occupied zones began to depend upon soldiers for their livelihoods as wartime deprivation and requisitioning robbed them of their means, so a certain measure of cordiality was required in commercial transactions. These interactions inevitably moved between hostility and familiarity; the Russian woman doing laundry for a Turkish prisoner of war over time became accustomed to his presence. The billeted soldier might gain a fondness for the family with which he was living, and vice-versa. While the war was in process, criticism of "fraternization" was muted by necessity, but when the war ended, often individuals faced public humiliation or violence if it was perceived by their communities that they had crossed invisible lines between service provider and collaborator.

Civilians performed a variety of tasks to keep the armies in the field, including service jobs such as running bath houses or doing laundry, serving as cooks or sutlers (vendors), and performing technical work. Local workers labored on projects for the armies as well, clearing debris, repairing roads or rails, working to unload supplies. In August 1918, the British army alone was employing more than sixteen thousand French civilians (more than ten thousand of whom were female) to work supporting operations in France and Belgium, while the Female Labor Bureau of the U.S. army in Tours employed twelve thousand local women.[68]

A good example of civilian complicity is the necessity for laundries for soldiers, officers, and other people attached to the war effort. Laundry was handled in many cases by civilian women hired by armies directly or by individuals engaged in war service. On the western front, the Australian Corps hired French and Belgian women on a weekly basis to staff their laundries and bath houses, but each woman was carefully screened by intelligence officers and supervised by regular army soldiers.[69] Where official laundries were not available, soldiers hired individual women to do their laundry at their own homes. American soldier Milford Manley wrote home to his mother about the French woman he had hired to do his laundry, noting that "[s]he ought to have [the laundry done], it's been there a week. Maybe I haven't got any by this time. It sometimes works that way. I guess all Yanks look alike to the French & the first fellow there gets the laundry."[70] For some women, doing soldiers' laundry and keeping billeted soldiers in their homes figured as their sole income during the war. A Flemish woman near Ypres (Belgium) could earn five francs per night for billeting a soldier and additional money on a piecework basis for taking in washing and ironing.[71] For example, Rachel Maelbrancke's mother took in soldiers' washing and mending in Flanders in order to feed her four children when her husband went to the United States to work at the Ford plant in Detroit.[72] Even soldiers in captivity often relied on laundry services provided by civilians. Mehmet Arif Ölçen, an Ottoman soldier taken prisoner by the Russians in 1916, described his laundress in the Russian village where he spent his first few months of captivity, writing, "An old Russian woman washed our clothes. She would bring the clean laundry to the door. She would read the name of the owner, and while giving back the clean clothes, write down in a notebook the soiled laundry that was given in return and the name of its owner."[73]

For the more basic needs, daily food and drink, laundry, shelter, and sex, the armies had to turn to civil populations. People of all social statuses billeted armies in their homes and outbuildings, some willingly but others only with coercion. Heber Alexander described the procurement of billets for officers and men with his Indian Mule Corps in France as they moved toward their assigned place at the front. In their first stop, villagers had just billeted Germans who had retreated hours earlier, and now they seemed quite willing to provide housing for the British officers and their Indian mule drivers. Alexander also noted with some surprise that the Indians got on quite well with many of the French children, and it was not unusual to see the soldiers playing with kids in the street. Later in the war he found French civilians sometimes unwilling to accommodate them, and he described one incident in Long Cornet:

> At the house which Moillis had selected for headquarters was a very truculent lady. On being asked for a room for two officers, she announced that her house was scarcely big enough for her own family, and that she was not going to find accommodation for anyone. I insisted on inspecting the house, and having done so, chalked upon the door of the selected room the mystic words "20 Indians." This had the desired effect. Madame had forgotten that she had such a room; of course it was exactly the thing for two officers, and she placed it gladly at our disposal.[74]

Reluctance to billet soldiers was not unusual, especially considering the fear some civilians felt for enemy troops. Many of the armies felt little compassion for their civilian hosts, and in fact, soldiers appear to have taken advantage of their hosts in many cases. A British regimental history hints at some of the problems that could occur in towns where soldiers were billeted:

> To be quite frank, it was stealing, but . . . it was easy, with a dozen men all clamouring to be served at once in a tiny shop, where the vendor was some old woman or a girl of 14, to fill one's pockets with three packets of biscuits and only pay for one. And when troops were billeted on farms, fowls, eggs, fruit, disappeared like magic, fences or doors were chopped up for firewood, interpreters distracted by complaints from frenzied Flemish and French farmers, resulting in masses of correspondence, enquiries from the base, hunts for the offenders, and (occasionally) reparation made. The general argument was that the farmer or shopkeeper was making fat profits out of the presence of the British Army (which was frequently true), and therefore members of the British Army were justified in getting their own back in any way that seemed good to them.[75]

In addition to the petty theft described in this account, the inconvenience of having to cook, clean, and fetch for soldiers was considerable. One American soldier described his excellent billet to his family in a letter, without much attention to the demands he was placing on the civilians to whom he was indebted. Walter Richter enthusiastically wrote to his mother,

> I am at a french home writing this letter. We are billeted at a french village and are certanly being treated fine by these french people, this is Sunday so we bought about 5 lbs of veal chops witch we had an old french couple cook for us, that is 3 of us, they fixed us a swell meal we also had a few bottles of wine we are allowed to drink wine and beer, but cannot get drunk, if you do, you go in the guard house. I am feeling fine and dont mind this army life.[76]

Richter's mention here of veal chops suggests a village away from the front lines. The worst place to be if one was a civilian billeting soldiers was often the operations zones, where "the villages were overrun by thousands of passing troops, going to and from the trenches. Absolute military law prevailed, without any of the mitigations that existed even in the etappen zone."[77]

Even in places where civilians were billeting their own troops, it was a relationship that could turn sour. Soldiers sometimes wrecked the houses where they stayed or got drunk and unruly, and even with well-behaved soldier-guests, the house's occupants were sometimes forced to give up their own rooms to create additional space. Piete Kuhr described her family's billeting experience in Schneidemühl (Germany). Just before her thirteenth birthday, a German captain and his batman (servant) were billeted in their house. Her mother was in a nearby city working, and her grandmother was ill, so she and her older brother took care of the billeted soldiers. Later, in August 1915, the town was full of soldiers, billeted in almost every house, and the townspeople gathered together to entertain these soldiers. As Piete notes in her diary, "In the evening we all sit on the Wegner's seat in front of the house, drag more chairs out and sing songs with the soldiers or listen to their stories from the front." The following summer, soldiers were again filling the town, and Piete got in trouble with her mother for playing piano for some of the older girls and the officers they had invited for tea. Her mother wrote to her in horror, "'I don't understand,' wrote Mummy. 'How you could do it: background music for what are obviously love-sessions of little Schneidemühl tarts! Has the war so confused your ideas of morality? I am furious with you!'"[78]

Piete's experience with billeting and interactions with soldiers point to one of the real dilemmas civilians faced during the war. Many provided services, often without a choice, to the armies passing through or staying in their towns, but these same civilians had to contend with charges of greedy war profiteering or, as with Piete, of collaboration or impropriety. Civilian women, in particular, were often seen as fair game for sexual liaisons. Piete herself was threatened by a soldier in town when she was thirteen:

Somebody else wanted to care for me in the summerhouse—namely, Aunt Otter's new billettee. He is blond and good-looking, really likeable. He came into the garden with Aunt's permission as I was swinging in the hammock on my own, reading. He wanted to know what I was reading, and I said, "Goethe!" He looked at me in a most interested way, as if he could not imagine me reading Goethe. Then he twisted one of my plaits in his hand. I let him do it because I thought he was playing. But it was quite another thing when he began to stroke my breast (I really don't have any yet) and then my hips and legs. I saw what he was up to, of course. I had a marvellous dodge. As quick as a flash, I swung round in the hammock and simply dropped out of it on to the ground. He hardly grasped what was happening as I shot past his legs on all fours out of the summerhouse. I ran out of the garden and slammed the garden door behind me. I'm just furious with this orderly! It is the first time a man has looked at me as a woman.[79]

While Piete was furious with these unwanted attentions, other civilians developed real relationships of friendship or even intimacy with those whom they billeted. Given the daily interactions, it was not surprising that some form of relationship would result. Virginie Loveling, who had a German orderly billeted with her in spring 1915, learned that he was well educated and could speak Russian and English. She also noted that he was polite, thanking her for her good treatment of him, but she never really befriended him because his views about German supremacy, what she deemed his "delusion," made any rapprochement with her impossible.[80]

Billeting was not the only location for interaction between soldiers and civilians, and indeed, more civilians probably met soldiers in restaurants, shops, and businesses than in their own homes. Many civilians worked as sutlers (vendors) for the armies directly, or opened their existing businesses up to soldiers. One example of the entrepreneurial spirit of some civilians near the fronts occurred while the Germans awaited a Japanese attack in the vicinity of Tsingtao in September 1914. Chinese shopkeepers tried to sell goods to the soldiers in the encampment, offering "beer, milk, sugar, canned pineapple, cigars, cigarettes," and other items. An enterprising sutler opened a café called "Ba Linna Fang Kuchen," and as one German soldier described it, the café sold coffee, cocoa, tea, and "real Berliner Pfannkuchen (jelly donuts) just like one gets them at home."[81] Soldiers and shopkeepers did not always interact in a cordial manner, and some memoirs suggest that soldiers injured shopkeepers. Ernst Nopper, a German soldier stationed in Poland, wrote a series of tirades about

Jewish shopkeepers in his diary: "You have to buy everything from the Jews, even matches. Hotels, chemists, cafes, they're all run by dirty, mean Jews."[82] On another day he punched a Jewish vendor for touching a picture he was drawing. Whatever the relationship that developed, it was clear that armies needed merchants and the merchants needed armies to keep their businesses afloat during wartime. Commercial transactions made the business of judging war "guilt," "profiteering," or "complicity" a difficult proposition.

Just as collaboration and complicity were often difficult to judge, resistance to the enemy could often be misinterpreted. Civilians sometimes resisted in ways not evident to most onlookers, by deliberately cooking poor meals for occupying forces or working slowly in order to irritate superiors. For instance, peasant agricultural workers in Montenegro slowed their production in a show of resistance to increased requisitions by Austrian occupiers.[83] Civilians also defied authorities by keeping diaries or drawing caricatures, neither of which overtly displayed their active resistance. In fact, resistance to authority, both of enemy or occupying forces and of their own countries, was a feature of civilian life in the war that played out in a multitude of ways.

Defiance allowed populations in occupied zones to maintain a level of personal security while still mocking their occupiers. For instance, one young man in Leuven, Belgium, spent ten days in jail for singing a patriotic song in public, while another man, aged forty-one, was incarcerated for a month for "having said publicly to a German soldier that it was [the Germans] who had massacred innocent civilians and deliberately burnt all the houses."[84] Small insults, work stoppages, and deliberate defiance of German rules were all forms of Belgian resistance to German occupation. One of the favored Belgian pastimes was undermining the November 1914 German decree that all live by "German time," which was an hour later than Belgian time. Civilians delighted in keeping "Belgian time" on their watches, marking invitations as "H.B. (heure belge)," and scorning German time when possible. Using Belgian time was an offense under German occupation rules, so some were fined or sent to prison for defying authorities.[85] The time wars rose to new absurdities in summer 1916, when the Germans adopted a "summer time" schedule to conserve energy, making German time different than Belgian time by two hours.[86]

One of the many posters instructing the occupied Belgian population how to behave. This 1915 poster bans the removal of potatoes from the city of Leuven. *Stadsarchief Leuven.*

For those caught between German and Belgian communities, this could be tricky. An English nurse wrote in her diary, "We were very undecided whether to go on duty Belgian or German time outside one had to have German time but inside the nuns insist on Belgian time, result most comical & we don't know where we are."[87] The Marquis de Villalobar, of the Spanish Legation in Brussels, began jokingly using "the hour of City Hall" to refer to the time, which was "German time" but on a "Belgian clock."[88]

The war created pockets of civilian resistance that featured not only small acts of defiance and mockery toward enemies but major sabotage actions. Zabel Bournazian described in her postwar memoir the ways in which her Armenian community sought to resist Ottoman armies. She and her seven-month-old child were among a group of about eight hundred taking shelter in an old fortress. They armed themselves, built shelters and barricades out of stones, rationed their meager food supply, and mobilized all men, women, and children for work. After three weeks, they had to surrender to the Turks, which meant execution for the men, rape and deportation for the women. Zabel saved herself, her child, and some family members by bribing a policeman to let them escape.[89] Beyond armed resistance, crime could sometimes function as a strategy for resisting occupiers. During the fall of 1917 in Vilna (Lithuania), German posters offered rewards for information leading to the arrest of unknown people responsible for a wave of crimes against German authorities, including robbery, arson, and murder. By the end of 1917, banditry was so bad that German authorities could barely control it, and some areas became totally lawless.[90]

Yves Congar, in Sedan, started his own defiance campaign during the war. In March 1915, he spat on a German private he saw in the street and got away with it, but in February 1918, he was called before the German authorities for calling an officer billeted with them a "Boche," a term of derision for German soldiers used by soldiers and civilians alike. He described in his diary the interrogation he received:

OFFICIAL: You caused great offence.

YVES: I didn't realise it at the time but now I do.

OFFICIAL: Where did you learn this word?

YVES: In the streets.

OFFICIAL: Do you go to school?

YVES: To college.

OFFICIAL: You were a schoolboy but now you are criminal. Follow me. [We go into a small stuffy room] You caused great offence.

YVES: I didn't mean anything wrong.

OFFICIAL: Do it again and you will get two years in prison, you little sod. Now off you go.

AND I LEFT VERY QUICKLY.[91]

Other forms of resistance to occupying authorities included smuggling of goods and foodstuffs, hiding requisitioned agricultural products and animals, running escape networks, and working for enemy intelligence organizations. Since communication was in such short supply in occupation zones, another valued form of resistance by civilians was the creation of underground newspapers and postal services. In Belgium, several such outlets developed during the war, but none of these was as celebrated as *La Libre Belgique,* which eventually had a nationwide distribution. The clandestine paper, which published in what it deemed a "regularly irregular" manner, began appearing in Brussels in 1915. *La Libre Belgique* featured scathing and humorous attacks on the German authorities, and it was known for its daring distribution feats, including that of managing to get a copy onto the desk of German governor-general Von Bissing without detection.[92] Networks for moving information and people arose throughout occupied zones and provided an outlet for the patriotic fervor of some civilians, despite the dangers of deportation, imprisonment, or death.

Intelligence services also operated where possible in front-line and occupation zones, and officials relied heavily on civilians as intelligence agents, couriers, and informants. An example of an unusual intelligence network developed by the British in Ottoman territory is NILI (Netzach Israel lo Ishakare, or the Eternity of Israel Will Not Lie).[93] Largely a family network created by Jewish scientist Aaron Aaronsohn, NILI included his siblings and many of their friends in Ottoman-occupied Palestine and Syria. Most of the members of the network were ardent Zionists who hoped that their contribution to the British war effort would prove helpful in their quest for postwar autonomy and would help undermine Ottoman control in the region. As Alex Aaronsohn, Aaron's brother, explained it, NILI saw Jewish Palestine's best hope as lying with British interests, not German or Ottoman. The spy network, once established, had more than thirty members, most of them under thirty years old. The work was directed by Sarah Aaronsohn (Aaron's sister) and Yossef Lishansky (a family friend).[94] NILI's most productive period of intelligence gathering came in late 1916 and in 1917 before the network was betrayed to Ottoman authorities and crushed in October 1917.[95]

Intelligence, perhaps more than many other wartime activities, depended on the blurred lines between civilian and soldier; without civilians spying on the enemy, the armies in the field would have incomplete information with which to strategize. In Belgium and northern France, multiple national intelligence-gathering operations were at work—German, French, Dutch, Belgian, and British, to name a few. Civilians, some motivated by patriotism or revenge, others by greed, offered their time and skills to aid these intelligence services. The networks tended to vary widely in effectiveness and personnel. Some British networks, such as La Dame Blanche (The White Lady), featured mostly Catholic and patriotic middle-class and aristocratic men and women in highly regimented train-watching and courier services throughout the occupied zones, while others, like Service Felix, took an entirely different tack and "employed women of doubtful reputation" to gather information. The Service Felix agents were paid in cash or drugs, while La Dame Blanche members hoped for postwar recognition of services rendered to the Allies.[96] Some intelligence networks featured thousands of civilians linked together by couriers, while others were quite small. La Dame Blanche enrolled more than a thousand people in its network from 1917 to 1918, while Lise Rischard developed a train-watching and information service for the British in Luxembourg that employed less than a dozen people (her first recruit was her husband).[97] The French used refugees to gain intelligence, while the British questioned those arriving at their ports from foreign countries.[98]

Intelligence networks, no matter what their size, provide a good example of the civilian-army cooperation that occurred during World War I. While most of the intelligence agents were civilians, many were paid by military officials from army or navy funds, some were provided with separation pay and military honors at the end of the war, and almost all considered themselves to be doing "war service." In fact, there is a blurring of the lines between civilians and soldiers with the gathering of military intelligence since civilians have access to more information, but analysts need to have some military knowledge to make such information useful. Belligerent nations tried to hedge their bets during the war by creating many types of overlapping information networks, hoping that some of them would pay off. As an example, in Belgium alone, more than 250 clandestine espionage services developed during the course of the war.[99]

La Dame Blanche (LDB), an unusual service in many ways, provides a useful instance of the ways in which intelligence services blurred the lines between soldiers and civilians. LDB actually militarized its members, enrolling them in battalions, extracting binding oaths, and providing identification badges. This group, which included teenaged boys and girls as well as the elderly, created soldiers of its spies. Members were encouraged to think of themselves as "soldats" (soldiers), not as agents or spies, which had a negative connotation. Many of those involved in the service wrote of their pride in serving as "soldiers like the 'others.'"[100] The loyalty oath that La Dame Blanche soldiers took underlines their seriousness about their role in the war: "I declare and enlist in the capacity of Soldier in the Allied military observation service, until the end of the war. I swear before God to respect this engagement."[101] In occupied territory where one had to escape across an electrified border into neutral territory in order to join the Belgian army, espionage work looked very much like an alternate form of military service. As typist Marguerite Blanckaert said of her wartime intelligence gathering and imprisonment in Germany, "I had as a motto: for my King, for my Fatherland, Always!"[102] Similarly, Jeanne Delwaide said of her service, "We have done our duty—as good British soldiers—and we have done it with . . . the assurance that our modest services would not be unnecessary to the great common cause."[103]

Some civilians in occupied territories combined their activities, often at great risk, providing intelligence, running escape networks, and helping with clandestine publications. The women of the de Radiguès family in eastern Belgium cared for and hid wounded Allied soldiers, then helped them escape to the Netherlands in the early part of the war, but then in the last year of the war began working for British intelligence.[104] In other cases, intelligence agents used their work, often for the occupying authorities themselves, as a front for espionage activities. In Tsingtao (China), German police developed an espionage service made up of Chinese men who took positions such as construction workers or cigarette sellers to hide their intelligence work.[105] Belgian Marthe Cnockaert worked as a nurse in a German hospital in Roubaix, served German soldiers in her parents' café in Roeselare at night, and worked as a British intelligence agent as well. In fact, Cnockaert won the Iron Cross for her service among German wounded before being arrested for espionage in late 1916; after the war, she was decorated by the British for her intelligence work.[106] Cnockaert's double duty for both Britain and Germany opened her up for postwar recriminations—was she a heroine or a collaborator? Collaboration and war profiteering were widely condemned after the war, yet in practice the lines between resistance and collaboration were frequently hard to interpret. This was a particular problem when it came to sorting out intimate relationships between soldiers and civilians.

Companionship, Sex, and the Soldier

Many of the soldiers longed for companionship outside of the trenches, and often the opportunity to talk with or be entertained by noncombatants was a treat. A British regiment recorded the conflict its soldiers felt when a divisional canteen opened in the village where they were billeted. Many could not decide whether to visit the canteen where English beer was sold or the Belgian café The Swan, where "the famous Emma dispensed hospitality."[107] The female performers hired by the YMCA and traveling theatrical troupes apparently lifted the spirits of men considerably. Rita Squire, a singer and performer, was the favorite of the 13th Australian Field Ambulance, who sent her fan letters such as one from July 1918, reporting that "[w]e have a number of your records out in our unit & we all know you well by voice . . . as your voice has been greatly admired by all the officers of our division, especially when you sing every evening at dinner for us."[108] The letter ended with a request for a signed photograph for the unit.

Relief organizations such as the YMCA tried to distract men from the hardships of war and from the more unsavory activities in which they might engage. Recreation huts provided food, hot coffee and cocoa, reading materials, games, and social events. Most importantly, these served as sites for conversation and "civilian interaction." Addie Hunton and Kathryn Johnson, two African-American women sent to work in the YMCA canteens in France, attributed the soldiers' interest in interacting with them to homesickness and loneliness. The men wanted sympathetic ears in which to pour their "joys and sorrows."[109]

The least complicated relationships that developed between soldiers and civilians often involved young children, and postwar oral histories and memoirs mention small kindnesses exchanged between billeted soldiers and their hosts. Elza Neel remembered as a child hanging around the barracks in Poperinge (Belgium) where British soldiers called her "Elsy, Little Ginger" and gave her gifts such as pieces of chocolate.[110] At the Berrima internment camp in Australia, the German naval officers imprisoned there made friends with village children, playing with them and constructing toys.[111] In these situations and many others, children reminded soldiers of their civilian lives and gave them a sense of familial surroundings. Civilian communities around battle fronts or in occupation zones had the ability to recreate home life for soldiers, to give them a taste of the pleasures of home. One of these pleasures that many soldiers longed for was companionship and sex, another area of civilian-soldier interactions fraught with contradictions.

Citizen-soldiers wanted the normalcy of relationships, and multiple postwar memoirs recount the marriage proposals that local girls received from billeted soldiers, many of which were nipped in the bud by irate parents.[112] In one case, postal censors were treated to a personal drama in letters home that followed the marriage of Mahomed Khan, a Hindustani Muslim from India who was serving with the British army in France, to a French woman in April 1917. Fellow soldiers and family members responded to this marriage with a mixture of curiosity and scorn, but at least one soldier found the whole situation proof of the acceptance of Indian troops in France. Zabur Shah wrote home of the incident: "The people of this country treat us with the greatest consideration and respect. One of our men has, with the consent of the French and British governments, married into these people and a daughter has been born to him."[113] This marriage and other relationships helped sustain soldiers who were far from home, and as with Mahomed Khan, it was sometimes worth the risk of incurring the wrath of superior officers and the derision of comrades. In short, civilians provided the link to home for many soldiers.

A different kind of civilian relationship was found in the African campaign, where soldiers often brought women and children with them, some of whom worked as support systems for their men and others of whom were hired directly as porters or laborers. German commander Paul Von Lettow-Vorbeck spent considerable time in his memoirs talking about the position of families in his army during the East African campaign. He worried about their safety but also fretted about the drag they might create on his mobility and about his men's dedication if they were busy with families. Yet his attempts to send the women away failed, as he noted somewhat ruefully in his memoir:

A crowd of Askari women had followed the force, and had attached themselves to various camps on the Rufiji, where they were very comfortable. I
was most anxious to send them south, where the question of supplies was
less difficult. The necessary transport was arranged for, and the women
were given rations for the march. After one short day's march, however, the
women simply lay down and declared that they could go no further. Their
rations, which were intended to last a considerable time, were all eaten by
the third day, and they were crying out for more. Some even went so far as
to attack and beat the European who was in charge of the transport.[114]

These were not "tender flowers" but seasoned campaigners, as it was
not uncommon for women to live with some African armies in barracks
and under military discipline during peacetime.[115] Von Lettow-Vorbeck
eventually decided to train the women to march faster and to use their
services to help maintain the morale of his askari (African soldiers). As
he recounted later in the book, the women played an important role in
camp:

Many Askari had their wives and children with them in the field, and many
children were born during the march. Each woman carried her own Mali
(property), as well as that of her lord, on her head. Often they carried on
their backs a small child, his woolly head peeping out of the cloth in which
he was wound. The women were kept in order and protected by a European
or a trustworthy old non-commissioned officer, assisted by a few Askari.
They all liked gay colours, and after an important capture, the whole convoy stretching several miles would look like a carnival procession.[116]

While it may have looked like a festive carnival, these women were
pursuing careers following the armies, providing vital services for soldiers, and marching between fifteen and twenty miles per day. In fact,
when Von Lettow-Vorbeck's army surrendered in November 1918, women
comprised one-fifth of his force.[117]

In other arenas of the war, the problem of female "followers" became
a policy issue for military commanders as well. Captain D. C. Thompson
wrote in his war diary for the Persian Labour Corps he commanded in
August 1918 that local property owners were complaining about female

followers of the corps squatting on their land and stealing food. When on August 28 Thompson received a formal petition complaining about the problem from a nearby landowner, he began a search for a place to erect a "Permanent Followers' Camp." After a short survey, Thompson

> went round the date-gardens adjoining my Camp with the Commandant, River Front Area, and selected a spot just behind the village of WAGAF in which to collect all the Persian women and children at present scattered in small parties in various places, pending the decision of the authorities re: the settling of a permanent Camp. I then started clearing the squatters away from their previous small encampments, and by the evening had rounded up all of them into the new site.[118]

Thompson's and Von Lettow-Vorbeck's problems with female "followers" were not unique. Armies found the "woman problem" an acute one in all theaters of war, and every belligerent had to develop rules governing access to wives and prostitutes. Men fighting near their homes often had the ability to travel home to visit wives and families while on leave, but others spent much of the war separated entirely from their families. Most British soldiers assigned to Mesopotamia and Palestine received no home leave, so holiday camps were set up on nearby beaches to provide a cheap and relaxing site for leave that was away from the dangers of the cities.[119] In the German-occupied Ober Ost on the eastern front, neither military nor civil officials could have their families with them. Visits from families were strictly forbidden, and apart from a female German secretarial staff, the entire administration of the Ober Ost (numbering between ten thousand and eighteen thousand) was male. The corresponding policy to this banning of families from the Ober Ost was the creation of military-run brothels with regulated and medically inspected prostitution.[120]

While some military establishments, such as the French, relied on *maisons tolerées* (regulated brothels), others, such as the American, sought to keep men from consorting with prostitutes altogether. The minutes from a meeting of Allied military personnel in July 1918 to discuss the problem of prostitution and venereal disease illuminates the differences between nations in their approach to the issue. It also highlights how military and civil personnel differed in their opinions about acceptable regulation of prostitution. For instance, when a major from the Canadian Expeditionary Force suggested that it "ought to be possible . . . to order that all women should be examined [for VD]," the British under-secretary for war (Ian McPherson) objected quite rigorously, saying, "I am quite sure that that would not be tolerated in this country." Later in the discussion, the French representative (a physician) detailed the regulated brothel system before an American army officer explained the U.S. policy established in May 1917, namely, that "no house of prostitution [was] permitted within five miles of a military camp," adding that alcohol was also forbidden and that any soldier contracting VD was court-martialed. After a long debate about varying methods, the archibishop of Canterbury pointed out the obvious lack of coordination, saying, "we are suggesting something which is exactly the opposite to what they are doing, because if I understand aright we were told just now that the French policy was at the moment to increase the *maisons de tolerance,* to inspect them more elaborately than before, so that it seems to be not a dimunition of activity if at the same time we are asking them to prevent the use of these places."[121] As the archbishop noted, the French were expanding their regulated brothels at the same time that the British and the Americans sought to abolish military brothels and make them off-limits to their soldiers. An Interallied Medical Committee came to a similar conclusion in its 1917 report, noting that U.S. theory was totally at odds with the French approach—where the Americans wanted "total abolition of prostitution," the French favored "highly supervised prostitution."[122] These disagreements led to a muddled policy indeed on the western front.

Beyond the problem of whether to control prostitutes was the issue of so-called clandestine prostitution. This was a much more serious issue for civil and military authorities, because clandestine prostitutes were often "amateurs" who became temporary sex workers in order to feed themselves or their families. The authorities could rarely identify, let alone regulate, such women, and rates of venereal disease rose quickly among clandestine prostitutes. Figures for Paris in 1917 suggest the differences in infection rate that occurred with regular medical exams and without them; fewer than 2 percent of women in *maisons tolerées* were infected with VD, but the rate for clandestine prostitutes was more than 35 percent.[123] Yet, dealing with the problem of clandestine prostitution was not a question upon which anyone really agreed. As Susan Grayzel has noted, "the dangers—prostitutes and amateurs—were defined as the same but the techniques used against them varied."[124] Complicating all questions of prostitution were consensual sexual relationships between soldiers and civilians, which sometimes skirted the line between consent and coercion. A soldier might bring "gifts" of food or clothing to a woman with whom he was having a sexual relationship, which made it hard for authorities to know whether these gifts were for services rendered or not. Regulating sex was no easy thing for either civil or military authorities in the war zones.

Prostitution developed wherever the military establishment went—occupation zones, staging areas, operations zones, training camps, and hospitals. While the military maintained "controlled" brothels such as a large center created by the Germans at Brussels, many young female workers made extra cash by engaging in casual prostitution. In occupied Ghent, where prostitution was particularly prevalent because of a large number of German soldiers, one area of town was renamed by local folks the "Microbe Boulevard." The price for sex with a Belgian prostitute varied, but it seems to have ranged from three to twenty marks for one-half hour and ten to fifty marks for the whole night.[125] For soldiers, both unauthorized and authorized prostitution was an option near most training camps, in large cities, and in the occupation zones, in particular. Brothels accommodated large numbers of soldiers in a day (one report cited an average of more than forty men per prostitute per day in French brothels), and it was not uncommon for queues to develop outside of regulated brothels.[126] In a year-long tally of brothel customers in Le Havre (France), figures suggested that about eighty men per day visited one of the brothels.[127]

In addition to military brothels such as the one in Brussels, where there was also a large hospital for women infected with venereal disease, centers of prostitution could be found in garrison towns and in the staging zone cities. Tours, France, was the supply headquarters for the U.S. army and what one medical officer called a "wide-open" town, with ready supplies of prostitutes and alcohol for men on leave.[128] Likewise, Freiburg, Germany, which was a command and staff headquarters during the war, recorded explosive increases in prostitution. Roger Chickering noted that in Freiburg, "close to 400 unregistered prostitutes were picked up in 1915" alone, and local hospitals saw a rise in rates of sexually transmitted diseases.[129] In the United States, vigilance squads arrested, inspected, and detained women accused of prostitution, especially near training camps full of young draftees.[130]

Most soldiers, despite regulations and vigilance squads, found access to prostitutes. Soldier Erwin Blumenfeld described an "authorized" German field brothel in occupied Valenciennes (northern France), noting the precautions taken to avoid disease:

> The brothel opened at ten in the morning; eighteen prostitutes lived there, six of whom only served officers; the standard price for their service was four marks, of which the prostitute and the owner of the house each got one mark. Every morning the prostitutes had a medical check-up, though not a very thorough one; for this duty the Red Cross, which took "medical moral responsibility" for the brothel, received the remaining two marks. Each prostitute received about twenty-five to thirty customers a day.[131]

Blumenfeld's description shows the alliance among army, civil authorities, and charitable organizations that made "regulated" brothels possible. Yet despite regulation and medical precautions, the sheer numbers of people involved in the sex trade, whether in official or in unofficial settings, made complete control of venereal disease virtually impossible.

The areas where brothels developed were at the heart of other forms of entertainment as well, and soldiers could drink liquor, buy drugs, and engage in other forbidden pleasures. Despite being officially "out of bounds" to troops, Egypt's brothels serve as a good example of the growth of prostitution in urban centers where lots of young soldiers congregated, especially in Cairo and Alexandria. Soldiers knew they could buy alcohol, cocaine, and hashish in Cairo, and prostitution was rife. When troops were stationed near the cities for long periods of time, VD infection rates rose considerably. For example, when the British front in 1916 was near Cairo, the VD rates were seventy-five per one thousand as compared to a rate during a comparable period in France of eighteen per thousand.[132]

Both Cairo and Alexandria had regulated and inspected brothels as well as clandestine prostitutes, but the situation was also complicated by the various nationalities represented in the brothels and the odd legal status of the British authorities in Egypt (as occupying authorities since 1882). In Cairo the police tried to use martial law regulations to shut down brothels and bars in "a nest of the worst type" where Australians had recently set fire to several houses. However, the police came up against a variety of problems, such as that "a good many of the premises . . . belong to the Coptic [Christian] Patriarch" and "there were some 1700 people of all nationalities involved and the question arose where they could go."[133]

As the police reports continued in 1915 and 1916, the scope of the prostitution in Egypt became more clear. In Alexandria, the police raided 280 clandestine brothels in 1914 and "saved" more than nine hundred young girls brought to the port as part of the "white slave traffic." These girls and women included Italians, French, Austrians, Greeks, Russians, British, Syrians, Armenians, and Turks. Cairo registered more than eleven hundred prostitutes by March 1916 and arrested several hundred other "unlicensed" prostitutes, and the police received permission to build a "new Quarter suitable in every way . . . to which . . . the whole of the public women will be removed."[134] Part of the reason for the police crackdown and reorganization of its policies came from an event that caused world attention to focus on Cairo. On "Good Friday 1915 the tension between the local population and the colonial troops exploded in the so-called Wassa riot, when the red-light district of Cairo was ransacked and set alight by Australians and New Zealanders aggrieved at the bad drink and 'diseased' Egyptian prostitutes supplied to them."[135] Another riot followed in July as authorities scrambled to contain and explain the violence. Even though official inquiries were held, the soldiers responsible for the violence were not punished; military officials instead responded by new controls on the brothels rather than on the soldiers.[136]

One other issue increased the vigilance about prostitution: fear regarding venereal disease. Despite differences in regulation and control of prostitution, all armies agreed upon the need to equip soldiers with information on venereal diseases and prophylactics to combat rising levels of syphilis and gonorrhea. Most armies built prophylactic stations such as the British "blue-light depots" and suggested attendance at a station after a sexual encounter.[137] The American Expeditionary Force, for example, set up "emergency stations" for men to go to for topical treatment after sex,

Card distributed to American soldiers in France showing the location of official prophylactic stations. U.S. military personnel were required to go to prophylactic stations within three hours after a sexual encounter or face court-martial. *National World War I Museum.*

mandating attendance. Those who were caught evading the stations could be court-martialed for neglect of duty. Treatment instructions were quite specific, and included washing genitalia with soap, then with bichloride of mercury. This cleansing was followed by an injection of a teaspoon of a protargol (derived from silver) solution into the urethra, which had to be held inside (the soldier was instructed to do so with thumb and forefinger) for five minutes. The treatment ended with calomel ointment and instructions not to urinate for at least four hours.[30] Other armies relied on mobile prophylactic kits, such as the French "dreadnought" or the Australian "blue packet," which were distributed to troops on leave.[39] Condoms were also distributed, but their cost and their possible use for contraception at home (thereby threatening the national birthrate) made them less popular official remedies until quite late in the war.

Civilians faced the reality of venereal disease in other ways. Soldiers brought the disease home with them on leave and after the war. In Britain, a soldier's family allowances were stopped, and he was put on half-pay while in hospital for venereal treatment, a particularly cruel punishment for the families at home.[140] Women particularly were targeted in the official attempt to stamp out prostitution, with testing for venereal diseases in some areas, criminalization of abortifacients, and curfews.[141] Some nations inspected women but not men for disease, and a clear double standard existed in regard to public conversations about wartime sex and venereal disease. "Evil" civilian women became the focus of army education pamphlets that warned soldiers not to trust women they met at the front. A U.S. army pamphlet, "The Red Souvenir," contrasted the virtuous lady waiting at home with the woman "with a mon cheri smile" who would give soldiers "a dirty body" to take home with a "red souvenir of lust."[142] Soldiers had to take care to avoid such voracious women.

Certainly it was easy for men to have their suspicions about civilian women confirmed when they visited brothel districts. For example, Anwar Shah, a member of the Camel Corps in the Suez region, described his disgust at seeing "nightingales" sitting with Egyptian men, indulging "in all kinds of lewd and obscure songs." He could not believe that Muslim men would "despoil" such awful women, especially since he was writing right at the end of a Muslim holy festival.[143] Officials, too, condemned women for losing all sense of modesty around men in uniforms, ignoring issues of poverty or other circumstances that might lead women to prostitution. In Britain, prostitution around training camps also led to a focus on women as destroyers of male health. In one case study of a woman whom officials were trying to confine to a hospital or prison, she was described as almost a national threat:

> This case suggests very strongly the desirability of providing means for restraining such a woman as this from mischief. With such determined proclivities as she appears to have she could do an immense amount of harm in a very short time. A power to hospital authorities to restrain for the purpose of medical treatment women only certified to be suffering dangerous contagious disease . . . might have good effect on the health of the troops.[144]

Restraint and confinement were considered the best way to protect soldiers from such civilians as this woman. Indeed, throughout the war and after it, civil and military officials sought to contain venereal disease and the prostitution that helped spread it through control of women, rarely taking measures to punish soldiers for having sex, only for refusing prophylactic treatment.

Conclusion

For civilians living close to the destruction of the war or under enemy control, the war was not a distant event. As they went for weekly registration at a "pass office" or queued up for soup at a relief kitchen, they recognized that their simplest daily activities were subject to the vagaries of war. In regions where war had taken an even deadlier toll, the search for food or fuel became secondary as populations struggled to survive epidemic disease. With the occupation of Romania in 1916, hundreds of thousands of refugees flooded into Moldavia, creating the environment for a devastating typhoid epidemic that killed more than one hundred thousand people.[145] In Poland, too, conditions were terrible in 1919. American Maurice Pate described the scene in a letter home in March: "At a time when the temperature was little above freezing I have seen women on the streets in their barefeet. In hospitals . . . doctors . . . wore aprons made of linen napkins pieced together, and the bandages used were rags torn from old shirts."[146] An observer in postwar Budapest (Hungary) described the aftermath of war, revolution, and occupation thus: "It was like a plague of locusts had devastated the place. Consumed and exhausted, the town lay on the rubbish heap."[147]

In 1918, when the war ended, many civilians felt like veterans of the conflict, seeing their war service and sacrifice as equal to that of the soldiers at the front. Misunderstandings, recriminations, and resentment were all common reactions to the reintegration of soldiers and refugees into civilian society. Add to the mix the revolutions, civil revolts, and continuing hardships of the period immediately following the cessation of hostilities, and the picture of volatile societies emerges. Even a cursory examination of politics and social change in the 1920s demonstrates the long-term psychological effects of the war on families and individuals, especially those who had spent multiple years in the trenches—whether at the battle front or along its edges. As to those traumatized by war, there is little possibility at this distance even of gauging that impact.

Yet the exhaustion of civil populations did not mean an immediate return to normalcy or a "laying to rest" of wartime issues. Questions of collaboration and resistance, equality of sacrifice, and wartime recriminations continued to fester in the immediate postwar world. The violence experienced by those living under occupation, in exile, or under fire had shaped their lives profoundly, and it was not an easy matter to forget what had occurred. A fitting conclusion to this tale of the civilian caught between the lines comes from Paul Valéry, a poet and essayist who witnessed the war from his desk job in Paris:

> The storm has died away, and still we are restless, uneasy, as if the storm were about to break. Almost all the affairs of men remain in a terrible uncertainty. We think of what has disappeared, we are almost destroyed by what has been destroyed; we do not know what will be born, and we fear the future, not without reason. We hope vaguely, we dread precisely; our fears are infinitely more precise than our hopes; we confess that the charm of life is behind us, abundance is behind us, but doubt and disorder are in us and with us. . . . One can say that all the fundamentals of the world have been affected by the war, or more exactly, by the circumstances of the war; something deeper has been worn away than the renewable parts of the machine. . . . But among all these injured things is the Mind.[148]

With the lingering effects of displacement, malnourishment, and influenza and the difficult return to home and so-called normal life, many civilian survivors of life between the lines of war, as Valéry predicted, "fear[ed] the future, not without reason."

[5]

Caring for the Wounded

Mourning brides besiege the hospitals for nurses' wear [while]
healthy men dressed for battle . . . with a red cross on their
jacket sleeves, rattle their swords in the cafeterias.

—Gyula Krúdy[1]

When the United States army sent out a call for a new group of
civilian employees called "Reconstruction Aides" in January 1918, both
Katrine Fairclough and Lena Hitchcock volunteered. These new "RAs"
provided specialized care for recuperating soldiers in the areas of massage
therapy, occupational therapy, and physical therapy. While Katrine Fairclough worked full-time at a hospital in Liverpool (U.K.) as a medical
masseuse, Lena Hitchcock was sent to France in 1918, where she worked
as a nurse's aide in the wards. As Hitchcock described it,

> I make beds, first sweeping them out with a whisk broom, twice daily; rub
> backs (black and white), sterilize the instruments, wash the rubber gloves,
> keep the dressing cart in order, hand Miss Knight and the surgeon what
> they need, take temperatures and fill out the charts. This is what we all do,
> and I love it. The boys are marvelous—when the horrible, gaping wounds
> are being dressed, there is never a word out of them.[2]

With all this other activity, she only managed to fit in her occupational therapy when there was extra time. The woodworking, weaving,
and sewing the men performed improved their dexterity, while exercises,
stretching, and massage helped rejuvenate muscles. Hitchcock and Fair-

A Reconstruction Aide helps wounded soldiers make wooden dolls as part of their rehabilitation. *U.S. Signal Corps, National Archives and Records Administration.*

clough, despite working with soldiers in militarized, uniformed settings, were civilian employees, trained specifically to retrain the bodies that war had broken. Applicants for the RA positions had to be twenty-five to forty years old, between one hundred and 195 pounds, with a high school diploma and training in physical massage. Although it consisted of civilian employees, this corps functioned under the auspices of the army, with living quarters, uniforms, and additional training provided as well as salaries of fifty to sixty dollars per month. Like tens of thousands of other civilians, these RAs spent their war trying to mend the broken bodies and souls that war created, rehabilitating them for further service in the war, or for return to civilian life.

Medical personnel, in all their variety, were among the most celebrated of all workers during the war. Medical services in World War I encompassed a broad range of functions and personnel, with military medical establishments, private charitable hospitals, ambulance corps run by private and public entities, and neutral medical services staffed and organized by international organizations such as the Society of Friends (Quakers), the Red Crescent, and the Red Cross. Many times during the war these various organizations clashed over ideology and over territory—caring for the wounded became a massive endeavor that strained resources and beliefs before the conflict came to a close.

Most medical personnel, whether they held military commissions or civilian posts, recognized that their role in the war was different from that of soldiers. Rather than taking lives, they were saving them. Yet many medical personnel were uniformed, protected, and often even housed and fed by armies, which were organized along national lines. Sometimes this led to conflict, as the needs of the wounded demanded a certain neutrality of perspective, but the demands of national Red Crosses or armies often called for partisan views. It was frequently hard for those working in hospitals to separate themselves from their national loyalties, and even neutrals sometimes got caught up in the nationalist fervor of those with whom they associated.

Doctors, nurses, orderlies, and ambulance drivers lived and interacted with soldiers on a daily basis, serving as a conduit between the worlds of the front and of the home. The gap between soldiers and those caring for them was certainly one of experience of killing, but in terms of exposure to danger and psychological trauma, they were closer together than either probably realized. Although deeply embedded in military life and culture and enmeshed in the war itself, doctors, nurses, ambulance drivers, and orderlies were often perceived as being separate from war, neutral, objective, somehow above the fray. This chapter examines the ambiguous role of medical services as accessories to war and as saviors of soldiers, an uncomfortable and difficult position to maintain.

Medicine under Fire

Medical services provide a useful insight into the problem of describing the divide between civilian and soldier. Many ambulance corps, nursing and hospital units, and rehabilitation clinics treated both civil and military patients, and they employed both civilian and military men and

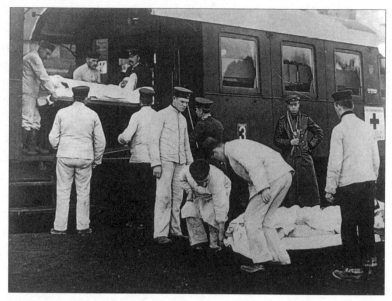

This German hospital train prepares to move and treat a group of wounded soldiers near Karlsruhe. *Library of Congress.*

women, some volunteers and some paid. Unlike earlier wars such as the Anglo-Boer War of 1899–1902, the First World War never maintained a real "separation between military and civilian medicine," chiefly because the need for medical care was complex, large in scope, and long-term.[3] Private charities set up medical trains, hospitals, and ambulance units with uniformed personnel, but they were often classified as civilian. For example, the Knights of Malta (Germany and Austria) created hospital trains to use as voluntary "ambulance service[s] in war time". Evelyn, Princess Blücher, described her pride at seeing her husband head out on his first medical mission with the Knights, "wearing his smart new uniform with the Red Cross band on his arm."[4] These hospital trains interacted with military medical units and civilian hospitals as part of their missions of mercy, with uniformed "civilian volunteers" caring for uniformed "soldiers" alongside "auxiliary nurses" and "contract doctors." Russian doctor Tatiana Alexinsky recalled her experiences on such a line, explaining, "Our hospital train is like a town on wheels—a little provincial town, with all its petty business, petty concerns, petty interests. . . . Except for [orderlies, stretcher bearers, etc.] the staff is 'civilian,' and is composed exclusively of women."[5]

Some medical units were civilian-military cooperative ventures, while others were considered strictly military or strictly civilian enterprises, but in most cases, the lines were blurred. Many of the medical facilities themselves were former civic buildings or estates owned by wealthy elites, and they retained their civilian look even as they were requisitioned for military purposes. Oftentimes convents were converted to medical facilities, especially since many female religious orders were used to nurse the sick. Other makeshift or purpose-built medical facilities were funded by the military but had to rely on a certain number of civilian personnel as nurses, doctors, or orderlies. In France a tuberculosis hospital for soldiers inhabited a series of five summer chalets at the seaside, with all the nursing and orderly work being assigned to hired civilian laborers from France's colony in Indochina.[6] Again, the mix of civil and military resources and personnel helped meet the medical needs of the war.

One young female nurse's anonymous memoir of the war illustrates the complex military-civil cooperation and changing arrangements that emerged during the war. The nurse, a British territorial nurse, volunteered for British service in August 1914 but was turned away, so she went to work in a Belgian hospital in a former school in Antwerp funded by Elisabeth, the Belgian queen. When Antwerp was taken by the Germans in October, she and the hospital staff retreated along with the Belgian army and numerous civilian refugees to Ghent, then Bruges, then Ostend. After a few days in England, she was back in Belgium, this time in a hospital in Furnes that was housed in an old Roman Catholic college. Here she nursed French troops, not only

the French "poilu," but [also] representatives from all the French colonies,—black, brown and yellow men. Great black, woolly-haired Senegalese from East Africa, savages and cannibals, lay stretched out on our beds, or oftener on the floors, for we were overflowing. These poor fellows could not even speak French, and they suffered bitterly from the cold. . . . There were also Turcos with red fezzes and baggy trousers, Zouaves with cutaway jackets, Algerians and Arab-Spahis with peculiar bowl-shaped turbans. Among them were Annamites from the Orient, members of the Legion-Étrangers, and French Alpinos with blue tam-o'-shanters.[7]

As this excerpt demonstrates, she interacted with all manner of soldiers, many of them probably as new to the war experience as she was. She remained at this hospital until it was destroyed by bombing in January 1915; then she moved to a new hospital at Hoogestade. Although this hospital began as a privately funded civilian venture under the Belgian Red Cross, by mid-1915 it had become a Belgian military hospital. She remained under the new regimen until she went home in October 1915.[8] Crossing civil-military lines as well as national lines repeatedly during the war, her experiences question the status of medicine in relationship to the civilian-soldier divide.

Outside of the European theaters of war, the lines between civilian and military medical personnel were also blurred. German-born Ludwig Deppe's improvised hospital in Tanga (Tanzania) at first treated both English and German casualties, but by 1916, he was working with the German East African forces and moving almost constantly as the army maneuvered, living off the land. His wife was his main surgical nurse and anesthesiologist, and his staff featured mostly local recruits, some of whom he could retain only by chaining them together to keep them from deserting. One of Deppe's diary entries for October 1916 sounds suspiciously similar to the entries from European military officers assigned to this war theater, with the problems of using "native conscripts" and feeding personnel from the land:

This sight of my retinue is enough to make you weep; at the front of the procession is my wheelbarrow with two men, harnessed to it like a team of horses. The wretched tracks are sandy, stony and rutted. To my left are two boys whose job it is to pick vegetables and mangoes and buy eggs, hens and pigeons. One carries a rifle and cartridge bag, a pith helmet and a lamp. The other carries the portable medicine chest and the hospital flag on a seven-metre-long bamboo stick. And then comes my caravan, which consists of 27 people. I have decided we must depart tomorrow morning at 4 a.m., because apparently we will have to march for nine hours through the barren steppe.[9]

Certainly Deppe's hospital experiences were far different from those of the stationary civil or military hospitals behind the lines; he was in fact embedded in the army in the field for much of the war.

Regardless of location, however, it was common for tensions to arise between military and civilian medical personnel, especially given the large number of untrained volunteer medical aides engaged in "war work." Military officials recognized their reliance on civilians for medical services but often sought to create situations where either military personnel provided supervision or where civilians could be marked as "separate" from military endeavors. When the Chinese Labour Corps of the British army came to France and Belgium to work as civilian contract laborers for the army, doctors with knowledge of Chinese were enlisted, many of them missionaries. E. J. Stuckey, hired to care for the Chinese on their voyage and in the special Chinese hospital in France, was required to wear civilian clothes on the voyage, as were the European military officers assigned to the corps in order to insure that "the venture was viewed as non-military."[10] In another charitable mission, the privately funded American Fund for French Wounded had been established to provide comforts, hospital supplies, clothing, and motor transport to wounded French soldiers in France. However, as time passed, many of the uniformed personnel in the AFFW began caring for civilians as well, making rounds to villages and towns where medical care had been absent since the war began. Dr. Alice Brown, a physician from Illinois, was visiting six towns, each twice per week, by 1917, mostly providing basic medical care and medicines to women and children.[11] Much of this work among civilians arose out of necessity as a real health crisis loomed. As Leo Van Bergen noted in his study of wartime medicine, "the voracious requirements of the medical services responsible for treating wounded and sick soldiers had a disastrous effect on civilian health care."[12]

The recruitment of many trained doctors and nurses into military medical service led civilian communities to face the loss of their medical care, and in some cases, major medical emergencies resulted. In Serbia, where a quarter of all trained doctors died in the war, the absence of widespread civilian medical care led to a public health disaster in 1915; an estimated hundred thousand civilians died of disease in that year alone.[13]

Australian nurse Edith Mackay described the sad situation she witnessed at a Serbian hospital:

> All day long sick, illfed & scantily clad Serbs flock around the little dispensary. Tottering old men. Weather worn pale & harrassed looking women. Sick children in their arms. The days work commenced at sunrise & ended some times long after sunset. People come long distances mostly on foot for treatment . . . & medicine & dressings for malaria, typhus, typhoid, influenza, diseases, accidents, dogbite, etc.[14]

Shortages of medical personnel and medicines led to disasters for civilian families such as these caught in the war's violence.

The medical crisis was not limited to war zones, however. In Germany during the war, there was one doctor for fifty-eight hundred people (as opposed to one per fifteen hundred prior to the war), and in France, the ratio was a shocking one doctor per fourteen thousand people. The armies' absorption of most doctors, nurses, dentists, and pharmacists left few resources for civilians. When combined with the lack of available medicines, poor sanitary conditions, and overcrowding in some zones, the results were disastrous. In Serbia, one of the major hospitals at war's outbreak was a barracks with no running water or anesthesia in August 1914.[15] With such conditions, it is unsurprising that an estimated two hundred thousand Serbians died of typhus in the first six months of the war alone.[16] Such epidemics affected not just the civil population but also soldiers, prisoners of war, and medical personnel who came into contact with civilians. For instance, novelist Mabel Dearmer died of typhus within weeks of volunteering as an orderly at a Serbian medical unit, as did another nurse from the same group of forty women.[17] Altogether approximately 125 of the 425 doctors in this Serbian zone died in the typhus epidemic.[18]

From Galicia to East Africa to Flanders, medical personnel used the resources they could find in order to aid the wounded and the sick. Sometimes they questioned their missions, as their calling to heal occasionally meant crossing lines of nationality or jurisdiction. In its end-of-the-war report, one Australian field ambulance baldly stated its activities, despite its role as a "military" ambulance designed to care for soldiers:

Medical personnel worked in a variety of locations throughout the war including such installations as this venereal treatment facility for U.S. soldiers in France. *U.S. Signal Corps, National Archives and Records Administration.*

> Ever since this unit landed in France medical attention has been accorded continually to French civilians. The latter have been visited professionally in their houses and generally cared for whenever circumstances precluded the attendance of French Medical men. During time of special stress and when civilians have been subjected to shell fire they have been frequently sheltered and fed in the dressing stations of this Ambulance.[19]

Other reports from Australian and British hospitals in the region also admitted to caring for civilians in the areas of gynecological care, venereal disease, and common diseases (especially in the period of the worst cases of influenza).

At home fronts, the medical needs of civilians and the public health concerns generated by war caused considerable difficulty as well. In some areas, military authorities combined forces with civilian medical personnel to deal with public health, as in France where treatment of venereal disease for soldiers and civilians was coordinated through one department from 1915 to the end of the war. This allowed for army surveillance of workers, both in munitions factories and in colonial labor contingents, but it also extended health care to civilians infected with venereal diseases.[20] A number of physicians saw the war as a large public health experiment, using wartime controls and propaganda to help promote moral or medical agendas. Doctor experts wrote articles and conducted studies of both soldiers and civilians as part of their wartime service.[21] In some areas, however, civilians were on their own. Almost all beds in France set aside for tuberculosis patients, for example, went to soldiers during the war, leaving women and children civilians with few options for care.[22]

In addition to the influenza pandemic in the last year of the war, civilian populations suffered from higher rates of tuberculosis and diseases related to hunger and poor sanitary conditions, such as scurvy, rickets, edema, and typhus. Some doctors and scientists used the war as a way of advancing medical knowledge, as German scientist Karl Mense noted in 1915: "The peoples of the world have thus set up an enormous epidemiological experiment, the likes of which scientists could never even have dreamed."[23] Other medical personnel fought for resources in the face of public health crises, especially in war zones where medications had been requisitioned. Romania, for example, saw a rise in malaria rates when quinine supplies were requisitioned for use by German troops. Compounding this problem was lack of soap, which led to increases in cases of typhus, scabies, and other illnesses.[24]

Even though military leaders often strived to maintain a strict separation between military and civilian medical care, adjuring their doctors and nurses to treat only soldiers, in practice, this became difficult, not merely because of the blurring of civilian and medical personnel in the war but also because it was often hard for medical providers to turn a blind eye to human suffering. In other cases, it was almost impossible to separate soldier and civilian care, for instance during an army's retreat, when many refugees marched alongside soldiers. While some populations did very well during the war, especially in major cities with adequate medical care and supplies, other groups found themselves fighting for survival against catastrophic disease outbreaks.[25] Epidemic diseases recognized no lines between soldier and civilian, and military doctors often realized that to control a local outbreak, they had to treat all those infected, not just the military or the civil population. Tensions in the medical profession continued throughout the war and beyond, affecting medical care and access for soldiers and civilians alike. Medical researchers, doctors, nurses, and other healthcare personnel gained much experience during their war service but also fought battles for the resources they needed to meet the enormous challenges the war brought in both military and civilian casualties. In short, war created a demand for access to medical care that transcended soldier/civilian divides, even when governments tried to create neat divisions in medical care.

Feminizing Medicine

Prior to World War I, major changes in the realm of medical treatment and training had transformed the field, professionalizing the occupations of both doctors and nurses and providing a new measure of respect and authority. In the nineteenth century, those interested in medical careers increasingly needed to have formal training, licenses, and access to professional organizations in order to establish themselves in the status-conscious world of modern medicine. With the outbreak of war, professional health care providers faced an onslaught of volunteers, some with rudimentary medical training, some with none. The dizzying array of Red Cross societies, military medicine corps, private ambulances (health care facilities), and civil hospitals meant a blurring of lines not only between military and civilian medical care but also between "real" doctors and nurses and "amateurs." Some trained nurses and doctors sought to protect their status, making decisions about their war service on the basis of their desire to maintain their professional identities. For instance, Hungarian doctor Josef Tomann expressed his disgust when in the Galician town of Przemyśl he witnessed the practice in hospitals of "recruiting teenage girls as nurses, in some places there are up to 50 of them! They get 120 crowns a month and free meals. That comes to 17,000 crowns a month! They are, with very few exceptions, utterly useless. Their main job is to satisfy the lust of the gentlemen officers and, rather shamefully, of a number of doctors, too."[26] While this undoubtedly misrepresents some of the girls' motives and usefulness, it does point to the problem many physicians and trained nurses faced, namely an influx of ill-prepared volunteers.

This became a particular issue for women during wartime, as trained nurses and doctors sought status and recognition and as female volunteers rushed to fill the role of nurses and aides. Given military preferences for male doctors, female physicians had to struggle for any access to military medicine. Many U.S. female doctors preferred working for civilian organizations such as the Red Cross rather than for militaries because they felt like second-class citizens with the armed services. For instance, the U.S. army wanted to hire females as civilian contract surgeons rather than give them commissions as regular personnel, so the women went to civilian-sponsored medical missions instead.[27] Likewise, female doctors in Britain, who faced an uphill battle for recognition, began their own hospitals under private charities or foreign regimes in order to maintain their autonomy.[28] In Germany, male physicians, particularly surgeons, closed ranks against women, and their war service among men reinforced prewar misogynist medical establishments that functioned as "bastions of masculinity."[29]

Female doctors who sought to volunteer often faced discrimination from military authorities, and several British efforts were privately organized, such as the Scottish Women's Hospitals. When Elsie Inglis approached the British War Office about staffing a hospital with women in 1914, she was turned down without much of a hearing, but she got favorable responses from other governments desperate for medical care.[30] Like Inglis, American Mary Borden took matters into her own hands even before the United States entered the war, and using her own money established a "frontline surgical unit under French military command in the Belgian zone."[31] Likewise, British women Elsie Knocker and Mairi Chisholm ran a surgical unit on the western front, while their countrywoman, Mabel St. Clair Stobart, organized a hospital in Antwerp in 1914 and in Serbia in 1915.[32] Other prominent women took on other medical roles. Austrian physicist Lise Meitner, for example, worked in L'viv as an x-ray technician, while Polish-born scientist Marie Curie developed mobile radiology labs for the French war effort.[33]

Female doctors were successful when they had the chance to perform their duties at the front, but they faced a problem of perception since popular images of women in medicine focused on their role as nurses.

Nursing was considered a nonthreatening role for females seeking to help the war effort, as it allowed them to fulfill their "natural" role of sacrifice and care giving. In fact, nursing became emblematic of women's war work (along with munitions); nurses were portrayed as selfless, pure, and patriotic. Male novels and memoirs of the period romanticize nurses—Ernest Hemingway's novels providing only one example—and feature elaborate fantasies involving nurses.[34] Of all the female war services between 1914 and 1918, nursing captured the public imagination in posters, novels, plays, and statuary; nurses, as Margaret Darrow argues, "would seem to have been the most worthy."[35] The public approval for female nursing led to large numbers of volunteers across the nations at war in addition to the mobilization of the trained nurses present in 1914.

In France, the government mobilized more than twenty thousand Red Cross–trained nurses in 1914, but they were quickly overwhelmed with casualties and had to seek volunteers, and eventually more than sixty thousand women served as nurses.[36] As in France, German Red Cross nurses were immediately called up for war service in 1914 and a call for women to volunteer for nursing training was also issued.[37] In Britain, army nurses were supplemented by the use of Voluntary Aid Detachments (VAD) of middle-class females with little practical nursing training. These women were deployed to home-front hospitals as well as to theaters of war in France and the Mediterranean.[38]

As with female doctors, however, nurses often resented the volunteers whom they perceived to be "playing at" nursing. In the decades prior to the war, professional nurses had been struggling to get recognition of their work as a respectable and needed vocation for women. Nurses in Catholic countries often mixed their role in nursing with their calling as nuns, creating a professionalized core of nurses but one that conformed to notions of women's proper nurturing role. In both Protestant and Catholic countries, nurses with a secular calling sought registration and state recognition of their professional lives. None of these nurses wanted a flood of volunteers devaluing their training, vocation, or postwar jobs, so many professional, trained nurses signed up for war service immediately, both for patriotic and for professional reasons. Elsa Brändström derided the stereotypical elite woman volunteer in her memoir of nursing work in Russia:

At the outbreak of the War a large number of Russian society women had themselves appointed as "sisters" after a short course in nursing. They flooded the hospitals in the country where they were supposed to supplement the inadequate number of the professional nurses. Some of these women were often a parody on the sister of mercy. Their main occupation was to shake the pillows, dry the foreheads and comb the hair of the wounded. . . . [O]nce their desire for sensation had been satisfied and the charm of novelty had gone, when, in the overcrowded military hospitals the truth in all its horror was revealed, they fled back to their dinners, bridge-parties and dances.[39]

Other women with training also resented the presence of volunteers out for a thrill. However, the war soon overwhelmed the small cadre of trained military nurses. Irish military nurse Evelyn Luard described the scene in September 1914: "You board a cattle truck, armed with a tray of dressings and a pail; the men were lying on straw, had been in trains for several days. . . . They were nearly all shrapnel-shell wounds more ghastly than I have ever seen or smelt; the Mauser wounds of the Boer War were pinpricks compared with them."[40] Caught between needing hands to deal with casualties and protecting their hard-won status as trained professionals, nurses often weeded out the volunteers with hard work and an unwelcoming mien. As Helen Beale found when she reported for duty as a volunteer in France, the "atmosphere is distinctly chilling; I say we are made to feel rather like pariahs and it is obvious that we are not to forget we are only V.A.D.s. In the ward it is alright though, I am merely treated as rather an ineffectual housemaid."[41] Such trials by fire separated those who romanticized nursing from those who could take the punishment the war and its personnel meted out.

For many women, in fact, volunteer nursing was much more grueling than they had expected, and some did give up. As British VAD Vera Brittain recorded after the war, "What did profoundly trouble and humiliate me was my colossal ignorance of the simplest domestic operations. . . . [M]ost of [the VADs] came to the hospital expecting to hold the patients' hands and smooth their pillows while the regular nurses fetched and carried everything that looked or smelt disagreeable."[42] While Brittain faced many of the same humiliations as Beale in her early days as a VAD, her perseverance paid off. When Brittain arrived in France to work in the military hospital at Étaples after a year of war work in Malta, she was greeted by a career military nurse from South Africa with some relief because of her experience in sick wards. The nurse welcomed her as "quite an old soldier," a significant difference from earlier encounters in which Brittain had been dismissed as a useless debutante out for a bit of excitement.[43]

In addition to their entry in large numbers into nursing and hospital work, women also found jobs in new specialties such as medical massage, occupational therapy, and rehabilitative work. While these fields were relatively new and therefore "open" to females, driving, especially with motor ambulances, became another proving ground for women. Amy Owen Bradley, a driver for the American Fund for French Wounded, wrote home that the French stared at her and her uniform as she drove around Paris in a Ford car named "Lizzie." As she noted in 1916 of this experience, "Nobody in Paris knows what it means" to see uniformed women driving automobiles and performing auto repairs on the roadsides of France.[44] Women ambulance drivers often found themselves in the midst of artillery attacks in the dead of night, risking their lives as surely as their male soldier relations. Perhaps the most astonishing thing about these ambulance corps is that they were often composed of volunteers who paid for the privilege of such work.[45] Young women from good families rolled along in ambulances between field hospitals for the whole course of the war. In her fictional account based on the experiences of a British female ambulance driver, Helen Zenna Smith described the experience: "Trainloads of broken human beings: half-mad men pleading to be put out of their misery; torn and bleeding and crazed men pitifully obeying orders like a herd of senseless cattle, dumbly, pitifully straggling in the wrong direction."[46] These women were certainly not separate from the experience of war—such hazardous occupations brought women right into the war front, placing them squarely within the combat framework, despite their official designation as "noncombatants."

Ambulance drivers were not the only women subject to the dangers of war, as many nurses and aides found themselves in medical units close to the fronts. The British nurses and VADs at Étaples faced bombardment at several times during the war, and Russian, Serbian, and Romanian hospitals were often totally destroyed by the changing lines of the front.

Tatiana Alexinsky, who served on a Russian hospital train in the Ukraine region, described their bombardment by an Austrian airplane as they tried to load seriously wounded soldiers onto the marked hospital train.[47] Other nurses and ambulance drivers described artillery bombardments, gas attacks, and outbreaks of infectious diseases, all of which threatened their lives as they worked to save the lives of soldiers. Even traveling to a new position could be treacherous, with the sinking of several ships carrying medical personnel in the course of the war; for example, fourteen British nurses died in the last three months of 1915 on ships sunk by mines or U-boats.[48]

What is particularly interesting about these attacks is their undermining of notions of protected categories of people in wartime. Both females and medical personnel were often portrayed in propaganda and popular media as separate from the war, yet many accounts show the deliberate targeting of both by armies. Governmental attempts to limit women's access to battlefields as medical personnel failed; armies needed female as well as male presence in the front lines, breaking down gendered notions of women's protection. Yet, women's presence in war zones also made them suspect, especially in regard to morals; young women were treating the bodies of young men, in close proximity to the masculine zone of battle. Historian Susan Grayzel sums up the mixed message women received through their medical work in the First World War: "The wartime world required this service [nursing] from women, but the postwar world was not always sure what to do with the women who had to perform it."[49]

Caring for the Sick

As women's role in relationship to war walked an ambiguous line, so too did the role of so-called neutral organizations. As medicine was changing in the late nineteenth century, a new idea had emerged to transform the treatment of the wounded during wartime—the International Red Cross. Founded in the wake of the Crimean War and during the American Civil War, the International Committee of the Red Cross embodied the ideas of Henri Dunant, a Swiss businessman who proposed the creation of a commission for the relief and care of the wounded. This "permanent committee" was free of custom duties and supported by "all civilized powers," and it resided in Switzerland, a neutral nation.[50] Dunant's idea built on the work of earlier reformers such as Florence Nightingale, whose ideas about improving sanitary conditions and instituting nursing training in the Crimea had saved countless lives. What made Dunant's committee unique was his plan that the Red Cross would be a universally recognizable symbol and a neutral organization, with medical personnel who were protected from attack.

As it emerged in the 1860s and 1870s, the Red Cross became a dual-concept organization dedicated primarily to the care of soldiers in wartime. On the one hand it was an international, neutral committee working out of Switzerland, but it also existed as a series of national Red Cross societies, with membership in and loyalty to individual nations. One difficulty the Red Cross faced, however, was with its organization on the national level. The International Committee could maintain its neutrality and distance from the conflict from the safety of Switzerland, but most of the hands-on work, particularly the medical care, was coordinated and financed through National Red Cross societies, many of whom had ties to their nation's militaries (for supply, transport, housing, etc.). In some cases, financing for national Red Cross societies was uneven, or political pressures made their work difficult.

The dual concept of national and international Red Cross created headaches for wartime planners throughout the world, and it meant that cooperation between national, often patriotic, subscribers in various countries and the "objective" and "neutral" committee in Geneva was difficult. Therefore, when war broke out in 1914, the national Red Cross societies mobilized for patriotic national service, while the International Red Cross prepared for its role as a neutral intermediary, as "watchdog, monitor and upholder of the Geneva Convention [its organizing principles]."[51] This arrangement created considerable flexibility but also set the stage for tensions and problems with maintaining protected status for Red Cross workers. A good example of this tension comes from the work of the Hilal-i Ahmer Cemiyeti (Ottoman Red Crescent, the Muslim version of the Red Cross), which faced funding shortages and lack of diplomatic help and representation. Critics charged that the Turkish Red Crescent even used its medical and humanitarian funds for intelligence and other nonauthorized work for the national war effort.[52] What this meant in practice is that the people for whom it was supposed to be responsible, particularly prisoners of war, suffered. In other cases, national Red Crosses feuded with existing charitable organizations or fought for turf, as in the case of the British Red Cross, which had considerable difficulties with the St. John's Ambulance until the two finally joined forces.[53] Perhaps even more problematically, sometimes civilians used the Red Cross flag and its neutrality to hide clandestine activities, as in Belgium, where an escape network used Red Cross facilities to hide fugitive soldiers from German occupying forces.[54] It is no wonder that some military officials saw Red Cross neutrality as suspect.

National Red Cross societies also functioned in some cases as branches of the military. For example in Germany, the Red Cross mobilized alongside the army in early August 1914, with collections of medical supplies, sewing circles, and outfitting of ambulances, hospitals, and supply depots.[55] This close connection with the military provided resources and transportation for the medical personnel involved in caring for the wounded, but it also called into question their "neutral" status. While military authorities often tried to delineate the separate status of the Red Cross in relationship to soldiers, it was difficult given the tortuous descriptions needed to explain this status. This example from the U.S. pamphlet for "Personnel en Route for Foreign Service in the Red Cross" demonstrates only one such attempt:

> Though you are not in the direct employment of the Government, you serve an organization which bears a close semi-official relationship to the Government, for the American Red Cross was created by Act of Congress and designated as a "medium of communication between the people of the United States of America and their armies". . . . From the moment that you put on the uniform you cease to be a private citizen in the ordinary sense; you are a representative of your country.[56]

At this point, male Red Cross members were instructed to salute members of the armed services. It was perhaps no surprise that Red Cross personnel, both men and women, often saw themselves as doing service equivalent to that of the soldiers they interacted with daily.

Sometimes the Red Cross personnel of the early years of the war became soldiers later in the conflict. Many neutrals from nations such as the United States later assumed military uniforms when the United States entered the war in 1917. Dr. Percy Smythe, a physician from Enid, Oklahoma, serves as a good example of how ordinary people could be drawn into Red Cross service, sometimes briefly, during the war and how their neutral status could be somewhat ambiguous. Smythe was invited to serve in an American Red Cross (ARC) hospital in Vienna (Austria) in 1914. As a citizen of a neutral nation, the United States, he could serve as a doctor in any combatant country where the Red Cross set up its operations.

Smythe's immediate impression on arriving in Vienna in January 1915 was that Austrians were not suffering too much, and he wrote home that conditions were good in the city, commenting specifically about details of his life. Such communication from a nonmedical man could have led to imprisonment or detention for espionage in another context. He also noted that ARC hospitals were not necessarily placed where they were most needed (near the fronts), again giving specific details about locations of hospitals. By April, his letters home contained references to bread shortages and high prices for some goods, and he reported on rumors of typhus outbreaks in other Red Cross hospitals in Serbia. By June, the nurses promised to the hospital had not yet arrived, food had gotten more expensive, and Smythe was ready to end his commitment to the ARC. Just before his departure, Smythe wrote his wife, "I'll be glad to get out of the Red Cross work I know—there has been a lot of soul-killing routine in it—just the same the experience has been great."[57] All in all, for Smythe, this was a service interlude that did little to change his outlook beyond giving him some sympathy for the German and Austrian war aims. Yet his experience also points to the ambivalent identities of Red Cross personnel. His time in Vienna gave him access to much information on the Austrian war effort that he communicated home in 1914 and 1915. This information and additional knowledge he gained while serving in Austria could have become quite useful to U.S. military planners when the United States entered the war in 1917, especially since he might have been subject to conscription into the regular army at that time. Such crossing of lines made Red Cross work difficult to defend as "neutral" and also helped justify later attacks on Red Cross personnel in war zones.

One way to bypass concerns about the use of national Red Cross personnel in enemy territory was to put power in the hands of women in these societies. As noncombatants who could not be conscripted for military service, women were considered more "neutral" than men in these organizations. For instance, German and Austro-Hungarian Red Cross nurses were allowed into Russian prisoner of war and civilian internment camps to inspect conditions in 1915 and in 1916 under the auspices of the Danish Red Cross. Many of these women had political clout and connections, which smoothed their way through the Russian wartime bureaucracy. Some of the "sisters" on these tours included Countess Nora Kinsky, Princess Cunigunde von Droy-Dülmen, and Baronin Andorine von Huszar, all well-connected members of the European nobility. As Alon Rachamimov argues, "their status, available time, connections, and political reliability [meant] these upper-class women were now entrusted also with official duties formerly reserved to men [but only] . . . for the duration of the war."[58] Gerald Davis also noted of the women's visits.

> These were educated women trained in nursing, experienced in medical administration and well informed about sanitation and nutrition. They managed large inventories of gift packages and substantial sums of money for which they had to account. . . . They were hard-driving and often abrasive and bossed men around, but they functioned within clearly understood roles of patriotic, upper-class women in a profession that was their own.[59]

These women functioned as part of a network of educated female elites engaged in the business of war, vital to the maintenance of soldiers and POWs, but rhetorically situated outside the lines of what constituted the "real" war. Russian "sisters," like their German and Austro-Hungarian counterparts, also visited camps in enemy countries under a reciprocal Red Cross agreement. These women were also highly capable and well-connected elites such as Catherine Samsonova, widow of a Russian general, and Princess Marie Galitsina.[60]

From its origins as an organization for the care of wounded soldiers, the Red Cross expanded its work to include civilians both during wartime and in peace, changing its mission forever. Eventually Red Cross work encompassed a whole variety of activities, including medical care, aid for and supervision of prisoners of war, refugee work, care of war orphans, and many other areas vital to the relief of civilians and soldiers in wartime situations. This expansion came less through a concerted plan to expand the reach of the Red Cross than through sheer necessity. Governments had made little provision for the problems civilians would face with a long war, so the rise in the number of orphans as well as food shortages, displaced peoples, and refugees led to a humanitarian crisis in many regions during and after the war. The Red Cross stepped in to deal with these crises.

The ARC's medical work spanned several continents during the war, and while much of it was financed by small donations, it also took on special projects funded by individual donors. One such example was a pediatric unit paid for by Mrs. William Lowell Putnam of Boston, which sent doctors, nurses, social workers, and child welfare specialists to France in 1917 under the direction of noted Berkeley professor Dr. William Palmer Lucas. Lucas had already performed humanitarian war work by doing a medical survey of civilian health under the auspices of the Commission for Relief in Belgium in 1916. His 1917 team's first task was to visit refugee centers and public health projects in France, but then they opened a children's hospital in Evian in October 1917. The head of nursing for this project, Elizabeth Ashe, described in a memoir the needs among children they found on their arrival in France:

> We inspected the refuge camp today which contains about three hundred children aged from two months to twelve years, and forty women. It has only been open two weeks and is really a herculean task. The place was an old barracks before and thoroughly infected. . . . The floors deep in mud and dirt, and the children covered with impetigo and pediculosis. . . . Each time here in France you imagine that you have witnessed the depths of misery until you take the next step. . . . Christ on his crucifix in many villages is the only thing erect, where women and little children by thousands must work in the fields under shell fire wearing gas masks to protect them.[61]

Ashe's experiences with the hardships of children in devastated zones mirrors other ARC reports of conditions in war zones. Edward Eyre Hunt, sent to Italy for refugee work in 1917 by the ARC, also wrote about the desperately poor conditions of refugees displaced by the war. As he noted, elite American women, such as Mrs. William Vanderbilt, worked with local authorities to develop crèches (daycare centers), hospitals, and canteens for the thousands of refugees streaming into Venice and its environs.[62]

The Red Cross societies, both national and international, saved millions of lives through their work in the war, but they also functioned in a sense because of the war. Unlike strict pacifists who worked to eliminate war, Red Cross personnel sought to alleviate suffering and reduce disease, death, and pain from the war. Therefore Red Cross medical personnel supported the war effort in countless ways, functioning alongside or under the auspices of militaries, perhaps extending the life of the war. Certainly their efforts at healing wounded soldiers sent many back to the fronts, and their work with civilians helped maintain morale at home fronts. Of all the "civilian" services of war, medicine may be the most crucial.

Conclusion

In World War I, medical services featured volunteer and paid professionals and relied on a complicated mix of local, national, and international cooperation. Some doctors, nurses, and assistants worked directly for armies, while others worked for nonprofit organizations or in private hospitals funded by individual patrons or groups. Still others worked in ambulance or medical transport corps, again in official capacities or in more privately funded organizations. The unprecedented opportunities for men and women to work in medical care expanded enormously during the war, making medicine a patriotic, respectable, and accessible career after the war ended. Some nurses and doctors were immediately employed in the postwar era, as medical crises such as the influenza outbreak consumed medical personnel's time and energies. Hospitals and clinics worldwide were crushed under the weight of the sick and dying. In Labrador (Canada), one-third of the population died from flu, while in Chiapas (Mexico), ten percent of the population perished. The total death toll from influenza remains unknown, but at least fifty million died globally in 1918–1919.[63]

Other diseases also found targets among civilians and returning soldiers, especially in war zones or areas where requisitions of men, animals,

Serbian refugees at the entrance to a Red Cross disinfection and treatment center in Uskut, ca. 1917. *U.S. Signal Corps, National Archives and Records Administration.*

and supplies created drought or shortages. For example, in Lille, France, which had been occupied by the Germans, a 1919 report found a massive problem of scabies, pediculosis, and rickets among young children in the city.[64] The American Red Cross dispatched teams to Harbin, China, in 1919 to help handle a cholera epidemic and to Vladivostock, Russia, to work on the health of refugee children.[65] One Red Cross doctor described the nightmares he developed at the end of 1919 after more than four years of medical work in Eastern Europe and Persia: "It is awful when you cannot keep from seeing this mass of hungry, staring, hollow-eyed, ghostly, ragged, verminous humans. When they stare at you from the walls of your locked room, from the sky, from the forest, from the rivers and from the books you are trying to read."[66] The stress and trauma of war visited medical personnel as it visited soldiers in the months and years after the conflict. Some medical and aid workers also found themselves continuing their work far past the end of the war. For example, Nancy Babb began as a student nurse in Russian Relief in 1917–1918, then worked for the American Red Cross, the YMCA, and the American Friends Service Committee. Barring a short period of relief work in the United States from 1919 to 1921, Babb spent almost a decade in Russia and the USSR working with refugees, returning home finally in the late 1920s.[67] While soldiers served as forces of occupation into the postwar period, medical personnel ministered to these forces and the civilian populations ravaged by years of war and disease.

World War I transformed medicine in a variety of ways, not least in personnel and medical knowledge. The overlaps between military and civilian medicine enriched both fields. Nursing, which had been associated with Catholic nuns or small cadres of elite professionals in many countries, opened its doors increasingly to women from a variety of backgrounds; as it expanded, it professionalized further as well.[68] Part of this shift, in nursing and all areas of medical care, reflected the sheer numbers of those involved in wartime medicine. Again, nursing provides a useful example. Just over one thousand British women served as nurses or aides during the Anglo-Boer War (1899–1902), but in World War I, almost thirty thousand women served as nurses or aides in official military organizations, not even including the British Red Cross and other private charities.[69]

The important role of caregivers helped forge a lasting memory from the war of the neutral goodness of such medical personnel. They inhabited novels and films, memoirs, and histories of the postwar period as romanticized figures, working tirelessly for the soldiers. Such praise led not only to their omnipresent role as ideal civilian war workers but also to the concretization of ideas of international medical aid organizations such as the Red Cross. As one American writer rhapsodized, providing a fitting commentary on the image of the Red Cross worker, "I lighten the horrors of the combat. . . . I bury the dead. . . . I cheer the sorrowful. . . . I am the saviour of death. I am my brother's keeper."[70]

[6]

Creating War Experts

I had, too, a long chat with von Moltke, who was curious about
Hoover and lost in admiration of the organization of the CRB
[Commission for Relief in Belgium]. What they simply cannot
understand is why men should work so for others and with no
financial end.

—Brand Whitlock, journal, June 25, 1915

More than any other war prior to 1914, the First World War
spawned the modern phenomenon of "expert" assistance in the management and maintenance of war. Scientists, humanitarians, diplomats,
clergy, social scientists, and voluntary aid workers devoted countless
hours, and sometimes their own lives, to the war, often not as patriots
for a particular nation but as international arbitrators, observers, and aid
workers. Like medical personnel, such civilian experts provided services
to the war effort but also had an uncertain identity within the wartime
establishment. This chapter focuses on the varied groups of people who
managed and inhabited the space between the civilian and the soldier.

Henry Shortt provides a useful instance of the blurring between civilian and military expertise, and his war service illustrates the ambiguity of
those working as part of this "third element" of experts. Born in India and
trained as a doctor in Scotland, Shortt spent part of the war in the military
as a medical officer in Basra (Iraq). Then, in 1916, he was reassigned to a
"research" unit on a ship in the Basra harbor. Here, he gave lectures on
public health and researched diseases such as malaria and "Oriental Sore"
(a parasitic skin disease). He was technically still an officer, but his duties

took him far from the war itself, and he spent more time with civilians than with soldiers. In effect, he became a traveling public health official in Mesopotamia and Persia, finding the time to meet and woo his future wife (a nurse working in Persia). Through his work, he moved from battle front to staging areas to civilian zones for the last two years of the war.[1] Shortt, while technically serving in the military, was no soldier, and he used his skills more for the protection of civilians in wartime than for the healing of soldiers.

Perhaps the most nebulous area of war service during the years 1914–1918 concerns armies of experts drawn into the lines of conflict to mitigate the damage of war. Like Henry Shortt, these scientists, diplomats, journalists, educators, and aid workers helped maintain a sense of normalcy for civilians drawn into the war, and they managed the human concerns generated by more than four years of conflict. Many of these individuals provided vital services in the regions where they were assigned, but their status was not always clearly defined and their ability to move between and among the various fronts, interacting with both civilians and soldiers, gave them a complex role to play in this global conflict. While some inhabiting this in-between space were celebrated for their war service, most notably humanitarian and charitable organizations, others were invisible in wartime and postwar accounts. Still others were vilified for their roles as collaborators. The work of this group of civilians exposes the ways in which war permeated the fabric of society and demonstrates the need for vast numbers of people to manage its impact.

Nurturing Expertise

The provision of clothing, "comforts," gifts, and educational material for soldiers, medical personnel, prisoners of war, and war laborers was a massive industry during the war, and it pulled in ordinary citizens from around the world. Women, especially, were mobilized for charitable activities that ranged from knitting and sewing at home to front-line nursing and driving. The American Red Cross in Latin America, for example, had chapters in Argentina, Bolivia, Brazil, Chile, Costa Rica, Cuba, Dominican Republic, Ecuador, Guatemala, Haiti, Honduras, Nicaragua, Paraguay, Peru, Uruguay, and Venezuela. The Latin American members "produced more than 5 million finished articles [of clothing] and contributed more than $2 million" to the war effort from 1917 to the end of the war.[2] These Red Cross participants, many of whom were female U.S. citizens living abroad, sponsored entertainments, sold war stamps, and ran knitting circles to do their part.[3]

Many of the funds and charitable projects that developed were focused on one particular group, for example, Russian prisoners of war or Australian soldiers in Egypt. Organizations emerged at the local, national, and international levels, and they varied from small-scale efforts to immense organizations providing bread and clothing. One very small effort involved one woman who created her own personal charitable project in Durban (South Africa). Ethel Campbell, "The Angel of Durban," donned a sailor suit and signaled from the shore "Welcome!" to every troop ship docking in the port, many of them filled with wounded Australians and New Zealanders. The daughter of a local doctor, Campbell gathered a group of young boys to help her, and they threw fruit and chocolates to soldiers on the ship. In some cases, she took parties of sixty to a hundred men home with her for tea.[4] While an unusual form of charitable activity, Campbell's personal mission demonstrates the depth of the call to service that many civilians felt during the war.

The sheer variety of the hospitality and service offered during the war is hard to capture. An example of the range of activity that emerged comes from Belgian civilian internee Henri Pirenne's mailbag for one day in April 1916 at Crefeld Camp (Germany). He found half a dozen packages waiting for him, a veritable bounty that day. They included a box of clothing and a separate package of cigars from his wife, foodstuffs from a friend, a case of eggs from a Swiss committee in Berne for the care of prisoners of war, and a package of food from a Maestricht committee to help Belgian prisoners of war. The last package, and his favorite that day, contained three "beautiful loaves of white bread" from a Belgian organization devoted to helping political prisoners and hostages taken to Germany.[5]

Societies sprang up around the world focused on specific needs of military and civil populations. In France, a special society (Les Amis des Soldats Aveugles) was developed for soldiers blinded by the war, while in Germany, multiple societies coalesced under a national women's service (Nationaler Frauendienst) to help "war families." The international

Green Cross provided aid to civilians and refugees, as did the Young Men's Christian Association. Nations also developed specific groups to help families contact prisoners of war or to facilitate mail and gifts between nations and fronts. There were also multiple charities for children, orphans, and widows. All of these organizations depended particularly on the labor of women of all ages and classes in order to function.

For example, the local comforts societies often mobilized women to make, pack, and ship textile "comforts" such as socks, mufflers, and hats. In the Punjab (India), Lady O'Dwyer organized a comforts fund that used Indian women and girls as a workforce to make bandages and to knit goods for overseas forces.[6] While not all of these gifts were always practical, such as the "body belts" that Indian mule drivers could find little use for at the front, letters and diaries suggest they contributed to morale and a sense that people at home supported those in the thick of the war. A member of the Indian Mule Corps, Ressaidar Ghulam Mahomed, expressed this sentiment in the thank-you letter he wrote to the comforts fund: 'We have great pleasure in expressing our gratitude to the gentry at home who have been taking much interest in sending presents with kind heartiness for the brave veterans at the front. . . . We accept all such presents very gladly, which we will not forget during the rest of our life."[7]

Local groups often coordinated their efforts with national associations, and networking across organizations was common. Some of these charitable efforts amassed large war chests, usually through the donations and time of societal elites. A good example of such local efforts comes from the British community in Shanghai (China). Spurred by the good work of local female elites, including President Lady Annie de Sausmarez, the British Women's Work Association created and shipped hundreds of thousands of bandages, dressings, and hospital garments to forces in Mesopotamia during the war, while a separate Mesopotamia Comforts Fund also sent gifts "for those engaged in Mesopotamia without distinction of race."[8] While these organizations gathered materials, the Shanghai Race Club barred German members and began raising money for the British Red Cross, both of which it considered patriotic war service. Another gathering of loyal British subjects in Shanghai raised money to create a British flower shop in order to force the "enemy" flower shops in Shanghai to close their doors. Perhaps the most unique of the Shanghai local associations was the "Fly Trap Fund," which raised money to provide "Japanese Automatic Fly Traps" to troops in the Near East. These "ingenious contrivance[s]" were revolving drums that were covered in a substance that attracted flies. Apparently the traps were a hit among troops in Mesopotamia, because the committee sent more than five thousand by the end of 1917.[9] Whatever their focus, simple food from home or fancy contraptions, these local charitable groups created a nexus of activity for the war effort that tied civilian volunteers imaginatively to the war itself.

All combatant countries created or mobilized national organizations to provide goods, foodstuffs, and entertainment for their soldiers, laborers, and other war workers. The Australian Comforts Fund (ACF), founded in 1915 in Egypt, where many of the Australians were based, hoped to improve the morale and morality of the Australian Expeditionary Force. The ACF became an umbrella organization for a plenitude of relief societies already functioning in the Australian cities and provinces.[10] Often the various organizations had to maintain territorial lines in order to protect "their" work from infringement by others. One ACF subsidiary, the Lady Mayoress's Patriotic League (Melbourne) had to keep reminding the public about its purpose:

> As much misconception still exists in the public mind as to this League's objects, it is to be clearly re-stated that our work is for the *well* soldier, in the training camp, on the troop ships, at the intermediate base, and in the trenches. So soon as he is ill in camp, or wounded, so soon is he in charge of the Army Medical and its auxiliary, the Red Cross, whose services and goods are, by their rules, not available until a man is sick or wounded.[11]

This work for the "well soldier" included the provision of food, sports equipment, books, clothing, and recreational huts. Many of the gifts were tailored to suit the needs of the climate where the soldiers were serving; ice cream freezers were sent to those in the "tropics" while mosquito nets were dispatched to New Guinea. Cigarettes were sent to all forces.[12]

Some of the comforts organizations began with charitable activities, but then moved into more substantial service for families and the state. In French West Africa, for example, the Comité d'Assistance aux Troupes Noires (CATN) provided blankets and couscous for Senegalese soldiers at the fronts but also took responsibility for distributing money to soldiers' wives and children. The CATN even banked funds for "families of soldiers killed in the war, even if for 'political reasons' local commandants intended to hold on to the money—and news of soldiers' deaths—until after the war had ended."[13] Indeed, after the war, the CATN was mobilized as a quasi-governmental service for helping to settle and ease demobilized soldiers back into their home societies. Such "comforts" went far beyond the work of a few women distributing gift boxes to soldiers to encompass political and social power.

Existing political and social connections were also mobilized for the war effort, and a good number of the funds created during the war had their origins in existing organizations or found themselves linked to such groups. One of the Indian Soldiers' Funds was a subsidiary of the Order of St. John of Jerusalem, and it focused its energies on Indian soldiers and laborers in all theaters of war and in POW camps. Like many of the other organizations, the Indian Soldiers' Funds provided parcels containing food, cigarettes, personal hygiene items, and clothing. They also tried to answer requests for specific items, such as Sikh combs, hockey sticks, wood-carving tools, and coconut oil.[14] For Chinese laborers, charitable groups sought culturally appropriate gifts such as Chinese New Year calendars.[15] The wide scope of such efforts meant that ordinary soldiers and laborers, who often felt unappreciated in their efforts, perceived the gifts as recognition of their service by the governments they served, not understanding that most charitable organizations were privately funded. One letter from an Indian Labour Company demonstrates this misconception about their gifts:

> We received your Indian Soldiers' Fund Committee articles with many thanks. We never forget your remembrance gifts, even we go back to India, and will proud [sic] before all men with your gifts and will explain to all men that there is no one who loves men as like as the British Government anywhere in this world.[16]

International organizations such as the Red Cross and Red Crescent and the Friends War Service Committee also provided services for soldiers, POWS, refugees, service families, orphans, and war invalids, to name only

Poster for a German charity designed to help civil and military prisoners of war. *National World War I Museum.*

some of the groups served. Much of this labor was voluntary or only nominally rewarded, but a good number of the workers wore uniforms and in some cases abided by military rules. The offices of the International Red Cross in Geneva played a particularly important advocacy role, encouraging governments and private organizations to spend money on relief but also coordinating the massive relief efforts of thousands of societies and individuals. In particular, the International Committee of the Red Cross (ICRC) created a massive agency for aid and information regarding prisoners of war, both military and civilian. Under the auspices of this work, the ICRC inspected camps (more than five hundred prisoner of war, labor, and civilian camps), brokered information and parcels between families and prisoners, and investigated missing persons. Thousands of personnel, the majority of whom were women, worked in the bureau during the war.[17]

This bureau was especially vital to the survival of many prisoners of war, both military and civilian, who relied upon parcels of food aid to survive. The Hague Convention of 1907 had made feeding war captives a responsibility of the nation holding prisoners, but as Heather Jones argues, "by the end of the First World War it had been largely accepted in practice that a prisoner's state of origin, as well as private charities and individuals, would supply him with food, through parcels."[18] Nations with poorly organized food relief programs for their POWs interned in enemy countries hoped charitable organizations would provide the needed food and clothing. When that did not happen, consequences were dire; nearly 20 percent of Italian POWs died in Austrian captivity. Not only did the prisoners receive no subsidies from the Italian government, but evidence suggests that the Italian military leadership tried to curtail the number of private packages sent from home to the camps.[19] The International Red Cross tried to intervene in such national cases, although not always with success.

In addition to the international bureau, neutral nations' Red Cross societies became especially important to humanitarian and relief work among civilians and prisoners of war because of their ability to move between belligerents. In this regard, both the Swedish and Danish Red Cross performed vital work in the Russian Empire, Austria-Hungary, Germany, and Serbia as camp inspectors and as clearinghouses for parcels and post. One of the best-known representatives in this work was Elsa Brändström, the daughter of the Swedish ambassador to St. Petersburg (Petrograd) and a tireless champion for better conditions in camps throughout Russia.[20] Her memoir, *Among Prisoners of War in Russia and Siberia,* outlined her impressions of the lives of prisoners of war in Russia and the relief workers like herself who ministered to them. She described a variety of activities for which the Swedish Red Cross served as an intermediary between belligerent governments, voluntary organizations, and individuals. For instance, the Swedish Red Cross set up an office in Petrograd as a clearinghouse for information, parcels, and permissions (to visit camps), and in addition, it sponsored conferences in Stockholm with Red Cross societies from Austria-Hungary, Turkey, Russia, and Germany to discuss issues concerning POWs. Brändström herself spent more than five years working as a delegate and "sister" for the Swedish Red Cross. She worked with transports of wounded prisoners, with camp inspection, with labor and hospital depots, to name a few of her responsibilities; before the war was over, she had traveled from Petrograd to Moscow to Siberia.[21]

Volunteers for Red Cross and other humanitarian positions often were motivated by patriotism or a desire to serve in some aspect of the war. Many saw this work as a duty of citizens in wartime in a modern nation. However, in other cases, voluntary societies had to guard against the types of volunteers they accepted. Many wives and sweethearts sought Red Cross work to get closer to their husbands or lovers. Gilbert Graham encouraged his wife to get a voluntary position in order to join him in Holland, where he was temporarily interned in 1918. As his wife Eunice found out by inquiring with a well-placed relative in England, the task of getting a position seemed unlikely: "At this moment they [Admiralty] are wild with rage because apparently about 16 wives have got over camouflaged as YMCA workers, & the several Government offices are being besieged with infuriated females wanting to know why they mayn't go too. I hear the YMCA has a waiting list of 200 or so, but it really seems the only chance."[22] In Russia, Countess O. V. Bennigsen took a position as a nurse in an ambulance squad of the Russian Red Cross so that, as she noted in her diary, she "could therefore follow my husband." The Bennigsens managed to meet fairly regularly, with the countess walking between her posting and her husband's along with several other wives who had also taken voluntary positions.[23]

Other groups associated with cross-national relief activities included religiously affiliated organizations such as the YMCA, YWCA, and the Society of Friends (Quakers). The "Y" movement functioned primarily to entertain and boost the well-being and morale of soldiers at the front, in training camps, and in prisoner of war camps. Conrad Hoffman, a YMCA worker in Germany, arrived in Berlin in 1915 to coordinate work in German prison camps. His work included serving as liaison between prisoners and German authorities, overseeing the development of a recreational hut, and providing reading materials for inmates.[24] Recreation and entertainment huts were quite popular not just in camps but in staging areas near the front lines, where soldiers could meet friends, play games, or buy refreshments while on leave. Many soldiers mention in unit histories or letters the pleasant hours they spent playing chess, smoking, writing let-

Soldiers drink hot coffee dispensed by a women's organization in Lötzen (today Giżycko), Poland, in 1915. *Library of Congress.*

ters, or drinking coffee with friends under the auspices of charitable societies and their "huts." Other Y activities included dances, concerts, cinema screenings, and sporting events, especially boxing and football. All of these events were designed to keep the soldiers happy and, it was hoped, healthy. An explicitly Christian organization, the YMCA saw its job as "pouring out tea and prayer in equal parts."[25] The YMCA and YWCA organizations in the British Empire and the United States published whole series of pamphlets on "manhood" and on morality. One Canadian brochure, "Facts for Fighters," described venereal disease in graphic terms, telling men that "it is not necessary to have intercourse with women to be manly and to develop the sexual organs," while an American pamphlet advised, "You can't play in the muck and keep clean."[26]

The YMCA was not the only organization to concern itself with the "health" of soldiers and civilians, particularly when it came to so-called racial health. Officials worried that infected soldiers would take their diseases home, thereby reducing the national birthrate. Protection of the "race," then, became a central plank in the anti-VD platform. The war provided a control mechanism and a captive audience for moral reformers, including feminists, social workers, physicians, and public officials. Many organizations and experts used the war to attack the scourge of venereal disease and to change habits. Some of these efforts by "experts" to combat venereal disease came into direct conflict with the work of voluntary societies such as the YMCA, which focused on abstinence and moral purity. Ettie Rout, "a one-woman campaign" against venereal disease, provides a good example of the tensions.[27] Rout, an Australian raised in New Zealand, wanted armies and charities to be more up front with soldiers about the dangers of VD, so she protested loudly against both from her canteens and medical facilities in Egypt and France. When officials appeared not to heed her warnings, she developed her own prophylactic kit of lotions and condoms, which the New Zealand Expeditionary Force adopted for its soldiers in 1917.[28] Rout continued work among soldiers in France and then later in a Red Cross depot, but her life provides a good instance of the ways in which war galvanized individuals into action.

Other individuals and groups also saw in the war an opportunity to address so-called racial problems, echoing prewar debates about eugenics and the health of the nation's children. In France, doctor "experts" wrote articles, spoke, and debated about what they deemed the "people's epidemic" of venereal disease. Measures for diagnosing and treating the disease at military hospitals were extended into civil hospitals, while the interaction of different nations' army medical personnel allowed for sharing of knowledge.[29] For many experts, the presence of so many young men in training camps, war and staging zones, and hospitals provided the perfect way to study their habits and perhaps to reeducate them.[30] Some of the military physicians even used their soldier VD patients to gain information on sexual habits in order to combat infection in the general population.[31]

Unlike the YMCA or racial hygiene experts, the Society of Friends (Quakers) focused its activities not on the morality of those caught up in war but on the casualties of war. They also created spin-off entities such as the Friends' Emergency Committee, the Friends' Ambulance Unit, and the War Victims Relief Committee. In particular, the Friends sought to help those who had fallen through the cracks of governmental or charitable assistance, especially enemy aliens. In a circular letter to supporters of their work, the Friends asked for help for "aliens of all nationalities who, having lived industriously and peacefully under the protection of the British Flag, have now fallen into dire distress."[32] Such pleas sometimes got the society into trouble with the public, as is evident in this August 1914 news article: "'Help our enemies!' is apparently the motto of a group of people who, in times of national crisis, seem to make it their first care to show their sympathy for countries with which Britain is at war."[33] As pacifists, too, the Quakers often had to pursue their wartime relief work while staving off criticism and, for some male Quakers, jail time for conscientious objection. For instance, Stephen Hobhouse, a leader among Quakers in London, was sentenced to prison in 1916 for his conscientious objection.[34] The Friends provided a variety of services for those who fell through the cracks of state and voluntary welfare provisions during wartime, not just "foreigners." For example, they provided trained craftsmen for the civilian internment camps, helped provide for the families of enemy aliens who were interned, and coordinated with other groups.

One such effort linked London Quakers with Dr. Elisabeth Rotten's organization in Berlin, the Auskunft- and Hilfstelle für Deutsche im Ausland und Ausländer in Deutschland (the Information and Help Service for Germans Abroad and Foreigners in Germany). The two groups corresponded and tried to provide assistance and news for those caught in the currents of nationality politics during wartime. In one 1916 case, Dr. Rotten and her counterpart in London, Mrs. Bridgwater, tried to help a separated family, the Kaplans. The Kaplan parents were in Germany, but their boy, who was born in England, remained there with a British foster family as the question of "papers" was settled. In another case, five children were cared for by the Quakers while their father was interned in England as an enemy alien; Dr. Rotten tried to help get the children to the man's sister in Berlin. Each of the cases exposes a variety of domestic dramas exacerbated by the war—divorce, abandonment, death of a parent, internment of a parent—and the relief societies did their part to deal in a humane way with the casualties that resulted.[35]

In all, charitable organizations worked to provide humane treatment for those affected by war, whether they were soldiers far from home or civilians displaced by the vagaries of battle or even anxious parents awaiting news of their beloved children in other countries. These civilian organizations developed a true expertise about how to manage societies in wartime, and many of these efforts spilled over into long-term relief work. Their contributions did help people, but enmeshed as they were in the war's infrastructure, charitable organizations also boosted national war efforts and allowed for military officials to plan for their help in waging war.

Feeding the Hungry

One of the specific humanitarian needs to arise from the First World War was food aid. Throughout most of the belligerent nations food scarcities occurred, and in some regions, hunger and starvation became common. Perhaps one of the most unusual food organizations to develop during the First World War was the Commission for Relief in Belgium, sponsored largely by American Herbert Hoover and a group of engineers and business leaders, who served as "volunteer professionals."[36] Developed in 1914 to help occupied Belgium feed its civilian population, the CRB promised neutrality and functioned under the auspices of both British and German promises, with American, Dutch, and Spanish personnel. Many of the leaders were independently wealthy, while the on-ground work was performed by young men fresh from collegiate life, who received a monthly stipend. In fact, the first group of ten CRB "delegates" were all Rhodes Scholars who traveled from England during their six-week Christmas term break in December 1914 to serve the Belgian relief agency. Many of the delegates were unprepared for the work they were asked to do, and although they were tested in French, some came to Belgium without the necessary linguistic skill to function well. Other aspects of the work also surprised the Americans, as Prentiss Gray, a young man working in his father's shipping business, explained,

> Frankly, I had but little idea what this work was I had come to do. I had rather pictured myself passing out loaves of bread to long lines of hungry people. . . . Besides having charge of the marine shipments through Antwerp, it seems that I was supposed to possess a knowledge of flour milling, baking, the manufacture of shoes, accounting, and Belgian legal procedure, this last qualifying me to officiate at the trials of recalcitrant bakers.[37]

Delegates of the Commission for Relief in Belgium pose with their automobiles in Brussels. *Herbert Hoover Presidential Library.*

Gray, who spoke virtually no French, found out that he had social obligations as well; the Belgian aristocracy wanted to entertain all the CRB personnel. Also, as informal diplomats, the CRB men were expected to dine with the various ministers and ambassadors, business leaders and bankers, and even with German occupying authorities. The delegates themselves understood the oddness of their position in this relief effort, and as CRB delegate John Simpson wrote in a spoof, "Once there was an organization without any. Its chiefs were mining and electrical engineers and its agents were anybody that happened to drop into the office."[38]

The CRB organized, shipped, and inspected foreign grain shipments destined for the civil populations of Belgium and, later, northern France. CRB representatives worked with more than seven thousand local and regional committees under the auspices of the Comité National (CN) in Belgium, but they also coordinated with the German civil and military authorities.[39] In some ways, the CRB was its own country, with its own flag, neutral identity, and head of state (Hoover).[40] From its beginning in late autumn 1914 until April 1917, the CRB helped provide food to occupied Belgium and northern France through its soup kitchens, mills, bakers, and shops.[41] Using tens of thousands of Belgian volunteers to do the cooking and distribution of food and assistance, the CRB was feeding close to 7.5 million Belgians by 1915.[42]

While world producers of grain sidestepped the British blockade and provided food to Belgium, Poland suffered terrible shortages. Humanitarian organizations did attempt to set up a CRB-style agreement for Poland at Hoover's urging, but with little success. A group of prominent leaders in Poland sent a petition to the CRB in 1915 asking for assistance, noting the destruction of crops, the requisitioning of crops and animals, and the widespread unemployment. Signed by the archbishop of Warsaw, the president of the Jewish Corporation in Warsaw, the president of the Protestant Evangelical Congregation, and the president of the Industrial Society, the letter outlined the dire predicament in which they found themselves and sought foreign assistance. The CRB sent one of their best men, Dr. Vernon Kellogg, to investigate conditions in November 1915, but all attempts to set up a food aid organization faltered in the face of diplomatic wrangling between the belligerent countries. Neither Britain, France, and Russia nor Germany and Austria-Hungary would provide the necessary guarantees that the food would not be requisitioned for military use.[43]

In Belgium, success bred additional relief services. Beyond its food provisioning, the CRB and its Belgium counterpart, the CN, organized several other charitable activities. These included clothing distribution centers with donated goods, a "discreet" assistance bureau for elites who were suddenly poor, and a restaurant program with vouchers for meals. One of the specific charities that developed was a program for unemployed female lace workers. With the help of several women in a variety of countries (Belgium, England, United States), lace workers were given materials to produce fine-quality Belgian lace, which was then shipped out to a special Belgian Lace Shop in London and to exhibitions and sales throughout the world. Altogether, almost fifty thousand Belgian lace workers found employment with the CRB lace industry.[44] The lace project in Belgium echoed other programs in various countries to help the destitute in wartime. For example, in France, the Institut de France developed sewing workshops in August 1914 for women reduced to destitution by the war.[45]

The volunteers of the CRB often included "experts" in nutrition, shipping, management, or education. One such "expert" was Philip S. Platt, who was asked to do a study of diets of working families in occupied Liège, Belgium. Using home visits, menus, and CRB ration cards, Platt compiled a careful picture of caloric intake and expenditures on food per week for families.[46] The CRB hoped to use this study to get a clear picture of whether their aid programs were sufficient, but they also wanted to provide a scientific basis for their calls for donations of food and funds. Another food scientist who worked for the CRB was Horace Fletcher, self-proclaimed "Vital Economist." Fletcher, who was already well-known for his system of "fletcherizing," was a proponent of chewing food. He advocated chewing thoroughly and eating only while in a pleasant frame of mind. He spent a year and a half with the CRB in Belgium promoting this system and studying food values and diet in occupied territory.[47] Other CRB experts provided reports on shipping and transport figures, on health and disease, and on unemployment. Hoover even commissioned studies of flour combinations and bread mixtures to determine nutrition and taste of the products they were producing for relief of Belgium.

Third Element

CRB experts provide only one example of the mobilization of expert personnel during the war. In an unprecedented way, the "third element" of social workers, economists, managers, engineers, scientists, educators, and medical personnel was mobilized. Intellectuals, too, were mobilized for war, and universities/schools involved themselves in recruiting, propaganda, relief work, etc. As early as September 1914, university scholars and public intellectuals began debating the merits of the war, the impact on civilization and culture, and the morality of war. In various countries, manifestos appeared in newspapers, and a famous debate over the heart of civilization was sparked by the October 1914 publication of the German manifesto, *Aufruf an die Kulturwelt*. In this document, ninety-three prominent German intellectuals signed a letter defending Germany's actions in the war. Calling Wilhelm II a defender of peace and Germany a cultured and civilized country, those signing the letter appealed to other intellectuals around the world to "Believe us! Believe that we will fight this war to the finish as a civilized people who are the heirs of Goethe, Beethoven, and Kant." This appeal was answered by widespread condemnation from professors in allied and neutral nations. French intellectuals responded simply with a series of questions such as "Who wanted the war?" and "Who violated the neutrality of Belgium?" and French scholarly organizations moved to exclude German members who had signed the manifesto.[48] In Britain, professors responded with similar questions and claims, adding,

> We see with regret the names of many German professors and men of science, whom we regard with respect and, in some cases, with personal friendship, appended to a denunciation of Great Britain so utterly baseless that we can hardly believe that it expresses their spontaneous or considered opinion. We do not question for a moment their personal sincerity when they express their horror of war and their zeal for "the achievements of culture." Yet we are bound to point out that . . . it is German armies alone which have, at the present time, deliberately destroyed or bombarded such monuments of human culture as the Library at Louvain and the Cathedrals at Reims and Malines.[49]

For scholars such as Henri Pirenne and Paul Fredericq in Belgium, who had studied in Germany and maintained ties with German scholars, the October manifesto felt like a major betrayal. Pirenne and Fredericq took their stand against German aggression at the University of Ghent, where they refused to cooperate with German occupying authorities who wanted to reopen the university as a pro-German Flemish-speaking university. At faculty meetings, both Fredericq and Pirenne led the opposition, with Fredericq saying he could teach his courses in Flemish, but he would not, and Pirenne declaring that "he would never lecture again until the Germans had departed."[50] Both men were deported to Germany, and the university reopened as a Flemish university under German auspices.

Other intellectuals put their talents to use for their governments. Sir James Headlam-Morley, for example, an eminent Cambridge-trained historian and classicist, worked for the British Propaganda Department from 1914 to 1917, then in intelligence, and as a member of the British delegation to the Paris Peace Conference.[51] Writers, poets, historians, mathematicians, and other scholars were recruited for positions in intelligence, censorship, propaganda, cryptography, and other war-related offices. A. D. "Dilly" Knox, a Cambridge mathematician, put his talents to use as a code breaker, while Oxford poet May Wedderburn Cannan worked in the British Mission in Paris.[52] Poets often helped sustain a sense of purpose or national identity in the face of war's destruction, as with Bulgarian poets Ivan Vazov and Kiril Hristov.[53] Other scholars investigated the war itself, such as Fernand Van Langenhove, who in 1915 and 1916 used German documents to investigate claims of widespread civilian resistance to the invasion of Belgium.[54]

Scientists used their skills in the service of the state as well. In the United States, chemists went to work on explosives and chemical warfare technologies in both university and corporate laboratories. For example, one of General Electric's factories in Cleveland worked for the army beginning in 1917; they developed gas masks and researched chemical warfare, x-rays, and other technologies, while eminent chemists from such universities as Johns Hopkins, Cornell, and Princeton volunteered to help with gas technology under the auspices of the Bureau of Mines. In France, the Ecole Normale Supérieure's physicists and chemists worked on research with direct impact on the war, conducting experiments on sonics, wireless telegraphy, and poison gas. Britain's J. S. Haldane, brother of the lord chancellor, was a noted physiologist hired by the War Office in 1915 to do research on effective gas masks.[55] In many combatant countries, academics at universities and military academies who were starved for students and resources put their efforts instead into war research or work, stimulating the development of fields as diverse as language study and medicine.[56] Experts in emerging fields such as prosthetics, plastic surgery, dental reconstruction, and radiology were needed, but also those with experience in infectious disease and pharmaceutical work.[57] Medical researchers and physicians saw major breakthroughs during the war in their ability to diagnose disease, perform surgeries, and advance their various specialties.

While scientific experts worked on such experimental breakthroughs, another sort of expert also answered the call: religious leaders. As chaplains with armies in the field, but also as humanitarian workers, community leaders, and sometimes as governmental representatives, the spiritual leadership of nations and villages stepped forward to do their part in the war. For national leaders, the burden of speaking for nations or groups within nations was sometimes great. Cardinal Mercier, the premier Roman Catholic cleric in Belgium, issued proclamations, open letters, and sermons on the problems of German occupation. His pastoral letter of Christmas 1914, for instance, urged people to resist the German authorities in their hearts.[58] In Turkey in November 1914, Ottoman religious authorities issued fatwas calling on Muslims around the world to take up arms against the enemies of the Ottomans.[59] Other clerics used their positions of authority to urge action—pulpits across Europe became platforms for the encouragement of patriotic sacrifice or, in some cases, rebellion against wartime authorities.

Missionaries, who served around the world, found themselves interned as enemies in some areas, but in others, they remained as observers, caretakers, and humanitarian workers. In Persia, for instance, in an October 1917 telegram, the Reverend Wilder P. Ellis reported famine conditions to an American Relief Committee in order to try to get foreign aid:

> If what I saw today in Sunni Mosque Urumiah could be transplanted ten hours Madison square every newspaper America ring with story most abject spectacle in world at war and millions for relief would follow straight away. Kurdish refugees from mountain villages, driven from ripening crops, living unsheltered on stones, indescribable rags, starvation sickness and filth, human beings in state of oriental street dogs with whom they compete for offal. Work is already done by Americans for Armenians, Syrians and Kurds in national triumph but vastness of continuing need is overwhelming.[60]

In their role as eyewitnesses, religious leaders tried to do their part by providing on-the-spot spiritual guidance and material relief when possible. For some, this meant officiating at executions of deserters, spies, or traitors, while for others the work called for sitting at hospital bedsides or at relief depots. After the war, some were judged "as accomplices to the war effort . . . implicated in the massive losses of the war" for their continued messages of "redemptive sacrifice" in the face of destruction.[61] Like scientists, intellectuals, and officials, religious figures sought to do their duty as citizens and to retain their ideals, without necessarily seeing their own collaboration with war itself.

One group that is omnipresent in wartime reports and integrally connected to wartime military and civilian personnel rarely appears as a category for examination: neutral diplomats. These men and women (wives and other family members were drawn into war service as well) functioned as negotiators between combatants, as financial and intelligence clearinghouses, and as inspectors of conditions in occupied territories and prisoner of war camps, to name a few of their often-unanticipated duties. Their work was dangerous, both physically and emotionally, and their ability to be sensitive to political forces was a paramount requirement for the job. Neutral diplomats from Switzerland, the Netherlands, Spain, Mexico, Denmark, and the United States left an illuminating record of letters, memoirs, and telegrams outlining their roles as observers and liaisons.

The neutral diplomatic communities during the war had to deal with their own citizens who had been caught up in wartime travel restrictions and other problems, but also they often assumed responsibility for other countries' citizens. For example, James Gerard, the American ambassador in Berlin in 1914, was looking after British, Russian, and Japanese interests after the outbreak of war as well as those of his own country. Gerard secured the release of a small community of Japanese citizens in Berlin in 1914 and got permission for them to leave the country through Switzerland. He also had to intervene when members of the Siamese legation were mistaken for Japanese by German authorities.[62] His assistant, Joseph Grew, described in his diary the exhausting days of August 1914. On August 1, 1914, the embassy processed "nearly 200 passports" and on August 3, Mrs. Gerard and Mrs. Ruddock (diplomatic wives) opened an office in the ballroom in order to deal with cases of destitution and panic. As Grew noted of the embassy activity, "Our relief department, composed of Mrs. Gerard, Mrs. Ruddock, Mrs. Gherardi, and Miss Kerr (the English girl) work as hard and long as we do, 9 till midnight daily. . . .

U.S. Diplomat Joseph Grew poses with some of his staff during World War I. *U.S. Signal Corps, National Archives and Records Administration.*

Mrs. Ruddock is a perfect wonder, taking entire charge of the sending of money to destitute Americans in different parts of the country, writing, telegraphing, listening to personal appeals for help."[63]

Likewise in Brussels, neutral diplomats sprang into action, and as in Berlin, the Americans were doing "a land-office business in passports."[64] U.S. minister Brand Whitlock assumed control of British, French, German, and Russian interests in Belgium at the outbreak of war in August, and then when the Danish and Italian diplomats left, they also turned over their affairs to him. As one official said to him, "Why . . . you'll be the greatest Minister in the world; you'll be representing America and all Europe!"[65] When Whitlock himself left in 1917 after the United States declared war, he turned American interests over to the Marquis de Villalobar (Spain) and Maurice Van Vollenhoven (Netherlands). Van Vollenhoven was in a particularly difficult position in August 1914 as German armies marched into neutral Belgian territory; his government was some-what nervous about the Netherlands' own neutrality, given its proximity to both Belgium and Germany. Van Vollenhoven also had a large group of people to care for in Belgium and northern France when war was declared. The more than sixty thousand Dutch nationals needed advice, financial assistance, and passports from their representative authority in Brussels.[66]

In addition to caring for citizens of their own and other nations, dip-lomats reported on local conditions to their national governments, often describing social and political conditions and providing local intelligence information. In Baghdad, Charles F. Brissel (American consul) reported on poor Ottoman preparations for war and local reaction to the declara-tion of war in November. Later he described the treatment of Christians and Jews by the Ottoman government. In a series of reports from Novem-ber 1915, Brissel informed the U.S. government that "the local police began to arrest a number of the leading Christian and Jewish gentlemen in this city. It appears [the men] . . . were sent to Samara and I understand from Samara they have been sent on toward Mosul with the possible destination of Desim."[67] Despite being technically "neutral," much of the information Brissel provided became vital when the United States joined the war in 1917.

While many of the officials felt themselves drawn into the conflict, oth-ers relished the protection that their "official" status allowed them. One British writer living in India told his aunt candidly in a letter,

> There is a general feeling abroad that danger threatens from the North & we luxurious bureaucrats may yet find ourselves entrained for Indus. . . . It is not at all pleasant to observe the callousness of highly-paid officials, (some of them) out here, about the war. You will find it hard to believe that men drawing £2000 a year give absolutely nothing to any war fund & pay 2 ¾ [percent] only as income tax, but it is true.[68]

The luxurious living of the diplomats in India described in this account differed significantly from the experiences of others, who faced real dan-ger. For example, Ulysses Grant-Smith, an American diplomat in Vienna, had a nervous breakdown from strain of work by late 1916, and Charles Brissel (Baghdad) died in a citywide cholera outbreak in October 1916.[69]

In addition to those formally employed by the diplomatic community, workers (both voluntary and paid) in quasi-governmental organizations also moved between the lines. Peter Gatrell has documented how in the Russian Empire by 1914, "voluntary organizations were in effect becoming substitutes for public agencies."[70] Using the Russian Red Cross and existing *zemstvos* (local unions), relief workers mixed voluntary and official personnel to meet the needs of those in dire straits. Russia's Tatiana Committee for the Relief of War Victims was formed in September 1914 to work with war widows, children, and refugees, no small task given the scope of war mobilization and refugee movement in the Russian Empire.[71]

In Russia's Ufa province in the Ural region, men and especially women were hired in the fields of adult education to help manage the war in local villages where peasants demanded news and information on the world conflict. These education experts opened lending libraries and developed adult education programs in order to take advantage of and capitalize on the possibility of wartime social change.[72] One peasant described the thirst for information among villagers:

> They read newspapers in the evenings and on holidays. Several people gather at a home and exert every effort to imagine, through the unfamiliar bookish language, distant military positions and foreign lands. . . . Inquisitiveness compels them to buy newspapers and books to learn about the geography and history of nations. They are no less interested in technology: automobiles, airplanes, dirigibles, cannons, machine guns, battleships, cruisers, submarines, mines.[73]

Adult education experts and local zemstvos were quick to pick up on the local mood, and by the end of 1914, they had nearly doubled the number of libraries in the region, added war news to their agricultural journal, and set up a series of lectures on history, literature, and the war. Throughout the war, these efforts continued to expand as librarians led the way in dispensing information on the war and in providing services such as "legal advice and assistance organizing peasant consumers' cooperatives to combat soaring inflation."[74]

Experts in social science, history, natural science, engineering, literature, and medicine were mobilized around the world to support the war effort. Scientists at universities were put to work designing weaponry, chemical agents, and machines for use in wartime. Humanities scholars were called to work in government information and propaganda ministries, helping to "educate" populations about the war. Engineers built bridges and railways across the fronts in areas as diverse as Mesopotamia, East Africa, and Poland. Social workers, dieticians, psychologists, and economists found work analyzing in great detail the impact of the war on civilian and military populations around the world, amassing volumes of data. Much of this expert effort came from civilians, and the importance of "experts" in legitimating and explaining the war should not be underestimated.

Conclusion

Were these "experts" complicit in helping the war last as long as it did? Certainly those maintaining the lines of war were drawn into the conflict in differing degrees, and they were implicated in different ways in the militarization of society. Civilians such as Elsa Brändström demonstrate the practical ways in which citizens around the world were mobilized to support and maintain the war in material ways, but they also signal the difficulty of identifying one "civilian" experience or perception of World War I. The sense of responsibility for war service that many officials, humanitarian workers, and others felt between 1914 and 1918 coexisted with a postwar uneasiness that their participation may have in fact prolonged or worsened the conflict. Among the last to be demobilized, these civilian humanitarians, experts, and officials did not disperse as the demobilized armies did. They became responsible at the end of the First World War for picking up the shattered pieces of humanity.

Although some offices and organizations did shrink in size, many national bureaucracies had been altered beyond recognition, many of them populated by "experts" recruited for the war effort. For example, in Britain the percentage of government employees changed from about 3 percent of the total workforce before the war to 23 percent in the 1920s.[75] This rise partly reflected the need for nations to maintain bureaucracies to deal with ballooning paperwork regarding pensions, new welfare provisions for ex-soldiers with physical and mental disabilities, and assistance to war widows and orphans. In areas devastated by war and famine, rebuilding efforts consumed the time of experts and diplomats. Relief organizations supplied temporary and permanent housing, set up refugee bureaus to help those returning to their homes after the war, developed employment assistance depots, and distributed food and clothing.

The work of war did not end in 1918 with the armistice, especially since many soldiers and prisoners of war did not return home until the early 1920s. Inspections of camps continued, and Red Cross workers spent considerable time working with those who were scheduled for repatriation. For soldiers still in camps or occupied zones, 1919 promised to be a year of waiting. The YMCA focused much of its energy on keeping the restive young men from rioting, getting drunk, or rebelling against their work orders. One of the Y's signal successes was the Interallied Games, held at the purpose-built Pershing Stadium in the Bois de Vincennes (in the Paris environs) in June–July 1919. The stadium could hold up to twenty-five thousand spectators, and more than fifteen thousand athletes from eighteen armies accepted invitations to participate.[76] Such events were designed to distract and entertain as the soldiers got increasingly impatient about their continued service away from home.

The humanitarian needs of the postwar period meant that the international aid organizations also remained large and active into the 1920s. One area that garnered world attention was the health of children. In Austria between 1919 and 1921, more than two hundred thousand children (one in three) were sent to recuperate from the war's effects in Switzerland or the Netherlands.[77] In Austria, Germany, Poland, and other former enemy zones, the United States sponsored the American Relief Administration (ARA) European Children's Fund, which provided food, clothing, and medical care for children. From a report in the Polish zone dated September 1919, the scope of the problem is clear. By this date, just under a million children were being fed supplementary rations by the ARA, and officials counted more than half a million more still in need of relief.[78] Many of the CRB delegates involved themselves in this work, which was run by Herbert Hoover. Likewise, the International Red Cross and many national Red Cross societies worked with war orphans, refugees, and those returning from war or internment.

Experts staved off social collapse, medical disaster, and revolution, but they also gave hope and help to millions affected by the war. Largely civilian, sometimes paid, these men and women took risks for other humans, yet they collaborated with governments and armies to make the war happen. Their crucial, yet largely undervalued, services to the war effort helped maintain the war for four years. The diplomats, aid workers, volunteers, and experts continued to shape the postwar world from 1918 into the 1920s and 1930s. Experts managed the postwar humanitarian crises of returning refugees, newly displaced people, hunger/inflation, and revolution. They also wrote histories and memoirs of their experiences, which in turn helped define a new generation of experts and which would later help shape policies of the Second World War. As Maurice Maeterlinck wrote in a wartime essay, "Humanity was ready to rise above itself. . . . Never before had nations been seen capable, for months on end, perhaps for years, of renouncing their repose, their security, their wealth, their comfort."[79] With this sentiment fueling the generation of 1914–1918, these in-between officials and volunteers provide evidence of continuing idealism in the face of the devastation of war.

[7]

Civilians behind the Wire

All the world's a cage,
And all the men within it weary players;
They have no exits, only entrances,
Where each spends many months 'ere he departs.
— L. E. Filmore, "The Seven Ages of a Kriegsgefangener,"[1]

The nightmares began almost as soon as he reached neutral territory. The dreams were vivid, featuring faceless officials wresting him from his comfortable Dutch hotel room and returning him to the horse stall where he'd spent the last three years. Gilbert Graham, a 28-year-old Australian electrical engineer released into Dutch custody in late April 1918 from a German civilian internment camp, wrote to his wife about the dreams:

Here I usually sleep too heavily to dream but when I do it is quite disturbing, because I always find myself back in Ruhleben, awake, with the knowledge that Holland was only a dream. It is always the same with slight variations, but I always have the same obsession, that is my brain worries and worries how to get back the letters which I wrote you and the Dad [sic] announcing my false freedom, such letters having been written under the dream impression that I was in Holland. It is quite disturbing while it lasts.[2]

Like many of his comrades also released into Holland during prisoner exchanges, Graham found himself unable to throw off the experience of confinement, longing alternately for solitude and for company, bothered by dreams, memories, and melancholy. At one point, he mused to his wife, "I shall indeed be like an Antarctic explorer returning to the world after this [experience]."[3]

Graham was certainly not alone in this experience of civilian internment in the First World War, and in fact, he was one of hundreds of thousands of ordinary civilians taken into custody by nations involved in the war. Millions more were displaced by the war, forced into refugee camps or housed in private homes and public institutions, either because they fled voluntarily or because military officials mandated movement from war zones. Enemy alien men of military age (roughly seventeen to forty-five years old) were particular targets, but men, women, and children around the world were affected by these policies of internment as well as by deportation and repatriation programs during and after the war. Altogether close to a million civilians spent at least part of their war behind barbed wire or in other forms of confinement.

While not a new invention in 1914, the widespread use and systematic organization of concentration/internment camps in the First World War was an innovation that became a precedent for later conflicts. The first to use concentration camps (reconcentrado) was Spanish general Valeriano Weyler in the fight against rebels in Cuba (1898), and such camps were also utilized by the British in South Africa during the Anglo-Boer War (1899–1902), when civilians were detained in camps or concentrated areas, supposedly in order to control support networks for guerilla fighters.[4] The major difference in World War I was that civilian internment was a deliberate state policy regardless of whether the nation in question was fighting on its own territory. Even nations as far removed from the battle lines as Canada, Australia, Brazil, and Chile interned civilians. Numbers of internees varied widely by country. For example, the Isle of Man housed more than twenty-five thousand civilian men interned by the British during the war, while in Germany, more than one hundred and ten thousand civilians were in captivity by 1918. Italy interned seventy thousand people in the Friuli and Dolomite border zones, sending the men of military age to Sardinia. In France, camps accommodated enemy men and women but also undesirable French and Belgian people from the military zones. In all, an estimated sixty thousand people spent some time in the French concentration camps of the war period.[5] In fact, internment camps existed in all combatant countries (Romania, Russia, Austria-Hungary, Ottoman Empire, Australia, Canada, United States, Chile), in neutral countries (Switzerland and the Netherlands), and in many colonial possessions (German East Africa, Malta, Singapore). Were these interned men and women still civilians when they were being held in military custody, guarded by soldiers, and subject to military control? The internment practices of World War I highlighted the difficulties in determining which civilians constituted military threats to the home population.

Those interned during the war were often outsiders or were living on the margins of society. Governments used various guidelines for internment of civilians, but the most common factor that led to internment was foreign birth. So-called enemy aliens who were purposefully or inadvertently residing in nations at war in 1914 often found themselves in camps or under supervision. Civilian internment exposed the problems of the civil/military divide, creating categories of people who did not fit neatly in either. Officials tried to categorize people by simple nationality, but national citizenship was neither simple nor static. People moved and their loyalties shifted, while in other situations, families stayed in the land in which they were born but their government (and therefore their nationality) changed.

The story of civilian internment in the First World War is the tale of thousands of ordinary individuals held in captivity for reasons that seemed oblique at best to most of them. Perhaps the best documented of the internment camp experiences are those in Western Europe, where the governments of Germany, Britain, and France paid close attention to the conditions in camps, publishing reports and inspections. In addition, the highly literate prisoners of high-profile camps such as Ruhleben and Knockaloe published stories, books, and letters detailing their experiences both during and after the war, creating a useful record for understanding camp life, the stresses of internment, and the larger impact of internment policies in World War I.

Their very status as civilians complicated their lives in multiple ways as international rules written to protect prisoners of war targeted soldiers and officers, not civilians. For men of military age, the purgatory of internment was difficult to endure; they could not fight and "prove" their masculinity, nor could they contribute work to their home or adopted country. This enforced passivity meant that civilian internees experienced the war behind wire, powerless to support or resist the war in any meaningful way.

The Internees

The war broke out at the height of the summer tourist season in 1914, so many on pleasure trips ended up staying in enemy territory longer than they had planned. In addition to tourists, travelers, workers and business people, political dissidents, or suspected subversives, unemployed or underemployed workers, prostitutes, religious leaders, and political hostages could also be subject to internment or supervision. In most countries that interned civilians, the bulk of those imprisoned were male, as officials reasoned that men of military age were "reservists" in their own countries, and if able to return to their natal homes, would bear arms. However, in some cases wives, children, single women, and the elderly were interned "for their own protection" or because of some action that made them suspect.

While Gilbert Graham dealt with life in a former horse stable because he was an Australian male of military age, another Australian located a world away was caught up in a living nightmare because she married the enemy. Detained by her own nation, Daisy Schoeffel tried to protect her family from what she saw as an absurdly tragic situation. Born in Australia to a well-established manufacturing family, Daisy technically "lost" her own nationality upon her marriage in 1913 to Alfred Schoeffel, a naturalized British citizen of German origin living in Fiji. Under Australian law, women took the nationality of their husbands. When war broke out, the Schoeffels continued their lives in Fiji, while Daisy's brother served in the Australian forces and her father, a boot manufacturer, supplied the army under a Defence Department contract. Their circumstances changed in 1917 when a panic about naturalized Germans in Fiji ensued, leading to accusations of espionage and trading with the enemy. All Germans, whether naturalized or not, were deported in the name of their own protection. They were sent to Australia under guard and in the hold of a ship, then to Bourke in New South Wales, a "family" internment center known for poor conditions and a "murderous climate."[6] Because all of their money and property had been seized in Fiji, they had no means to make their lives more bearable and could purchase no additional food or clothing. As Daisy wrote to a government official after the war, "The first week at Bourke was hell on earth. . . . About six weeks after we arrived in Bourke we all got dysentery . . . and for two months one time we received absolutely nothing but bread and meat, the latter being flyblown."[7]

Daisy and her two small children (aged three years and fifteen months, respectively, in 1917) were among hundreds of civilians sent to Australian internment camps from British colonies and territories, including Fiji, Ceylon, Hong Kong, and Singapore. China even applied in 1917 to send its enemy aliens to Australia, but that plan never reached fruition. In all, close to seven thousand people were interned in Australia during the war, most of them residents and some of them even Australian citizens under suspicion merely for having a German surname or ancestry.[8] Other British colonies in Asia and the Pacific also maintained internment centers at various times during the war, with the largest being those in New Zealand, at Stonecutters Island in Hong Kong, in India, and in Singapore. These camps often housed a wide range of individuals from all over the Pacific and Indian Ocean regions; one camp in Rajputan, India, housed approximately three thousand men from a dozen language groups, including Afghan, Persian, Kurd, Armenian, Greek, Turk, etc.[9]

Other nations far from the front lines also interned civilians, albeit in fairly small numbers. In the United States, rather than interning all German-born males of military age, officials targeted naturalized or enemy citizens accused of disloyalty. Karl Muck (1859–1940), director of the Boston Symphony Orchestra, was among four thousand civilians interned in the United States during World War I.[10] Muck spent close to a year in internment at Fort Oglethorpe, Georgia, as a "dangerous enemy alien"; his crime was a false accusation of espionage and "refusing to play the Star-Spangled Banner" at a concert in October 1917. On this occasion, Muck stated publicly that: "Art is a thing by itself, and not related to any particular nation or group." His concerts led to protests and eventually to his arrest in spring 1918.[11] Muck shared his confinement with scholars, scientists, musicians, and poets, a mere handful of "dangerous" men held captive in a nation with more than four and a half million citizens who had been born in countries tied to the Central Powers. With what seemed

Civilian men wait for transfer to the U.S. internment camp
at Fort Oglethorpe in Georgia. *Library of Congress.*

to be arbitrary policies toward those of German or Austrian descent, the
United States only interned those who had been denounced for pro-
German or anti-American activities or those considered too influential
to remain free citizens.[12] This policy led to the captivity of a strange mix
of prominent German-born men, including Muck, bankers Rudolf Hecht
and Ernst Fritz Kuhn, scientist Richard Goldschmidt (who was on a temporary appointment at Yale when he was arrested), and Ernst Kunwalt,
a concert pianist and conductor of the Cincinnati Orchestra.[13] Many of
these men had only vague ideas about the charges against them, and they
had to suffer the uncertainty of not knowing why they were incarcerated
or for how long they might remain behind barbed wire.[14] Like the United
States, Canada also operated enemy alien internment camps during the
First World War, but its camps held few prominent bankers, scholars, or
musicians. Rather, its concern was with unemployed and underemployed
recent immigrants, many of whom were Ukrainians who had been invited
to Canada as workers prior to the war. Most of these workers had little
education and few ties in Canada, and their status was uncertain in 1914.
Arrested as enemy aliens and officially classified as part of the Austro-

Hungarian Empire, these worker-immigrants comprised the bulk of the more than eight thousand people interned by the Canadian government during the war. Others interned included political dissidents and sailors from merchant vessels taken from ports in Canada and British colonies of the Caribbean (Jamaica, Barbados, Bermuda, etc.). Perhaps because of their class status or Canada's unwillingness to create protective policies, the civilian internees in Canada were among the few in the First World War to be forced into hard labor.[15]

Labor projects varied for those interned, but a large number were sent to camps in the Rocky Mountains to build roads using hand tools such as picks, shovels, and wheelbarrows. Their labor was part of a scheme in the fledgling national parks system to make these wilderness areas more accessible to tourists. Internees were engaged in road, bridge, and other building projects, but weather conditions were harsh, and the remote location of these camps meant poor access to fresh water and difficult supply issues. For most of the civilian internees and their keepers, this life was hellish, as is evident in this description of the camp at Banff:

> [T]he prisoners and their guards put in exceptionally long days walking to and from the project sites. In some cases they marched from four to six miles each way; according to the inspection report [February 1916], this amounted "practically to a day's work in itself," especially given the snow conditions that winter. To make matters worse, the distance from the camp precluded a warm midday meal and the men had to choke down frozen food.[16]

Canada ran more than two dozen internment centers during the war, with most of them requiring work from inmates. Yet many of the civilians refused to accept the conditions offered them by Canadian authorities. In a November 1916 report on another internment work camp at Spirit Lake in Quebec, U.S. consul G. Willrich found a majority of the civil inhabitants on strike, claiming that as civilians they should be provided with wood for heat and good food. Willrich recorded pitiful stories of inadequate food and heat, guard brutality, and poor lodging, as with this account from Oftude Boka (interned for more than a year): "Do not want to work any more, did not get enough to eat. Corporal hit me, nobody lets me see the Colonel, nor the orderly officer. Worked all winter getting wood on sleighs, and when sick, was not permitted to go to the hospital. Do not care whether I die or not."[17] This treatment was a far cry from the life of better-educated, mostly German internees, who were assigned to nonwork internment centers in Ontario, where they were put in a "privilege camp."[18]

This class division, based on wealth, occupation, and education, was a feature of civilian internment in all the combatant countries, leaving some internees in distinctly better situations than others. Wealthier interned civilians even managed to use their own funds to hire servants from among the poorer internees. Artist Paul Cohen-Portheim described Knockaloe, an ordinary internment camp on the Isle of Man, as having "[t]wo sharply divided classes, the £1 a week class and the moneyless class," but he himself was soon transferred to a "gentleman's camp" at Wakefield, England, for a more privileged existence.[19] Other internment sites purposefully separated social classes, such as Fort Oglethorpe (United States). This center in Georgia had three camps, one of which was known as the "millionaires' camp" because it included internees who could afford to pay for better food, servants, and little luxuries.[20] The French had two categories of special camps—those for "notables" or famous people, and those for the wealthy or privileged.[21] In India, some of the colonial administrators held in concentration camps there lived quite well, with servants, household amenities, and whole family groups in one place. As one inspector noted in his 1917 report, the civilian internees "seemed like visitors on a holiday rather than enemy subjects in captivity."[22] Likewise in Australia two camps for elite internees emerged as the war progressed, one at Berrima and one at Trial Bay. Trial Bay held "merchants, physicians, priests" as well as the German consuls from all the Australian states and many British colonies in the Pacific. Two foreign scientists who were interned because they were in Australia attending a professional meeting also became well-known inhabitants of Trial Bay.[23]

Perhaps one of the greatest examples of the contrast between the work camps and "privilege camps" was the internment center at Berrima in New South Wales, which even became a tourist attraction during the war. The German concentration camp at Berrima was a privilege camp mostly reserved for sailors and ships' officers taken from vessels in the region but housing a few civilians as well. The crew of the SMS Emden, famously captured by a British warship in the Indian Ocean, was held here along with other German civilians and military personnel captured from naval and commercial vessels. Unlike many others interned in Australia, the Berrima inmates slept in cells of an old prison at night but had free run of the small village and its river during the day. Amazingly, the internees developed friendly relations with the townspeople, helping them with chores, gardens, and building projects, and in return, the village allowed the internees to make the river their playground. The interned men built huts and gardens on the shores of the river, a footbridge, a dam, and an "American-style water chute," and eventually they constructed small boats for racing regattas.[24]

The mariners' aptitude for carpentry was apparent in their created village within a village, but other skilled internees helped develop the town even further. Friedrich Machotka, a 34-year-old farmer and agricultural expert from Bohemia (Austria at that time, the Czech Republic now), brought his whole family to live in Berrima while he was detained. His American wife and three young daughters set up house in the village, and Machotka and his daughters, with the later help of other internees and villagers, created astounding vegetable and flower gardens that became showplaces in the region. Not only did they gain fame but the gardens (called New Pomerania) provided an almost continuous supply of fresh produce for the camp, a boon many internees in other countries and indeed in Australia coveted.[25] Berrima, like many of the other privilege camps, still limited its inhabitants' freedom, but its advantages over "regular camps" were multiple and visible. As one of the Australian guards noted in his history of Berrima, "It is a charming site for a concentration camp, and . . . internees generally are very satisfied and recognise that this is the best concentration camp to be found anywhere."[26]

The differences between the privilege camps at Berrima and Trial Bay and the large multipurpose camp, Holdsworthy, in the Sydney suburb of Liverpool, underline the ways in which class and occupational status provided benefits, even in internment settings, in the First World War. Friedrich Machotka, who had spent time in both Berrima and Holdsworthy, petitioned the U.S. Embassy for a transfer to Berrima, where Mrs. Machotka and the children would be allowed to live under internment conditions as well. In Holdsworthy, wives and families were not allowed, and in fact, they were often sent to the dreaded outpost at Bourke.[27] Another internee, H. Sauerbeck, who was living at the privilege camp at Trial Bay, explained the difference between Holdsworthy and Trial Bay in a written description:

> In our camp [Trial Bay] there is a very good institution, called "Genossenschaft [The Cooperative]" which has a monopoly for selling all kinds of provisions: coffee, beer, milk, sausages, fruits, etc. The profit from this endeavor provides upkeep for the theater, the orchestra, etc., and each month the chef receives a large portion for improving our menu. Thus the prices are fixed for all things and the camp benefits from each penny that one spends. Sadly, there is no equivalent institution in the large camp at Liverpool [Holdsworthy] where nearly 5000 Germans are interned.[28]

Another internee, Georg Boysen, wrote to his family expressing gratitude for a cell (in an old jail) at Trial Bay over the barracks at Liverpool, where "it was rightly said, that a coolie in Ceylon would when dead have more room on the Cemetry [sic] than we have here in the barracks. . . . [Liverpool] is a dreadful place."[29] Even the Holdsworthy camp commandant, Lt. Col. R. S. Sands, recognized that the general camp conditions were harsher than those at the privilege camps. Despite having no official approval for mandatory work, Sands instituted "working gangs of prisoners" at Liverpool, "[t]o keep the prisoners physically fit I insisted at that time that all should do 4 hours work daily, and I put them on to congenial work such as clearing bush lands, grubbing trees, building fences, etc." Sands also created a "feeding system" borrowed from cattle yards that funneled men through mazelike races toward the food. He admitted that "[t]he prisoners at first did not take kindly to the change and to vent their displeasure they used to 'bah' like sheep as they went through the races."[30] No wonder the men were unhappy; in addition to mandatory work programs, regimented "feeding," and crowded barracks, there were only forty-two cold showers, all in the open air, and open pit latrines with no privacy for the more than six thousand men interned there in 1918.[31]

While internment camps featured divisions based on class, camp officials also divided prisoners on the basis of their nationalities. Certain enemy aliens could escape internment entirely if their nationality was termed a "friendly" one, or if they were perceived to be a subject people within a larger empire. For example, the United Kingdom often exempted Arabs or Greeks from the Ottoman Empire or Czechs and Poles living under Austro-Hungarian rule.[32] The French also made allowances for Syrians and Armenians who were technically Ottoman subjects, but they initially interned most men from Alsace and Lorraine because of the difficulty in determining their loyalties (French or German).[33] Within the camps themselves, certain nationalities were quarantined. At Ruhleben, which was filled with British nationals, the "PGs," or pro-Germans, among the internees were segregated in a special barracks called "the Tea House" for their own protection.[34]

In some cases having an indeterminate nationality or a confusing family history could lead to internment as surely as being a clear enemy alien subject, and mistakes were made. Internment seemed an almost arbitrary decision when men with almost similar backgrounds found themselves on opposite sides of the barbed wire. One instance of such national difficulty is the case of Paul Waller, an internee at Knockaloe on the Isle of Man, who was arrested while trying to arrange travel from the UK back to France to join the army. Technically he was a German because of his birth in the territory of Lorraine in 1886 (under German control after 1871), but his sympathies and family background were French. His family had lived in London since he was a teenager, and in 1914, he was engaged to marry a British woman. The complexity of his national background and his age (thirty years, or military age) seems to have occasioned his arrest, despite his fifteen-year residence in London and the fact that all his "interests and associations are in Great Britain."[35] Like Daisy Schoffel in Australia, some civilians found themselves interned through accidents of birth or circumstance, victims of modern definitions of citizenship in the nation-state.

Nationalism reared its head in other ways, most notably through purposeful reprisals, which became a feature of internment experiences. When certain nations were perceived to be treating internees badly, their counterparts might retaliate in kind. For example in Austria-Hungary, stories about British mistreatment of Germans and Austrians in its camps led to an 8:00 p.m. curfew for British internees in Austrian camps and a policy whereby Russian and French prisoners were allowed walks outside the wire, while British prisoners were not.[36] Germany and France developed a particularly nasty policy of reprisals over the course of the war, while early internment policies in Germany and Britain were partly shaped by government orders for reprisal.[37] Local camp commandants were told not to order reprisals without clearance from their states, but camp officials sometimes found such restraint difficult in the heightened wartime atmosphere. The commandant at Holdsworthy camp in Australia explained his feelings about reprisals in a report:

> The instructions issued to me by the Minister for Defence in connection with the treatment of internees, was to treat them with the consideration that I would desire to be treated if I was interned, and not to let my feelings be influences [sic] by rumours and reports of bad treatment upon our own men, but to remember that it was an Englishman's privilege and his desire to carry into effect the dictates of his own conscience. Any reprisals which were to be made were not to be of a local nature but would be ordered by the Secretary of State to Great Britain. These instructions I have faithfully tried to carry into effect, and I have endeavoured not to let my temper overrule my judgment, but I must say reading the reports from other camps in enemy countries furnished by Mr. Gerard the Ambassador for the United States in Germany, I have often been tempted to give them as it is commonly observed "one to go on with", but I have refrained.[38]

Beyond the national question, countries divided internment camps by language and ethnicity as well. In Germany, most British civilians were sent to Ruhleben while Belgian and French civilians found themselves at Holzminden or Gütersloh. Those minority nationalities who were interned often petitioned for separate accommodations in camps, so, for instance, at the Isle of Man camps Austrian prisoners often were segregated from Germans. In France, there were three different kinds of internment camps for those from the disputed French-German territories of Alsace and Lorraine, depending on the level of security risk each person was assigned.[39] Ethnic groups were sometimes targeted for unique treatment, as with gypsies who were forcibly deported as suspect aliens by the Russians and who were confined to special camps for nomads by the French.[40]

In other circumstances, some of the warring nations tried to use nationalist or ethnic allegiances to their advantage. Germany set up special "propaganda" camps for Ukrainians and for Muslims from the Russian Empire, Africa, and India, hoping to find recruits for their armies on the eastern front (Ukrainians) and in the Middle East (Muslims).[41] Irish prisoners were a special source of concern in both Germany and the United Kingdom. The Germans held special meetings of all Irish Roman Catholics from various internment centers and tried to entice them to join the German army or to fight against England in other ways. At one such meeting, "Sir Roger Casement[42] and five Irish priests from Rome . . . [proposed] that these Irishmen should form a special corps . . . to 'fight for their country' (against England, of course)."[43] Meanwhile, the British tried to find special internment accommodations for "ringleaders" from the Irish Easter Rebellion of 1916 who were awaiting trial, but with mixed success. The Isle of Man refused to house Irish revolutionaries because of proximity to the Irish mainland and fears of sympathy from the mainly Irish camp guards, so many of the male revolutionaries were sent to prisons in northern England, and female revolutionaries spent their internment at a former inebriates' reformatory in Aylesbury and at Holloway prison in London.[44]

More ominously, separate Ottoman camps for Armenians in Mesopotamia and Syria were used to isolate this minority group as part of a genocidal plan that led to the extermination of more than a million Armenian civilians.[45] Those Armenians who tried to flee into surrounding territories sometimes found themselves little better off, as they were taken as civilian prisoners again. One Ottoman prisoner of war described with pity these civilian refugees who arrived in Russia by rail convoy only to be "held" in internment centers "mostly wearing old, tattered clothes. Sinking to their knees in mud and dragging themselves along, they were taken to sheds" as holding centers.[46] On the eastern front, deportation and internment sometimes became an excuse for pogroms against Jewish or other minority communities.[47]

Religion often dictated separate accommodation as well. The Douglas Internment Camp (Isle of Man) provided three different subcamps within its facilities: a class-based "privilege camp," an ordinary camp, and a Jewish camp.[48] The camp for the "better class of prisoners" cost each man ten shillings per week, but these men got choice lodging (even private tents, if they paid extra) and personal servants. At the Jewish subcamp within camp compound 2, there was a "separate kitchen where Kosher food is prepared for orthodox Jews," of which there were more than four hundred by 1917.[49] Likewise, at Ruhleben Camp in Berlin, Jewish prisoners were segregated in a special barrack with its own kitchen and many of its own activities.[50] The French provided separate kitchen facilities and food for Ottoman Muslims interned in their camps, when it was possible.[51] If an internee died, many of the camps tried to make arrangements for proper funeral rites and burials.[52] Despite some sensitivity to religious issues regarding rites, food preparation, and housing, religious tension remained in many internment facilities.

Colonial subjects faced different accommodations and treatment from their metropolitan counterparts during internment also, and often racism was a feature of life in the camps. Ruhleben housed a large contingent from the British Empire, most of whom were confined to one barrack, the "Negerbaracke," and whose presence was described in a memoir by 24-year-old Irish internee John Patrick Bradshaw:

> The tropical quarters of the British Empire were represented by some 150 of his Majesty's dusky subjects. The great majority of these were Africans, and most of the remainder came from Jamaica. With the exception of about half a dozen who had been living in Germany and had arrived in the camp along with different parties of white men, they lived in a barracks where no white face was to be seen. . . . [F]ew of them could speak any English. . . . [A] number had their tribal marks burned or cut on their cheeks. . . . [T]heir greatest earthly bliss appeared to be a cricket match. . . . They played cricket daily, regardless of wind and weather.[53]

As this account suggests, European internees often depicted black inmates as childlike and simple, and there are multiple accounts, some paternalistic and some hostile, of the music and sport-loving internees, suggesting a pervasive racial prejudice that accompanied anti-Semitism and class distinctions in many of the camps.[54] Although a number of imperial internees like those at Ruhleben found themselves eventually in European internment camps, some unfortunates were interned in colo-

Photographs showing prisoners in German internment camps. These photos were taken by camp officials as documentation of the diversity of prisoners in their custody. *Library of Congress.*

nies that were ill-prepared to intern civilians. The primary predictors of civilian internment camp conditions in World War I were the readiness of the facility and the organizational level of the government's war office. Some of the worst internment experiences were in Russia and the Ottoman Empire, where the general level of societal preparation for war was low, but the internment experiences in colonial settings could also be particularly harsh. Otto Wienecke, a German living in the Cameroons, complained bitterly of his treatment when the British rounded up civilians and kept them interned on a ship docked in port for several weeks while they decided on a course of action.[55] While Wienecke was loud in his complaints, his ordeal was of relatively short duration. In fact, the thing that seemed to make him most angry was that he and his fellow German colonial officials and their families were marched through the streets past their colonized subjects, who shouted abuse at them. Nonetheless, Wienecke's charges were investigated, and rumors of poor treatment in the colonies often affected policy elsewhere. The U.S. ambassador in Berlin,

James Gerard, was asked to conduct further investigation of allied treatment of Germans after Berlin officials heard that "Germans taken prisoners in German African Colonies were forced to work in the sun, watched and beaten by coloured guards."[56] In many cases, the accounts of poor treatment became just one more weapon in the propaganda war being waged.

Like the German Otto Wienecke, British missionary John Williams left a compelling account of his time in internment centers in Africa. This account shows how very different internment experiences could be depending on location. While some men lived it up on the river in Berrima and others played cricket in Ruhleben, some civilians suffered hard labor in Canada's western wilderness or, like Williams, battled tropical disease and starvation diets. Williams, along with four women and three men, was interned in early 1915 as an enemy alien in German East Africa. His group was marched on foot through difficult terrain for hundreds of miles as they were moved between internment sites during his two years of captivity. His first long-term internment center, Kiboriani, was an old mission station located at six thousand feet above sea level. The internees included medical personnel, missionaries, planters, and businesspeople, both men and women, from the region. Williams described the diet and conditions in his diary:

> We had nothing to eat but millet (Kaffir corn) & a few poor European potatoes, with now & then a little rice, and meat. Drink milk & coffee. The millet was old, & disgustingly dirty, had been overrun by rats, and smelt badly. It was made into bread, the crust of which when burnt was passably eatable. With this bread we were given a piece of butter as big as a nut for breakfast and tea. To drink with this we had coffee—the great amount of 4 dessert's spoons' full of coffee for 40 people. For lunch we had millet made up into small dumplings and boiled—they were nauseous & one could only eat them by holding one's nose and swallowing one quickly. It was often that even one made one sick, & there were serious epidemics of diarrhea from time to time.[57]

Williams was eventually moved along with several others to the civilian camp at Tabora, which held British, French, Belgian, Greek, and Italian civilians and some soldiers. While conditions were somewhat better at Tabora for the British such as Williams, African-born missionaries were treated particularly badly in these camps, often whipped, put in chains, and forced into hard labor. Zacharia Mazengo, a teacher for the Church Missionary Society, testified in 1916 to the treatment he had received from the Germans when he was interned. He told a magistrate in Mombasa, "There we were stretched out on the ground and greatly beaten, each of us receiving 110 strokes with a kiboko [rhinoceros-hide whip]; again we were bound with cords and our hands tied behind from 8 a.m. till 3 p.m. until we fainted and were nearly dying." Despite such torture, Mazengo and the four other "native" teachers so punished refused to admit to trumped-up charges of learning signaling from the English.[58]

The experience of internment varied widely according to nation, age, and status of internee, and period of the war, but in all cases, internees were removed from society and placed in a strange state of limbo for the duration of the war or until their repatriation. Civilian internees, like military prisoners of war, fought a different war of boredom and confinement, leaving them in an uneasy spot upon their release as bystanders to the conflict with little power to serve their nations or to refuse service.

The Camps

As all these accounts demonstrate, internment of civilians could vary greatly according to their wealth, location, sex, age, race, nationality, and sometimes even luck. A trip at the wrong time, a stray word disparaging the government, or an accident of birth was enough to lead to internment of an individual. In one unusual case, several hundred Turkish families returning from pilgrimage to Mecca were interned in Cairo in 1917, with men in an internment camp while their wives and children were housed in an old citadel.[59] Here bad luck and poor timing were both factors in the internment of these individuals.

One of the most important issues for most internees was their housing situation. Privacy, or more accurately, lack of privacy, was a great strain for most internees, but for older prisoners, the physical hardships of some of the camps' housing made internment a torture. The worst luck for an internee came with an early arrest because as camps were being built and furnished, many of the earliest prisoners were forced into building their own lodgings, or they had to make do with very inadequate conditions. Israel Cohen, interned at Ruhleben from November 1914 to June 1916, described his first impressions of the camp, noting that they slept on straw alone for the first six weeks:

> The Camp was in a lamentable state of unpreparedness when we were first interned, and we had many hardships to endure throughout the winter. We suffered not only because of the insalubrious quarters in which we were housed, or rather stabled, but also because of the insufficient heating and lighting, the lack of hot water, and the vast swamps that formed through the Camp whenever there were heavy rains.[60]

Another internee at Ruhleben, John Patrick Bradshaw, also landed there in early November 1914 when many of the British in Germany were interned, and like Cohen was astonished at how ill prepared the camp was for their occupation. He described the stables where they were housed:

> It was about 70 or 80 feet long, and about 25 feet broad. The ground floor consisted of a row of loose boxes. . . . [A]nd also two little rooms which were occupied by the soldiers in charge. The corridor was about six feet wide and had a door at each end and one side door in the middle. . . . In each loose box six men were lodged, and as we stood outside parties of six were told off and ordered into the boxes until all were filled. The remainder of the party, which included myself, were sent upstairs . . . [to the] hayloft. . . . The floor was concrete covered with straw—not too thickly covered. Each of us chose a spot, reserved it by depositing our luggage on it, and thus we were installed.[61]

Bradshaw humorously noted that all his fellow loft inmates were unanimous in wishing for a nice jail cell instead of this accommodation. Conditions at Ruhleben in 1914 were primitive, but as the camp grew, adjustments were made to the lodging arrangements. In fact, Ruhleben was seen as one of the better of the internment camps because of the solidity of the stables, and in fact, the U.S. ambassador arranged the transfer of some British subjects from the camp at Wittenberg to Ruhleben in order

Paul Fredericq poses in his room at Gütersloh prison camp in Germany. His position as a professor and political prisoner meant he had nicer accommodations and more privileges than poorer civilians in the camps. *Universiteit Gent, Manuscript Collection.*

to improve their situation.[60] Also, some of the crowding was alleviated by the latter years of the war, when the German and British government managed to negotiate a better exchange system that allowed for some internees to be released into neutral territory or to their home countries. By the end of 1916, for example, the stable boxes at Ruhleben housed only four men per box rather than the six per box ratio that obtained in 1915.[61]

Other civilian internment camps in Germany had varied housing for prisoners, with social class again being an important factor. For famous political prisoners, such as consuls, mayors, and religious or educational leaders, internment facilities were of a much better quality than those for ordinary folk. Paul Fredericq, historian at the University of Ghent, was interned for his refusal to support German plans to create an all-Flemish university at Ghent in spring 1916. His first internment at the camp in Güt-

ersloh was surprisingly comfortable, as he shared a double room of a dor-
mitorylike structure with a Belgian industrialist from Liège. [64] Rather than
sharing a horse box with five others unknown to him, Fredericq spent his
days in relative privacy, reading, writing letters, and visiting with the tight-
knit group of fellow "notables" housed at the camp. Fredericq's colleague
and fellow scholar, Henri Pirenne, found similar accommodations when
he was interned in Germany on the same day as Fredericq for the same
crime. Pirenne, an internationally known historian in 1916, was housed
very comfortably at first at a camp for military officers in Crefeld. Here,
he was the only civilian and was treated as a star. When in May 1916 he
was moved to the general civilian camp at Holzminden, things changed
for him. As he was led down the main avenue of the camp, he was dis-
tressed to see wooden barracks in poor repair, and could only describe
the camp atmosphere as "dismal." The camp, unlike the socially elite
Crefeld, accommodated men, women, and children of all social classes
from a variety of countries, and this mish-mash of humanity was disconcerting for Pirenne. When he arrived at barrack 82, his new home, he was
housed with two unknown Frenchmen, given an iron campbed with a
stuffed straw mattress and some bed linen. Pirenne described the camp in
his diary by comparing it to mining camps in the United States, especially
those hastily constructed in the Klondike. It is no wonder that after less
than a week at Holzminden, Pirenne confided to his diary, "I miss Crefeld
with all my heart."[65]

Like the internees in the German camps, many of those interned in
Britain had little idea in 1914 what kind of homes they would inhabit for
the duration of the war. As with the early arrivals at Ruhleben, the first
internees in Britain found poorly organized and often unlivable facilities.
Some of the first internment centers were holiday camps, docked cruise
ships, prisons, and pleasure centers, hastily converted to lodging for
enemy aliens. A few of the accommodations were permanent structures,
but many used bell tents to house internees until barracks could be built.
Most internees in Britain ended up at some point in the war on the Isle of
Man, where the main two internment facilities were located. The Douglas
Camp, a holiday camp in the capital, housed well-to-do and ordinary prisoners (about three thousand normally), while the purpose-built Knockaloe accommodated more than twenty-five thousand at its busiest point.

Both camps suffered early on from poor ventilation, anemic light fixtures, and overcrowded facilities, but Knockaloe had the additional problem of location. It was built facing the sea on clay, and the wet climate made for miserable conditions in the camp itself and in the barracks, which were hardly watertight.[66]

The housing problems at Knockaloe led to the gathering of depositions from prisoners for inspectors of the American embassies, which in turn led to diplomatic intervention for better housing. One of these depositions provides a glimpse at the conditions the internees found so intolerable. Ferdinand Schoelle, interned in 1915 at age forty-eight, described the housing he encountered at Knockaloe:

> The huts are defective in construction, of single match boardings with no upper ventilation and the fresh air can only come in through the windows and doors. The walls show leaks and gaps. According to the direction of the wind, part of the huts is exposed to bad weather. . . . I slept for the whole six months of my internment on a straw mattress. The Government gave out no pillows and at the beginning only two blankets.[67]

Although some of these conditions improved over the course of the war, camp inspectors in 1917 were still commenting on the overcrowded barracks, wet and muddy conditions, and lack of personal space. One of these reports noted that at Knockaloe airspace was about 140–225 cubic feet per prisoner as compared with 670 cubic feet in Austria.[68] Part of the difficulty for camp officials was the changing governmental policies toward internment, which led to an expansion of Knockaloe to hold more than twenty thousand people, when its original size was planned for five thousand.[69] However, some problems were insoluble, such as the climate—as one inspector noted, he spent a week on the Isle of Man and had only one day when it was not "pouring with rain and a gale of wind blowing, which is typical weather during the autumn season."[70] At Douglas Camp, which also suffered from the weather, even the camp commandant noted in his diary of November 1914, "an appallingly wet day. . . . I must say I sympathize the camp is quite unfit to live in as it is at present."[71]

Despite the draughty and wet lodgings on the Isle of Man and the stable smell at Ruhleben, these facilities were still an improvement over the hodge-podge of internment facilities used in other parts of the world. Canadian prisoners at Banff began the winter of 1915 in tents, before moving in the snow to poorly heated bunkhouses in a nearby town, while in Russia, several hundred thousand civilians were lodged in the Russian interior, Siberia, and the Caucasus in private homes or schools, barns, and prisons, with few amenities.[72] In New Zealand, the governor of Samoa found his accommodation on Motuihe Island to be an abandoned mental hospital with little sanitary accommodation and a poor water supply.[73]

While housing was an important concern for internees, food quality and quantity claimed even more of their attention and concern. Not only was the food often monotonous and bland, but it was sometimes spoiled, infested with insects, or even inedible. The Douglas Riot of 1914 on the Isle of Man is a dramatic testament to the food problems, especially as the camps were organizing. The disturbance on November 19, 1914, left five internees dead and nineteen more wounded after a food riot broke out in the communal cafeteria of the camp and the panicked guards opened fire.[74] The camp was designed to hold about twenty-four hundred prisoners, but by November, the population had swelled to more than thirty-three hundred. In addition to overcrowding, the food was provided by the owner of the holiday camp, Joseph Cunningham, but some suggested that he might be profiteering by pocketing some of the money and providing subpar rations. In October, spoiled meat was served, resulting in more than 120 cases of diarrhea, and then after that, a problem surfaced with potatoes infested with wire-worms, which the camp kitchen continued to serve for two weeks. Added to all this was miserably wet weather and the continued reliance on tents while more permanent huts were built. The men protested on November 18 by refusing to eat, and then apparently rushed the guards at dinner time on November 19, throwing food, furniture, and utensils.[75] At the inquest that followed in late November, the jury found the deaths "justifiable" by the circumstances, but the incident did lead to closer scrutiny of internment conditions in the United Kingdom and to kitchen arrangements that put more control of food preparation in the hands of prisoners themselves.[76]

Early supply problems with food were ironed out by 1915, but as the war progressed and nations felt the squeeze of military demands and the Allied blockade, the rations meted out to prisoners dropped, causing additional distress regarding food. In 1916, U.S. camp inspector Alonzo Taylor was barred from visiting Ruhleben after he published a report calling the internees' food rations "a starvation diet," and the rations actually dropped again later in the war.[77] At Ruhleben, prisoners ate almost all their meals from the white enameled bowls they were given for washing, eating, and drinking, and so their diets consisted mostly of soups and bread.[78] As John Patrick Bradshaw recounted, this bowl "was a breakfast cup; at noon it held our soup—and our meat if we were lucky enough to get any; in the evening it was a cup or bowl according to the fluid supplied for the evening meal."[79] Israel Cohen also commented on the poor rations and especially the poor quality of the "war bread," which he thought could easily be used as a projectile.[80] Even this dubious diet was restricted as time went by and the food scarcity in Germany deepened. As P. C. Sarell, former British consul at Dunkirk, noted of the food at Ruhleben, "the rations were gradually reduced to 200 grammes per man per day. The coffee was an indescribable mixture, always served without sugar and milk." Sarell thought that for most men the ration was insufficient without canteen supplements.[81] The uneven quality of the food meant epidemics of stomach ailments at various points in the camp's history, and in 1917, a dysentery outbreak.[82] In France, the bread ration at the internment camps plummeted from six hundred grams per day early in the war to only two to three hundred grams daily by 1918.[83]

In England, too, the food disintegrated in quality as the war proceeded. As Paul Cohen-Portheim pointed out in his memoir, the food was determined by "scientific" means, often calculated by number of calories. This method did not take into account tastes or variety, and often it ignored issues of weather, work status, and age.[84] Particularly abhorrent to many of the men were the frequent salt-herring rations that they were fed. As one Swedish camp inspector noted in his report on the Isle of Man camps, the food depressed most of the prisoners, but "some prisoners complain about the amount of salt herrings they frequently get, which are rather hard to digest. They are grateful to have them at present replaced by potatoes and vegetables."[85] At one point the British camps shared recipes for salted fish with each other, perhaps hoping for a more palatable menu item. All the camps agreed that at least forty-eight hours of soaking and then lots of onions and spices seemed to make the herrings more palatable, but the cook at Lofthouse Park noted that "Salted Smelts [another fish used in the camps] are the abomination of Desolation. Nothing can be done with them."[86] Herrings became more important as a staple as the bread and meat ration dropped by the end of the war—at Knockaloe camp by early 1919, the bread ration was only five ounces per day, with three to four ounces of meat on five days of the week, and three pounds of herrings per week.[87] Additionally, this was only the published dietary, which did not always reflect the true ration prisoners received.

Given the monotony, poor quality, and limited quantities of food, the civilian internees lived for their canteens, where prisoners with money could supplement their diets, and for parcels, which could be sent from relatives through a prisoners of war bureau or through charitable organizations. In addition, many governments supplied extra rations to their internees at points during the war. This varied greatly by country, and in fact, could cause genuine distress over inequities. The English government supplied its civilians at Ruhleben with sugar, margarine, and white bread in January 1917, while Australian prisoners such as Gilbert Graham received parcels that same month that were "an insult," with "no tea, butter, margarine or jam."[88] The British government, which had hired bakeries in Holland to supply bread for internees, was particularly adept at keeping its parcels of white bread and tinned food on schedule for those held in Germany.[89] Prisoners also received parcels of clothing, cigarettes, and food items from relief organizations at the local and national level, including the Red Cross. On special occasions, charities arranged for parcels for poor prisoners, and Conrad Hoffman remembered in his memoir of YMCA work the gratitude of destitute Russian internees who lined up for Christmas presents in January 1917 (Orthodox Christmas is on January 7); each drew a lot for a gift, then left with an orange or a cake or some cigarettes. That same year at Holzminden, the YMCA sponsored a party for more than two hundred interned children, giving each a small book or game and goodies.[90] For many of the prisoners, the comforts they received helped make life bearable, but also the parcels and gifts themselves were an important psychological reminder that they had not been forgotten. As the camp commandant at Holdsworthy (Australia) noted in a report, "I wish to emphasise the fact that it is not realised by the general public what joy is expressed by a prisoner on the receipt of a parcel from his relatives or friends, even if it contain the merest trash."[91]

An enormous amount of time was taken up in internees' diaries, letters, and memoirs discussing their correspondence with the outside world and worrying about the location of letters, packages, and postcards. Henri Pirenne, who was separated by his wife of twenty-eight years when interned, fretted when he did not receive her correspondence, a vital lifeline for him with his old life. Indeed, some of the letters he exchanged with his wife are truly touching—such as his joyful recounting in his diary of the letter he received notifying him that he would become a grandfather soon. He immediately responded, but also recorded in his diary how hopeful this new life would make him after the death of one of his sons at the front in 1914: "And I am delighted here all alone in my heart, knowing our blood continues through our son. . . . My blessing and my thoughts are with them."[92] Like Pirenne, Paul Fredericq kept a close watch for his correspondence. He started his daily diary with an accounting of the letters and parcels he had received, sometimes copying the letters he wrote and received into the narrative. These letters were treasured connections, as he noted in a letter two weeks after his internment: "I have received with infinite pleasure the cards [from family and friends]." He admitted to being particularly charmed by a note from two of his young pupils, Denise Voortmanck and Henriette Buysse.[93]

Fredericq and Pirenne, along with other Belgian political "hostages" sent to German internment camps to insure the good behavior of the occupied regions, received packages from a special bureau set up to provide help and information. Pirenne wrote almost reverentially about the "three beautiful white loaves of bread" he received from them.[94] Other prisoners were "adopted" by local charities, and they sometimes received parcels from unknown good Samaritans. The International Red Cross alone handled more than "20 million items of post in total, on top of 1,884,914 individual parcels, 1813 collective relief packages and the equivalent of over 18 million Swiss francs in cash."[95] Many local villages or communities also sent socks, food items, and cigarettes to prisoners of war.

Another form of charitable work benefiting the prisoners was the establishment of recreation facilities by such organizations as the YMCA and the Society of Friends. Both Ruhleben and Holzminden had YMCA recreation huts, with libraries, lecture rooms, and lounges for games and socializing. One of the best-organized examples of these activities was the placement of James T. Baily as "Industrial Advisor" at the Isle of Man internment camps by the Friends' Emergency Committee, who hoped to combat "moral rot" in the camps.[96] Baily spent the years from 1915 to 1919 organizing craft activities in the camps, particularly at Knockaloe, and he set up numerous artistic, artisanal, and craft workshops. Some of the more impressive creations from the prisoners included exquisitely carved bonework vases (made from the leftover animal bones created by a camp of twenty-five thousand men), but there were also workshops for weaving, shoemaking, and sewing. Baily's biggest success came in his own area of expertise, woodworking, when he set up a studio of master cabinetmakers to craft furniture. This studio, run by Charles Malt, not only produced goods for use in camp, but also crafted furniture from designs by architect Charles Rennie Macintosh for an industrialist's home in Northampton.

In an even more unusual scenario, Malt and his craftsmen also used Manx timber to create cupboards, buffets, and tables for displaced families in the north of France. While the Quakers provided new prefabricated housing, the German internees at the Isle of Man crafted furniture for the French peasant refugees to use in the houses.[97] Again, this illustrates the contradictions inherent in the idea of "civilians" protected by soldiers being separate from war. In this case, interned civilians whose lives and jobs were disrupted by war were voluntarily making furniture for other civilians whose lives and jobs had been disrupted by war.

The camps became centers of industry and retail in fact, as barber shops, dentists' offices, cafés, and clothing stores emerged. In Holdsworthy Camp, a "shopping center" arose, where one of the most successful shops was the pawn broker's.[98] At Ruhleben, the main shopping street was known as "Bond Street," and one could purchase a variety of services and goods. In a letter to his wife written in 1916, Gilbert Graham recognized that there were benefits to captivity:

> I am finished with the Dentist who has done a wonderfully fine job for me. He is one of ourselves and has a surgery which we fitted up and equipped for him with all the most modern appliances. I now no longer have to wear a plate as everything is now arranged by gold bridges fitted on to my own

This snapshot from Ruhleben in Germany shows one of the prisoners who took the opportunity of setting up shop in camp. *Documentariecentrum Ieper, In Flanders Fields Museum.*

strong teeth. . . . This man who is a specialist in high class mechanical work of that nature did it for me for four hundred and forty marks.[99]

Not only were services provided to internees by internees, but many of the clothes, furniture, and everyday products used in camp were produced by internees. At Knockaloe, a tailoring department turned out most of the socks, towels, shirts, etc., and at many of the camps around the globe, gardens were tended by internees. In France, camps had a variety of workshops—bakeries, brickworks, and a clog-making workshop.[100] In fact, the French, German, and British camps, all used wooden clogs for their internees, as they were the only suitable footwear for the often muddy and poorly drained camps.

In addition to the mercantile and craft pursuits in camps, other entertainments sprang to life in these miniature camp cities, including sporting clubs, theaters, musical ensembles, debating clubs, and universities. At Ruhleben, "Grand Stand University" offered a whole range of courses in natural sciences and the humanities, and some men in camp gained degrees, qualified for Oxford or Cambridge, or learned new languages. Books loaned from the Royal Library in Berlin or donated from outside sources helped boost the curriculum offered.[101] Pirenne taught history courses at both Crefeld and Holzminden, and he was delighted at the large turnout for his lectures and the attendees' "exemplary attention." The camp also allowed university studies for women in the camp—Pirenne signed on to do history, with other professors taking responsibility for additional subjects. For Pirenne, his most important project was the Belgian history course he began on June 16, 1916, whose audience felt to him comfortably "familial and national"—a bit of Belgium "transplanted here."[102]

Like Pirenne, other experts who were used to lives of conversation and scholarship shared their knowledge with fellow internees or tried to pursue their studies. At Ruhleben, 23-year-old James Chadwick and 19-year-old Charles Ellis set up a physics laboratory by depending on the generosity of German scholars such as Lise Meitner and Max Planck, who donated equipment for the internment camp. They also created instruments from objects in the camp when necessary, and Chadwick taught a course in camp on "radio-activity." While interned, the two young men "worked on the ionization which occurs in the oxidation of phosphorus and also on photo-chemical reaction of carbon monoxide and chlorine," and after the war, each pursued successful careers as scientists. In fact, Chadwick won the Nobel Prize in Physics in 1935 for discovering the neutron.[103]

Theater was a surprisingly omnipresent feature of civilian and military prisoner camps. The camp theaters, often built with charitable donations or with proceeds from camp canteens, produced a variety of fare, from "high" theater to pantomime and musical theater. All the costumes and scenery for these productions were manufactured by the internees, and men usually performed all the parts. Popular plays included works by George Bernard Shaw, Henrik Ibsen, and Gotthold Lessing (especially Minna von Barnhelm), but theater companies chose plays their audiences could recognize. The Ruhleben Irish Players performed a lot of Irish drama, including Playboy of the Western World, Spreading the News, and Cathleen Ni Houlihan.[104] Many of the productions were open to the public, as with Ruhleben's production of The Mikado at New Year's 1917, mentioned in multiple memoirs, diaries, and letters. The camp produced the popular operetta (and a parody called "The Makeado") with Ernest Macmillan conducting. Macmillan, only twenty-three years old at the time, later went on to become the conductor of the Toronto Symphony and a composer. The star of the show was 41-year-old George Webber, an opera singer and conductor. He maintained later in life that one of his "greatest triumphs . . . was in singing the role of the Mikado at the internment camp at Ruhleben with Sir Ernest Macmillan conducting."[105] These theatrical productions were written up in a plethora of camp magazines, which were a mix of political commentary, literary and cultural pieces, gossip, advertising, and sport reporting. Some of the journals were handwritten and poorly produced, while others were typeset and printed, with large circulations inside the camps and to family and friends in the outside world.

Sport was also a consuming passion for some in the camps because it combated a sense of physical inertia and created a sense of camaraderie. A sailor whose merchant ship had been captured in a German harbor was excited to find daily football and rugby matches as well as games such as "leap-frog" when he arrived at Ruhleben in November 1914.[106] Another Ruhlebenite appreciated not only the boxing, football, and cricket matches but also the fact that a well-known footballer, Steve Bloomer, was interned there as well.[107] Camps developed facilities for sporting events, including tennis courts, golf pitches, and badminton courts. At Berrima, internees spent most of their days in the mild climate of New South Wales on the river—swimming, boating, resting on the banks. At Knockaloe, a recreation field was provided for each of the four camp compounds, and Douglas had a large swimming pool for its internees.[108] Bored internees developed their own fitness plans; for example, Joseph Pilates created the basics for his popular exercise program while interned at Knockaloe in the First World War. Pilates, born in Germany to Greek parents, was traveling in England with a circus when he was interned as an enemy alien. To amuse himself in camp, he tutored fellow inmates in wrestling and self-defense while compiling the exercises that would later make up his "contrology" series.[109]

Sometimes work itself could be a way to stave off boredom. During later years of the war, many internees were paroled outside camp for agricultural work; this was true in France, Germany, Russia, Canada, and Australia, for example. Canadian internees wintering in Banff provided work for the city by building a toboggan run and "an elaborate ice palace, complete with interior maze, for the Banff winter carnival."[110] For Pirenne and Fredericq, who were moved in fall 1916 from their internment camps to the university town of Jena and interned in a local hotel, the lack of activity after the stimulation of the camps was hard to accept. When they were separated again the following year, Pirenne vowed to fight his feeling of isolation and uselessness by setting a strict work schedule for his days. He began the mornings studying Russian, then took a long walk after lunch, and spent his evenings working on a manuscript, which became a social and economic history of Europe. As he wrote in his diary, these occupations "constructed a barrier to a wandering imagination, calmed anxieties and dispelled boredom."[111]

Finding occupation was extraordinarily important for combating the "barbed wire sickness" that began appearing in the camps. This illness, which manifested itself in a variety of ways, arose when the strain of captivity became too much for an individual. Quaker James Baily described the symptoms as "moroseness, avoidance of others, and an aimless promenading up and down the barbed-wire boundary of the compound, like a wild animal in a cage."[112] An internee in the United States wrote in the Camp Oglethorpe magazine, "All of those who have spent more than a short time behind barbed wire are more or less crazy and peculiar things grow out of their lame imaginations," but he thought hobbies helped, since the idle had brains "more certain to petrify."[113] Barbed wire psychosis was no imagined malady. According to the Swiss doctor A. L. Vischer, who published a paper about it in 1917 based on interviews with prisoners, the illness led to irritability, memory loss, and other abnormal behaviors.[114] Even those who didn't have "clinical" symptoms of barbed wire disease got tired of their lack of privacy, their confined space, and the monotony of camp life. Paul Cohen-Portheim explained in his memoir, "It is not the men of bad character or morals you begin to hate, but the men who draw their soup through their teeth, [and] clean their ears with their fingers at dinner."[115] All the prisoners agreed—time was the enemy and occupation or distraction was their friend.

For those who could not find occupation for themselves, trouble usually followed. Serious riots occurred in some camps, and in some areas, gangs developed to prey on other prisoners. In the Australian camp at Holdsworthy (Liverpool), a camp mafia developed that called itself the Black Hand Society. Several dozen men joined the association and spent their time forcing others to pay for "protection." A change finally came when a group of new internees was brutally beaten when they arrived in April 1916, and with the tacit agreement of camp officials, a group of prisoners "took revenge on their tormentors who had now become victims themselves. Some twenty Black Handers were beaten up and the bodies were thrown over the seven foot-high fence to the feet of Commandant Sands and his officers who had been observing what was happening in the camp from just outside the camp gate." One of the Black Hand members died, several others were treated for severe injuries, and their reign of terror ended.[116] At other camps, more spontaneous violence erupted as at Knockaloe Camp III in October 1916, when "stone-throwing and hooliganism" ensued over a long weekend period, followed by the brutal beating of three internee "captains" in the camp.[117] E. C. Kny, chairman of the Central Committee at Knockaloe Camp 4, was attacked several times by prisoners who thought he was too pro-British and too accommodating to camp authorities, and "on at least one occasion the attack assumed grave proportions."[118]

Some camps witnessed endemic problems, such as Fort Douglas in Utah. Preferential treatment of military prisoners at the camp, including better recreation facilities and new clothes, led to simmering resentment among civilians. Strikes, rallies, and even fire bombs in the barracks soon followed, with the last straw being the discovery of a plot to blow up the guard towers. Force and solitary confinement became the order of the day for troublemakers, and calm never really emerged. As William Glidden recorded, "Fort Douglas was the worst of the camps, and in time it came to resemble more of a combat zone than a detention center."[119] In France, special disciplinary camps were created for habitually uncontrollable offenders, while minor problems continued in the other camps. For example, female prostitutes interned at Précigné had to be moved because of widespread fraternization with the guards, and at this same camp, internees poisoned the guard dogs deployed to stop escape attempts.[120]

Disciplinary problems took several forms, with the most common being hunger strikes or demonstrations over food, refusals to work or to line up for inspections, and escape attempts. In some camps, escapes were more common. Although several tried to escape the Isle of Man camps primarily through a series of tunneling attempts, none succeeded in getting off the island. At Ruhleben, Geoffrey Pyke and Edward Falk escaped in July 1915, then made their way to the Dutch border by train and foot.[121] One of the most dramatic escapes came in New Zealand, where Felix von Luckner and a group of prisoners stole the commandant's launch in order to escape from the internment camp of Motuihe Island. They were at liberty for about a week before being recaptured.[122] Several of the internees in the Canadian parks eluded guards and escaped, probably trying to improve their conditions and get out of the harsh climate and long work days that were their lot.[123] Work stoppages and strikes also broke out in camps in multiple countries, and it was not uncommon for internees to need institutionalization for nervous breakdowns or attempted suicide.

The emotional toll of civilian internment could be severe, and one of the worst parts for many was separation from family, friends, and communities. Particularly hard for many of the men was the thought that their families had no provider while the war continued or that wives would be forced into work, and indeed, destitution among wives and children of internees was rampant. Despite schemes for charity such as those designed by the Society of Friends in Great Britain or "family camps" for internee families such as Bourke in Australia, hundreds of thousands of families found themselves without means, sometimes in strange countries, given the common policy of deporting women and children. These families also faced violence from their neighbors, especially in periods when propaganda battles raged. As Lotte Hahn wrote in a letter to the governor-general in Australia,

> Being an Alien Subject and in deep trouble, I am writing asking your help and protection. My landlord has given me notice to leave the cottage with my three little children, because I am a German. The prejudice here is so

bitter that I cannot send my two little boys to school. . . . I beg of you to have me and my children interned with my husband.[124]

While short visits were allowed to the camps, for most distance, cost, and the war itself made visiting impossible. YMCA secretary Conrad Hoffman poignantly described the emotional cost of family separation, saying that when he brought his four-year-old daughter with him on a German camp visit, the men all wanted to see her, give her treats, and hold her on their knees. "As we left the camp the little one asked me why the men had cried, and I told her that no doubt they had been thinking of their own little girls and boys at home."[125] In some cases the men chided their wives for not writing more often, as with R. H. Sauter, who was interned at Alexandra Palace Camp in Britain:

It is not the time—to most people, time has almost ceased to exist, except for the regular beating of the inevitable food-clock . . . Herrings—bacon— nothing: Herrings—bacon—nothing . . . and the weekly chime of a short two hours visit to brighten the day. No, not the time: but the waiting, the tension, the suppressed excitement. . . . I wonder if there are many of the wives who so little realize what the lack of that of those few short words means, whose correspondence is so shut off from the outside.[126]

The interned men may have missed their families, but they also developed ways of coping emotionally with the strain of camp life. Many formed lifelong friendships with other internees, through bonds formed by shared living space, theatrics, and clubs. Others developed intense same-sex relationships, and in all the camps, the female impersonators of the camp theaters received much lavish attention. In Russian camps, for instance, performers in drag "received passionate poems and letters from other prisoners on a regular basis."[127] Paul Cohen-Portheim called these "affectionate friendships" almost inevitable, and many of the internees saw the ideals of fraternal bonding in the domestic arrangements that developed, often between elder and younger men. Some sexual encounters undoubtedly occurred despite the lack of privacy, and camp records do show disciplinary actions taken after complaints about "unnatural conduct" and the forcing of "pederastic and homosexual desires upon

... fellow internees."[128] However, few mention sex in relationship to the camps in their writing about internment, and the camp administrations themselves often acted as if sex was not an issue.[129]

Conclusion

For those who survived civilian internment with their health (especially after the influenza epidemic of 1918), the postwar period was not always easy. The sense of choice in shops, the spaciousness, the privacy of homes—all of these were unfamiliar sensations. Paul Cohen-Portheim describes the months he spent at partial liberty in Holland with former internees, noting that "we dared not stand alone and face the unknown." Cohen-Portheim, like Gilbert Graham, suffered from vivid dreams and a terrible sense that he did not know how to regain his "self."[130] Graham and Cohen-Portheim both awaited release in neutral Holland, unable to find a place where they felt comfortable. As Graham wrote to his wife about another change in lodging, "I am really very glad that I have made the change, because although at first I had a great desire to be absolutely alone, I began to find it rather trying." And, of course, he could not quite shake "these rotten Ruhleben dreams" of being sent back to the camp.[131]

Cohen-Portheim's and Graham's dreams attest to the immediate aftermath of incarceration, but more nightmarish was the continued internment of some internees after the armistice or their forced repatriation/deportation to the nations from which they had immigrated. Many of the internment camps only ceased operation in 1920–1921, when treaties and release arrangements were all tied up. At the British-run internment camp for Ottoman prisoners at St. Clement's, Malta, Lt. Col. H. A. Strachan tried to keep order while the slow repatriation process continued into the early 1920s. Strachan wrote to the quartermaster general in February 1920 that the prisoners were angry at their continued incarceration, and he said that they responded by refusing to work, breaking crockery, and damaging equipment. One inmate of St. Clement's explained the problem of continued imprisonment after the war had ended in a 1919 letter to Strachan:

Internees at St. Clement's Camp in Malta amuse themselves and try to stave off boredom. St. Clement's was one of the camps that did not close down until well after the end of the war, in the early 1920s. *Library of Congress.*

Once I led a peaceful and modest life working hard as a bank clerk in order to earn a living for me and my wife, till I came to Malta as a P.o.W. . . . to-day I am a dying man and I feel I shall not live till next spring if I have to remain here another winter—the sixth already in Malta. . . . I have not seen my wife for seven years, [and] five years imprisonment have deprived me of all means to support her, . . . I have to live in close confinement without any friends.[132]

James Baily thought the last year at Knockaloe was the worst of the war, especially given what he called "the stupid and cruel attitude taken by the Government Office in Douglas" who refused Christmas trees and extra food to the internees in December 1918.[133] For those who were released, the months and years of reestablishing themselves in a new country, claiming property confiscated during the war, finding work, and reacquainting themselves with their families had just begun. Those who landed in Germany in the midst or aftermath of revolution or in newly minted nations of Eastern Europe had a particularly rough time.

For those who were released and who got permission to stay in the countries in which they were interned, prejudice often followed. Friedrich Machotka, finally released from internment in late 1919, got a job as the head gardener at an Australian property, but lost the job when anonymous threats to his employer for hiring a "Hun" led to his dismissal. Later, the employer set up a different arrangement whereby Machotka bought land and ran a farm in Berrima with this employer's support, but sadly, a weakened constitution from the war years and a rough winter storm led to Machotka's early death in July 1921. His wife and four children (one of whom had been born in internment at Berrima) were forced to sell their land and move back to her home in Los Angeles, California.[134]

The concentration camps built in 1914–1918 were often utilized again in the Second World War, and internment camps were a feature of the Spanish Civil War as well as subsequent twentieth-century conflicts. While nowhere near as brutal as many of the subsequent concentration camps experiences nor as deliberately harmful, internment camps of World War I were a rehearsal for later policies. As Heather Jones has written, "It was in these camps during the First World War that states gained the know-how regarding how to build, house and confine large numbers of military men."[135] In many ways, the First World War functioned as a "practice run" for the use of prisoner labor in national and local economies, for forced work schemes, for food rationing and supply, and for the management of large-scale prisoner camps.

For the real people involved in internment during World War I, they were civilians, yet they were militarized as well, a cog in the war machine living neither behind the lines officially nor at the front but in a true "No Man's Land" of barbed wire enclosures. Paul Cohen-Portheim captured this in-between feeling perhaps best when writing of the sense of "complete futility" internees experienced: "The civilian prisoners were an uncomfortable sideshow and, at a time when numbers were everything, not important enough to bother about. . . . [For internees] there is no leave, there is no 'behind the line,' there is no dismissal."[136] The ultimate victory for civilian internees after the war was a modest goal, which Gilbert Graham outlined for his wife: "Merely to maintain one's equilibrium and not to become demoralised is somewhat of an achievement under the circumstances."[137]

[8]

Civil War and Revolution

Rumour has it that the strikers wanted to blow up the Renault munitions factory last night. We are living on a volcano and everyone is complaining. The example of the Russians bodes no good.

—French Postal Censors' Report on Morale, 1917[1]

Between August 1914 and the signing of the peace treaty in June 1919, civil revolts, rioting, and revolutions broke out in dozens of countries around the world as the strain of wartime demands pushed crowds to desperate actions while also creating opportunities for dissident groups. Because many of these disturbances were civilian in nature, they have often been treated as separate from the war, but in fact, most of them were shaped fundamentally by the events of 1914–1918. Historians have categorized revolutions and revolts as "civilian" and as separate from the First World War for a century. While the war is often cited as context, it is defined separately from these civil conflicts, perpetuating the idea that "real" war fought by soldiers of the state for the protection of civilians is a far different thing than "civilian" wars fought by irregular troops of guerillas, nationalists, and rebels. This chapter tries to integrate civil conflict into the larger narrative of the civilian experience of the war, suggesting that these violent confrontations were born of wartime militarization of whole populations. Civilians, adjusted to lives of violence, perpetuated the violence in attempting to reconstruct their societies in the midst of and in the aftermath of war.

War weariness and economic distress helped create an environment in which violence appeared to be the answer to a whole host of woes, while militarization of society and prevalent war rhetoric engendered violence as a means to solve all sorts of problems. The revolts, disturbances, and revolutions of the war period and its immediate aftermath varied widely in intensity, violence, and impact, but all pointed to the destabilizing forces unleashed in societies around the world by the years of industrialized warfare. The conflicts can be grouped mainly around three large themes: (1) identity politics (race, ethnicity, nationalism); (2) social and political revolution; and (3) anticolonial revolts, which include conscription and antiwar concerns. In all cases, men and women, civilians and soldiers were drawn into the fray, and many conflicts were either complicated or prolonged by the needs of the wartime situation. This chapter will briefly examine some of these wars within the war, demonstrating that violence was never limited to the formal battle fronts nor to regular soldiers.

Identity Politics

World War I called into question expressions of identity on a number of levels around the world. National or colonial allegiance, racial and sexual identity, age, ethnicity, personal loyalty—all these concepts were tested as millions of civilians were mobilized to serve the needs of states at war. Some of the first tensions regarding identity emerged at the personal level as families and individuals sought to cope with the demands of the state for their sacrifices. These personal identity struggles played out in a variety of private and public situations, in the form of pension applications, conscientious objectors' entreaties, and drawing-room battles. For families with divided loyalties regarding the war, assertion of a united identity was often impossible, and this led to cleavages. Even in families or communities with the same surface loyalty, different interpretations of war, sacrifice, and patriotism could spark tensions or even violence. War meant choosing sides and taking stands, and for individuals, the expression of individual loyalties was often the first hard task.

As for larger-scale identity politics, communities at war fragmented along a number of lines; most commonly, the fractures appeared over questions of class, race, ethnicity, language, nation, gender, and religion. As war made demands on society, the fragile bonds connecting people together often were severed, and differences became a focal point for the violence and bitterness of war. In France, for example, the importation of colonial and foreign workers led to workplace violence, escalating personal attacks in the streets, and, in some cases, collective violence or rioting. As historian Tyler Stovall has written about these attacks, the patterns of racial violence suggest a close correspondence with "the crisis of morale and the rise of war weariness in France" but also with a wave of strikes and working-class agitation after 1917.[2] In this case, race might have served as a visible marker of other anxieties surrounding class status or gender issues such as protection of French women, who had entered the workplace in larger numbers by 1917. Uncertainty over jobs certainly fueled much fear in the minds of male workers at the front and behind the lines.

Indeed, workers' agitation and strikes, along with subsistence riots, were a staple of the latter years of the war in almost all nations involved in the conflict, even those on the periphery, such as Argentina, Chile, and Peru.[3] In Germany, France, Russia, Austria-Hungary, and Britain, industrial strikes undermined the war effort, and bread riots also contributed to a dangerous atmosphere in cities. Unemployment was a significant problem in many urban areas in 1919, and strikes were common occurrences in large cities such as Paris and London in the latter years of the war and into the early postwar period. Even combatant countries far from the physical damage of the war, such as the United States and Australia, faced significant labor unrest. For instance, a general strike in Sydney shut down much of the city for the month of August in 1917, while in the United States a civilian "Protective League" deported and interned an estimated twelve hundred men, women, and children in New Mexico in order to stop a mining strike in Bisbee, Arizona, in 1917.[4]

Those on the margins of society—foreigners, Jews, gypsies, and refugees—were often most at risk in the violence that sometimes ensued from labor agitation or civil war. As historian Christopher Capozzola has observed, sometimes the line between national defense or patriotic vigilance and vigilante violence was blurred. War's emphasis on sacrifice and vigilance fed the flames of extra-legal justice.[5] In the United States the reorganization of the Ku Klux Klan in 1915 and a wave of anti-German sentiment led to lynchings and other violence against minority groups and perceived internal enemies. Such mob violence was only exacerbated with conscription in 1917, when African Americans and recent immigrants were called to national service alongside "white Americans." The concentration of young men of all races in training camps around the country led to clashes with civilian populations near the camps. This violence did not stop with the end of the war, and in fact, it escalated in the immediate aftermath with race riots throughout the country between 1919 and 1922. In 1919 alone, there were more than twenty-five documented race riots in U.S. cities, from Chicago to Washington, D.C., to Tulsa to Omaha.[6]

Racial, religious, and ethnic violence became particularly severe and prolonged in regions where order had completely collapsed, such as the Russian/Austro-Hungarian borderlands. In East Galicia, which had suffered through occupations by more than one army over the course of the war, violence followed in 1918 amidst terrible economic hardships and lack of effective leadership. Armed bands of looters, army deserters, and criminals terrorized villages and towns, while quickly formed paramilitaries sought to regain control. In the Polish-Ukrainian border wars that plagued the region in late 1918, Jews tried to remain "neutral," but this policy was a dismal failure, with Jews targeted again and again by both sides in the conflict. In one of the most egregious episodes of the conflict, Polish forces attacked the Jewish community in L'viv over several days in November 1918. The pogrom resulted in hundreds of casualties, including more than a hundred dead. In addition to the human casualties, the pogrom led to property damage and the loss of irreplaceable historical buildings and artifacts (including a seventeenth-century synagogue).[7] A prominent scholar of the event, Carol Fink, called the 1918 attack on L'viv "the most prolonged and extensive carnage against civilians in Eastern Europe since 1906."[8] Despite an international investigation of this incident, violence against Jews continued, especially as a feature of the Soviet war with Poland and the Ukraine between 1919 and 1921.

Spontaneous violence in regions still more or less at war continued into the 1920s, but a more calculated unrest also resulted from the war. In some regions occupied by foreign powers, the wartime occupation policies had sought to inflame racial or ethnic tensions, or to create collabo-

Flemish activists in Belgium march with their slogan "Flanders for the Flemish." German occupiers encouraged the split between Flemish and French speakers in Belgium during World War I, fueling a dispute that continues into the twenty-first century. *U.S. Signal Corps, National Archives and Records Administration.*

rators among certain groups in the occupied zones. German occupiers in Belgium encouraged the development of Flemish separatism, arguing that the Flemish speakers were "Germanic" and belonged as allies of the Germans. The occupiers targeted young Flemish-speaking men in internment or POW camps in Germany but also tried to create Flemish-only laws within occupied Belgium. In Ghent, they closed the French-language university and opened it again only for Flemish-language coursework. Flemish activism and sense of separateness from the French-speaking Belgian communities existed prior to the war, but the occupation policies ignited many of the issues that had only simmered before. At one point in the war, opportunistic Flemish leaders tried to declare an independent Flemish nation, but the Germans balked at such autonomy, wanting only Flemish allegiance to a German federation. With the end of the war and the return of the Belgian king, Flemish activism was checked (at least temporarily), but Belgium's postwar political decisions reflected an ever-increasing politicization of identity politics surrounding issues of language, national identity, war service, and collaboration.[9]

Nationalism created tense political standoffs even in areas that were counted among the victors in the war, particularly when the promises of wartime diplomacy failed to deliver land or concessions that were expected by weary civilian populations. Hans Ulrich Gumbrecht described this process in Italy as a perceived "national slight." Allied promises that Trieste would become a free city and that Italy would gain territory in Dalmatia disappeared in the postwar peace negotiations, leaving Italians feeling angry and betrayed. The subsequent uprising, an odd occupation of the city of Fiume (now in Croatia) by poet Gabriele d'Annunzio and a band of rebels in September 1919, symbolized Italy's sacrifices and its postwar claims. Gumbrecht cites d'Annunzio, who captured this sentiment in his public speeches: "Not only has our war not ended—it has only now reached its climax."[10] D'Annunzio's claims initially captured Italian and world attention and some measure of sympathy, but as the crisis unfolded, civilians in the city fled to avoid Italian dictatorship and privation. Throughout 1920, those civilians still living in the city itself turned on d'Annunzio and helped undermine public support outside of Fiume for this action.[11] Civilian nationalism in the aftermath of World War I helped create the Fiume revolt while civilian nationalism in response to the revolt helped end it.

In other areas with complicated linguistic and cultural divides, the war led to tension over citizenship and war patriotism as well. Canada had to call in troops to pacify a rebellion in Quebec in 1918 after the nation introduced mandatory conscription. The "Easter Riots" of March and April 1918 in Quebec City and other parts of Quebec province led to property destruction and more than 150 casualties before the state reestablished control by declaring martial law and putting an occupying military force in place until spring 1919. As historian Martin Auger wrote, "It was, at the time, the largest military force ever assembled in aid to the civil powers in Canada."[12] The suppression of these anticonscription riots meant that the draft was established in all provinces of Canada, but it also helped quell the possibility of a larger civil uprising in 1918 or 1919 amid fears of bolshevism and Quebecois nationalism.[13] As in Belgium, revolution did not follow the war, but the linguistic, cultural, and political divides deepened with the actions of the wartime state.

While Canada struggled with its attempt to introduce conscription, other regions of the world dealt with social transformations from foreign occupation. The presence of wartime settlers in occupied zones often reconfigured societies to meet the needs of occupiers disrupting social, religious, and political traditions. Japan's occupation of Micronesia during the war led to a "Japanization" of society with mandatory Japanese-language training, Japanese-style education, and an aggressive policy for moving Japanese, Okinawan, and Korean settlers to the islands. By 1920, just over a quarter of the population of the major town of Saipan was Japanese.[14] Similarly, in the German occupied Ober Ost (Baltic region), the long-term impact of German "reshaping" policies was hard to calculate since the Germans had classified, regulated, and moved populations to fit its notion of order. Ultimately, though, German attempts to "Germanize" the region with university and secondary educational institutions, German-language publications, and intense propaganda failed. Instead, historian Vejas Liulevicius suggests that the postwar Freikorps violence in the zone expressed better the German crisis of identity occasioned by defeat in the war rather than a crisis among the multicultural populations of the Ober Ost.[15] Yet regardless of whether these occupation policies failed or succeeded, in every case the attempts at social engineering led to dislocations and conflicts.

Clearly the war sparked identity crises for many of the individuals and communities involved as they sought to make sense of victory or defeat, the dissolution of empires, and the assumed return to normalcy. The forces unleashed by World War I shaped the twentieth century, often lighting the fuse for conflicts that would simmer well into the contemporary period. In some cases, however, the resentments and perceived injustices of the war boiled over into outright revolutions or civil wars in the midst of the First World War and in its aftermath.

Revolution

The most significant of these was the Russian Revolution of 1917, a crisis sparked by and shaped by the First World War. The first stage of the revolution in February 1917 (Russian calendar) began after a series of shortages, strikes, and unrest surrounding food and work pressures.

The catalyst was a demonstration marking International Women's Day in one district of St. Petersburg.[16] These food demonstrations were not necessarily more severe than or markedly different from those in Berlin or Vienna during the war, but what made them escalate to revolution was the Russian Empire's political failure in managing the wartime mobilization of resources effectively.[17] Added to this was the difficulty in mobilizing and sustaining a population largely "disengaged from the war effort," especially by 1917.[18] The combination of poor central war planning, lack of rationing, and tensions based on class and ethnicity helped the Russian riots escalate into a full-scale conflict in 1917.

Eyewitness Countess O. V. Bennigsen described the early days of the revolution in a town near St. Petersburg:

> In the afternoon of the 27th [February] processions of workers and large crowds of people were passing along. . . . [They] carried banners, sang but without causing any serious disturbances. . . . On March 2, as soon as I and my mother woke up our maid came running into our room saying: "Mistress, soldiers are coming along the street with red banners and machine guns." . . . There were also women in the motor cars; they also carried cartridges, revolvers and were sitting arm in arm with the soldiers; they were yelling and waving small red banners.[19]

As Bennigsen described it, the revolution incorporated a disparate group of angry women, weary soldiers, and disaffected workers into a revolutionary crowd, which seized rail stations, munitions, and public buildings.

Perceived inequities in distribution and ineptitude by wartime leaders probably fueled support for movements calling for an end to the tsarist regime and to the eventual rise of a Socialist solution.[20] Civilian perceptions that their needs were not being met reflected the reality of grain shortages, rising prices for food and fuel, and very unorganized (and only localized) food controls and rationing. The Russian government made the decision not to ration in a nationwide manner, which most other combatant nations were doing, and tried to control producers instead. This was a disastrous policy that alienated rural producers and probably contributed to shortages. By 1917, civilians felt justified in believing that the "tsarist regime made only haphazard provision for civilian consumers."[21] As housewives, workers, and soldiers joined forces in the street, the tsar abdicated in favor of his brother, who chose not to accept the invitation. Sheila Fitzpatrick described this surprising turn of events in spring 1917, noting that "[d]e facto, then, Russia was no longer a monarchy."[22] Civil unrest that many felt would topple the current tsar, but not destroy the monarchy entirely, suddenly led to a politically unstable and volatile situation in wartime Russia.

The February Revolution led not just to the abdication of the tsar and the creation of a provisional government at the national level but also, and importantly, to a radicalized local soviet system, particularly in Petrograd. The two saw themselves with different tasks and constituencies, but they also clashed over how to manage the war and the economic problems. Continuing tensions between these two "authorities" helped create a situation for a second phase of revolution in October, with the Bolshevik coup.[23] The German interest in fomenting rebellion among its enemies contributed, with Germany helping to provide transport for Vladimir Lenin and other Bolsheviks in exile to return to Russia. Here too the war played a role, as the pressures that had sparked the February Revolution had not disappeared, and the provisional government continued to try to fight the war. Many civilians and soldiers alike had expected that the February Revolution would lead to an end of war. Instead, the provisional government launched a war loan drive in spring 1917, and it "ro dedicated the country to the cause of war," which became its most damaging mistake.[24]

As the months progressed, and the war did not end, morale plummeted in army training camps, rural villages, and urban workplaces. Dissent within army units deepened as well, inspiring the institution of Order Number 1 by the Petrograd Soviet, which called for election of officers and "democratization of the Army."[25] This order sparked class conflict and violence in some units of the army, exacerbating problems with discipline and morale. Added to these underlying problems, the disastrous failure of a summer offensive in Galicia led to hundreds of thousands of casualties, sparking mass desertions and major unrest. Demonstrations in Petrograd during the "July Days" highlighted the ongoing wartime pressures and dissatisfaction with the provisional government's policies, setting the stage for further revolutionary activity in October.[26] Led by the Petrograd Soviet and a small vanguard of Bolsheviks, the October Revolution toppled the provisional government and attempted to create a workers' state. Revolutionaries occupied governmental offices in Petrograd and surrounded the Winter Palace in a coordinated series of actions, leading to a mostly bloodless coup.[27] By the end of the month, Lenin had established a one-party system with himself at the head, and he called for an armistice on November 19, 1917.[28]

Despite the Bolshevik success in ending the Russian role in World War I by March 1918, their October Revolution unleashed more violence than it cured. The Treaty of Brest-Litovsk ceded Russian territory in Poland, Ukraine, Belarus, and the Baltic to its wartime enemies, setting the stage for nationalist struggles and eventually civil war within the Soviet Union and in these former territories. Estonia, Latvia, Lithuania, and Finland all declared independence in 1918 with the withdrawal of the armies of the Central Powers, and in many cases, German authorities set up local administrative bodies to provide a semblance of "national self-determination."[29] The promise of independence, however tentative, combined with the disintegration of the Central Powers' authority on the eastern front and led to a situation in which many nationalist groups sought permanent autonomy. Soviet forces hoping to reabsorb these territories found themselves fighting multiple insurgencies throughout the Baltic areas, Poland, Belarus, and Ukraine as well as civil war within their own borders by the early 1920s.[30]

The civil wars and rebellions that broke out in 1918 and 1919 lasted well into the early 1920s, in effect extending the war beyond the "peace" in the Soviet Union.[31] As Peter Holquist has astutely noted, the "Soviet Union never really demobilized from 'total mobilization'. . . . [T]he remobilization of society for revolution continued for several decades longer."[32] Those hurt most by this unending state of war were civilians, many of whom faced starvation from 1916 to the 1920s. While hardships abounded, the war itself probably made possible the intensity and length of the civil wars that followed. The 1917 revolution benefited enormously from the wartime militarization of society that had already regulated much economic activity, and Bolshevik leaders quickly understood that they already had an "apparatus capable of being deployed for revolution-

Polish children wait for soup from the American Relief Administration after World War I, as civil war continues to create hardships for civilians. *Herbert Hoover Presidential Library.*

ary work."[33] In many ways this continuing societal mobilization made it possible for the Soviets to fight the civil wars that would fester until the early 1920s.

One result of the "success" of the October Revolution was a fear among other nations in Europe that international Marxism was on the march. The fear that Bolshevik sentiment might spread and infect countries around Europe and Asia was not unfounded. Even in tiny Luxembourg, which had spent the entire war under German occupation, a group of revolutionaries proclaimed a republic and created a Committee of Public Safety in Luxembourg City in November 1918. Demanding the dissolution of the monarchy, leftists sought to use the end of the war crisis and the perceived Germanophilia of the grand duchess, Marie Adélaïde, to reshape the political and social order. The short revolt was abruptly stopped by the threat of French troops, which the revolutionaries called a fratricidal act, and the abdication of the grand duchess in favor of her younger sister, Charlotte.[34] Like Luxembourg, the neutral Netherlands also experienced a few days of revolutionary tumult in November 1918. Led by Social Democrat Pieter Troelstra, meetings and processions calling for revolutionary change escalated with a march to military barracks in Amsterdam on November 14. Shots were fired from the barracks into the crowd, killing a handful of people and injuring a dozen more. What looked like a possible revolutionary impetus ended abruptly by November 18, with the threat by the Allies of an end to the importation of food into the Netherlands. On the 18th, a large pro-monarchical demonstration was staged at the Hague to reaffirm "the popularity of the Queen."[35]

In nearby occupied Belgium, Belgian Socialists joined German soldiers with red flags in the streets in early November as well. A Brussels diarist described the scenes of November 9–11, 1918:

> The Kaiser has abdicated & the Kronprinz has renounced the throne! ... Bavaria has proclaimed the Republic. . . . All the big military men have vanished & the soldiers are doing as they like. They hoisted the red flag on the ministères, plucked off their German imperial insignia from caps & uniforms & threw them on the ground. . . . Mme W went to Louvain to-day with Vollenhoven, in his motor. She says the "revolution" there was much more serious than here. There was firing in the streets, the soldiers stopped them several times, wanting to take the motor, but refrained, as it was the Dutch minister's....Weareanxiousaboutwhatmayensue...thereisnotsufficientpolice, no established authority here just now, capable of controlling the masses. . . . [S]ome Belgian Socialists having manifested against the King . . . the revolutionary movement may spread amongst the Belgians. I consider that if the armistice is signed, we should have a powerful military Allies' forces here <u>at once</u>, to keep the Germans & our socialists in order, & make the former realise that we master the situation & "boss the show" now.[36]

In Belgium much of the revolutionary tumult ended with the departure of German troops and the triumphal return of King Albert and his family. Other nations suffered much longer from the revolutionary chaos of the war's end.

In Hungary, three successive waves of revolution and a period of foreign occupation followed the collapse of the Habsburg Empire in 1918. The first stage, a moderate revolution with a coalition government, gave way to Communist Bela Kun's new pro-Bolshevik republic in Hungary in March 1919. This second coup led to the Hungarian invasion of parts of Slovakia and the establishment of a Soviet Republic there as well.[37] It also sparked a showdown with nearby Romania, who occupied Budapest for several months, ignoring demands by its allies that it leave.[38] Finally, a popular counterrevolution helped defeat Kun in November 1919, leaving a new state under a military dictator, Admiral Miklós Horthy, who would remain in control of Hungary until 1944.[39]

Other regions in the Balkans saw civil unrest or continuation of wartime situations, such as Greece, Bulgaria, Romania, and the Balkan coast. War between Greek forces and Turkish troops lasted until 1923, creating millions of refugees and forced migrants, reopening old wounds from the Balkan wars of 1912 and 1913.[40] Guerilla fighters in the mountains of Montenegro battled Austrians and Bulgarians in an armed resistance movement that began in 1916. The fighting eventually culminated in the Toplice Rebellion of February 1917, in which more than twenty thousand civilians perished in the quelling of the uprising.[41]

Various national armies invaded nearby territories in all these conflicts in order to jockey for land in the peace treaties of 1919 and the following years. Italy, for instance, administered Trento, Trieste, and other coastal territories—an American ambassador described this occupation as organized chaos: "All Government had vanished in these regions save the military rule of the occupying Italian forces. All food-supplies had been exhausted, or were on the point of being so; and all the customary means of renewing such supplies had ceased to function."[42] At the same time, Italy was trying to maintain control of a volatile situation at home, where continued shortages and urban unrest were threatening the political status quo. By the end of the postwar conflicts in the Balkan region, a massive population shift had occurred in much of the eastern Mediterranean as a result of wartime violence and displacement, negotiated peace treaties that forced emigration of whole groups of people, and political change.

Perhaps unsurprisingly, the empires of the Central Powers dissolved in revolutionary activity in 1918 as well. Germany exploded in violence in

October and November 1918 as scarce resources and war weariness fueled popular anger and organized revolutionaries sought to extend the Communist revolution beyond Russia. The event that triggered the revolutionary wave was a sailors' mutiny in Kiel on November 3, 1918, but workers, soldiers, and housewives had all shown signs of discontent prior to this period; Kiel merely moved this vague and unorganized rage into a new stage. The wartime context, with its shortages, and increasing demands for loyalty and sacrifice, had led to widespread war weariness and disillusionment. As Richard Bessel has argued of the German situation in 1918, "In failing to provide the basic necessities to the working population, Germany's wartime rulers had broken the unspoken contract they had made with the German people at the outbreak of the war."[43] There was little loyalty left to the kaiser's regime by 1918.

The revolution in Leipzig is a good example of the ways in which authority crumbled in a number of locations throughout the Wilhelmine Empire in October and November 1918. In Leipzig, rioting and striking were common occurrences by the end of the war, but they intensified by October 1918 as the economic, military, and political situations deteriorated. That same month, Socialist groups began to call openly for revolution as elites seemed unable or unwilling to control the situation. News of the events in Kiel seemed to be the last straw. By the first days of November, not only had workers come out into the streets to protest, but they had been joined by sailors and soldiers. Leipzig's revolution officially began on November 8, and it inspired revolutionary activity in the nearby big cities of Dresden and Chemnitz as well as in many other small Saxon municipalities.[44] Australian Ethel Cooper recorded her reaction to seeing the hoisting of the red flag by soldiers in Leipzig, where she had been living during the war:

> Republic of Germany! . . . I have seen the red flag! I think long before this reaches you, you will have seen it too. It began last Monday—we read in the evening papers that the sailors in Kiel had risen, disarmed their officers, hoisted the red flag on all the ships, and that the Government had given in to practically all their demands. . . . On Tuesday and Wednesday, the other great ports, Lubech Bremen and Hamburg followed suit—on Thursday Munchen and with it all Bavaria.[45]

Marchers in 1918 Berlin carry placards with this demand: "Give back our fathers!" *Library of Congress.*

Cooper went on to talk about the development of worker and soldier councils and the abdication of the kaiser. When the peace terms were published, Cooper reflected with dismay on the depressing reality of continued blockade, noting that German civilians were just crushed and shocked. Cooper noted sadly, "I have not dared to speak to a German since, but one thing is clear to me—that everything must be accepted, and yet humanely speaking can't be fulfilled."[46] Cooper concisely summarized the problem, namely, that Germany had to accept peace conditions in order to end the Allied blockade and stave off starvation, but acceptance of Allied terms might further destabilize Germany itself and lead to other problems.

By the time Berlin's revolution occurred, Bremen, Hamburg, Württemberg, Saxony, Hanover, and Bavaria had already experienced revolutionary violence.[47] In the capital itself, women and radical youth were joined by workers in street demonstrations on November 9. Evelyn Blücher recorded in her war diary her impressions of the first stirrings of revolution in Berlin:

(24 Oct 1918) Last evening there was another demonstration going on under our windows, caused by the triumphal procession accompanying the notorious Socialist, Liebknecht, who has returned from prison, where he has been for the last two years. He was seated in a carriage with his wife, surrounded by flowers, and they drove slowly by the Reichstag and through some by-streets, landing finally at the Russian Embassy. There Liebknecht addressed his assembled friends in a speech tainted with Bolshevism. . . . (9 Nov 1918) And here we are right in the midst of the tumult of a great revolution. After all our expectations, it has in reality fallen on us like a bomb— the Kaiser's abdication and the revolution.[48]

She described mobs of soldiers and youth in the streets shouting, waving flags, and exhorting others to join their cause. As they sought a "bread peace," demonstrators demanded an end to war and privation. Many thought the 1918 revolt would lead to a widespread Socialist revolution that would transform German society. Instead it toppled the kaiser and his government, and it created a new republic replete with promises, albeit not the kind of revolutionary transformation for which many hoped.[49]

The crushing of these hopes led to further outbreaks of violence and revolution in the 1918–1919 Spartacist uprisings in Berlin and Munich. The radical Berlin revolt ended with the lynching of its leaders, Karl Liebknecht and Rosa Luxemburg, on January 15, 1919, as well as a vicious counterrevolution.[50] German revolutionary instability continued, and the new republic unleashed thousands of demobilized soldiers organized into Freikorps, whose job it was to crush the revolutionary instability. In Munich, more than a thousand civilians died in the Freikorps assault on the city in early May 1919.[51]

The violence in Munich was particularly surprising to observers since the political transition there in November 1918 had been relatively peaceful and had led to a moderate Socialist leader, Kurt Eisner. However, by early 1919 he had been ineffective at creating a viable state coalition, and on February 21, 1919, he was murdered in the street.[52] Violence erupted in the wake of the assassination and eventually a Soviet Republic was declared in April 1919, leading to a power struggle between the deposed Bavarian government and the new Soviet Republic. The national provisional government in Berlin provided troops in the form of twenty thousand Freikorps volunteer units, who proceeded to sack the city.[53] As with the Spartacist uprising in Berlin, the Bavarian Soviet leaders were murdered and brutal repression was the order of the day. Scholar MacGregor Knox noted in his study of postwar Europe that the Freikorps, composed of demobilized soldiers and young men who "missed" the war, wanted "less to reestablish republican order than to revenge defeat upon the 'internal enemy.'"[54] What emerged as a major difference between revolution in Germany and revolution in Russia was the reaction of soldiers; in Russia, soldiers joined the revolutionaries to turn the tide at crucial times, while in Germany enough soldiers became forces of repression to stop the revolutionary impetus.

The German revolutionary wave of 1918–1919, which ultimately failed in its radical aims, provides an excellent example of the role of the war in uniting soldiers and civilians for revolution. Defeat mixed with four years of wartime sacrifices to create a volatile political and social situation. The impact of these revolutions lasted well into the twentieth century, shaping the nation-states that would fight again a mere two decades later. However, it is also important to remember the context of the civil disturbances of 1918 and 1919—nations were attempting to demobilize large numbers of men, which would inevitably lead to unemployment and social dislocation at first. Even though not all states experienced revolution or even major civil disturbance, the threat of such activity remained in the forefront of official concerns.[55] So revolution, wherever it occurred, loomed large in the minds of leaders around the world in 1918. These revolutions questioned the very basis of imperial authorities throughout the warring states, and they both reflected and catalyzed notions of revolutionary upheaval in the broader colonial setting of the European overseas empires.

Anticolonial Revolt

While those in Europe felt betrayed by their wartime leaders and expressed their rage in civil revolt, many living in colonial situations felt a much different sense of anger over their use by colonial authorities for war service with few promises in return for extension of citizenship or rights. Imperial authorities often took for granted the notion that their subjects around the world would want to support their war efforts. When resistance occurred, officials within these empires often resorted to coercion to fulfill their labor and resource needs during the war. Inevitably, coercive practices and the drain of wartime requisitioning led to unrest and violence in colonial regions of empires.

One of the major sparks for localized rioting and broader rebellions was resistance to labor recruitment for the war and to conscription, especially in areas poorly integrated into multinational empires. Minority groups, often targeted for aggressive recruitment by officials, felt particularly aggrieved by exploitative strategies designed to use their labor, and they suspected government officials of trying to use their men as "cannon fodder" in the war effort. Such fears and suspicions led to attacks on recruitment offices and widespread rebellions around the world during the war. In South Africa, not only did more than eleven thousand Boers rise up in rebellion in 1914 to protest conscription for a British cause, but another thousand fled to German territory in order to enlist against the British.[56]

Perhaps the most serious and longest-lasting revolts against conscription took place in the Russian Empire's Central Asian provinces (modern Kyrgyzstan and Kazakhstan). The rebellion featured several stages and a variety of peoples, both nomadic groups and agricultural laborers. Many of those involved were poorly integrated into the empire, with their own languages and cultural/political traditions. When war was declared, the peoples of Central Asia provided supplies of money and goods for the Russian war machine as "donations" or as required by requisition orders, but they were not subject to conscription. This changed in 1916 with increased demands for soldiers and laborers for the war effort. Revolts immediately broke out in summer 1916, and the rebellion was not entirely suppressed until 1917, with dire consequences for the region as refugees fled into China to escape atrocities by occupying Russian troops. For some areas affected by the revolt, estimates range as high as 20 percent of the population killed as a result of the revolt.[57]

The French also experienced a violent rebellion as they attempted to impose conscription in some of their colonies. In the Haut-Senegal-Niger region (today, Mali and Burkina Faso), a group of villages revolted against France in 1915 in the face of conscription demands and perceived insults by French administrators toward Muslim leaders. The French raised an army to fight an estimated army of ten thousand but were repulsed several times by an armed federation of villages. It was not until the end of 1917 that France "pacified" the region at great cost; more than thirty thousand locals died in the fighting as well as hundreds of soldiers from the French Empire.[58] While their resistance was not as widespread or bloody, colonized peoples in British areas also rebelled against conscription, with uprisings in Nyasaland, Gold Coast, Nigeria, and Southern Rhodesia. "Coercive military recruitment of local labor" in Portuguese East Africa also led to rioting and rebellion.[59] Those in colonies who chose not to rebel often fled recruiters, "feigned illness," or went into hiding.[60] Throughout European colonies, migration functioned as a further form of resistance to conscription into colonial armies, as men decided to flee rather than fight either in state uniforms or against them.[61]

Anticonscription agitation sometimes assumed a purely political character, with some street violence, but more often with wars of words. The Australian case is a good example of a prolonged and wrenching public debate about conscription over the course of 1916. The anticonscription victory achieved by a narrow margin in the first national referendum on the issue shocked many in Australia and in the British Commonwealth (as did the subsequent failure of the second referendum in 1917), but it also suggested the war weariness that had begun to characterize many of the nations at war by late 1916.[62] Had the conscription bill passed, it is unclear whether Australia would have faced some of the same violence witnessed by other regions where conscription was imposed. Certainly the outbreak of serious labor agitation in Australia by 1917 suggests that anticonscription rebellion would not have been outside the realm of possibility. As one British official noted in 1916 regarding possible Irish conscription, it is not "feasible to demand national service from any community without a general measure of consent."[63] The violence surrounding proposed conscription of nonwilling populations supports his claim, especially in the Irish case.

One of the earliest uprisings during the war, which had revolutionary potential if not success, was Ireland's Easter Rising in 1916. General resistance to the demands of the British wartime state and the possibility of conscription played some role in the mobilization of Irish resistance in 1916, but more importantly, the leaders of the rising saw the war as an opportunity to reinitiate their demands for independence. Thwarted in earlier risings beginning in the eighteenth century and denied the peaceful moderation of Home Rule, Irish rebels in 1916 assumed that Britain's absorption with the war effort and German assistance with arms would provide the means for successful rebellion. Germany promised, through John Devoy (leader of the American Clan na Gael), to deliver rifles, machine guns, and explosives to the Irish rebels. Poor planning and communication led to the seizure of the ship carrying the German arms by the British navy, with a loss of all the arms.[64] The revolutionaries decided to move forward with the rising anyway.

A small group of revolutionaries took control of several buildings in Dublin for a week in April 1916 before British forces broke the rebellion. The rising disrupted life in Dublin but had little effect on Irish forces on the western front at the time, and it seemed destined to be forgotten quickly in Dublin until British mishandling of the aftermath.[65] There was little popular support for the rising, but widespread anger at the brutal and summary execution of the leaders at the hands of the British government, and the resumed threat of mass conscription in 1918 helped change the mood of the populace. Even then, however, the rising did not assume its mythic nationalist importance until the postwar period, when it helped construct the alliance that would lead to an independent Irish Free State by the early 1920s.[66]

The memory of the Easter Rising, along with the anticonscription riots in 1918 in Ireland, led to a protracted war between revolutionaries and British authorities from 1916 to 1923, in which more than ten thousand people were killed or wounded. The use of former World War I soldiers as forces of order in Ireland (Black and Tans), plus the availability of men on both sides with military training and possession of weapons, made the revolution and civil war an extension of wartime trauma. In one of the most publicized incidents of the Irish Civil War, Field-Marshal Sir Henry Wilson was assassinated in June 1922 in London on his way home from unveiling a war memorial to those who died between 1914 and 1918; the two Irish assassins had both served as British soldiers in the war.[67] Was it any wonder that civilians had difficulty knowing where the lines of loyalties were drawn?

As in Ireland, India experienced postwar violence, a sign perhaps that Britain's hold on its empire was weakening around the world. Just as Ireland had hoped for Home Rule on the eve of the war and then felt betrayed by Britain, India had pinned its hopes for independence on the 1917 Montagu Declaration and subsequent reforms, which pledged that Britain would help India develop self-government with an eye towards devolution of power. However, little real change was realized in the last years of the war, and severely repressive measures followed in 1919 to control Indian nationalism. By 1919, Indian "disaffection was widespread."[68] It was in this charged postwar atmosphere that a well-known example of colonial repression of a peaceful protest occurred—India's Amritsar massacre. In April 1919, British troops fired into a peaceful gathering in the Punjab town of Amritsar, killing several hundred and wounding more than a thousand in what became known locally as the Jallianwala Bagh massacre.[69] This controversial event occurred during a festival period, but many were gathered for two alternate reasons: the continuation of a general strike and the funeral of strikers killed earlier in the week.[70] The general in charge, Reginald Dyer, ordered the shootings into the crowd of twenty thousand because of a recent law barring gatherings, which he had read out publicly two days before the incident. Dyer, unrepentant after the event, justified his actions by saying the violence was necessary to teach a moral lesson to all who thought to defy the British Empire in the wake of war, saying famously that "there could be no question of undue severity."[71]

Although widely publicized and condemned in the world media, Amritsar was only the most egregious of a series of repressive measures in India aimed at suppressing anti-British sentiment. Many of the punishments inflicted on "offenders" were humiliating, such as public flogging, "making people skip," or public recitations of poetry. Dyer was also responsible for the infamous "Crawling Order," which forced pedestrians to crawl through filth. These acts and other repressive British measures, such as the Rowlatt Bills, led to the development of a new phase of Indian nationalism.[72] Amritsar, some scholars argue, radicalized Indian nationalist leaders such as Jawaharlal Nehru.[73] Perhaps more importantly, it allowed Mahatma Gandhi to move from being one of a group of prominent nationalist leaders to the unquestioned spokesman for the Indian nationalists by the early 1920s. Amritsar was clearly the turning point in this process.[74]

The war unleashed many protests and revolts in other dependencies and colonies as well, particularly in areas that had suffered physically because of the war or that felt cheated by the terms of the postwar peace treaties. For the former, the harsh effects of colonial conscription of labor and soldiers, famine, and influenza combined to spark rebellions. A peasant rebellion that broke out in Egypt in spring 1919 reflected hardships and shortages caused by British army demands on the population. The violence focused mostly on supply networks, with the smashing of rail lines and looting of supply depots. While undoubtedly much of the anger was directed at the British as a colonial occupying force, there is no doubt that fear of hunger helped drive the protests. The Egyptian revolt required thousands of British troops to suppress it.[75] In other colonial areas, rebellion as such did not occur, but all political and social order disappeared, leaving "ungovernable" populations. In central Tanzania's Dodoma region, colonial requisitioning of men, food, and cattle led to a multiyear and devastating famine called the Mtunya, in which approximately one-fifth of the population perished.[76] As one official described the situation, there was "no system of administration at all. The Gogo chiefdoms gone—the German system had gone—and the famine had so churned up the population that some chiefs had no people at all."[77]

Such traumatic breakdowns of sustenance and political authority had long-term consequences for colonial regimes. After the war, further unrest occurred as demobilized soldiers and carriers found their way home. When the war ended, in many cases men were released with few provisions and left to fend for themselves in getting home. In Nyasaland (today, Malawi) not only did soldiers return home malnourished and in rags, but they brought with them venereal disease and influenza, contributing to postwar misery. While Malawians did not resort to overt violence, they expressed their postwar frustrations and fears in a series of new social and cultural institutions, which in turn helped feed nationalism as the interwar period progressed.[78] Veterans associations, in Malawi and other former colonies, also became sites for social and political discussion that helped feed the emergent independence movements of the twentieth century.

In other regions, Woodrow Wilson's championing of principles of self-determination warred with colonial powers' determination to contain and retain their imperial possessions. Wilson's pronouncement that the fate of people around the world should be determined according to "free, open-minded, and absolutely impartial adjustment" met with anger from his allies, who had no intention of releasing their colonies or of granting independence to many colonies of defeated nations.[79] Protests against the peace treaties and unfair colonial obligations led to violence and long-term bitterness in many of these states, and the British Empire alone saw major nationalist pressure in Ireland, India, Egypt, Palestine, and Iraq, just to name a few regions.[80] In many African colonies, returning veterans often had few services to depend upon, and this led not only to difficulties of reintegration into village life but also to looting and crime. Colonial authorities in the midst of world war and its aftermath had little patience or real understanding of the claims of colonized peoples in the period, and the result was massive repression of anticolonial revolts.

While China was technically not a colonial possession of any other nation at the end of World War I, it experienced a reaction to the "turbulent new forces unleashed by the First World War."[81] Most historians agree that the May Fourth Movement of 1919 shared characteristics of anticolonial revolts and that it was sparked by the war and its immediate aftermath. When the armistice was signed, the Chinese media signaled high hopes for the postwar settlements and called on Wilson as a champion. One journalist wrote in November 1918, "Wilson is the best qualified statesman to assume the role of champion of human rights generally and of the rights of China in particular," as the Chinese version of Wilson's "Fourteen Points" became a bestseller.[82] When the treaty terms of 1919 favored Japanese territorial ambitions by awarding former German holdings in China to Japan, popular protests broke out among students in

Beijing and then spread to the countryside. Specifically, the Chinese protested both the terms of the Versailles Peace Treaty and Japan's "Twenty-One Demands" issued to China in 1915, which called for China to cede territory in Manchuria and Shandong province to Japan. The revolt helped crystallize opposition in China to foreign control and altered the political landscape, leading to a reorganization of nationalists (Guomindang) and the founding of the Chinese Communist Party in 1921.[83] For China, the result of World War I was a sense of betrayal by and alienation from Europe and the United States, and the creation of political forces that would shape China's future to the present day.[84]

In China, as in many cases of popular protest during and just after the war, civilian resentment at the perceived disregard of their sacrifices during wartime played a role. Many ordinary men and women thought that war service, in all its variety, would entitle them to some measure of respect and independence from colonial authorities and foreign governments. What they discovered, however, was that Wilson's promises of "self-determination" had limits, and that in the fraught postwar environment of the peace negotiations, some nations and peoples were more entitled than others.

Although many of the revolts and civil disturbances of the late-war and postwar periods were later obscured by the negotiations at the Paris Peace Conference and by the treaties, the number of regions affected by civil violence remained astonishingly high, ranging through Europe, the Americas, Africa, and Asia. Table 8.1 demonstrates the variability and scope of some of the major revolts.

In addition to the revolutions and revolts listed here, many other nations suffered waves of strikes, marches, and riots throughout the second half of the war, requiring the use of armies against civilians on the home front. For some soldiers, demobilization was postponed as they were posted to rebellion zones. Others made a postwar career out of violence, such as the Black and Tans in Ireland or the Freikorps of Germany and the eastern front. Some nations saw a rise in the politics of hate, with the development of antiliberal and increasingly violent ideologies such as fascism and national socialism and the emergence of white supremacist organizations such as the newly reconstituted Ku Klux Klan in the United States.

TABLE 8.1.
Civil revolts, wars, and revolutions

State	Type of Disturbance	Years
Austro-Hungarian Empire	Austrian Revolution	1918
	Hungarian Revolution	1918–1919
Baltic zone (Lithuania, Latvia, Estonia)	Civil War	1918–1919
Bulgaria	Civil Revolt and Coup	1918
Canada	Anticonscription Revolt	1918
China	May Fourth Movement	1919
Egypt	Civil Revolt	1919
Finland	Civil War	1918
France	Mutinies	1917
Germany	Revolution	1918–1919
Greece	Turko-Greek War	1920–1922
India	Amritsar Massacre	1919
	Afghan War	1919
Ireland	Easter Rebellion	1916
	Anticonscription Riots	1918
	Independence War, Civil War	1919–1923
Italy	Conflict in Fiume	1919–1920
Luxembourg	Civil Revolt and Coup	1918
Mali	Volta-Bani War	1915–1917
Montenegro	Rebellion	1916
Morocco	Rif Rebellion	1921–1926
Netherlands	Civil Revolt	1918
Nyasaland	Chilembwe's Revolt	1915
Ottoman Empire	Armenian revolt	1915
	Azerbaijian Rebellion	1918–1920
	Hejaz War	1919–1926
	Iraqi Rebellion	1920–1921
	Oman Revolt	1913–1920
Poland	Civil War	1918–1923
Portugal	Rebellion	1919
Russian Empire	Central Asian Rebellion	1916
	Revolution	1917
	Civil War	1917–1920
Serbia	Toplice Rebellion	1917
Singapore	Mutiny	1915
South Africa	Boer Rebellion	1914–1915
Turkey	Turko-Greek War	1920–1922
United States	Caco Revolt (in U.S.-occupied Caribbean)	1918–1920
	Race Riots	1917–1921

The disruptions of postwar demobilization and the continued economic pressures on civilian populations meant that the civil revolts, strikes, revolutions, and disturbances created a never-ending state of war. For civilians, the militarization that had marked their lives from their nations' entry into the war continued well into the next decade in both subtle and occasionally overt, and violent, ways.

Conclusion

In spring 1916, Mary Martin recorded in her diary the shambles of Dublin's General Post Office and general vicinity in the aftermath of the Easter Rising, noting that amidst soldiers and barricades, the city was a shocking sight:

> Troops & artillery have arrived in large numbers. . . . Although prepared for great havoc it is much worse than I anticipated From O'Connell Bridge to Cathedral Lane past Earl St is utterly destroyed being only a heap a smouldering rubbish with a few facades standing to mark where some of the more important buildings stood. The GPO is only a skeleton front the interior being complete [sic] gone & the house down to the Coliseum also.[85]

Martin's diary, which recounts the anxious days of the revolt and its aftermath, was intended as an eventual letter for her son, Charlie, who was missing in action after Salonika. Martin, a civilian living far from the battle fronts, describes to her citizen-soldier son scenes of pitched battle more reminiscent of soldiers' letters than those of noncombatants. Later, as she dealt with the news of her son's death and the ensuing grief for him and anxiety over her other children, still overseas, Martin witnessed further nationalist unrest, conscription riots, and the outbreak of full-fledged civil war in Ireland by 1919.

For Martin and other civilians caught up in new wars, the lines between World War I and the conflicts it spawned were ephemeral at best. Violence, whether officially sanctioned and managed by the nation-state or not, disrupts civilian lives, threatens their physical safety, and destroys their peace of mind. Millions of people experienced little change in their

This Russian
refugee in the
early 1920s
clutches a piece
of bread, her
face showing the
ravages of years of
war, revolution,
and civil strife.
Herbert Hoover
Presidential
Library.

circumstances with the armistice of 1918; instead the war ground on, just
with different trappings. Most had no notion of when "normalcy" might
return. Especially for those who watched their identities shift before their
eyes, the disappearance of governments and whole empires spurred not
only violence but confusion and disillusionment. The ends of historic
empires in Russia, Austria-Hungary, Turkey, and Germany created instability and dislocation for millions of people for years after the "official"
end of war in 1918. As Aviel Roshwald has observed, "Political and insti-
tutional responses to these dilemmas were hastily improvised . . . amidst
the often violent clash of conflicting interests . . . yet many of the resulting
arrangements were to remain in place for years to come, with far-reaching
consequences."[86]

By 1919, the world had changed irrevocably, and the political and social upheaval of the war and its aftermath reshaped global relationships for good. World War I set the stage for the emergence or revitalization of nationalist movements around the colonized world in the interwar period, it provided ammunition for budding ethnic and cultural separatists, it ushered in the era of successful Communist revolution, and it unleashed new right-wing political ideologies in the form of fascism and national socialism that spawned even more violence and destruction. Certainly one should not draw a straight line from 1914 to the tragedies of the 1940s or the independence movements of the post–World War II period, but many of the political and social changes unleashed by the First World War shaped irrevocably a generation of men, women, and children, all of whom would determine the future of the twentieth century.

Conclusion:

Consequences of World War I

And what is even more true is that the idea of the soldier remains as a fixture of all our thought, so that in some way each of us is both civilian and soldier. In the full understanding of ourselves, the story of the soldier is also our own.

—Susan Griffin, *A Chorus of Stones:*
The Private Life of War[1]

Countless times over the past few years as I have worked on this book, the following scenario has played out with friends, colleagues, and acquaintances. They ask me about my current project, and when I reply that I am writing a civilian history of the First World War, the common response elicited is, "Oh, the home front." For most people who consider the history of war at all, "civilians" equal "home front"—people removed from the battle front. This book has demonstrated that while home fronts do help create the lifelines that make modern war possible, they constitute only a part of the work of war performed by "civilians." A civilian history of war must encompass all the ideological and practical work of war, which concerns not just the munitions worker behind the lines or the nurse on the hospital train, but the citizen-soldier or laundress at the front, the civilian behind wire, and the refugees clogging the roads to the trenches. The gendarme who delivered the call to conscripts by riding from village to village was no less central in the creation of armies in 1914 than the quartermaster who handed out shirts and trousers. The charitable organizations who posted care packages of food and clothing helped maintain armies in the field, prisoners in camps, and families in their homes. In World War I, citizens' lives were militarized, their imaginations and lives drawn into the war experience, whether they wore uniforms or not.

Civilians were and are crucial to the waging of warfare in the twentieth and twenty-first centuries, and without their willingness to serve as soldiers, producers, and reproducers for the nation, wars of the scope and length of World War I would not have been possible. Most fascinating, however, was the way in which civilians became central to the conflict as real targets and as justification for war, yet they also became marginal to the war experience. In this conflict, the lines between home and front were more blurred than they had ever been, particularly in occupied zones such as Poland or Belgium, yet state and societal propaganda sought to maintain a clear line between soldier and civilian, home front and battle front. The ultimate result was massive reliance on civilians for funding, labor, and other material support for the war effort, with an accompanying invisibility of those efforts. In postwar commemoration, often only the "victims" (the dead) figure in memorials and monuments to the war effort, and civilians often seem an afterthought in histories of the war.

This process of making sense of the war and rebuilding the shattered landscapes and relationships the conflict had forged was neither easy nor quick. Käthe Kollwitz described the impact of the war in a letter to her soldier son, Hans: "Everywhere beneath the surface are tears and bleeding wounds. And yet the war goes on and cannot stop. It follows other laws."[2] While the First World War officially ended with an armistice in November 1918 amid claims to be the "war that would end war," for Kollwitz and others like her, peace was illusory. The work of war continued far past 1918, but more significantly, the logic of war and its structuring of politics, society, and culture continued. The peace negotiations at Versailles and other treaty locations were contentious, more likely to perpetuate violence and punishment than to resolve fundamental issues raised by the war. As this "peace" was being negotiated, war raged around the world—civil wars, nationalist revolts, border conflicts. Soldiers, prisoners of war, and volunteer aid workers often waited months or years for their release from service or imprisonment, and some went straight from world war into civil war or revolutionary situations. In private homes, the war continued as families came to terms with bereavement and with the reintegration into civilian life of citizen-soldiers, some of whom were deeply scarred both physically and mentally by war. Civilians who had suffered from rape or other personal violence or who were pregnant with "enemy" children suffered particularly difficult postwar situations.

For civilians, demobilization was an elusive concept. After an intense but short period of exhilaration and hope with the signing of the armistice, many civilians found themselves still standing in bread lines or mending their frayed clothing, waiting for loved ones to come home. For most nations the challenges of the postwar world were new, as none had experience in administering the massive systems of pensions, taxation, and health care that had become expected by citizen-soldiers. Medical establishments, too, had to retool to repair the shattered bodies and minds returning from war. For those in empires that had dissolved before their eyes, these problems were magnified by the lack of solid political authorities, continued occupations by foreign forces, and the simmering disputes unleashed by the peace treaties.

Reiterating and memorializing the heroism of the soldier provided one solid branch to which postwar populations could cling. Political leaders spent time and money to enable the raising of local and national monuments, and workers spent countless hours digging up, identifying, labeling, and reburying the dead. As Kurt Piehler has noted, "the war dead were still being pressed into service by their governments. . . . Since they were silent, the war dead could offer their complete allegiance to the nation."[3] The commemoration of soldiers' service sometimes sparked political battles over national, ethnic, religious, racial, and familial identities, but few opposed the notion of marking the sacrifice of heroic male combatants.

For civilian participants, the promise of postwar recognition and commemoration was a much more difficult proposition. Some felt that civilian sacrifice should also be celebrated with medals, commemorative stones, and, in some cases, government payments or pensions. Others argued that civilians were merely supplemental to the "real" war and that it would be impossible to reward the sacrifice of a munitions worker on the home front or the victim of an air raid or a civilian contract worker. Refugees also had a different story of war, one that shared little with the kind of narrative of sacrifice that those in occupied or war zones told. Some refugees faced destruction of their property and new displacement by wartime or postwar conflict. Other returnees exacerbated tensions by questioning the loyalty of those who remained in their homes with occupying armies surrounding them, wondering if those who stayed profited from the war.[4] The millions displaced by war fit poorly into its postwar narrative, except as a side note and object of pity, certainly not as a heroic group to be commemorated.

While refugees faced an uncertain return, those deemed civilian collaborators or war profiteers experienced even harsher treatment at the hands of fellow civilians and demobilized soldiers. Especially in occupation zones like Belgium or northern France, civil tribunals were held in the postwar period to punish suspected collaborators or profiteers. Such collaborators ranged from those accused of "trading with the enemy" to those who had "intimate relations" with occupying forces. Rancorous public denunciations marked the postwar period, but authorities realized almost immediately that sorting out "good" civilians from "bad" would be difficult. The very ambiguity of civilian participation in war, in the zones of both allies and enemies, complicated commemoration of the civil side of the war: victims, collaborators, patriots, or heroes—it was difficult to find a singular narrative of civilian life in the war.

In the rush to "prove" war service, the lines were rarely clear. Service to nation implied special treatment by postwar governments as well, and the interwar governments who had trouble meeting pension claims from soldiers looked with horror upon the prospect of civilian claims for compensation, payment, and recognition for their war service. Part of the collective forgetting of civilian sacrifice and service emerged from real concerns that a "return to normalcy" must be the order of the day. Civilians had to provide stability and support as the massive war machines demobilized, but they were also required to rebuild and inhabit the new nations rising from the ashes of war. Civilians were urged to look to the future, not to the past. More importantly, the postwar period saw a regendering of family and society that required a story of war in which masculine heroism was central. Civilian women and men wrote in their memoirs about the erasure of their service, as throughout the involved nations, civilian service was downplayed. A Romanian nurse, Jeanna Fodoreanu, captured this feeling well in her war memoir, *The Woman-Soldier* (1928). At the end of the war official ceremonies were held to celebrate the return of the king and queen, but Fodoreanu wrote, "I am not going to the parade. I am no longer anything more than a poor woman who lost her father, mother, brothers, relatives, friends."[5] In the end, the civilian dropped away from most memories of the war, becoming an object of war and a presence in war but rarely an actor on the wartime stage, except in safely confined areas "behind the lines."

Despite little commemoration of civilian participation, the First World War created an image of the civilian that in many ways is still with us today. Policy makers remembered civilians' roles and used these experiences from 1914 to 1918 to shape future wars. Both civilians and soldiers were complicit in making war in a whole host of ways, which many military and civil officials realized. It is hard not to see echoes of the bombing of civilian targets in World War I in the firebombing of Dresden or the nuclear attack on Hiroshima. Likewise, state experience with widespread internment of civilians helped usher in the world of Japanese-American internment in the United States, as well as the labor and death camps of Nazi Germany. Civilian war service was taken for granted as world war approached again in the 1930s, and military planners sought to use civilians to an even greater extent in industry and at fronts than in the First World War. Once again states mobilized civilian contractors (both corporations and laborers), controlled consumer needs, and reused concentration camps—in small and large ways, World War I changed the nature of civilian service and the expectations about the nature and demands of wartime states and societies.

It is not an exaggeration to say that the period of World War I fundamentally reshaped the geopolitical situation for a century, especially given the revolutions that toppled empires in its aftermath. The treaties and conflicts of the wartime and postwar periods established newly created nations and reassigned imperial responsibilities. If one considers the "hot spots" in twentieth-century world history, the First World War looms large in the development of these situations: Poland, Yugoslavia, Cyprus, Iraq, Israel, Ireland, India, China, Japan, for example. Civilian officials, for the most part, divided the world according to ideas of self-determination and power politics, but they also created an international movement resisting imperial dominance. Erez Manela demonstrates this broad movement of resistance to colonial control in 1919 in India, Korea,

China, and Egypt. He writes, "Rather than bolster or expand the imperial order, the events of 1919 in fact laid the groundwork for its demise."[6] World War I opened up a dialogue about the nature of nationalism, imperialism, and self-determination that shaped both war and peace in the twentieth and twenty-first centuries.

In addition, the war itself created a generation of leaders whose understandings of nation and war reflected their direct experiences in 1914–1918. Most of the civilian leaders of the 1920s to the 1950s had served in the war as citizen-soldiers or as civilians. Political leaders such as Harry Truman (United States), Adolf Hitler (Germany), Clement Attlee (Britain), Winston Churchill (Britain), Charles de Gaulle (France), Gyula Gömbös (Hungary), Benito Mussolini (Italy), and Mustafa Kemal Atatürk (Turkey) all served as citizen-soldiers in the war. Some politicians spent the war in civilian service, including Nikita Khrushchev (Soviet Union), Franklin Roosevelt (United States), and Chaim Weizmann (Israel). Still other leaders spent their time opposing the First World War, setting up their later activities: Mohandis Gandhi (India), Jomo Kenyatta (Kenya), John Curtin (Australia), and Eamon de Valera (Ireland). Their war experiences helped frame their view of politics, society, and culture, shaping international institutions such as the League of Nations but also international relations.

Beyond political elites, however, ordinary people saw their lives being transformed by World War I and its aftershocks. Even in areas where borders were not redrawn or societal upheaval did not occur, civilians felt the continued militarization of their lives. Intelligence services, which had ballooned in size during the war, remained as smaller but permanent fixtures in the political landscape. State control mechanisms for societies did not disappear; passports became a regular part of people's lives, as did daylight savings time (summer time), income taxes, and liquor regulations (the U.S. 18th Amendment establishing Prohibition being the most restrictive example). Veterans groups and civilian service organizations arose, helping to shape remembrance of war and providing a continued focus on service in wartime as a duty of citizens. States developed pension schemes for ex-soldiers and their dependents as well as widows and orphans of fallen soldiers. In addition, governments devoted time and money to the care of those with disabilities from the war. When benefits

As her child clutches a shell, this woman represents the civilian populations militarized by war. *Library of Congress.*

were insufficient or promised entitlements did not appear, citizens often took to the streets to protest, as with the U.S. Bonus March on Washington D. C. in 1932.

Civilians often bore the brunt of the postwar reintegration of soldiers into society. Women and adolescents who had been employed in well-paid war work found themselves put out on the streets to make room for returning soldiers in need of jobs. Grieving families had to face not only the ongoing pain of loss but also the difficulties of supporting themselves in the absence of a major breadwinner, especially in states where payments to dead soldiers' families were nonexistent or insufficient. Some families joyously welcomed home veterans only to witness men working through physical or psychological trauma, or worse, bringing home contagious diseases, such as tuberculosis or venereal disease. Marina Larsson gives voices to these families "shattered" by war, citing that in Australia alone, ninety thousand ex-servicemen received war disability pensions and at the outbreak of World War II, seventy-seven thousand were still living with disabilities from World War I.[7] Britain supported sixty-five thousand "neurotics" in hospitals and countless more with mental disability outside of its institutions; France denied aid to mentally ill veterans, while Germany declared "neurotics" ineligible for pensions in 1926. Even with such restrictions, approximately "10 percent of German society was reliant on pensions."[8] With such large numbers of ill or disabled men, families often assumed primary care for these veterans, not for a year or two but for decades. These civilians certainly experienced only a partial demobilization.

Families living with the wounded and scarred certainly faced the trauma of war, but for those whose homes disappeared, the postwar period functioned as war on another front. Many refugees found it difficult to return home in the postwar era given the redrawing of lines of citizenship and state, and other families were forcibly removed from their homes in a deliberate policy of resettlement. The best and most tragic example of these policies was the Treaty of Lausanne (1923), which mandated a "compulsory exchange of Turkish nationals . . . and of Greek nationals."[9] This treaty meant the deliberate uprooting of Muslims in Greece and Christians in Turkey; altogether, approximately 1.2 million Christians in Turkey and about four hundred thousand Muslims in Greece had to relocate to states to which they had no ties, no common language, and little knowledge.[10] These mass deportations extended the logic of the wartime displacements and deportations, making them an acceptable solution in twentieth-century political conflicts, especially after World War II when twelve million Germans were forcibly deported.[11] It also set the stage for more insidious forms of ethnic cleansing of populations in the years to come, conducted in the name of purity and nationalism.

The First World War unleashed a new level of technological and psychological violence on the world stage, but it also drew unprecedented numbers of people into its reach; wartime logic became normal logic for all those involved. The corporatist economic strategies pioneered during the war became the basis for many states in the interwar period, while the ethos of struggle permeated political movements around the world in the same time frame. Genocide and ethnic cleansing became thinkable, and industrial killing became possible. As Omer Bartov has argued,

[T]he distinction between soldiers and civilians, whether they belonged to the enemy's camp or constituted one's own human reservoir, became increasingly blurred, and . . . various categories of human being could more easily be defined as expendable or harmful and therefore eliminated in large numbers without any major technical difficulties or moral qualms. . . . [T]he Great War . . . created the preconditions for indiscriminate bombing of civilian targets, slave labor, state-controlled famine and depopulation, deployment of nuclear weapons, and death camps.[12]

Bartov's claims reinforce the arguments of this book, namely, that civilian lives in the First World War and their experiences in that conflict profoundly shaped world history in the century that followed. The histories and experiences of Hiroshima or My Lai or Abu Ghraib are far different than what happened in Przemyśl or Ypres, but the logic used in each of these later cases is recognizable in the experiences of World War I civilians.

The use of civilians for rhetorical and actual maintenance of war in 1914–1918 established the practices that would become acceptable means of waging war in the future. Civilians are not merely confined to a separate and protected home front space in times of war, nor does the war follow the rules of armistice for civilians; noncombatant populations work and fight to maintain the war, and then they deal with its consequences, often for a long time. Eventually civilians become part of the landscape of war, objects of pity or possibly derision, but objects nonetheless, subject to relocation, control, or torture. They fade into the background of war, denied the postwar accolades, treated with suspicion, but carrying the weight of war into the postwar period. In this book, I have argued that we create an artificial dichotomy and construct too many barriers in our understanding of war— by defining civilians as objects of war rather than active participants, we create a vision of war that is profoundly gendered, "raced," and in many ways, imaginary. This works pleads for a broader conceptualization of military history that moves beyond the lines of battle to consider the fundamental ways in which civilian lives constructed and maintained war in the twentieth century and continue to do so in the twenty-first century.

Notes

INTRODUCTION

1. Piete Kuhr, *There We'll Meet Again,* trans. Walter Wright (Gloucester, UK: Walter Wright, 1998), 9.

2. Cited in *Intimate Voices from the First World War,* eds. Svetlana Palmer and Sarah Wallis (New York: Morrow, 2003), 55.

3. Dorothy Scannell, *Mother Knew Best: Memoir of a London Girlhood* (New York: Pantheon, 1974), 56.

4. Hugo Slim, *Killing Civilians: Method, Madness, and Morality in War* (New York: Columbia University Press, 2008), 19.

5. For a concise overview of some of the changes, see Michael Howard, *War in European History,* updated edition (Oxford: Oxford University Press, 2009).

6. Scott N. Hendrix, "In the Army: Women, Camp Followers, and Gender Roles in the British Army in the French and Indian Wars, 1755–1765," in *A Soldier and a Woman: Sexual Integration in the Military,* eds. Gerard J. DeGroot and Corinna Peniston-Bird (Harlow, Essex: Pearson Education, 2000), 35, 38; Myna Trustram, *Women of the Regiment: Marriage and the Victorian Army* (Cambridge: Cambridge University Press, 1984), 2–3; Colonel Noel T. St. John, *Judy O'Grady and the Colonel's Lady: The Army Wife and Camp Follower since 1660* (London: Brassey's Defence Publishers, 1988), 1, 11–12.

7. Holly A. Mayer, *Belonging to the Army: Camp Followers and Community during the American Revolution* (Columbia: University of South Carolina Press, 1996), 6–8, 122.

8. Barton Hacker, "Women and Military Institutions in Early Modern Europe: A Reconnaissance," *Signs: Journal of Women in Culture and Society* 6:4 (1981): 676, 681.

9. Hacker, "Women and Military Institutions," 645.

10. Trustram, *Women of the Regiment,* 3, 12–13.

11. John Horne, "Introduction: Mobilizing for 'Total War,' 1914–1918," in *State, Society, and Mobilization in Europe during the First World War,* ed. John Horne (Cambridge: Cambridge University Press, 1997), 1–3.

12. Slim, *Killing Civilians*, 209.

13. It is important to note that the term "total war" was coined after World War I in Erich Ludendorff's 1935 memoir, *Der Totale Krieg*, as an explanatory term for the 1914–1918 conflict in the postwar reexamination. For more on the term "total war," see Jeremy Black, *The Age of Total War, 1860–1945* (Westport, CT: Praeger Security International, 2006), 1–11.

14. John Brocklesby, "Escape from Paganism," 1958, pp. 29–33; TEMP MSS 412, Society of Friends Library, London (SFL).

15. Ernest Louis Meyer, *Hey! Yellowbacks! The War Diary of a Conscientious Objector* (New York: John Day, 1930), 43–44. Thanks to Brian DeSantis for this reference.

16. As quoted in *Nurses at the Front: Writing the Wounds of the Great War*, ed. Margaret Higonnet (Boston: Northeastern University Press, 2001), 21.

CHAPTER 1

1. Joanna Bourke, ed., *The Misfit Soldier: Edward Casey's War Story, 1914–1918* (Cork, Ireland: Cork University Press, 1999), 14–18.

2. In Britain, as Adrian Gregory notes, officials ended Poor Law payments to "able-bodied" men in August 1914, compelling many to enlist. Bribery was also quite common. See Adrian Gregory, *The Last Great War: British Society and the First World War* (Cambridge: Cambridge University Press, 2008), 74–81.

3. On this process of self-mobilization, see John Horne, ed., *State, Society, and Mobilization in Europe during the First World War* (Cambridge: Cambridge University Press, 1997). Especially useful are the chapters by John Horne and Wolfgang Mommsen.

4. As quoted in Nicoletta Gullace, *"The Blood of Our Sons": Men, Women, and the Renegotiation of British Citizenship during the Great War* (New York: Palgrave Macmillan, 2002), 129.

5. Ute Frevert, *A Nation in Barracks: Modern Germany, Military Conscription, and Civil Society*, trans. Andrew Boreham with Daniel Brückenhaus (Oxford: Berg, 2004), 12.

6. Frevert, *A Nation in Barracks*, 12.

7. Eliot A. Cohen, *Citizens and Soldiers: The Dilemmas of Military Service* (Ithaca, NY: Cornell University Press, 1985), 45.

8. Cohen, *Citizens and Soldiers*, 50–51.

9. Geoffrey Best, *Humanity in Warfare* (New York: Columbia University Press, 1980), 99.

10. Michael Howard, *War in European History*, updated edition (Oxford: Oxford University Press, 2009), 75–76.

11. Karma Nabulsi, *Traditions of War: Occupation, Resistance, and the Law* (Oxford: Oxford University Press, 1999), 21–22, 48–52.

12. Daniel Moran, "Arms and the Concert: The Nation in Arms and the Dilemmas of German Liberalism," in *The People in Arms: Military Myth and National Mobilization since the French Revolution*, eds. Daniel Moran and Arthur Waldron (Cambridge: Cambridge University Press, 2003), 49–74.

13. Robert A. Graham, "Universal Military Training in Modern History," *Annals of the American Academy of Political and Social Science* 241 (September 1945): 8–9.

14. Jan Lucassen and Erik Jan Zürcher, "Conscription as Military Labour: The Historical Context," *International Review of Social History* 43 (1998): 415.

15. Edward M. Spiers, *The Late Victorian Army, 1868–1902* (Manchester, UK: Manchester University Press, 1992), 2, 30, 61; Anne Summers, *Angels and Citizens: British Women as Military Nurses* (London: Routledge and Kegan Paul, 1988), 204, 275; A. J. A. Morris, *The Scaremongers: The Advocacy of War and Rearmament, 1986–1914* (London: Routledge and Kegan Paul, 1984), 226.

16. Helen McCartney, *Citizen Soldiers: The Liverpool Territorials in the First World War* (Cambridge: Cambridge University Press, 2005), 19.

17. John Mackenzie, "Introduction," in *Popular Imperialism and the Military*, ed. John Mackenzie (Manchester, UK: Manchester University Press, 1992), 20.

18. H. L. Wesseling, *The European Colonial Empires, 1815–1919*, trans. Diane Webb (Harlow, Essex: Pearson Longman, 2004), 32–33.

19. Benito Mussolini, *My Diary, 1915–17* (Boston: Small, Maynard, 1925), 59.

20. Best, *Humanity in Warfare*, 128–35.

21. I. S. Bloch, *The Future of War*, trans. R. C. Long (New York: Doubleday & McClure, 1899), 30.

22. Jack Snyder, "Civil-Military Relations and the Cult of the Offensive, 1914 and 1984," in *Offense, Defense, and War: An International Security Reader*, eds. Michael Brown, Owen R. Coté Jr., Sean M. Lynn-Jones, and Steven E. Miller (Cambridge, MA: MIT Press, 2004), 120.

23. "Russian Circular Note Proposing the First Peace Conference," August 1898, in *The Hague Peace Conferences of 1899 and 1907 and International Arbitration: Reports and Documents*, ed. Shabtai Rosenne (The Hague: Asser Press, 2001), 23.

24. Michael Walzer, *Just and Unjust Wars: A Moral Argument with Historical Illustrations* (New York: Basic Books, 1977), 137.

25. Rosenne, ed., *The Hague Peace Conferences of 1899 and 1907*, xvii.

26. Nicoletta Gullace, "Sexual Violence and Family Honor: British Propaganda and International Law during the First World War," *American Historical Review* 102:3 (1997): 716.

27. Isabel V. Hull, *Absolute Destruction: Military Culture and the Practices of War in Imperial Germany* (Ithaca, NY: Cornell University Press, 2005), 120.

28. Hull, *Absolute Destruction*, 121.

29. Alan Kramer, *Dynamic of Destruction: Culture and Mass Killing in the First World War* (Oxford: Oxford University Press, 2008), 329.

30. Best, *Humanity in Warfare*, 147.

31. Margaret Darrow, *French Women and the First World War: War Stories of the Home Front* (Oxford: Berg, 2000), 55.

32. "Evening of 25 September 1914," as quoted in *Lines of Fire: Women Writers of World War I*, ed. Margaret Higonnet (New York: Penguin, 1999), 457.

33. Decie Denholm, ed., *Behind the Lines: One Woman's War, 1914–18; The Letters of Caroline Ethel Cooper* (London: Jill Norman & Hobhouse, 1982), 133–34.

34. Harry Hamilton Snively, *The Battle of the Non-Combatants* (New York: Business Bourse Publishers, 1933), 30.

35. My thanks to the members of the International Society for First World War Studies for their help in compiling this mobilization table.

36. Joanna Bourke, *An Intimate History of Killing: Face-to-Face Killing in Twentieth-Century Warfare* (New York: Basic Books, 1999), 60.

37. Stéphane Audoin-Rouzeau and Annette Becker, *14–18: Understanding the Great War*, trans. Catherine Temerson (New York: Hill and Wang, 2002), 34.

38. B. E. Sargeaunt, *The Isle of Man and the Great War* (Douglas, Isle of Man: Brown and Sons, 1920), 12–13.

39. David McGill, *Island of Secrets: Matiu/Somes Island in Wellington Harbour* (Wellington, New Zealand: Steele Roberts & Silver Owl Press, 2001), 44–45.

40. Luc De Vos, J. Du Chau, W. Steurbaut, and G. Van Huffel, *Leuven: Ook een Garnizoensstad* (Leuven, Belgium: Peeters, 1989), 17–20; Albert Fuglister, *Louvain Ville Martyre* (Paris: Editions Delandre, 1916), 57–69; Posters 1–21, Box 3791, Affiches Collection (Verzameling), Stadsarchief Leuven (SL). All translations in text are mine unless noted.

41. John Horne, "Remobilizing for 'Total War': France and Britain, 1917–1918," in Horne, ed., *State, Society, and Mobilization*, 195.

42. Jon Lawrence, "The Transition to War in 1914," in *Capital Cities at War: Paris, London, Berlin, 1914–1919*, eds. Jay Winter and Jean-Louis Robert, vol. 1 (Cambridge: Cambridge University Press, 1999), 139–41.

43. "Bankers Here Confer on War," *New York Times* (31 July 1914), 1.

44. "South America Affected," *New York Times* (3 August 1914) and "Week's Holiday in Argentina," *New York Times* (4 August 1914).

45. Bent Blüdnikow, "Denmark during the First World War," *Journal of Contemporary History* 24:4 (October 1989): 685.

46. Charles Nelson Spinks, "Japan's Entrance into the World War," *Pacific Historical Review* 5:4 (1936): 298; Frederick R. Dickinson, *War and National Reinvention: Japan in the Great War, 1914–1919* (Cambridge, MA: Harvard University Press, 1999), 61.

47. Nicholas Hiley, "Counter-espionage and Security in Great Britain during the First World War," *English Historical Review* 101:400 (July 1986): 637.

48. Martha Hanna, *Your Death Would Be Mine: Paul and Marie Pireaud in the Great War* (Cambridge, MA: Harvard University Press, 2006), 6–7.

49. Slavka Mihajlović diary in *Intimate Voices from the First World War*, eds. Svetlana Palmer and Sarah Wallis (New York: Morrow, 2003), 15.

50. Donald C. Savage and J. Forbes Munro, "Carrier Corps Recruitment in the British East Africa Protectorate, 1914–1918," *Journal of African History* 7:2 (1966): 315–16.

51. Josh Sanborn, "The Mobilization of 1914 and the Question of the Russian Nation: A Reexamination," *Slavic Review* 59:2 (2000): 272.

52. Sanborn, "The Mobilization of 1914," 275–77.

53. Mohammad Gholi Majd, *Iraq in World War I: From Ottoman Rule to British Conquest* (Lanham, MD: University Press of America, 2006), 50.

54. Sandra Swart, "'A Boer and His Gun and His Wife Are Three Things Always Together': Republican Masculinity and the 1914 Rebellion," *Journal of Southern African Studies* 24:4 (December 1998): 737, 745–51; Tim Stapleton, "The Impact of the First World War on African People," in *Daily Lives of Civilians in Wartime Africa: From Slavery Days to Rwandan Genocide*, ed. John Laband (Westport, CT: Greenwood Press, 2007), 119.

55. Bill Nasson, *Springboks on the Somme: South Africa in the Great War* (Johannesburg: Penguin, 2007), 39–48.

56. Quoted in Keith Watenpaugh, *Being Modern in the Middle East: Revolution, Nationalism, Colonialism, and the Arab Middle Class* (Princeton, NJ: Princeton University Press, 2006), 119.

57. Joshua A. Sanborn, *Drafting the Russian Nation: Military Conscription, Total War, and Mass Politics, 1905–1925* (Dekalb: Northern Illinois University Press, 2003), 29–35, 78–79.

58. Sanborn, *Drafting the Russian Nation*, 35.

59. Sanborn, *Drafting the Russian Nation*, 38–39, 44–47.

60. Benjamin Ziemann, *War Experiences in Rural Germany, 1914–1923*, trans. Alex Skinner (Oxford: Berg, 2007), 18–20.

61. Siegfried Debaeke, *Ik was 20 in '14* (Kortrijk, Belgium: De Klaproos, 1999), 143.

62. As quoted in Bourke, *An Intimate History of Killing*, 230–31.

63. Peter Singer, *Pushing Time Away* (Sydney: Fourth Estate, 2003), 142–46.

64. This was particularly hard for multinational empires with no strong sense of shared nationalism. See Aviel Roshwald, *Ethnic Nationalism and the Fall of Empires: Central Europe, Russia, and the Middle East, 1914–1923* (London: Routledge, 2001), 71–72.

65. Robert Crossley, ed., *Talking across the World: The Love Letters of Olaf Staple-don and Agnes Miller, 1913–1919* (Hanover, NH: University Press of New England, 1987), 106.

66. Gullace, *"The Blood of Our Sons,"* 73.

67. Margaret Levi, "The Institution of Conscription," *Social Science History* 20:1 (Spring 1996): 142.

68. Roland Philipps to Arthur Gaddum, 8 August 1915, TC/248, Scout Association Archives, Gilwell Park, UK (SA).

69. Roland Philipps to Arthur Gaddum, 13 February 1915, TC/248, SA.

70. Typescript of Stanley Ince's Wireless Talk (BBC Boy Scout Programme), 7 July 1927; Roland House File, TC/168, SA.

71. Tammy Proctor, *On My Honour: Guiding and Scouting and Interwar Britain* (Philadelphia: American Philosophical Society, 2002), 88–89; "Captain the Hon. Roland E. Philipps," *Headquarters Gazette* 10:8 (August 1916): 203, SA.

72. Vera Brittain, *Testament of Youth* (New York: Penguin, 1989), 307.

73. Quoted in Higonnet, ed., *Lines of Fire*, 321.

74. Dennis Showalter, "'It All Goes Wrong!': German, French, and British Approaches to Mastering the Western Front," in *Warfare and Belligerence: Perspectives in First World War Studies*, ed. Pierre Purseigle (Leiden, Netherlands: Brill, 2005), 51.

75. Hanna, *Your Death Would Be Mine*, 29.

76. Graf Adam Pavlovich Bennigsen papers, Hoover Institution, Stanford (HI).

77. Quoted in Higonnet, ed., *Lines of Fire*, 323–24.

78. Michael Roper, *The Secret Battle: Emotional Survival in the Great War* (Manchester, UK: Manchester University Press, 2009), 93–94.

79. Denise De Weerdt, *De Vrouwen van de Eerste Wereldoorlog* (Ghent: Stichting Mens en Kultur, 1993), 51.

80. As quoted in McCartney, *Citizen Soldiers*, 78–79.

81. HS3708A Paul Fredericq Wegvoeringsdagboeken, vol. 14; Universiteit Gent, Manuscript Collection, Belgium (UGMC).

82. Photos from Richard Dodson (Ruhleben) accompanying Mary Thorp diary; Documentariecentrum Ieper, In Flanders Fields Museum, Belgium (DI).

83. Alon Rachamimov, "The Disruptive Comforts of Drag: (Trans)Gender Performances among Prisoners of War in Russia, 1914–1920," *American Historical Review* 111:2 (April 2006): 374.

84. For an excellent discussion of the psychological impact of leave and its shaping of soldiers' civilian identities, see Ziemann, *War Experiences in Rural Germany*, 48–51.

85. Lt. Col H. C. Taylor-Young to C.O. Third A.G.H., 10 March 1918, 27 370/153 Treating Belgian/French civilians, Australian War Memorial, Canberra, Australia (AWM).

86. Alon Rachamimov, *POWs and the Great War: Captivity on the Eastern Front* (Oxford: Berg, 2002), 108–9.

87. Gary Leiser, trans. and ed., *Vetluga Memoir: A Turkish Prisoner of War in Russia, 1916–1918* (Gainesville: University Press of Florida, 1995), 71–75.

88. The story is engagingly and painstakingly told in Ben Macintyre, *The Englishman's Daughter: A True Story of Love and Betrayal in World War I* (New York: Farrar, Straus, Giroux, 2001).

89. Hubertus F. Jahn, *Patriotic Culture in Russia during World War I* (Ithaca, NY: Cornell University Press, 1995), 118–22.

90. Arthur E. Barbeau and Florette Henri, *The Unknown Soldiers: African American Troops in World War I* (New York: Da Capo Press, 1996), 40–41.

91. Addie W. Hunton, and Kathryn M. Johnson, *Two Colored Women with the American Expeditionary Forces* (Brooklyn: Brooklyn Eagle Press, 1920), 24, 29–31, 152.

92. Maureen Healy, *Vienna and the Fall of the Habsburg Empire: Total War and Everyday Life in World War I* (Cambridge: Cambridge University Press, 2004), 88–89, 118.

93. Letters from Mrs. Arado and Josie Yeockel, Walter Arthur Richter collection, File 5, National World War I Museum Archives, Kansas City, MO, USA (LMM).

94. Piete Kuhr, *There We'll Meet Again*, trans. Walter Wright (Gloucester, UK: Walter Wright, 1998), 109, 118.

95. Edith O'Shaughnessy, *My Lorraine Journal* (New York: Harper & Brothers, 1918), 3–5, 46–51, 115. Another American woman described a similar outing with a group of friends to see the devastation of Verdun in May 1917; Amy Owen Bradley, *Back of the Front in France* (Boston: Butterfield, 1918), 41–50.

96. Heather Jones calls this a "network of militarised prisoner of war and civilian internment camps . . . established across the world." Heather Jones, "A Missing Paradigm? Military Captivity and the Prisoner of War, 1914–18," *Immigrants and Minorities* 26:1/2 (March/July 2008): 24.

97. Heather Jones, "Encountering the 'Enemy': Prisoner of War Transport and the Development of War Cultures in 1914," in Purseigle, ed., *Warfare and Belligerence*, 142, 144, 152.

98. Best, *Humanity in Warfare*, 285.

99. Bloch, *The Future of War*, 37.

100. Horne, "Remobilizing for 'Total War': France and Britian, 1917–1918," and Richard Bessel, "Mobilization and Demobilization in Germany, 1916–1919," in Horne, ed. *State, Society, and Mobilization*, 210, 216.

101. Bourke, ed., *The Misfit Soldier*, 69.

102. Audoin-Rouzeau and Becker, *14–18*, 34.

CHAPTER 2

1. Quoted in Norman Clothier, *Black Valour: The South African Native Labour Contingent, 1916–1918, and the Sinking of the Mendi* (Pietermaritzburg, South Africa: University of Natal Press, 1987), 27.

2. Clothier, *Black Valour*, 28.

3. Clothier, *Black Valour*, 21, 118.

4. Albert Grundlingh, *Fighting Their Own War: South African Blacks and the First World War* (Johannesburg: Ravan Press, 1987), 57.

5. Martin van Creveld, *Supplying War: Logistics from Wallenstein to Patton*, 2nd ed. (Cambridge: Cambridge University Press, 2004), 233.

6. See, for example, Pradeep Barua, "Inventing Race: The British and India's Martial Races," *Historian* 58 (1995): 107–16; Timothy H. Parsons, "'Wakamba Warriors Are Soldiers of the Queen': The Evolution of the Kamba as a Martial Race, 1890–1970," *Ethnohistory* 46:4 (Autumn 1999): 671–701; and Jeffrey Greenhut, "Sahib and Sepoy: An Inquiry into the Relationship between the British Officers and Native Soldiers of the British Indian Army," *Military Affairs* 48:1 (January 1984), 15–18.

7. Hebert Maitland Alexander, *On Two Fronts: Being the Adventures of an Indian Mule Corps in France and Gallipoli* (London: Heinemann, 1917), 247–48.

8. Some of these were battalions in the armed services. For example, the British already used Pioneers in its Indian army and had experimented with pioneer-type corps in the Crimea and other conflicts, so they created a formal pioneer corps in late 1914. Such battalions were attached to army divisions, and they included "diggers" but also skilled tradesmen such as carpenters, blacksmiths, masons, etc. For more information, see K. W. Mitchinson, *Pioneer Battalions in the Great War: Organized and Intelligent Labour* (London: Leo Cooper, 1997).

9. Thanks to Tim Parsons for this insight.

10. W. D. Downes, *With the Nigerians in German East Africa* (London: Methuen, 1919), 272.

11. Daryl Klein, *With the Chinks* (London: John Lane Bodley Head, 1918), 31.

12. Peter Gatrell, *Russia's First World War: A Social and Economic History* (Harlow, Essex: Pearson Longman, 2005), 177, 182, 190.

13. Col. E. D. Anderson report from 1918, quoted in Arthur E. Barbeau and Florette Henri, *The Unknown Soldiers: African-American Troops in World War I* (New York: Da Capo Press, 1996), 33.

14. U. N. Chakravorty, *Indian Nationalism and the First World War, 1914–1918: Recent Political and Economic History of India* (Calcutta: Progressive Publishers, 1997), 10–11.

15. Nicholas J. Griffin, "Britain's Chinese Labor Corps in World War I," *Military Affairs* 40:3 (October 1976): 104.

16. Nicholas J. Griffin, "Scientific Management in the Direction of Britain's Military Labour Establishment during World War I," *Military Affairs* 42:4 (December 1978): 199.

17. As quoted in Clothier, *Black Valour*, 27.

18. As quoted in Clothier, *Black Valour*, 166, 1, 80–81, 126–30.

19. Scott P. Rosenberg, "Promises of Moshoeshoe: Culture, Nationalism, and Identity in Lesotho, 1902–1966" (Ph.D. diss., Indiana University, 1998), 46–47.

20. Rosenberg, "Promises of Moshoeshoe," 47.

21. Clothier, *Black Valour*, 19.

22. Clothier, *Black Valour*, 21.

23. Timothy H. Parsons, *The African Rank-and-File: Social Implications of Colonial Military Service in the King's African Rifles, 1902–1964* (Portsmouth, NH: Heinemann, 1999), 63; Downes, *With the Nigerians*, 97; Ross Anderson, *The Forgotten Front: The East African Campaign, 1914–1918* (Stroud, UK: Tempus, 2004), 185.

24. B. P. Willan, "The South African Native Labour Contingent, 1916–1918," *Journal of African History* 19:1 (1978): 68. A proposal to send prisoners from South African jails to the SANLC, however, was never implemented.

25. Grundlingh, *Fighting Their Own War*, 58.

26. Parsons, *The African Rank-and-File*, 63–64.

27. Richard Smith, *Jamaican Volunteers in the First World War: Race, Masculinity, and the Development of National Consciousness* (Manchester, UK: Manchester University Press, 2004), 5.

28. Xu Guoqi, *China and the Great War: China's Pursuit of a New National Identity and Internationalization* (Cambridge: Cambridge University Press, 2005), 148.

29. Contract for Chinese Labour Corps (Form F13), WO 106/33, National Archives, UK (PRO); Sample Identification paper for CLC, WO 32/11345, PRO.

30. Guoqi, *China and the Great War*, 130; Michael Summerskill, *China on the Western Front: Britain's Chinese Work Force in the First World War* (London: Michael Summerskill, 1982), 55, 65, 205. Guoqi's recent book has sorted through the muddle of differing statistics to come up with solid numbers of about 140,000 Chinese laborers in France and Belgium (western front) and perhaps six thousand more on Britain's fronts in Mesopotamia and Egypt.

31. Guoqi, *China and the Great War*, 114–16.

32. Guoqi, *China and the Great War*, 117–19.

33. Summerskill, *China on the Western Front*, 1; Guoqi, *China and the Great War*, 123.

34. Guoqi, *China and the Great War*, 130; Wendy M. Fisher, "Dr. E. J. Stuckey and the Chinese Hospital at Noyelles-sur-Mer: A Biographical Fragment of World War I" (1978), 94; MSS1174, Australian War Memorial (AWM).

35. Fisher, "Dr. E. J. Stuckey," 42 n.24; Guoqi, *China and the Great War*, 126–30.

36. Xu Guoqi notes that the British treatment of their Chinese laborers was much harsher than that of the French. The French paid better, provided better-quality food, and allowed more freedom. Guoqi, *China and the Great War*, 132–33.

37. Gwynnie Hagen, "Eenen Dwazen Glimlach aan het Front: Chinese koelies aan het westers front in de Eerste Wereldoorlog," (Licentiate thesis, Katholieke Universiteit Leuven, Belgium, 1996), 78–82. For more discussion of the interaction between civilians and soldiers/workers of the various armies around Ypres, see: Dominiek Dendooven, "The Multicultural War in Flanders," in *Une Guerre Totale? La Belgique dans la Première Guerre mondiale*, ed. Serge Jaumain et al. (Brussels: Algemeen Rijksarchief, 2005), 377–89.

38. Tyler Stovall, "The Color Line behind the Lines: Racial Violence in France during the Great War," *American Historical Review* 103:3 (June 1998): 753.

39. Summerskill, *China on the Western Front*, 175.

40. Susan R. Grayzel, "'The Souls of Soldiers': Civilians under Fire in First World War France," *Journal of Modern History* 78 (Setpember 2006): 602.

41. War Diary for September 1917, WO 95/83, PRO.

42. Col. B. Fairfax to Director of Labour, GHQ (25 December 1917), WO 106/33, PRO.

43. "A Grave Issue." *Daily News* (14 Sept. 1917); Draft reply; War Diary September 1917, WO 95/83 Director of Labour, PRO.

44. Klein, *With the Chinks*, 7.

45. Fisher, "Dr. E. J. Stuckey," 55.

46. Fisher, "Dr. E. J. Stuckey," 64, 72, 75–82, 85.

47. Summerskill, *China on the Western Front*, 2; Fisher, "Dr. E. J. Stuckey," 32.

48. Stovall, "The Color Line behind the Lines," 744–45.

49. Brian C. Fawcett, "The Chinese Labour Corps in France, 1917–1921," *Journal of the Hong Kong Branch of the Royal Asiatic Society* 40 (2000): 59.

50. Guoqi, *China and the Great War*, 143–45.

51. Fisher, "Dr. E. J. Stuckey," 83.

52. "Restrictions on the Employment of Various Classes of Labour administered by the Labour Directorate (Nov. 1917)," War Diary 1917 Appendix, WO 95/83, PRO.

53. War Diary May 1918, WO 95/83, PRO.

54. John Horne, "Immigrant Workers in France during World War I," *French Historical Studies* 14:1 (1985): 59.

55. Richard S. Fogarty, *Race and War in France: Colonial Subjects in the French Army, 1914–1918* (Baltimore, MD: Johns Hopkins University Press, 2008), 63–65.

56. Stovall, "The Color Line behind the Lines," 741–42.

57. Horne, "Immigrant Workers in France," 86–87.

58. Stovall, "The Color Line behind the Lines," 755–56.

59. Dominiek Dendooven, "The British Dominions and Colonies at the Front in Flanders," in *World War I: Five Continents in Flanders,* eds. Dominiek Dendooven and Piet Chielens (Tielt, Belgium: Lannoo, 2008), 105.

60. Christopher Pugsley, *Te Hokowhitu a Tu: The Maori Pioneer Battalion in the First World War* (Auckland, New Zealand: Reed, 1995), 9, 35–36, 45, 54–55.

61. Alexander, *On Two Fronts,* 147.

62. Ellis Goldberg, "Peasants in Revolt: Egypt 1919," *International Journal of Middle Eastern Studies* 24:2 (May 1992): 269–71.

63. Mohammand Gholi Majd, *Iraq in World War I: From Ottoman Rule to British Conquest* (Lanham, MD: University Press of America, 2006), 353.

64. J. Fitzgerald Lee, *Blacklead and Whitewash: A Side-Show of the Great War* (Karachi, Pakistan: G. A. Holdaway, [1923]), 87.

65. Barbeau and Henri, *The Unknown Soldiers,* 102.

66. Barbeau and Henri, *The Unknown Soldiers,* 89–102.

67. Barbeau and Henri, *The Unknown Soldiers,* 101–6.

68. As quoted in Barbeau and Henri, *The Unknown Soldiers,* 89.

69. Mark Thompson, *The White War: Life and Death on the Italian Front, 1915–1919* (New York: Basic Books, 2008), 141.

70. Hew Strachan, *The First World War,* vol. 1: *To Arms* (Oxford: Oxford University Press, 2001), 690–91.

71. Gatrell, *Russia's First World War,* 72–73, 156.

72. Vejas Liulevicius, *War Land on the Eastern Front: Culture, National Identity, and German Occupation in World War I* (Cambridge: Cambridge University Press, 2000), 72–75.

73. Diary entries from April 8 to April 18, 1915, as quoted in Svetlana Palmer and Sarah Wallis, eds., *Intimate Voices from the First World War* (New York: Morrow, 2003), 70, 83, 86–88.

74. TS extracts from Henry S. Gullett diaries and notebooks, Jerusalem, p. 1; AWM 40/62.

75. Gatrell, *Russia's First World War,* 114–15, 156, 189.

76. Gatrell, *Russia's First World War,* 188–91.

77. Avis No. 151, 30 May 1915, Box 2792 Affiches Collection 1914–1918, Stadsarchief Leuven (SL).

78. Anderson, *The Forgotten Front,* 186.

79. Palmer and Wallis, eds., *Intimate Voices from the First World War,* 307.

80. Annette Becker, *Oubliés de la Grande Guerre* (Paris: Éditions Noêsies, 1998), 68–69; Margaret Darrow, *French Women and the First World War* (Oxford: Berg, 2000), 117–20. See also, René Deruyk, *1914–1918, Lille dans les Serres Allemandes* (Lille, France: La Voix du Nord, 1992).

81. Isabel V. Hull, *Absolute Destruction: Military Culture and the Practices of War in Imperial Germany* (Ithaca, NY: Cornell University Press, 2006), 254–55.

82. Maurice Pate diary (transcription), 21–30 October 1916, pp. 40–45; Pate Papers, Box 1, Herbert Hoover Presidential Library, West Branch, Iowa, USA (HHPL).

83. Jens Thiel, "Forced Labour, Deportation, and Recruitment: The German Reich and Belgian Labourers during the First World War," in Jaumain et al., eds., *Une Guerre Totale?*, 235–45. For a fuller analysis of this issue, see Jens Thiel, *Menschenbassin Belgien: Anwerbung, Deportation und Zwangsarbeit im Ersten Weltkrieg* (Essen, Germany: Klartext, 2007).

84. Thiel, *Menschenbassin Belgien*, 32.

85. Hull, *Absolute Destruction*, 252–53.

86. The official statistics also include Belgian carriers. Geoffrey Hodges, *The Carrier Corps: Military Labor in the East African Campaign, 1914–1918* (New York: Greenwood Press, 1986), 99–100, 110–11.

87. David Killingray, "Labour Exploitation for Military Campaigns in British Colonial Africa, 1870–1945," *Journal of Contemporary History* 24:3 (July 1989): 489–90.

88. Gregory Maddox, "Mtunya: Famine in Central Tanzania, 1917–20," *Journal of African History* 31:2 (1990): 183–84.

89. Human porterage had been a mainstay of transport in East Africa since the early nineteenth century, with the development of a professional labor force of carriers. However, the forced labor of porters even before the war and in great numbers during the war constituted a different phenomenon. For more information on porterage in East Africa, see Stephen J. Rockel, *Carriers of Culture: Labor on the Road in Nineteenth-Century East Africa* (Portsmouth, NH: Heinemann, 2006).

90. Downes, *With the Nigerians*, 187–88.

91. Hodges, *The Carrier Corps*, 145, appendix 5.

92. Killingray, "Labour Exploitation for Military Campaigns," 493.

93. Downes, *With the Nigerians*, 125.

94. As quoted in Palmer and Wallis, eds., *Intimate Voices from the First World War*, 180–83.

95. Grundlingh, *Fighting Their Own War*, 87–88.

96. "Forced Labor Bill Passed," *New York Times* (10 April 1918).

97. Alon Rachamimov, *POWs and the Great War: Captivity on the Eastern Front* (Oxford: Berg, 2002), 31, 60, 72, 107.

98. Heather Jones, "A Missing Paradigm? Military Captivity and the Prisoner of War, 1914–18," *Immigrants and Minorities* 26:1/2 (March/July 2008): 28.

99. Rachamimov, *POWs and the Great War*, 108–15.

100. Gatrell, *Russia's First World War*, 184.

101. Gerald H. Davis, "Prisoners of War in Twentieth-Century War Economies," *Journal of Contemporary History* 12:4 (October 1977); 628–29.

102. Kai Rawe, "Working in the Coal Mine: Belgians in the German War Industry of the Ruhr Area during World War I," in Jaumain et al., eds., *Une Guerre Totale?*, 224. See also, Kai Rawe, *'... wir werden sie schon zur Arbeit bringen': Ausländerbeschäftigung und Zwangsarbeit im Ruhrkohlenbergbau während des Ersten Weltkrieges* (Essen, Germany: Klartext, 2005).

103. Niall Ferguson, *The Pity of War* (New York: Basic, 1999), 267, 371.

104. Edith O'Shaughnessy, *My Lorraine Journal* (New York: Harper & Brothers, 1918), 9.

105. Maureen Healy, *Vienna and the Fall of the Hapsburg Empire: Total War and Everyday Life in World War I* (Cambridge: Cambridge University Press, 2004), 276.

106. M. S. Leigh, *The Punjab and the War* (Lahore, Pakistan: Government Printing, 1922), 51–52.

107. Chakravorty, *Indian Nationalism and the First World War*, 15.

108. W. B. Lane, *A Summary of the History, with Suggestions, and Recommendations of the Seven Jail Labour and Porter Corps, Employed in Mesopotamia from October 1916 to July 1919* (Baghdad: Government Press, 1920), 1.

109. Lane, *A Summary of the History*, 7–8.

110. Thomas C. Kennedy, *The Hound of Conscience: A History of the No-Conscription Fellowship, 1914–1919* (Fayetteville: University of Arkansas Press, 1981), 83–84.

111. The papers of many of these conscientious objectors are held at the Society of Friends Library in London.

112. Tammy Proctor, *On My Honour: Guides and Scouts in Interwar Britain* (Philadelphia: American Philosophical Society, 2002), 87.

113. See Cynthia Enloe, *Does Khaki Become You? The Militarisation of Women's Lives* (London: South End Press, 1983), 4–7.

114. Melissa Stockdale, "'My Death for the Motherland Is Happiness': Women, Patriotism, and Soldiering in Russia's Great War, 1914–1917," *American Historical Review* 109:1 (February 2004): 92, 95. See also Laurie Stoff, "They Fought for Russia: Female Soldiers of the First World War," in *A Soldier and a Woman: Sexual Integration in the Military*, eds. Gerard J. DeGroot and Corinna Peniston-Bird (Harlow, Essex: Pearson Education, 2000), 66–82.

115. Quoted in Laurie Stoff, *They Fought for the Motherland: Russia's Women Soldiers in World War I and Revolution* (Lawrence: University Press of Kansas, 2006), 37.

116. Stoff, *They Fought for the Motherland*, 53, 77, 114.

117. Bianca Schönberger, "Motherly Heroines and Adventurous Girls: Red Cross Nurses and Women Army Auxiliaries in the First World War," in *Home/Front: The Military, War, and Gender in Twentieth-Century Germany*, eds. Karen Hagemann and Stefanie Schüler-Springorum (Oxford: Berg, 2002), 91; and Susan Zeiger, *In Uncle Sam's Service: Women Workers with the American Expeditionary Force, 1917–1919* (Ithaca, NY: Cornell University Press, 1999), 2.

118. A. Lincoln Lavine, *Circuits of Victory* (Garden City, NY: Doubleday, Page, 1921), 272–77.

119. Zeiger, *In Uncle Sam's Service*, 51.

120. Krisztina Robert, "Gender, Class, and Patriotism: Women's Paramilitary Units in First World War Britain," *International History Review* 19:1 (February 1997): 59.

121. Ute Daniel, *Arbeiterfrauen in der Kriegsgesellschaft: Beruf, Familie undPolitik im Ersten Weltkrieg* (Göttingen, Germany: Vandenhoeck & Ruprecht, 1989), 91–93.

122. Pate, 11 March 1917, 82; Box 1, HHPL.

123. Pam Maclean, "War and Australian Society," in *Australia's War, 1914–1918*, ed. Joan Beaumont (St. Leonard's, Australia: Allen & Unwin, 1995), 80.

124. Stockdale, "My Death for the Motherland ," 84. Stockdale notes that complaints about unofficial women's units appear in the official records after November 1917.

125. Healy, *Vienna and the Fall of the Hapsburg Empire*, 204.

126. Nancy Loring Goldman and Richard Stites, "Great Britain and the World Wars," in *Female Soldiers—Combatants or Noncombatants? Historical and Contemporary Perspectives*, ed. Nancy Loring Goldman (Westport, CT: Greenwood Press, 1982), 29; and F. Tennyson Jesse, *The Sword of Deborah: First-Hand Impressions of the British Women's Army in France* (New York: Doran, 1919), 27.

127. Army Council Instruction [pamphlet] No. 537 of 1917, "Employment of Women with the Armies Abroad," WO32/5251, PRO.

128. Minute sheet, May 1917, Status of WAAC file, WO32/5253, PRO.

129. Women's Overseas Service File, WO 32/5251 Public Record Office (PRO). See also Elizabeth Crossthwait, "'The Girl behind the Man behind the Gun': The Women's Army Auxiliary Corps, 1914–18," in *Our Work, Our Lives, Our Words*, eds. Leonore Davidoff and Belinda Westover (Basingstoke, UK: Macmillan Education, 1986), 161–81.

130. Jesse, *The Sword of Deborah*, 93.

131. Yves Pourcher, "La fouille des champs d'honneur," *Terrain* 20: *La mort* (March 1993), available at http://terrain.revues.org/document3057.html. Consulted 20 October 2006.

132. O'Shaughnessy, *My Lorraine Journal*, 105.

133. Daniel, *Arbeiterfrauen in der Kriegsgesellschaft*, 91.

134. Healy, *Vienna and the Fall of the Hapsburg Empire*, 241–42, 263–64.

135. Koenraad Dumoulin, Steven Vansteenkiste, and Jan Verdoodt, *Getuigen van de Grote Oorlog: Getuigenissen uit de frontstreek* (Koksijde, Belgium: De Klaproos, 2001), 83.

136. Civilian Labour Returns, AWM25 101/23 Baths and Laundries; War Diary August 1918, WO 95/83, PRO.

137. Guoqi, *China and the Great War*, 146.

138. Barbeau and Henri, *The Unknown Soldiers*, 165–66.

139. Barbeau and Henri, *The Unknown Soldiers*, 166–67.

140. Guoqi, *China and the Great War*, 146.

141. Ian Gleeson, *The Unknown Force: Black, Indian, and Coloured Soldiers through Two World Wars* (Rivonia, South Africa: Ashanti, 1994), 45.

142. Clothier, *Black Valour*, 172–77.

143. Maddox, "Mtunya," 181.

144. Yucel Yanikdag, "Ottoman Prisoners of War in Russia, 1914–1922," *Journal of Contemporary History* 34:1 (January 1999): 80.

145. Gatrell, *Russia's First World War*, 80.

146. Maurer Maurer, "The Court-Martialing of Camp Followers, World War I," *American Journal of Legal History* 9:3 (1965): 204.

147. Lavine, *Circuits of Victory*, xix.

CHAPTER 3

1. Walter Arthur Richter collection, File 5, National World War I Museum Archives, Kansas City, MO, USA (LMM).

2. Piete Kuhr, *There We'll Meet Again*, trans. Walter Wright (Gloucester, UK: Walter Wright, 1998), 4.

3. Kuhr, *There We'll Meet Again*, 3, 14, 20.

4. "War Precautions Act 1914," in *The Acts of the Parliament of the Commonwealth of Australia Passed during the Years 1914 and 1915* (1916), National Archives of Australia (NAA); Mark Thompson, *The White War: Life and Death on the Italian Front, 1915–1919* (New York: Basic Books, 2008), 212; Victor S. Mamatey, "The Czech Wartime Dilemma: The Habsburgs or the Entente," in *War and Society in East Central Europe*, eds. Béla Király and Nándor F. Dreisziger (New York: Columbia University Press, 1985), 103.

5. In Spain, for instance, the government outlawed political gatherings to discuss Spanish neutrality in an attempt to stave off civil conflict and a move by some to push Spain into war. Later, in 1917, the Spanish government also instituted censorship and suspended many constitutional rights. See Francisco J. Romero Salvadó, *Spain, 1914–1918: Between War and Revolution* (London: Routledge, 1999), 9, 109.

6. Gerard J. DeGroot, *Blighty: British Society in the Era of the Great War* (London: Longman, 1996), 234–35; Susan R. Grayzel, *Women's Identities at War: Gender, Motherhood, and Politics in Britain and France during the First World War* (Chapel Hill: University of North Carolina Press, 1999), 151–52; and Philippa Levine, *Prostitution, Race, and Politics: Policing Venereal Disease in the British Empire* (New York: Routledge, 2003), 163–65.

7. "Emergency Laws and Rules," *Times* (London) (26 November 1918).

8. Eberhard Demm, "Propaganda and Caricature in the First World War," *Journal of Contemporary History* 28:1 (1993): 165–67.

9. Richard Smith, *Jamaican Volunteers in the First World War: Race, Masculinity, and the Development of National Consciousness* (Manchester, UK: Manchester University Press, 2004), 43–44.

10. Laura E. Nym Mayhall, *The Militant Suffrage Movement: Citizenship and Resistance in Britain, 1860–1930* (Oxford: Oxford University Press, 2003), 118; Susan Kingsley Kent, "The Politics of Sexual Difference: World War I and the Demise of British Feminism," *Journal of British Studies* 27 (July 1988): 232.

11. Nicoletta Gullace, *"The Blood of our Sons": Men, Women, and the Renegotiation of British Citizenship during the Great War* (New York: Palgrave Macmillan, 2002), 123.

12. For further discussion of this phenomenon in Britain, see Claire A. Culleton, *Working-Class Culture, Women, and Britain, 1914–1921* (New York: St. Martin's Press, 1999), 140, 146–47.

13. K. F. Tegart, "Charles Tegart: Memoir of an Indian Policeman," unpublished TS; MSS EUR/C235, Oriental and India Office Library, British Library (OIO-BL).

14. David Mitrany, *The Effect of the War in Southeastern Europe* (New Haven, CT: Yale University Press, 1936), 64.

15. Eric Lohr, *Nationalizing the Russian Empire: The Campaign against Enemy Aliens during World War I* (Cambridge, MA: Harvard University Press, 2003), 18.

16. John Braeman, "World War One and the Crisis of American Liberty," *American Quarterly* 16:1 (Spring 1964): 110.

17. John Horne, "Introduction: Mobilizing for 'Total War,' 1914–1918," in *State, Society, and Mobilization in Europe during the First World War*, ed. John Horne (Cambridge: Cambridge University Press, 1997), 11.

18. Frederick Luebke, *Germans in Brazil* (Baton Rouge: Louisiana State University Press, 1987), 169–96.

19. Joseph C. Grew, "Why Germany Must Be Defeated" (1917), Folder: Addresses by Grew, Merrill, Pearl, Smith, Taylor, Wilbur, Box 7, U. S. Food Administration Files, Herbert Hoover Presidential Library (HHPL).

20. Maurer Maurer, "The Court-Martialing of Camp Followers, World War I," *American Journal of Legal History* 9:3 (1965): 203.

21. Nate Williams, "German-Americans in World War I," Western Front Association-Phi Alpha Theta Essay Prize 2001, available at http://www.wfa-usa.org/new/germanamer.htm. Last accessed October 30, 2009.

22. Christopher Capozzola, *Uncle Sam Wants You: World War I and the Making of the Modern American Citizen* (Oxford: Oxford University Press, 2008), 117.

23. Capozzola, *Uncle Sam Wants You*, 184–85.

24. Unpublished MS, pp. 9–10; PR 91/048, Item 55, Papers of Gilbert Graham, Australian War Memorial (AWM).

25. Martha Hanna, *Your Death Would Be Mine: Paul and Marie Pireaud in the Great War* (Cambridge, MA: Harvard University Press, 2006), 38; Lohr, *Nationalizing the Russian Empire*, 13.

26. Miss R. A. Neal MS (October 1914), 87/26/1, Imperial War Museum (IWM).

27. David French, "Spy Fever in Britain, 1900–1915," *Historical Journal* 21:2 (1978): 365.

28. Quoted in Jean-Jacques Becker, *The Great War and the French People*, trans. Arnold Pomerans (New York: St. Martin's Press, 1986), 50.

29. Thompson, *The White War*, 212.

30. Demm, "Propaganda and Caricature in the First World War," 166.

31. Christa Hämmerle, "'You Let a Weeping Woman Call You Home?' Private Correspondences during the First World War in Austria and Germany," in *Epistolary Selves: Letters and Letter-Writers, 1600–1945*, ed. Rebecca Earle (Aldershot, UK: Ashgate, 1999), 153–54; Mark Graham, *British Censorship of the Civil Mails during World War I, 1914–1919* (Bristol, UK: Stuart Rossiter Trust Fund, 2000), 26, 37.

32. Lohr, *Nationalizing the Russian Empire*, 31–43; Tammy Proctor, *Female Intelligence: Women and Espionage in the First World War* (New York: New York University Press, 2003), 39. For an excellent account of the motivation and impact of the Lusitania riots in Britain, see Nicoletta Gullace, "Friends, Aliens, and Enemies: Fictive Communities and the Lusitania Riots of 1915," *Journal of Social History* 39:2 (December 2005): 345–67.

33. Kuhr, *There We'll Meet Again*, 73.

34. George Butling to his father, 6 August 1917, 1/27, Butling Correspondence, Con Shelf, IWM.

35. Maureen Healy, *Vienna and the Fall of the Habsburg Empire: Total War and Everyday Life in WWI* (Cambridge: Cambridge University Press, 2004), 244.

36. Stéphane Audoin-Rouzeau, "Children and the Primary Schools of France, 1914–1918," in Horne, ed., *State, Society, and Mobilization*, 45.

37. Sabine Hake, "Chaplin Reception in Weimar Germany," *New German Critique* 51 (Autumn 1990): 87–111.

38. "What the Players Are Doing for Their Country," *Opera House Reporter* (26 April 1918), Liberty Theaters correspondence, LMM.

39. Ephemera from the American Committee for Relief in the Near East Collection, LMM.

40. Ephemera from German Home Front Collection, LMM.

41. Feroz Ahmad, "War and Society under the Young Turks, 1908–1918," in *The Modern Middle East: A Reader*, eds. Albert Hourani, Philip Khoury, and Mary C. Wilson (London: Tauris, 2004), 133.

42. C. Paul Vincent, *The Politics of Hunger: The Allied Blockade of Germany, 1915–1919* (Athens: Ohio University Press, 1985), 11, 20; Ljuben Berov, "The Bulgarian Economy during World War I," in Király et al., eds., *War and Society in East Central Europe*, 172.

43. Stephen Broadberry and Peter Howlett, "The United Kingdom during World War I," in *The Economics of World War I*, eds. Stephen Broadberry and Mark Harrison (Cambridge: Cambridge University Press, 2005), 229–30.

44. Avner Offer, *The First World War: An Agrarian Interpretation* (Oxford: Clarendon Press, 1989), 1.

45. Vincent, *The Politics of Hunger*.

46. Axel Robert Nordvall, "Sweden's Food Supply," *Annals of the American Academy of Political and Social Science* 74 (November 1917): 58–61.

47. A. G. A. Van Eelde, "The Case for Holland," *Annals of the American Academy of Political and Social Science* 74 (November 1917): 77.

48. Francois Monod, "Food for France and Its Public Control," *Annals of the American Academy of Political and Social Science* 74 (November 1917): 87–88; Benjamin Ziemann, *War Experiences in Rural Germany, 1914–1923*, trans. Alex Skinner (Oxford: Berg, 2007), 156–57.

49. Şevket Pamuk, "The Ottoman Economy in World War I," in Broadberry and Harrison, eds., *The Economics of World War I*, 122.

50. Hanna, *Your Death Would Be Mine*, 52

51. Serao, "Contadine," in *Lines of Fire: Women Writers of World War I*, ed. Margaret Higonnet (New York: Plume, 1999), 120–21.

52. Kuhr, *There We'll Meet Again*, 191.

53. Kuhr, *There We'll Meet Again*, 227.

54. Offer, *The First World War*, 29, and Vincent, *The Politics of Hunger*, 45.

55. *Notre Labeur: La Région de Louvain pendant la Guerre* (Brussels: De Bruycker, n.d.), 120–21; Vincent, *The Politics of Hunger*, 129.

56. Peter Gatrell, *Russia's First World War: A Social and Economic History* (Harlow, Essex: Pearson Longman, 2005), 26; Josh Sanborn, "The Mobilization of 1914 and the Question of the Russian Nation: A Reexamination," *Slavic Review* 59:2 (Summer 2000): 276.

57. John Turner, "State Purchase of the Liquor Trade in the First World War," *Historical Journal* 23:3 (September 1980): 593.

58. Hämmerle, "'You Let a Weeping Woman Call You Home?'," 170.

59. As quoted in Offer, *The First World War*, 29.

60. Thierry Bonzon and Belinda Davis, "Feeding the Cities," in *Capital Cities at War: Paris, London, Berlin, 1914–1919*, vol. 1, eds. Jay Winter and Jean-Louis Robert (Cambridge: Cambridge University Press, 1997), 324–25.

61. Press release digest 21 April 1917 to 29 November 1918, Box 2, and Food Saving and Sharing folder, Box 8, US Food Administration documents, HHPL.

62. Rose Kerr, *The Story of a Million Girls* (London: Girl Guides Association, 1937), 290.

63. This statement refers to Germany, but it could be any number of nations in the war. Richard Bessel, "Mobilization and Demobilization in Germany, 1916–1919," in Horne, ed., *State, Society, and Mobilization*, 219.

64. Pamuk, "The Ottoman Economy in World War I," 124.

65. As quoted in Svetlana Palmer and Sarah Wallis, eds., *Intimate Voices from the First World War* (New York: Morrow, 2003), 43.

66. Secret intelligence report (filed by Capt. General Staff—L of C. area)—Confidential IS1656 (30 August 1917) from Hector Lambrechts (Directeur de l'Industrie et du Travail at Brussels); Folder Belgium, General Conditions; Brand Whitlock Papers, Library of Congress (LC).

67. Police report quoted in Belinda J. Davis, "Homefront: Food, Politics, and Women's Everyday Life during the First World War," in *Home/Front: The Military, War, and Gender in Twentieth-Century Germany*, eds. Karen Hagemann and Stefanie Schüler-Springorum (Oxford: Berg, 2002), 126. On the Italian riot, see Paul Corner and Giovanna Procacci, "The Italian Experience of 'Total' Mobilization, 1915–1920," in Horne, ed., *State, Society, and Mobilization*, 230.

68. Barbara Alpern Engel, "Not by Bread Alone: Subsistence Riots in Russia during World War I," *Journal of Modern History* 69:4 (December 1997): 697, 708–10, 721.

69. Pamuk, "The Ottoman Economy in World War I," in Broadberry and Harrison, eds., *The Economics of World War I*, 124–25.

70. Mohammed Gholi Majd, *The Great Famine and Genocide in Persia, 1917–1919* (Lanham, MD: University Press of America, 2003), 17–22.

71. As quoted in Majd, *The Great Famine and Genocide in Persia*, 40.

72. Gregory Maddox, "Mtunya: Famine in Central Tanzania, 1917–20," *Journal of African History* 31 (1990): 181.

73. Dániel I. Szabó, "The Social Basis of Opposition to the War in Hungary," in Király et al., eds., *War and Society in East Central Europe*, 139.

74. Ian F. W. Beckett, *The Great War, 1914–1918* (Harlow, Essex: Pearson Education, 2001), 269–71.

75. Kuhr, *There We'll Meet Again*, 142.

76. Engel, "Not by Bread Alone," 703–4.

77. Keith Allen, "Sharing Scarcity: Bread Rationing and the First World War in Berlin, 1914–1923," *Journal of Social History* 32:2 (Winter 1998): 371.

78. Allen, "Sharing Scarcity," 383–84.

79. Healy, *Vienna and the Fall of the Habsburg Empire*, 45.

80. Peter Pastor, "The Home Front in Hungary, 1914–1918," in Király et al., eds., *War and Society in East Central Europe*, 127.

81. Belinda Davis, *Home Fires Burning: Food, Politics, and Everyday Life in World War I Berlin* (Chapel Hill: University of North Carolina Press, 2000), 190–204.

82. Offer, *The First World War*, 58–59.

83. Many of the essays in Horne, ed., *State, Society, and Mobilization*, deal with this particular issue. See essays by Mommsen, Horne, Bessel, and Corner/Procaccia.

84. Healy, *Vienna and the Fall of the Habsburg Empire*, 54–55.

85. Ute Daniel, *The War from Within: German Working-Class Women in the First World War*, trans. Margaret Ries (Oxford: Berg, 1997), 197–98.

86. As quoted in Vincent, *The Politics of Hunger*, 21.

87. Davis, *Home Fires Burning*, 49–50, 71–75.

88. Roger Chickering, *The Great War and Urban Life in Germany: Freiburg, 1914–1918* (Cambridge: Cambridge University Press, 2007), 227.

89. Healy, *Vienna and the Fall of the Habsburg Empire*, 65–68.

90. Margaret H. Darrow, *French Women and the First World War: War Stories of the Home Front* (Oxford: Berg, 2000), 199.

91. Davis, "Homefront," 125, and Healy, *Vienna and the Fall of the Habsburg Empire*, 49.

92. Healy, *Vienna and the Fall of the Habsburg Empire*, 116.

93. Monica Krippner, *The Quality of Mercy: Women at War, Serbia, 1915–1918* (Newton Abbot, UK: David and Charles, 1980), 29, 35.

94. Darrow, *French Women and the First World War*, 240.

95. Bianca Schönberger, "Motherly Heroines and Adventurous Girls: Red Cross Nurses and Women Army Auxiliaries in the First World War," in *Home/Front: The Military, War, and Gender in Twentieth-Century Germany*, eds. Karen Hagemann and Stefanie Schüler-Springorum (Oxford: Berg, 2002), 89.

96. Women's Reserve Ambulance flyers and booklets, Eunice Graham's Green Cross Society WRA Cards, Gilbert Graham to Eunice Graham, 2 March 1916; Folders 1 & 3—3DRL/4149 and 3DRL/6545B (Mrs. G. E. Graham), Papers of Gilbert Graham, AWM.

97. Darrow, *French Women and the First World War*, 81. Darrow (pp. 82–83) also points out that not all *marraines* were women, but that some civilian men and convalescing soldiers could also take on that role. Belgium also had a *marraines de guerre* scheme, developed along French lines during the war (thanks to Sophie de Schaepdrijver for this information).

98. Grayzel, *Women's Identities at War*, 30–33; Darrow, *French Women and the First World War*, 79–82.

99. *La Baïonnette* [Special Issue on Marraines], 14 October 1915, 230–231; Cartoon Research Library, Ohio State University (CRLOSU).

100. Kuhr, *There We'll Meet Again*, 100, 112, 114, 122–23, 155, 170, 217.

101. Walter Arthur Richter collection, Files 5 and 6, LMM.

102. Angela Woollacott, *On Her Their Lives Depend: Munition Workers in the Great War* (Berkeley: University of California Press, 1994), 21–22.

103. Susan Zeiger, *In Uncle Sam's Service: Women Workers with the American Expeditionary Force, 1917–1919* (Ithaca, NY: Cornell University Press, 1999), 17. See also Maurine Weiner Greenwald, *Women, War, and Work: The Impact of World War I on Women Workers in the United States* (Westport, CT: Greenwood Press, 1980).

104. Thierry Bonzon, "The Labour Market and Industrial Mobilization, 1915–1917," in Winter and Robert, eds., *Capital Cities at War*, vol. 1, 185.

105. Bonzon, in Winter and Robert, eds., *Capital Cities at War*, vol. 1, 188; Laura Lee Downs, *Manufacturing Inequality: Gender Division in the French and British Metalworking Industries, 1914–1939* (Ithaca, NY: Cornell University Press, 1995), 192.

106. Daniel, *The War from Within*, 65–66, 73–84; Richard Bessel, "Mobilization and Demobilization in Germany, 1916–1919," in Horne, ed., *State, Society, and Mobilization*, 214.

107. Healy, *Vienna and the Fall of the Habsburg Empire*, 204.

108. Vera Brittain, *Testament of Youth* (New York: Penguin, 1989), 231–36.

109. Regina Schulte, "Käthe Kollwitz's Sacrifice," trans. Pamela Selwyn, *History Workshop Journal* 41 (Spring 1996): 195, 197, 204.

110. Mary Martin Diary, MS 34256A, Manuscripts Collection, National Library of Ireland (NLI).

111. Mary Martin Diary (NLI).

112. Hugh Gibson, *A Journal from Our Legation in Belgium* (New York: Doubleday, Page, 1917), 146.

113. Vejas Gabriel Liulevicius, *War Land on the Eastern Front: Culture, National Identity, and German Occupation in World War I* (Cambridge: Cambridge University Press, 2000), 19.

114. Christian Geinitz, "The First Air War against Noncombatants: Strategic Bombing of German Cities in World War I," in *Great War, Total War: Combat and Mobilization on the Western Front, 1914–1918*, eds. Roger Chickering and Stig Förster (Cambridge: Cambridge University Press, 2000), 207, 212.

115. Susan R. Grayzel, "'The Souls of Soldiers': Civilians under Fire in First World War France," *Journal of Modern History* 78 (September 2008): 595.

116. R. J. Wyatt, *Death from the Skies: The Zeppelin Raids over Norfolk* (Norwich: Gliddon Books, 1990), 1–2.

117. Charles B. Burdick, *The Japanese Siege of Tsingtau* (Hamden, CT: Archon Books, 1976), 76–77, 122–23.

118. Harold C. Swan (Acting Vice-Consul) to J. H. Towsey (Consul—Milan) 13 Sep 1916, /566 Air raids over Venice, AIR 1/657/17/122 Air Historical Section, National Archives UK (PRO).

119. Alan Kramer, *Dynamic of Destruction: Culture and Mass Killing in the First World War* (Oxford: Oxford University Press, 2008), 56.

120. "French Air Mastery on Bulgarian Frontier," *Times* (London) (13 June 1916).

121. Joseph Green 1915 diary, Box 20, Joseph C. Green Papers, Hoover Institution, Stanford (HI).

122. London County Council Report by Chief Engineer, 11 Oct 1917, MEPO 2/1657 Air Raid Shelters, PRO.

123. War Diary for September 1917, WO 95/83 Director of Labour November 1916 to March 1919, PRO.

124. Albert Chatelle, *Calais pendant la Guerre (1914–1918)* (Paris: Librairie Aristide Quillet, 1927), 69.

125. Elizabeth H. Ashe, *Intimate Letters from France during America's First Year of War* (San Francisco: Philopolis Press, 1918), 80–81.

126. Clipping, "Eggs at Zep. Funeral," *Daily Sketch* (14 September 1916) in papers of Mrs. E. Fernside, Con Shelf, IWM.

127. "Sinking of a Hospital Ship," *Times* (London) (29 April 1916).

128. "Hospital Ship Sunk," *Times* (London) (28 February 1918).

129. "Great Explosion near Archangel," *Times* (London) (22 November 1916).

130. "Halifax Dead at 1500," *New York Times* (25 December 1917).

131. Woollacott, *On Her Their Lives Depend*, 85–86.

132. 20 January 1917, Letters of Mrs. E. Fernside, Con Shelf, IWM.

133. 30 January 1917, Letters of Mrs. E. Fernside, Con Shelf, IWM.

134. Proctor, *Female Intelligence*, 61.

135. See, for example, Pierre Purseigle, "Warfare and Belligerence: Approaches to the First World War," in *Warfare and Belligerence: Perspectives in First World War Studies*, ed. Pierre Purseigle (Leiden, Netherlands: Brill, 2005), 13.

136. Healy, *Vienna and the Fall of the Habsburg Empire*, 313.

CHAPTER 4

1. Mildred Aldrich to Harriet Levy, 11 February 1916; Mildred Aldrich collection, folder 1, Hoover Institution, Stanford (HI).

2. Quoted in Ludo Stynen and Sylvia Van Peteghem, eds., *In Oorlogsnood: Virginie Lovelings Dagboek, 1914–1918* (Ghent: Koninklijke Academie voor Nederlandse Taal-en Letterkunde, 1999), 407–8.

3. Hugo Slim, *Killing Civilians: Method, Madness, and Morality in War* (New York: Columbia University Press, 2008), 39.

4. Philippe Nivet, "Réfugiés," in *Encyclopédie de la Grande Guerre 1914–1918: Histoire et culture*, eds. Stéphane Audoin-Rouzeau and Jean-Jacques Becker (Paris: Bayard, 2004), 799.

5. Michaël Amara, *Des Belges à l'épreuve de l'Exil: Les Réfugies de la Première Guerre mondiale, France, Grande-Bretagne, Pays-Bas 1914–1918* (Brussels: Editions de l'Université de Bruxelles, 2008), 12.

6. Otto Wiesinger, *Als Kriegsfreiwilliger in Tsingtau* (Shanghai: Nössler, 1915), 24.

7. Peter Gatrell, "Refugees and Forced Migrants during the First World War," *Immigrants and Minorities* 26:1/2 (March/July 2008): 84–85.

8. Mohammad Gholi Majd, *The Great Famine and Genocide in Persia, 1917–1919* (Lanham, MD: University Press of America, 2003), 30.

9. Nivet, "Refugiés," 801, 807.

10. Mitchell A. Yockelson, *Borrowed Soldiers: Americans under British Command, 1918* (Norman: University of Oklahoma Press, 2008), 122.

11. Vejas Gabriel Liulevicius, *War Land on the Eastern Front: Culture, National Identity, and German Occupation in World War I* (Cambridge: Cambridge University Press, 2000), 20, 30.

12. Peter Gatrell, *Russia's First World War: A Social and Economic History* (Harlow, Essex: Pearson Longman, 2005), 19.

13. Vasily Mishnin as quoted in *Intimate Voices from the First World War*, eds. Svetlana Palmer and Sarah Wallis (New York: Morrow, 2003), 106–7.

14. Mildred Aldrich, *A Hilltop on the Marne* (Boston: Houghton Mifflin, 1915), 86.

15. Stynen and Van Peteghem, eds., *In Oorlogsnood*, 57.

16. Stynen and Van Peteghem, eds., *In Oorlogsnood*, 66.

17. Quoted in *Strangers in a Strange Land: Belgian Refugees, 1914–1918* (Leuven, Belgium: Davidsfonds, 2004), 119.

18. Amara, *Des Belges à l'Épreuve de l'Exil*, 154–55.

19. Peter Cahalan, *Belgian Refugee Relief in England during the Great War* (New York: Garland, 1982), 17, 231; Michaël Amara, "Ever Onward They Went: The Story of a Unique Belgian Exodus," in *Strangers in a Strange Land*, 7.

20. Cahalan, *Belgian Refugee Relief*, 262, 274. The militarization of munitions production was a measure adopted by several nations. In Italy, for instance, army officers provided discipline and oversight for armaments factories; workers became subject to military discipline, including court-martial for desertion in the case of insubordination or strikes. See Paul Corner and Giovanna Procacci, "The Italian Experience of 'Total' Mobilization, 1915–1920," in *State, Society, and Mobilization in Europe during the First World War*, ed. John Horne (Cambridge: Cambridge University Press, 1997), 227.

21. Peter Gatrell, *A Whole Empire Walking: Refugees in Russia during World War I* (Bloomington: Indiana University Press, 1999), 21, 52; Amara, "Ever Onward They Went," 20.

22. Dragolioub Yovanovitch, *Les effets économiques et sociaux de la guerre en Serbie* (New Haven, CT: Yale University Press, 1930), 30.

23. Alan Kramer, *Dynamic of Destruction: Culture and Mass Killing in the First World War* (Oxford: Oxford University Press, 2008), 59, and Mark Thompson, *The White War: Life and Death on the Italian Front, 1915–1919* (New York: Basic Books,

2008), 139–40. Kramer (p. 55) notes that more than four hundred thousand refugees fled into Italy in the aftermath of the 1917 disaster at Caporetto, further worsening the situation.

24. M. Wandel quoted in *Strangers in a Strange Land*, 69.

25. Isabel V. Hull, *Absolute Destruction: Military Culture and the Practices of War in Imperial Germany* (Ithaca, NY: Cornell University Press, 2006), 255.

26. Tracy B. Kittredge, "The History of the Commission for Relief in Belgium, 1914–1917" (1918), 318; CRB Collection, 530:1, HI.

27. Annette Becker, *Oubliés de la grande guerre* (Paris: Editions Noêsis, 1998), 68–70.

28. Quoted in Margaret R. Higonnet, ed., *Lines of Fire: Women Writers of World War I* (New York: Plume Books, 1999), 127–28.

29. Jens Thiel, "Forced Labour, Deportation, and Recruitment: The German Reich and Belgian Labourers during the First World War," in *14–18 Une Guerre Totale? La Belgique dans la Première Guerre mondiale*, ed. Serge Jaumain et al. (Brussels: Algemeen Rijksarchief, 2005), 241. See also Jens Thiel, *Menschenbassin Belgien: Anwerbung, Deportation, und Zwangsarbeit im Ersten Weltkrieg* (Essen, Germany: Klartext, 2007).

30. CRB Diary of Maurice Pate [transcript], 42–45; Box 1, Folder: Belgian Relief CRB Correspondence 1916–17, Herbert Hoover Presidential Library (HHPL).

31. Louis Gille, Alphonse Ooms, and Paul Delandsheere, *Cinquante Mois d'Occupation Allemande, 1916*, volume 2 (Brussels: Librairie Albert Dewit, 1919), 331–32.

32. Robert A. Jackson, Handwritten Relief Memoir, Part 3, pp. 4–5; Jackson collection, HI.

33. Sophie de Schaepdrijver, *La Belgique et la Première Guerre mondiale* (Brussels: Peter Lang, 2004), 224–25.

34. Eric Lohr, "The Russian Army and the Jews: Mass Deportation, Hostages, and Violence during World War I," *Russian Review* 60 (July 2001): 409–10; Nivet, "Réfugiés," 800.

35. Alexander Victor Prusin, *Nationalizing a Borderland: War, Ethnicity, and Anti-Jewish Violence in East Galicia, 1914–1920* (Tuscaloosa: University of Alabama Press, 2005), 28–30.

36. Quoted in Palmer and Wallis, eds., *Intimate Voices from the First World War*, 87–88.

37. John Horne and Alan Kramer, *German Atrocities, 1914: A History of Denial* (New Haven, CT: Yale University Press, 2001), 83–84.

38. Liulevicius, *War Land on the Eastern Front*, 20.

39. Fernand Van Langenhove, *Hoe een Cyclus van Legenden Ontstaat: Franc-Tireurs en Gruweldaden in België* (Leiden, Netherlands: De Flaamsche Boekenhalle, 1916), 18, 95.

40. Horne and Kramer, *German Atrocities, 1914*, 138.

41. Horne and Kramer, *German Atrocities, 1914,* 74–76.

42. Kramer, *Dynamic of Destruction,* 61; Horne and Kramer, *German Atrocities, 1914,* 85.

43. Katie Pickles, *Transnational Outrage: The Death and Commemoration of Edith Cavell* (New York: Palgrave Macmillan, 2007), 76.

44. See, for example, Stéphane Audoin-Rouzeau and Annette Becker, *14–18: Understanding the Great War,* trans. Catherine Temerson (New York: Hill and Wang, 2002), 53, and Nicoletta Gullace, "Sexual Violence and Family Honor: British Propaganda and International Law during the First World War," *American Historical Review* 102:3 (1997): 714–47.

45. See Stéphane Audoin-Rouzeau, *L'Enfant de l'Ennemi, 1914–1918* (Paris: Aubier, 1995).

46. Eric Lohr, *Nationalizing the Russian Empire: The Campaign against Enemy Aliens during World War I* (Cambridge, MA: Harvard University Press, 2003), 17.

47. Nancy M. Wingfield and Maria Bucur, "Introduction," in *Gender and War in Twentieth-Century Eastern Europe,* ed. Wingfield and Bucur (Bloomington: Indiana University Press, 2006), 7.

48. Kramer, *Dynamic of Destruction,* 246.

49. Hermann Joseph Hiery, *The Neglected War: The German South Pacific and the Influence of World War I* (Honolulu: University of Hawaii Press, 1995), 72–73.

50. Kramer, *Dynamic of Destruction,* 246–47, and Thompson, *The White War,* 350.

51. See Ruth Harris, "The 'Child of the Barbarian': Rape, Race, and Nationalism in France during the First World War," *Past and Present* 141 (November 1993): 170–206.

52. Susan R. Grayzel, *Women's Identities at War: Gender, Motherhood, and Politics in Britain and France during the First World War* (Chapel Hill: University of North Carolina Press, 1999), 60–63.

53. Stephane Audoin-Rouzeau, *L'Enfant de l'Ennemi (1914–1918): Viol, avortement, infanticide pendant la Grande Guerre* (Paris: Aubier, 1995), 30.

54. Audoin-Rouzeau and Becker, *14–18,* 58.

55. Lohr, *Nationalizing the Russian Empire,* 144; Liulevicius, *War Land on the Eastern Front,* 15.

56. Prusin, *Nationalizing a Borderland,* 49.

57. Lohr, "The Russian Army and the Jews," 413–14.

58. Horne and Kramer, *German Atrocities,* 15, describe several documented instances of the use of human shields in the invasion of Belgium in 1914.

59. Tim Stapleton, "The Impact of the First World War on African People," in *Daily Lives of Civilians in Wartime Africa: From Slavery Days to Rwandan Genocide,* ed. John Laband (Westport, CT: Greenwood Press, 2007), 122.

60. Grigore Antipa, *L'Occupation ennemie de la Roumanie et ses conséquences économiques et sociales* (New Haven: Yale, [1929]), 41.

61. Mohammad Gholi Majd, *Iraq in World War I: From Ottoman Rule to British Conquest* (Lanham, MD: University Press of America, 2006), 193.

62. Luc De Vos, J. Du Chau, W. Steurbaut, G. Van Huffel, *Leuven, Ook een Garnizoensstad* (Leuven, Belgium: Peeters, 1989), 15.

63. Quoted in Palmer and Wallis, eds., *Intimate Voices from the First World War*, 57–58.

64. Quoted in Palmer and Wallis, eds., *Intimate Voices from the First World War*, 312.

65. Thompson, *The White War*, 348.

66. Antipa, *L'occupation ennemie de la Roumanie*, 30.

67. Mary Thorp, "Local Gossip and 'side-shows' of the war during the German occupation of Belgium," unpublished diary, Documentariecentrum Ieper, In Flanders Fields Museum, Belgium (DI).

68. War Diary for August 1918, WO95/83 GHQ Director of Labour November 1916–March 1919, National Archives UK (PRO); Johnson Hagood, *The Services of Supply: A Memoir of the Great War* (Boston: Houghton Mifflin, 1927), 167.

69. "Returns of Civil Labour Employed in the Australian Corps Laundry," AWM25 101/23 Baths and Laundries, Australian War Memorial (AWM).

70. Robert N. Manley and Elaine Manley McKee, eds., *The World War I Letters of Private Milford N. Manley* (Gardner, KS: Dageforde, 1995), 110.

71. Celina Wullepit, *Souvenir de la guerre 1914–1915* [unpublished] (1949), 92; MI 1544, DI.

72. Koenraad Dumoulin, Steven Vansteenkiste, and Jan Verdoodt, *Getuigen van de Grote Oorlog: Getuigenissen uit de frontstreek* (Koksijde, Belgium: De Klaproos, 2001), 81–83.

73. Gary Leiser, trans. and ed., *Vetluga Memoir: A Turkish Prisoner of War in Russia, 1916–1918* (Gainesville: University Press of Florida, 1995), 56.

74. Heber Maitland Alexander, *On Two Fronts: Being the Adventures of an Indian Mule Corps in France and Gallipoli* (London: Heinemann, 1917), 55, 93, 108.

75. John Aston and L. M. Duggan, *The History of the 12th (Bermondsey) Battalion East Surrey Regiment* (Finsbury: Union Press, 1936), 54–55.

76. Walter Richter to mother, 27 October 1918; File 3, Walter Richter Collection, National World War I Museum Archives, Kansas City, MO, USA (LMM).

77. Kittredge, "The History of the Commission for Relief in Belgium, 1914–1917," 31, HI.

78. Piete Kuhr, *There We'll Meet Again*, trans. Walter Wright (Gloucester, UK: Walter Wright, 1998), 129, 186, 189.

79. As quoted in Palmer and Wallis, eds., *Intimate Voices from the First World War*, 63–64.

80. Stynen and van Peteghem, *In Oorlogsnood*, 176–83.

81. Wiesinger, *Als Kriegsfreiwilliger in Tsingtau*, 30–31.

82. As quoted in Palmer and Wallis, eds., *Intimate Voices from the First World War*, 112–13.

83. Yovanovitch, *Les effets économiques et sociaux de la guerre en Serbie*, 74.

84. Records for Office Central Belge pour les prisonniers de guerre, File 3236, cases 88660/1 3984 and 83922/1 0947; Stadsarchief Leuven (SL).

85. Larry Zuckerman, *The Rape of Belgium: The Untold Story of World War I* (New York: New York University Press, 2004), 98.

86. Schaepdrijver, *La Belgique et la première guerre mondiale*, 119.

87. Manuscript diary 1914, Folder 1, Margaret W. Netherwood Mills Collection, HI.

88. Brand Whitlock, *Belgium: A Personal Narrative*, volume 2 (Toronto: McClelland & Stewart, 1919), 269.

89. Quoted in Higonnet, ed., *Lines of Fire*, 168–71.

90. Various posters (*Bekanntmachungen*) from October to November 1917, Box 28, World War I Subject Collection, HI; Liulevicius, *War Land on the Eastern Front*, 78–79.

91. As quoted in Palmer and Wallis, eds., *Intimate Voices from the First World War*, 315.

92. Jean Massart, *La Presse Clandestine dans la Belgique Occupée* (Paris: Berger-Levrault, 1917), 9; and Schaepdrijver, *La Belgique et la première guerre mondiale*, 121.

93. Anthony Verrier, ed., *Agents of Empire: Anglo-Zionist Intelligence Operations, 1915–1919; Brigadier Walter Gribbon, Aaron Aaronsohn, and the NILI Ring* (London: Brassey's, 1995), 320 n.1.

94. Alex Aaronsohn, "The NILI or 'A' Organisation," in Verrier, ed., *Agents of Empire*, 307–11.

95. Eliezer Tauber, "The Capture of the NILI Spies: The Turkish Version," *Intelligence and National Security* 6:4 (1991): 702.

96. Sir Ivone Kirkpatrick, "The War 1914–1918," unpublished memoir, 79/50/1, Imperial War Museum (IWM); Tammy Proctor, *Female Intelligence: Women and Espionage in the First World War* (New York: New York University Press, 2003), 76–77.

97. Janet Morgan, *The Secrets of Rue St. Roch: Hope and Heroism behind Enemy Lines in the First World War* (London: Penguin, 2005), 52–53, 338–43.

98. Douglas Porch, *The French Secret Service: From the Dreyfus Affair to the Gulf War* (New York: Farrar, Straus, Giroux, 1995), 90.

99. Emmanuel Debruyne, "Les services de renseignements alliés en Belgique occupée," in *14–18 Une Guerre Totale? La Belgique dans la Première Guerre mondiale*, ed. Serge Jaumain et al. (Brussels: Algemeen Rijksarchief, 2005), 143.

100. Proctor, *Female Intelligence*, 89–91.

101. "Serment," Service Patriotiques Historical Notices, P-212, Archives Générale du Royaume (AGR).

102. Denise De Weerdt, *De Vrowen van de Eerste Wereldoorlog* (Ghent: Stichting Mens en Kultuur, 1993), 175.

103. News clipping from *Moniteur*, 31 January 1919, La Dame Blanche Box 2, folder 13, IWM.

104. Proctor, *Female Intelligence*, 87–88.

105. Charles B. Burdick, *The Japanese Siege of Tsingtau* (Hamden, CT: Archon Books, 1976), 133–34.

106. Proctor, *Female Intelligence*, 143.

107. Aston and Duggan, *The History of the 12th*, 64–65.

108. 22 Jul 1918 from F. R. Foster (13th Field Ambulance), PR86/173 Letters to Rita Squire, AWM.

109. Addie W. Hunton and Kathryn M. Johnson, *Two Colored Women with the American Expeditionary Forces* (Brooklyn: Brooklyn Eagle Press, 1920), 141–42.

110. Dumoulin et al., *Getuigen van de Grote Oorlog*, 73.

111. John Simons, *Prisoners in Arcady: German Mariners in Berrima, 1915–1919* (Bowral, New South Wales: Berrima District Historical and Family History Society, 1999), 40.

112. Dumoulin et al., *Getuigen van de Grote Oorlog*, 164–65.

113. David Omissi, *Indian Voices of the Great War: Soldiers' Letters, 1914–1918* (New York: St. Martin's Press, 1999), letters 492, 535, 568, 588.

114. General [Paul] Von Lettow-Vorbeck, *My Reminiscences of East Africa* (London: Hurst and Blackett, 1920), 177.

115. For example, the King's African Rifles allowed women to live in barracks. See Timothy Parsons, "'All Askaris Are Family Men': Sex, Domesticity, and Discipline in the King's African Rifles, 1902–1964," in *Guardians of Empire: The Armed Forces of the Colonial Powers c. 1700–1964*, eds. David Killingray and David Omissi (Manchester, UK: Manchester University Press, 1999), 170.

116. Von Lettow-Vorbeck, *My Reminiscences*, 234.

117. David Killingray, "Gender Issues and African Colonial Armies," in Killingray and Omissi, eds., *Guardians of Empire*, 228.

118. August 8, 28, 31, 1918 entries, War Diary L of C Persian Labour Corps (1918 Aug–1920 Jan), WO95/83, PRO.

119. David R. Woodward, *Hell in the Holy Land: World War I in the Middle East* (Lexington: University Press of Kentucky, 2006), 98.

120. Liulevicïus, *War Land on the Eastern Front*, 57–58, 80.

121. Minutes, "Venereal Disease and Its Treatment in the Armed Forces," 11 July 1918, WO 32/5597 Brothels at Havre, PRO.

122. Summary of Proceeding of Permanent Board of Inter-Allied Medical Committee Sanitary Commission for December 1917, WO 32/5597 Brothels at Havre, PRO.

123. Haig to Secretary of the War Office, 4 June 1918, WO 32/5597 Brothels at Havre, PRO. For more information on French regulation of sexuality and venereal disease, see Judith Surkis, *Sexing the Citizen: Morality and Masculinity in France, 1870–1920* (Ithaca, NY: Cornell University Press, 2006).

124. Susan R. Grayzel, *Women's Identities at War: Gender, Motherhood, and Politics in Britain and France during the First World War* (Chapel Hill: University of North Carolina Press, 1999), 152.

125. De Weerdt, *De Vrouwen van de Eerste Wereldoorlog*, 87–90.

126. George Walker, *Venereal Disease in the American Expeditionary Forces* (Baltimore, MD: Medical Standard Book Co., 1922), 84; Yockelson, *Borrowed Soldiers*, 55–56. Walker's interviews with soldiers who contracted VD suggested that they averaged only five to fifteen minutes with a prostitute during a sexual encounter.

127. Leo van Bergen, *Before My Helpless Sight: Suffering, Dying, and Military Medicine on the Western Front, 1914–1918*, trans. Liz Waters (Farnham, UK: Ashgate, 2009), 154.

128. Walker, *Venereal Disease in the American Expeditionary Forces*, 155.

129. Roger Chickering, *The Great War and Urban Life in Germany: Freiburg, 1914–1918* (Cambridge: Cambridge University Press, 2007), 358–59.

130. Christopher Capozzola, *Uncle Sam Wants You: World War I and the Making of the Modern American Citizen* (Oxford: Oxford University Press, 2008), 133.

131. As quoted in Lutz D. H. Sauerteig, "Sex, Medicine, and Morality during the First World War," in *War, Medicine, and Modernity*, eds. Roger Cooter, Mark Harrison, and Steve Sturdy (Stroud, UK: Sutton, 1998), 177.

132. Woodward, *Hell in the Holy Land*, 27–29.

133. J. G. Maxwell to High Commissioner, 29 Sep 1915, folder 2, FO 141/466 Prostitution and Venereal Disease, PRO.

134. H. Hopkinson to J. G. Maxwell, 19 March 1916 and Geo. Harvey, "Report," 20 March 1916, folder 2, FO 141/466 Prostitution and Venereal Disease, PRO.

135. Joan Beaumont, "Australia's War," in *Australia's War, 1914–1918*, ed., Joan Beaumont (St. Leonard's, Australia: Allen & Unwin, 1995), 9.

136. Philippa Levine, *Prostitution, Race, and Politics: Policing Venereal Disease in the British Empire* (New York: Routledge, 2003), 155–57.

137. Levine, *Prostitution, Race, and Politics*, 148–49.

138. "Instructions for Administering Venereal Prophylaxis 1918," WWI Medical Department Records, RG120, Entry 2115, Box 5249, National Archives and Records Administration (NARA).

139. Walker, *Venereal Disease in the American Expeditionary Forces*, 29.

140. Woodward, *Hell in the Holy Land*, 30.

141. Susan R. Grayzel, "The Enemy Within: The Problem of British Women's Sexuality during the First World War," in *Women and War in the Twentieth Century:*

Enlisted with or without Consent, ed. Nicole Ann Dombrowski (New York: Garland, 1999), 80–81.

142. "The Red Souvenir," VD leaflet, Miscellaneous Ephemera collection, LMM.

143. Omissi, *Indian Voices*, letter 383.

144. Minutes Sheet 1915; VD and Camp Followers, HO 45/10724/251861/63, PRO.

145. Maria Bucur, "Women's Stories as Sites of Memory: Gender and Remembering Romania's World Wars," in Wingfield and Bucur, eds., *Gender and War in Twentieth-Century Eastern Europe*, 173.

146. Maurice Pate to father [1 March 1919]; Maurice Pate Papers, Box 4, Folder: Polish Relief Correspondence 1919, HHPL.

147. Quoted in Eliza Ablovatski, "Between Red Army and White Guard: Women in Budapest, 1919," in Wingfield and Bucur, eds., *Gender and War in Twentieth-Century Eastern Europe*, 70.

148. Paul Valéry, *On the European Mind*, 1922; Internet History Sourcebook, available at http://www.fordham/edu/halsall/mod/valery.html. Last accessed 30 October 2009. Thanks to Joe O'Connor for this suggestion.

CHAPTER 5

1. Quoted in Tibor Hajdu, "Army and Society in Hungary in the Era of World War I," in *War and Society in East Central Europe*, volume 19, eds. Béla Király and Nándor F. Dreisziger (New York: Columbia University Press, 1985), 118.

2. Lena Hitchcock, "The Great Adventure," unpublished TS, National World War I Museum Archives, Kansas City, MO, USA (LMM); Katrine Rushton Fairclough Kimball collection, Hoover Institution, Stanford (HI).

3. Roger Cooter and Steve Sturdy, "Of War, Medicine, and Modernity: Introduction," in *War, Medicine, and Modernity*, eds. Roger Cooter, Mark Harrison, and Sturdy (Stroud, UK: Sutton, 1998), 11.

4. Evelyn Blücher, *An English Wife in Berlin* (New York: Dutton, 1920), 45–46.

5. Quoted in Margaret Higonnet, ed., *Lines of Fire: Women Writers of World War I* (New York: Plume, 1999), 197.

6. Amy Owen Bradley, *Back of the Front in France* (Boston: Butterfield, 1918), 32–33.

7. *A War Nurse's Diary: Sketches from a Belgian Field Hospital* (New York: Macmillan, 1918), 64.

8. *A War Nurse's Diary*, 3–5, 9, 31, 35–36, 40, 52, 79, 85, 101, 115.

9. As quoted in Svetlana Palmer and Sarah Wallis, eds., *Intimate Voices from the First World War* (New York: Morrow, 2003), 183.

10. Wendy M. Fisher, "Dr. E. J. Stuckey and the Chinese Hospital at Noyelles-sur-Mer: A Biographical Fragment of World War I," Ph.D. diss., 32; MSS1174 Wendy M. Fisher Thesis, Australian War Memorial (AWM).

11. Bradley, *Back of the Front in France*, 87–91.

12. Leo Van Bergen, *Before My Helpless Sight: Suffering, Dying, and Military Medicine on the Western Front, 1914–1918*, trans. Liz Waters (Farnham, UK: Ashgate, 2009), 24.

13. Dragan Živojinović, "Serbia and Montenegro: The Home Front, 1914–1918," in Király and Dreisziger, eds., *War and Society in East Central Europe*, 243.

14. Sister Edith Mackay PR 89/27, file 89/0396, Australian War Memorial Collection (AWM).

15. Katherine Burger Johnson, "Allied Medical Personnel in World War I," in *Personal Perspectives: World War I*, ed. Timothy C. Dowling (Santa Barbara, CA: ABC-CLIO, 2006), 163.

16. Van Bergen, *Before My Helpless Sight*, 23–25.

17. Mabel Dearmer, *Letters from a Field Hospital* (London: Macmillan, 1915), 59–60, 109, 175.

18. Elsie Inglis, "The Tragedy of Serbia," in *Women's Writing of the First World War: An Anthology*, ed. Angela K. Smith (Manchester, UK: Manchester University Press, 2000), 264.

19. Report from 19 Dec 1918. From 2nd Australian Field Ambulance; 27 370/154 Treating Belgian/French civilians, AWM.

20. Judith Surkis, *Sexing the Citizen: Morality and Masculinity in France, 1870–1920* (Ithaca, NY: Cornell University Press, 2006), 236–38.

21. Susanne Michl, *Im Dienste des "Volkskörpers": Deutsche und französische Artze im Ersten Weltkrieg* (Göttingen, Germany: Vandenhoeck & Ruprecht, 2007), 11, 82, 105–6.

22. Van Bergen, *Before My Helpless Sight*, 25.

23. Wolfgang U. Eckart, "'The Most Extensive Experiment That the Imagination Can Conceive': War, Emotional Stress, and German Medicine, 1914–1918," in *Great War, Total War: Combat and Mobilization on the Western Front, 1914–1918*, eds. Roger Chickering and Stig Förster (Cambridge: Cambridge University Press, 2000), 137.

24. Grigore Antipa, *L'Occupation ennemie de la Roumanie et ses conséquences économiques et sociales* (New Haven, CT: Yale University Press, [1929]), 30.

25. A good comparison of public health conditions in Berlin, Paris, and London can be found in two articles by Catherine Rollet in this edited collection: Jay Winter and Jean-Louis Robert, eds., *Capital Cities at War: Paris, London, Berlin, 1914–1919*, volume 1 (Cambridge: Cambridge University Press, 1997), 421–86.

26. As quoted in Palmer and Wallis, eds., *Intimate Voices from the First World War*, 78.

27. Kimberly Jensen, "Physicians and Citizens: U.S. Medical Women and Military Service in the First World War," in Cooter et al., eds., *War, Medicine, and Modernity*, 112.

28. Janet S. K. Watson, "Wars in the Wards: The Social Construction of Medical Work in First World War Britain," *Journal of British Studies* 41 (October 2002): 487–90.

29. Michael H. Kater, "Professionalization and Socialization of Physicians in Wilhelmine and Weimar Germany," *Journal of Contemporary History* 20:4 (October 1985): 685–86. As Kater notes, Germany was the last European country to train and license female doctors.

30. Monica Krippner, *The Quality of Mercy: Women at War, Serbia, 1915–1918* (Newton Abbot, UK: David and Charles, 1980), 10, 29.

31. Margaret Higonnet, ed., *Nurses at the Front: Writing the Wounds of the Great War* (Boston: Northeastern University Press, 2001), viii, ix.

32. Higonnet, ed., *Nurses at the Front*, x, and Krippner, *The Quality of Mercy*, 19.

33. Ruth Lewin Sime, *Lise Meitner: A Life in Physics* (Berkeley: University of California Press, 1996), 59–60; Marie Curie, *Autobiographical Notes*, trans. Charlotte Kellogg and Vernon Kellogg (New York: Macmillan, 1923), 208–11.

34. Klaus Theweleit, *Male Fantasies*, vol. 1, trans. Stephen Conway (Minneapolis: University of Minnesota Press, 1989), 126.

35. Margaret H. Darrow, *French Women and the First World War: War Stories of the Home Front* (Oxford: Berg, 2000), 134.

36. Darrow, *French Women and the First World War*, 137–41.

37. Bianca Schönberger, "Motherly Heroines and Adventurous Girls: Red Cross Nurses and Women Army Auxiliaries in the First World War," in *Home/Front: The Military, War, and Gender in Twentieth-Century Germany*, eds. Karen Hagemann and Stefanie Schüler-Springorum (Oxford: Berg, 2002), 89.

38. Anne Summers, *Angels and Citizens: British Women as Military Nurses* (London: Routledge and Kegan Paul, 1988), 237–270.

39. Elsa Brändström, *Among Prisoners of War in Russia and Siberia*, trans. C. Mabel Rickmers (London: Hutchinson, 1929), 40.

40. Quoted in Yvonne McEwen, *"It's a Long Way to Tipperary": British and Irish Nurses in the Great War* (Dunfermline, Scotland: Cualann Press, 2006), 59.

41. Quoted in Watson, "Wars in the Wards," 486.

42. Vera Brittain, *Testament of Youth* (New York: Penguin, 1989), 165–67.

43. Brittain, *Testament of Youth*, 373.

44. Bradley, *Back of the Front in France*, 4.

45. Jane Marcus, "Afterword: Corpus/Corps/Corpses; Writing the Body in/at War," in Helen Zenna Smith, *Not So Quiet . . . Stepdaughters of War* (New York: Feminist Press, 1989), 243.

46. Smith, *Not So Quiet*, 29. Smith was the pen name of Evadne Price.

47. Quoted in Higonnet, ed., *Lines of Fire*, 202.

48. McEwen, *"It's a Long Way to Tipperary,"* 113.

49. Susan R. Grayzel, *Women and the First World War* (London: Pearson Education, 2002), 41.

50. Caroline Moorehead, *Dunant's Dream: War, Switzerland, and the History of the Red Cross* (London: HarperCollins, 1998), 16.

51. Moorehead, *Dunant's Dream*, 207.

52. Yucel Yanikdag, "Ottoman Prisoners of War in Russia, 1914–22," *Journal of Contemporary History* 34:1 (January 1999): 82–84.

53. Moorehead, *Dunant's Dream*, 209.

54. Katie Pickles, *Transnational Outrage: The Death and Commemoration of Edith Cavell* (New York: Palgrave Macmillan, 2007), 23–24.

55. Jean H. Quataert, "Women's Wartime Services under the Cross," in Chickering and Förster, eds., *Great War, Total War*, 453–54.

56. "Information for Personnel en Route for Foreign Service in the Red Cross," Aug. 1918, 1–3; Miscellaneous Ephemera, LMM.

57. Telegram 1914; Letters to wife 9 January 1915, 1 June 1915, 17 July 1915; letter to son Ernest 9 April 1915; Dr. P. A. Smythe papers, LMM.

58. Alon Rachamimov, "'Female Generals' and 'Siberian Angels': Aristocratic Nurses and the Austro-Hungarian POW Relief," in *Gender and War in Twentieth-Century Eastern Europe*, eds. Nancy M. Wingfield and Maria Bucur (Bloomington: Indiana University Press, 2006), 25.

59. Gerald H. Davis, "National Red Cross Societies and Prisoners of War in Russia, 1914–1918," *Journal of Contemporary History* 28:1 (January 1993): 35–36, 40.

60. Davis, "National Red Cross Societies," 41.

61. Elizabeth H. Ashe, *Intimate Letters from France during America's First Year of War* (San Francisco: Philopolis Press, 1918), 5, 21, 26, 35.

62. "The American Red Cross in Italy," n.d.; Box 4, Edward Eyre Hunt Collection, Herbert Hoover Presidential Library (HHPL).

63. John Barry, *The Great Influenza: The Epic Story of the Deadliest Plague in History* (New York: Viking, 2004), 362–63, 450.

64. Elmira W. Bears, "Report of Child Welfare Department, Commission for Relief in Belgium and Northern France at Lille" (1 July 1919), 3–5; Folder 93.16 Department of Child Welfare Reports, Box 93, CRB Collection, HI.

65. Scrapbook from Dr. George Washington Davis papers, LMM; "Children's Ark," TS, n.d.; Hannah Campbell Collection, HI.

66. Harry Hamilton Snively, *The Battle of the Non-Combatants* (New York: Business Bourse Publishers, 1933), 143.

67. "Some Small Contributions toward Goodwill and Understanding," TS, n.d.; Folder 2 Nancy Babb collection, HI.

68. Katrin Schultheiss, *Bodies and Souls: Politics and Professionalization of Nursing in France, 1880–1922* (Cambridge, MA: Harvard University Press, 2001), 3–4, 6.

69. Grayzel, *Women and the First World War*, 39–40; Summers, *Angels and Citizens*, 231.

70. As quoted in Moorehead, *Dunant's Dream*, 244.

CHAPTER 6

1. H. E. Shortt, "In the days of the Raj, and after, Doctor, Soldier, Scientist, Shikari" [ca. 1968]; MSS EUR/C435 Henry Shortt, Oriental and India Office, British Library (OIO-BL).

2. Frank M. Chapman, *The American Red Cross in Latin America* [Washington, c. 1920], 5–6; Frank Chapman Collection, Hoover Institution, Stanford (HI).

3. Hope Cox Pope, "History of Montevideo Chapter, American Red Cross," 4–5, 21; Hope Cox Pope Collection, HI.

4. Clippings books, 3DRL/2110, Australian War Memorial (AWM). Campbell's war service was recognized formally with an MBE, but she was also feted in an Australian tour in 1923 in which ex-soldiers from all over Australia came out to see her public appearances and lectures.

5. Bryce Lyon and Mary Lyon, eds, *The Journal de Guerre of Henri Pirenne* (Amsterdam: North-Holland, 1976), 66–67.

6. M. S. Leigh, *The Punjab and the War* (Lahore, Pakistan: Government Printing Office, 1920), 69–70.

7. Heber Maitland Alexander, *On Two Fronts: Being the Adventures of an Indian Mule Corps in France and Gallipoli* (London: Heinemann, 1917), 85–86.

8. H. Phillips (H. M. Consul Shanghai), "National War Museum: Shanghai Report" (23 March 1918), 28; MSS EUR/C591 Shanghai Report, OIO-BL.

9. H. Phillips (H. M. Consul Shanghai), "National War Museum: Shanghai Report" (23 March 1918), 5–10; MSS EUR/C591 Shanghai Report, OIO-BL.

10. "The Australian Comforts Fund: Its Aims, Achievements, and Constitution." 2/1/1, Records of the Australian Comforts Fund Souvenirs 8, AWM.

11. "Report of the Lady Mayoress's League," August 1915, 2/4/1, Records of the Australian Comforts Fund Souvenirs 8, AWM.

12. 2/4/1 and 2/1/1 AWM.

13. Gregory Mann, *Native Sons: West African Veterans and France in the Twentieth Century* (Durham, NC: Duke University Press, 2006), 81–82.

14. The Order of St. John of Jerusalem, "Fifth Report of the Indian Soldiers' Fund for the Period 1 January 1918 to July 1919" (London: 1919), 6, 10–11; MSS EUR/F120 Indian Soldiers Fund, OIO-BL.

15. Memo suggesting New Year's Gift for Chinese Labor Corps from Lt. Remington, Jan. 1918; WO106/33, National Archives UK (PRO).

16. The Order of St. John of Jerusalem, "Fifth Report of the Indian Soldiers' Fund for the Period 1 January 1918 to July 1919" (London: 1919), 18; MSS EUR/F120 Indian Soldiers Fund, OIO-BL.

17. Comité International de la Croix-Rouge, *L'Agence Internationale des Prisonniers de Guerre, Genève 1914–1918* (Geneva, 1919); Caroline Moorehead, *Dunant's Dream: War, Switzerland, and the History of the Red Cross* (London: HarperCollins, 1998), 257.

18. Heather Jones, "A Missing Paradigm? Military Captivity and the Prisoner of War, 1914–18," *Immigrants and Minorities* 26:1/2 (March/July 2008): 36.

19. Mark Thompson, *The White War: Life and Death on the Italian Front, 1915–1919* (New York: Basic Books, 2008), 351–52, and Alan Kramer, *Dynamic of Destruction: Culture and Mass Killing in the First World War* (Oxford: Oxford University Press, 2008), 65–66.

20. Gerald H. Davis, "National Red Cross Societies and Prisoners of War in Russia, 1914–1918," *Journal of Contemporary History* 28 (1993): 37.

21. Elsa Brändström, *Among Prisoners of War in Russia and Siberia* (London: Hutchinson, [1929]), 5–6, 170, 186.

22. S. Fremantle to Eunice Graham, 16 May 1918 (Folder 4), Gilbert Graham Papers 3DRL/4149; AWM.

23. Count Bennigsen diary, spring 1915, pp. 44, 50–51 (Folder 1) and Countess Bennigsen diary, p. 1 (Folder 2); Bennigsen collection, HI.

24. Conrad Hoffman, *In the Prison Camps of Germany: A Narrative of 'Y' Service among Prisoners of War* (New York: Association Press, 1920), vii, 31, 50, 78–79.

25. E. W. Hornung, *Notes of a Camp-follower on the Western Front* (New York: Dutton, 1919), 6.

26. Oswald C. J. Withrow, "Facts for Fighters" [Manhood Series Number Three] (Toronto: YMCA, 1918), 3, and Charles Larned Robinson, "Don't Take a Chance" (New York: Sex Education Bureau of the National War Work Council of the YMCA, 1918), 3; Miscellaneous Ephemera, National World War I Museum, Kansas City, MO (LMM).

27. Philippa Levine, *Prostitution, Race, and Politics: Policing Venereal Disease in the British Empire* (New York: Routledge, 2003), 152–53.

28. Jane Tolerton, "Rout, Ettie Annie 1877–1936," *Dictionary of New Zealand Biography*, updated 22 June 2007. Available at http://www.dnzb.govt.nz/. Last accessed 1 November 2009.

29. Susanne Michl, *Im Dienste des "Volkskörpers": Deutsche und französische Ärtze im Ersten Weltkrieg* (Göttingen, Germany: Vandenhoeck & Ruprecht, 2007), 105–6, 120–24.

30. See, for example, Nancy K. Bristow, *Making Men Moral: Social Engineering during the Great War* (New York: New York University Press, 1997).

31. George Walker, *Venereal Disease in the American Expeditionary Forces* (Baltimore, MD: Medical Standard Book Co., 1922), 127–30.

32. Circular Letter from the Society of Friends of Foreigners in Distress, 1914; FEWVRC/EME/1, Society of Friends Library, London (SFL).

33. "Aid for the Enemy Only," *Daily Express* (31 August 1914); FEWVRC/EME/1, SFL.

34. John V. Crangle and Joseph O. Baylen, "Emily Hobhouse's Peace Mission, 1916," *Journal of Contemporary History* 14:4 (October 1979): 740.

35. Rotten and Bridgwater correspondence, Records of the Friends' Emergency & War Victims Relief Committee (1914–1923), FEWVRC/EME/3; SFL.

36. Robert D. Cuff, "Herbert Hoover, the Ideology of Voluntarism, and War Organisation during the Great War," *Journal of American History* 64:2 (September 1977): 359.

37. Prentiss Gray diary, 24 February 1916, pp. 8–9; Prentiss Gray papers Box 1, Herbert Hoover Presidential Library (HHPL).

38. John Simpson untitled TS, John L. Simpson folders, Prentiss Gray papers Box 1, HHPL.

39. Herbert Hoover, "Benevolent Department (From October 26, 1914 to April 1, 1917)," (London: CRB, 1917), 8–9; WWI Subject File 128:18; HI.

40. Sophie de Schaepdrijver, *La Belgique et la Première Guerre mondiale*, trans. Claudine Spitaels and Vincent Marnix (Brussels: Peter Lang, 2005), 112.

41. Tracy B. Kittredge, "The History of the Commission for Relief in Belgium, 1914–1917," 1918; CRB Collection, 530:1, HI.

42. Charles De Lannoy, *L'Alimentation de la Belgique par Le Comité National (Novembre 1914 à November 1918)* (Brussels: Office de Publicité, 1922), 153.

43. Petition to the CRB [1915], 128:11; "Dr. Kellogg's Note on Warsaw and Poland," [1915], 128:9; Herbert Hoover to Sir Edward Grey, 22 Dec 1915, 128:8; WWI Subject File, Box 128, HI.

44. Belgian Lace Correspondence, Box 12, Lou Henry Hoover Subject Collection, HHPL; Elaine Merritt, "War Lace: Commemorating Victory and Determination," *Piecework* 7:4 (July/August 1999): 24–29.

45. Martha Hanna, *The Mobilization of Intellect: French Scholars and Writers during the Great War* (Cambridge, MA: Harvard University Press, 1996), 54.

46. Philip S. Platt, "A Social, Economic, and Dietetic Study of Twenty-Seven Families of the Working Class in the Province of Liège, November–December 1916," Folder 126:11, Box 126 London Office, CRB Collection, HI.

47. Brand Whitlock, *Belgium: A Personal Narrative* (New York: Appleton, 1919), 174; "War Has Nourished Belgium into Health," *New York World* (26 December 1915) and "Post-card Propaganda," Folder 314.22, Box 314, CRB Collection, HI.

48. *Manifeste signé par 93 Savants allemands aux Nations civilisées [and responses]* (Paris: Imprimerie Descamps, 1915); Christophe Prochasson, "Les intellectuels," in *Encyclopédie de la Grande Guerre 1914–1918: Histoire et culture*, eds. Stéphane Audoin-Rouzeau and Jean-Jacques Becker (Paris: Bayard, 2004), 666–67; Hanna, *The Mobilization of Intellect*, 78–80.

49. "Reply to German Professors," *Times* (London) (21 October 1914).

50. Bryce Lyon and Mary Lyon, eds., *The Journal de guerre of Henri Pirenne*, 10; Bryce Lyon, *Henri Pirenne: A Biographical and Intellectual Study* (Ghent, Belgium: E. Story—Scientia, 1974), 224; E. C. Coppens, *Paul Fredericq* (Ghent: Gent Liberal Archief, 1990), 219.

51. Curriculum Vitae, HDLM Acc 727 34, Sir James Wycliffe Headlam Morley papers, Churchill College Archives, Cambridge University (CCAC).

52. Tammy Proctor, *Female Intelligence: Women and Espionage in the First World War* (New York: New York University Press, 2003), 66–68.

53. Ian F. W. Beckett, *The Great War, 1914–1918* (Harlow, Essex: Pearson, 2001), 285.

54. Fernand Van Langenhove, *Hoe een Cyclus van Legenden Ontstaat: Franc-Tireurs en Gruweldaden in België* (Leiden, Netherlands: De Flaamsche Boekenhalle, 1916).

55. "The Story of the Development Division Chemical Warfare Service" (General Electric Company, 1920), 164; "The War-Gas Controversy," *New York Times* (7 June 1918); Hanna, *The Mobilization of Intellect*, 179–80; Steve Sturdy, "War as Experiment: Physiology, Innovation, and Administration in Britain, 1914–1918; The Case of Chemical Warfare," in *War, Medicine, and Morality*, eds. Roger Cooter, Mark Harrison, and Steve Sturdy (Stroud, UK: Sutton, 1998), 66.

56. Elizabeth Fordham, "Universities," in *Capital Cities at War: Paris, London, Berlin, 1914–1919*, volume 2, eds. Jay Winter and Jean-Louis Robert (Cambridge: Cambridge University Press, 2007), 270.

57. Catherine Rollet, "The 'Other War' I: Protecting Public Health," in *Capital Cities at War: Paris, London, Berlin, 1914–19*, volume 1, eds. Jay Winter and Jean-Louis Robert (Cambridge: Cambridge University Press, 1999), 432.

58. Schaepdrijver, *La Belgique et la première guerre mondiale*, 121.

59. Mohammad Gholi Majd, *Iraq in World War I: From Ottoman Rule to British Conquest* (Lanham, MD: University Press of America, 2006), 77–79.

60. As quoted in Mohammad Gholi Majd, *The Great Famine and Genocide in Persia, 1917–1919* (Lanham, MD: University Press of America, 2003), 30.

61. Patrick Porter, "New Jerusalems: Sacrifice and Redemption in the War Experiences of English and German Military Chaplains," in *Warfare and Belligerence: Perspectives in First World War Studies*, ed. Pierre Purseigle (Leiden, Netherlands: Brill, 2005), 101, 123.

62. James W. Gerard, *My Four Years in Germany* (New York: Doran, 1917), 155–56.

63. Joseph Grew Diary 1914 (vol. 5), MS Am 1687, Grew Papers, Houghton Library, Harvard. My thanks to Molly Wood for this reference. For more information on the "careers" of diplomatic wives during war and peace, see Molly Wood, "Diplomatic Wives: The Politics of Domesticity and the 'Social Game' in the U.S. Foreign Service, 1905–1941," *Journal of Women's History* 17:2 (2005): 142–65.

64. Hugh Gibson, *A Journal from Our Legation in Belgium* (New York: Doubleday, Page, 1917), 6.

65. Brand Whitlock, *Belgium: A Personal Narrative* (New York: Appleton, 1919), 63–68, 259.

66. M. W. R. Van Vollenhoven, *Memoires: Beschouwingen, Belevenissen, Reizen en Anecdoten* (Amsterdam: Elsevier, 1948), 274, 289.

67. As quoted in Majd, *Iraq in World War*, 171–76.

68. Charles Godrey Chenevix-Trench to Aunt Francie, 23 November 1915, MSS EUR/B271, OIO-BL.

69. Ulysses Grant-Smith to Irwin Laughlin, 12 April 1916, Box 13, Irwin Laughlin Papers, HHPL; Majd, *Iraq in World War I*, 404.

70. Peter Gatrell, *Russia's First World War: A Social and Economic History* (Harlow, Essex: Pearson Longman, 2005), 40–42.

71. Peter Gatrell, *A Whole Empire Walking: Refugees in Russia during World War I* (Bloomington: Indiana University Press, 1999), 40–41.

72. Scott J. Seregny, "Zemstvos, Peasants, and Citizenship: The Russian Adult Education Movement and World War I," *Slavic Review* 59:2 (Summer 2000): 290–94.

73. As quoted in Seregny, "Zemstvos, Peasants, and Citizenship," 294.

74. Seregny, "Zemstvos, Peasants, and Citizenship," 300, 309.

75. Rodney Lowe, "Government," in *The First World War in British History*, eds. Stephen Constantine, Maurice W. Kirby, and Mary B. Rose (London: Edward Arnold, 1995), 29.

76. Program—Interallied Games, Paris, 1919. Pershing Stadium—Joinville-Le-Pont, Paris (June 22–July 6, 1919); *Service with Fighting Men: An Account of the Work of the American Young Men's Christian Associations in the World War*, volume 2 (New York: Association Press, 1922), 49; Miscellaneous Ephemera, LMM.

77. Maureen Healy, *Vienna and the Fall of the Hapsburg Empire: Total War and Everyday Life in World War I* (Cambridge: Cambridge University Press, 2004), 255.

78. Maurice Pate to ARA, 6 November 1919, Box 4: Folder on Polish Relief, Maurice Pate Papers, HHPL. It is interesting to note that Pate was again involved in ameliorating hunger in World War II and its aftermath, and he became the first director of UNICEF when it was founded. World War I was in many ways the model for the development of food aid, especially for children, in the twentieth century.

79. Maurice Maeterlinck, *The Wrack of the Storm* (New York: Dodd, Mead, 1916), 297.

CHAPTER 7

1. L. E. Filmore, "The Seven Ages of a Kriegsgefangener," *In Ruhleben Camp* no. 1 (6 June 1915), 7; Documentariecentrum Ieper, In Flanders Fields Museum, Belgium (DI).

2. Gilbert Graham to Eunice Graham, 9 May 1918 (Folder 2), Gilbert Graham Papers 3DRL/4149; Australian War Memorial (AWM).

3. GG to EG, 2 Feb 1918 (Folder 1), Gilbert Graham Papers 3DRL/4149; AWM.

4. Hugo Slim, *Killing Civilians: Method, Madness, and Morality in War* (New York: Columbia University Press, 2008), 78, and Michael Walzer, *Just and Unjust Wars: A Moral Argument with Historical Illustrations* (New York: Basic Books, 1977), 102, 191.

5. J. C. Bird, *Control of Enemy Alien Civilians in Great Britain, 1914–1918* (New York and London: Garland, 1986), 132; Jean-Claude Farcy, *Les Camps Concentration Français de la première guerre mondiale 1914–1920* (Paris: Anthropos-Economica, 1995), 129; Richard B. Speed III, *Prisoners, Diplomats, and the Great War: A Study in the Diplomacy of Captivity* (New York: Greenwood Press, 1990), 151; Matthew Stibbe, *British Civilian Internees in Germany: The Ruhleben Camp, 1914–18* (Manchester, UK: Manchester University Press, 2008), 23; Mark Thompson, *The White War: Life and Death on the Italian Front, 1915–1919* (New York: Basic Books, 2008), 136, 139.

6. Report of Otto Johannsen (1917), 1918/89/443, CA 1/A11803 Governor-General's Office War Files, National Archives of Australia (NAA).

7. Daisy Schoeffel to the Hon. H. Gregory as quoted in Gerhard Fischer, *Enemy Aliens: Internment and the Homefront Experience in Australia, 1914–1920* (St. Lucia: University of Queensland, 1989), 320.

8. Fischer, *Enemy Aliens*, 86, 139–45, 152.

9. Caroline Moorehead, *Dunant's Dream: War, Switzerland, and the History of the Red Cross* (London: HarperCollins, 1998), 198.

10. About twenty-three hundred enemy alien civilians were interned but another two thousand or so nonmilitary sailors from merchant vessels and luxury liners caught in U.S. ports were also detained.

11. Gerald H. Davis, "Orgelsdorf: A World War I Internment Camp in America," *Yearbook of German-American Studies* 26 (1991): 257; Joan M. Jensen, *The Price of Vigilance* (Chicago: Rand McNally, 1968), 163; Christopher Capozzola, *Uncle Sam Wants You: World War I and the Making of the Modern American Citizen* (New York: Oxford University Press, 2008), 184.

12. Mark Ellis, "German-Americans in World War I," in *Enemy Images in American History*, eds. Ragnhil Fiebig-von Hase and Ursula Lehnkuhl (Providence, RI: Berghahn, 1997), 194–95.

13. Davis, "Orgelsdorf," 257.

14. William B. Glidden, "Internment Camps in America, 1917–1920," *Military Affairs* 37:4 (December 1973): 138.

15. Bohdan Kordan, *Enemy Aliens, Prisoners of War: Internment in Canada during the Great War* (Montreal: McGill-Queen's University Press, 2002), 5, 36, 60–61, 84.

16. Bill Waiser, *Park Prisoners: The Untold Story of Western Canada's National Parks, 1915–1916* (Saskatoon, Canada: Fifth House Publishers, 1995), 3–4, 26.

17. Peter Melnycky, "Badly Treated in Every Way: The Internment of Ukrainians in Quebec during the First World War," in *The Ukrainian Experience in Quebec*, ed. Myroslaw Diakowsky (Toronto: Basilian Press, 1994), reprinted and cited from www.infoukes.com.

18. Melnycky, "Badly Treated in Every Way." See also W. D. Otter, *Internment Operations, 1914–1920* (Ottawa: Mulvey, 1921), 4–6.

19. Paul Cohen-Portheim, *Time Stood Still: My Internment in England, 1914–1918* (New York: Dutton, 1932), 44, 65.

20. Davis, "Orgelsdorf," 254.

21. Farcy, *Les Camps Concentration Français*, 169–73.

22. *Reports on British Prison-Camps in India and Burma* (New York: Doran, 1918), 13–14.

23. Fischer, *Enemy Aliens*, 246–49.

24. John Simons, *Prisoners in Arcady: German Mariners at Berrima, 1915–1919* (Bowral, New South Wales: Berrima District Historical and Family History Society, 1999), 35, 45–49, 106.

25. Simons, *Prisoners in Arcady*, 178–81.

26. Lt. Edmond Samuels, *An Illustrated Diary of Australian Internment Camps* (Goulburn, Australia: Argyle Press, 1983), 8. This booklet is a reprint of part of a 1919 book that examines three Australian camps—this part only looks at Berrima.

27. Simons, *Prisoners in Arcady*, 180. Late in the war, in May 1918, a family camp was opened at Molonglo (outside Canberra), and the Bourke families were moved.

28. H. Sauerbeck, "Le camp des prisonniers de guerre à Trial Bay, NSW Australie" (22 June 1917), Box 7, Papers of Enemy Aliens, MLMSS261, Mitchell Library, Sydney (MLS).

29. Georg Boysen to Winnie (Nov. 1917), Box 1, Papers of Enemy Aliens, MLMSS261, MLS.

30. Lt. Col. R. S. Sands, "Concentration Camps NSW Report" (9 Feb 1917), AWM27 425/7, AWM.

31. Fischer, *Enemy Aliens*, 202.

32. Bird, *Control of Enemy Alien Civilians*, 46–47.

33. Farcy, *Les Camps de Concentration Français*, 41–42, 60–62.

34. Conrad Hoffman, *In the Prison Camps of Germany: A Narrative of "Y" Service among Prisoners of War* (New York: Association Press, 1920), 44.

35. Paul Waller to Lt. Col. F. W. Panzera (6 September 1916), Box 11, Folder: Paul Waller, Government Office Papers, Aliens/Internees 1914–1918, Manx National Library (MNL).

36. Ulysses Grant-Smith to Irwin Laughlin, 6 Jan 1915, Box 13 Irwin Laughlin Papers—Professional Correspondence, Herbert Hoover Presidential Library (HHPL).

37. Stibbe, *British Civilian Internees in Germany*, 127.

38. Lt. Col. R. S. Sands, "Concentration Camps NSW Report" (9 Feb 1917), AWM27 425/7, AWM.

39. Farcy, *Les Camps Concentration Français*, 180.

40. Peter Gatrell, *A Whole Empire Walking: Refugees in Russia during World War I* (Bloomington: Indiana University Press, 1999), 23; Dominiek Dendooven, "The European Armies: No Ethno-Cultural Monoliths," in *World War I: Five Continents in Flanders*, eds. Dominiek Dendooven and Piet Chielens (Tielt, Belgium: Lannoo, 2008), 39.

41. Hoffman, *In the Prison Camps of Germany*, 81–82.

42. Casement was an Irish revolutionary nationalist who was later tried and hung in 1916 by the British for his role in the Easter Rising in Dublin.

43. P. C. Sarell papers, 92/10/1, Imperial War Museum (IWM); James Gerard, *My Four Years in Germany* (New York: Doran, 1917), 190.

44. B. E. Sargeaunt to Under-Secretary of State (22 June 1916), Government Office Papers, Aliens/Internees 1914–1918, MNL; Hanna Sheehy-Skeffington, "Home Again in 1918," MS33621 (12), National Library of Ireland (NLI); "Irish Rebellion Prisoners in England," *Times* (London) (16 October 1917), 3.

45. Vincent Duclert, "La Destruction des Arméniens," in *Encyclopédie de la Grande Guerre 1914–1918: Histoire et culture*, eds. Stéphane Audoin-Rouzeau and Jean-Jacques Becker (Paris: Bayard), 381–85.

46. Gary Leiser, trans. and ed., *Vetluga Memoir: A Turkish Prisoner of War in Russia, 1916–1918* (Gainesville: University Press of Florida, 1995), 53.

47. Eric Lohr, *Nationalizing the Russian Empire: The Campaign against Enemy Aliens during World War I* (Cambridge, MA: Harvard University Press, 2003), 146–47.

48. B. E. Sargeaunt, *The Isle of Man and the Great War* (Douglas, Isle of Man: Brown and Sons, 1920), 64.

49. Leland Littlefield (Special Attaché) to Walter Hines Page (U.S. Ambassador, London), 12 October 1915, HO 45/10946/266042/100; "Report on Camps by Lt. Col. Mossberg," 31 May 1917, HO 45/10947/266042/261, National Archives UK (PRO).

50. Israel Cohen, *The Ruhleben Prison Camp: A Record of Nineteen Months' Internment* (London: Methuen, 1917), 41–46.

51. Farcy, *Les Camps Concentration Français*, 45.

52. At Knockaloe camp, there was a burial committee composed of internees to deal with funerals and burial of the dead; "Final Report and Statistical Record" (15 March 1919), HO 45/10947/266042/361, PRO.

53. John Patrick Bradshaw, "An Innocent Abroad (with apologies to the late Mark Twain). Being a Painfully Truthful Account of the 'Innocent's' Experience of German Gaol and Camp," 1916, MS 35288 (1/2), NLI.

54. Matthew Stibbe, "A Community at War: British Civilian Internees at the Ruhleben Camp in Germany, 1914–1918," in *Uncovered Fields: Perspectives in First World War Studies*, eds. Jenny Macleod and Pierre Purseigle (Leiden, Netherlands: Brill, 2004), 87–90.

55. *Alleged Ill-Treatment of German Subjects Captured in the Cameroons* (London: HMSO, 1915), 7–9.

56. Gerard, *My Four Years in Germany*, 288.

57. Rev. J. T. Williams, "African Diary," 95/32/1, IWM.

58. *Reports on the Treatment by the Germans of British Prisoners and Natives in German East Africa* (London: HMSO, 1917), 2–4, 12, 19–21.

59. Moorehead, *Dunant's Dream*, 197.

60. Cohen, *The Ruhleben Prison Camp*, 72.

61. Bradshaw , "An Innocent Abroad," 56–57.

62. Gerard, *My Four Years in Germany*, 174. Wittenberg camp was the subject of an investigation because of widespread complaints about poor treatment of internees and because of a deadly typhus outbreak.

63. Mary Thorp, "Local Gossip and 'side-shows' of the war during the German occupation of Belgium," September 17, 1916, DI.

64. Paul Fredericq Wegvoeringsdagboeken, vol. 2, 20 March 1916, HS 3708A, UGMC.

65. Bryce Lyon and Mary Lyon, eds., *The Journal de Guerre of Henri Pirenne* (Amsterdam: North-Holland, 1976), 99–108.

66. "Confidential. Destitute Aliens Committee. Report on Isle of Man Camps," 4 December 1914; HO 45/10946/266042/38, PRO.

67. "Series of depositions transmitted to Foreign Office from American Ambassador about conditions in camps, 1916; HO 45/10946/266042/141, PRO.

68. "Report on Camps by Lt. Col. Mossberg," 31 May 1917, HO 45/10947/266042/261, PRO.

69. Sargeaunt, *The Isle of Man and the Great War*, 67.

70. "Report on Camps by Capt. Unander," 5–12 November 1917, HO 45/10947/266042/261, PRO.

71. Journal of H. W. Madoc, MD 15028/1, MNL.

72. Elsa Brandstrom, *Among Prisoners of War in Russia and Siberia*, trans. C. Mabel Rickmers (London: Hutchinson, 1929), 160.

73. Dr. Erich Schultz to Secretary of State for Colonies, 12 Feb 1915, FO383/30, PRO.

74. Telegram to Under Secretary, Home Office, 19 November 1914, Box 13, Folder Acc 9845, Government Office Papers, Aliens/Internees 1914–1918, MNL.

75. Robert Fyson, "The Douglas Camp Shootings of 1914," *Proceedings of the Isle of Man Natural History and Antiquarian Society* 11:1 (April 1997–March 1999): 116–21, MNL.

76. "Official Report of the Inquest Proceedings," November 1914, HO 45/10946/266042/38, PRO.

77. Gerard, *My Four Years in Germany*, 184.

78. Geoffrey Pyke, *To Ruhleben and Back: A Great Adventure in Three Phases* (Boston: Houghton Mifflin, 1916), 126–27.

79. Bradshaw, "An Innocent Abroad," 60–61.

80. Cohen, *The Ruhleben Prison Camp*, 178.

81. P.C. Sarell papers, 92/10/1, IWM.

82. Stibbe, "A Community at War," 91.

83. Farcy, *Les Camps Concentration Français*, 230–31.

84. Cohen-Portheim, *Time Stood Still*, 163–64.

85. "Report on Camps by Capt. Unander," 5–12 November 1917, HO 45/10947/266042/261, PRO.

86. "Methods of Treating Salted Herrings" from Lofthouse Park to Home Office, 8 May 1917, HO 45/10835/329066/32, PRO.

87. E. C. Kny, Knockaloe Civilian Prisoners of War Internment Camp Final Report, 15 March 1919, p. 10, HO 45/10947/266042/361, PRO.

88. Thorp, "Local Gossip and side-shows," January 13, 1917; Gilbert Graham to Eunice Graham, 4 January 1917, Gilbert Graham Papers PR 91/048; AWM.

89. Percy Brown, "My Three Years in Rat-Infested Ruhleben," in *The Great War: I Was There*, ed. John Hammerton (London: Amalgamated Press, 1938), 2002.

90. Hoffman, *In the Prison Camps of Germany*, 91 96.

91. Lt. Col. R. S. Sands, "Concentration Camps NSW Report" (9 Feb 1917), AWM27 425/7, AWM.

92. Lyon and Lyon, *The Journal de Guerre*, 67.

93. Paul Fredericq Wegvoeringsdagboeken, vol. 4, 3 April 1916, HS 3708A, Universiteit Gent Manuscript Collection (UGMC).

94. Lyon and Lyon, *The Journal de Guerre*, 67.

95. Matthew Stibbe, "The Internment of Civilians by Belligerent States during the First World War and the Response of the International Committee of the Red Cross," *Journal of Contemporary History* 41:1 (2006): 10.

96. Leslie Baily, *Craftsman and Quaker: The Story of James T. Baily, 1876–1957* (London: Allen & Unwin, 1959), 88–91.

97. J. T. Baily Diary 1915–1919, pp. 19, 23–28, James T. Baily personal papers, MS 10417, MNL.

98. Lt. Col. R. S. Sands, "Concentration Camps NSW Report" (9 Feb 1917), AWM27 425/7, AWM.

99. Gilbert Graham to Eunice Graham, 2 October 1916 (Folder 1), Gilbert Graham Papers 3DRL/4149; AWM.

100. Sargeaunt, *The Isle of Man and the Great War*, 75, and Farcy, *Les Camps Concentration Français*, 252–56.

101. Hoffman, *In the Prison Camps of Germany*, 45, 79.

102. Lyon and Lyon, *The Journal de Guerre*, 117, 128–29.

103. Obituaries for "Sir James Chadwick," 25 July 1974, and "Sir Charles Ellis," 15 January 1980, *Times* (London).

104. The Ruhleben Irish Players, *First Annual General Meeting* (Berlin: Preuss, 1916), 9–11.

105. Obituaries for "Mr. Charles Webber," 29 July 1954, and "Sir Ernest Macmillan," 8 May 1973, *Times* (London); Thorp, "Local Gossip and side-shows," January 15, 1917; Gerard, *My Four Years in Germany*, 180.

106. Capt. H. S. Gulston diary, 7–12 November 1914, 91/30/1, IWM.

107. K. M. Gwynn to M. T. Bacon Phillips, 21 July 1915, 99/3/1, IWM.

108. Yvonne M. Cresswell, ed., *Living with the Wire: Civilian Internment in the Isle of Man during the Two World Wars* (Douglas, Isle of Man: Manx National Heritage, 1994), 30.

109. "Joseph H. Pilates, Body Builder, 86," *New York Times* (10 October 1967).

110. Waiser, *Park Prisoners*, 43.

111. Henri Pirenne, *Souvenirs de Captivité en Allemagne, Mars 1916–Novembre 1918* (Brussels: Maurice Lamertin, 1920), 64–65.

112. Baily, *Craftsman and Quaker*, 93.

113. Erich Posselt, *Orgelsdorfer Eulenspiegel* no. 5 (15 December 1918), as quoted in Davis, "Orgelsdorf," 259.

114. Bird, *Control of Enemy Alien Civilians*, 157–58, and Alon Rachamimov, "The Disruptive Comforts of Drag: (Trans)Gender Performances among Prisoners of War in Russia, 1914–1920," *American Historical Review* 111:2 (April 2006): 372–73.

115. Cohen-Portheim, *Time Stood Still*, 89.

116. Fischer, *Enemy Aliens*, 208–9.

117. F. W. Panzera to B. Sargeaunt, 6 October 1916, and cutting from *Isle of Man Weekly Times*, 28 October 1916; HO 45/10947/266042/208.

118. Special Assistant Madigan to Commandant re: repatriation, 23 August 1919, Box 11, Folder: Cecil Kny, Government Office Papers, Aliens/Internees 1914–1918, MNL.

119. Glidden, "Internment Camps in America, 1917–1920," 140.

120. Farcy, *Les Camps Concentration Français*, 187–98.

121. Pyke, *To Ruhleben and Back*, 171.

122. James N. Bade, *Von Luckner: A Reassessment; Count Felix von Luckner in New Zealand and the South Pacific, 1917–1919 and 1938* (Frankfurt am Main: Peter Lang, 2004), 84–94.

123. Waiser, *Park Prisoners*, 15–16.

124. Fischer, *Enemy Aliens*, 270.

125. Hoffman, *In the Prison Camps of Germany*, 92.

126. R. H. Sauter to wife, 4 August 1918, R. H. Sauter Collection, Con Shelf, IWM.

127. Rachamimov, "The Disruptive Comforts of Drag," 378.

128. Journal of H. W. Madoc, MD 15028/1; MNL, and Berthold Schwarz to Governor-General, 1 November 1917, Complaints by Prisoners of War 1917/89/413, CA 1/A11803 Governor-General's Office "War Files," NAA.

129. Stibbe, "A Community at War," 90–91.

130. Cohen-Portheim, *Time Stood Still*, 184, 213–15.

131. Gilbert Graham to Eunice Graham, 12 May 1918 and 18 June 1918 (Folder 2), Gilbert Graham Papers 3DRL/4149; AWM.

132. Angelus Twoboda to Strachan, 25 August 1919, and Strachan to Quartermaster General, 16 February 1920, Papers of Lt. Col. H. A. Strachan, 78/23/1, IWM.

133. J. T. Baily Diary 1915–1919, pp. 109–10, James T. Baily personal papers, MS 10417, MNL.

134. Simons, *Prisoners in Arcady*, 205–9.

135. Heather Jones, "A Missing Paradigm? Military Captivity and the Prisoner of War, 1914–18," *Immigrants and Minorities* 26:1/2 (March/July 2008): 40.

136. Cohen-Portheim, *Time Stood Still*, 82–83.

137. GG to EG, 2 Feb 1918 (Folder 1), Gilbert Graham Papers 3DRL/4149; AWM.

CHAPTER 8

1. Jean-Jacques Becker, *The Great War and the French People*, trans. Arnold Pomerans (New York: St. Martin's Press, 1986), 220.

2. Tyler Stovall, "The Color Line behind the Lines: Racial Violence in France during the Great War," *American Historical Review* 103:3 (June 1998): 754, 759.

3. For more information on strikes in South America, see chapter 6 of Bill Albert's *South America and the First World War* (Cambridge: Cambridge University Press, 1988).

4. Robert Crossley, ed., *Talking across the World: The Love Letters of Olaf Stapledon and Agnes Miller, 1913–1919* (Hanover, NH: University Press of New England, 1987), 240–44; Christopher Capozzola, "The Only Badge Needed Is Your Patriotic

Fervor: Vigilance, Coercion, and the Law in World War I America," *Journal of American History* 88:4 (2002): 1366–67.

5. Capozzola, "The Only Badge Needed ," 1354, 1359.

6. Capozzola, "The Only Badge Needed," 1375; Arthur E. Barbeau and Florence Henri, *The Unknown Soldiers: African American Troops in World War I* (New York: Da Capo Press, 1996), 175–78.

7. Alexander Victor Prusin, *Nationalizing a Borderland: War, Ethnicity, and Anti-Jewish Violence in East Galicia, 1914–1920* (Tuscaloosa: University of Alabama Press, 2005), 75–76, 82–85, 102, 107, 111–12.

8. Carol Fink, *Defending the Rights of Others: The Great Powers, the Jews, and International Minority Protection, 1878–1938* (Cambridge: Cambridge University Press, 2004), 111.

9. Sophie de Schaepdrijver, *La Belgique et la Première Guerre Mondiale* (Brussels: Peter Lang, 2005), 297–306. The *Flamenpolitik* of the First World War would leave a lasting imprint on Belgium, and indeed, its legacy was particularly apparent in the German occupation of Belgium again in the Second World War.

10. Hans Ulrich Gumbrecht, "I redentori della vittoria: On Fiume's Place in the Genealogy of Fascism," *Journal of Contemporary History* 31:2 (April 1996), 260–61.

11. Series of articles in the *Times* (London) from September 1919 to December 1920.

12. Martin F. Auger, "On the Brink of Civil War: The Canadian Government and the Suppression of the 1918 Quebec Easter Riots," *Canadian Historical Review* 89:4 (December 2008): 504.

13. Auger, "On the Brink of Civil War," 538.

14. Hermann Joseph Hiery, *The Neglected War: The German South Pacific and the Influence of World War I* (Honolulu: University of Hawaii Press, 1995), 137–42.

15. Vejas Gabriel Liulevicius, *War Land on the Eastern Front: Culture, National Identity, and German Occupation in World War I* (Cambridge: Cambridge University Press, 2000), 228–33.

16. Sheila Fitzpatrick, *The Russian Revolution, 1917–1932* (Oxford: Oxford University Press, 1982), 38–39.

17. Peter Holquist, *Making War, Forging Revolution: Russia's Continuum of Crisis, 1914–1921* (Cambridge, MA: Harvard University Press, 2002), 44–46.

18. Peter Gatrell, "Poor Russia, Poor Show: Mobilising a Backward Economy for War, 1914–1917," in *The Economics of World War I*, eds. Stephen Broadberry and Mark Harrison (Cambridge: Cambridge University Press, 2005), 262.

19. Countess Bennigsen's Papers, Diary pp. 2–3; Bennigsen Collection, Hoover Institution (HI).

20. Mary McAuley, *Bread and Justice: State and Society in Petrograd, 1917–1922* (Oxford: Clarendon Press, 1991), 35; Peter Gatrell, *Russia's First World War: A Social and Economic History* (Harlow, Essex: Pearson Longman, 2005), 170; Barbara Alpern

Engel, "Not by Bread Alone: Subsistence Riots in Russia during World War I," *Journal of Modern History* 69:4 (Dec 1997): 720.

21. Peter Gatrell and Mark Harrison, "The Russian and Soviet Economies in Two World Wars: A Comparative View," *Economic History Review* 46:3 (August 1993): 443–45.

22. Fitzpatrick, *The Russian Revolution*, 39.

23. McAuley, *Bread and Justice*, 24–26.

24. Gatrell, *Russia's First World War*, 198.

25. Fitzpatrick, *The Russian Revolution*, 41.

26. Fitzpatrick, *The Russian Revolution*, 39, 46–51.

27. Fitzpatrick, *The Russian Revolution*, 56–58.

28. Ian F. W. Beckett, *The Great War, 1914–1918* (Harlow, Essex: Pearson, 2001), 377.

29. James D. White, "National Communism and World Revolution: The Political Consequences of German Military Withdrawal from the Baltic Area in 1918–19," *Europe-Asia Studies* 46:8 (1994): 1357.

30. Beckett, *The Great War, 1914–1918*, 377–78.

31. Fitzpatrick, *The Russian Revolution*, 61–63.

32. Holquist, *Making War, Forging Revolution*, 240.

33. Gatrell, *Russia's First World War*, 238.

34. Gilbert Trausch, *Le Luxembourg entre la France et la Belgique, 1914–1922* (Luxembourg: Imprimerie Saint-Paul, 1975), 21–23.

35. *Times* (London), 18 November 1918 and 22 November 1918.

36. Mary Thorp, "Local Gossip and 'side-shows' of the war during the German occupation of Belgium," unpublished diary, vol. 5, 9–11 November 1918; Documentariecentrum Ieper, In Flanders Fields Museum, Belgium (DI).

37. Peter A. Toma, "The Slovak Soviet Republic of 1919," *American Slavic and East European Review* 17:2 (April 1958): 203–7.

38. John R. Lampe, *Balkans into Southeastern Europe: A Century of War and Transition* (London: Palgrave, 2006), 53.

39. Istvan Deak, "Budapest and the Hungarian Revolutions of 1918–1919," *Slavonic and East European Review* 46:106 (January 1968): 129–34.

40. Lampe, *Balkans into Southeastern Europe*, 60–61; André Andréadés, *Les effets economiques et sociaux de la guerre en Grèce* (New Haven, CT: Yale University Press, 1929), 3.

41. Dragan Živojinović, "Serbia and Montenegro: The Home Front, 1914–1918," in *War and Society in East Central Europe*, eds. Béla Király and Nándor F. Dreisziger (New York: Columbia University Press, 1985), 255–56.

42. Thomas Nelson Page, *Italy and the World War* (New York: Scribner's, 1920), 387.

43. Richard Bessel, *Germany after the First World War* (Oxford: Clarendon Press, 1993), 41.

44. Sean Dobson, *Authority and Upheaval in Leipzig, 1910–1920: The Story of a Relationship* (New York: Columbia University Press, 2001), 174–82, 219–20.

45. Decie Denholm, ed., *Behind the Lines: One Woman's War, 1914–18; The Letters of Caroline Ethel Cooper* (London: Jill Norman & Hobhouse, 1982), 284–85. Letter dated Nov. 10, 1918.

46. Denholm, ed., *Behind the Lines*, 284–85.

47. Rudolf Coper, *Failure of a Revolution: Germany in 1918–1919* (Cambridge: Cambridge University Press, 1955), 13.

48. Evelyn Blücher, *An English Wife in Berlin* (New York: Dutton, 1920), 256, 279, 282.

49. Belinda Davis, *Home Fires Burning: Food, Politics, and Everyday Life in World War I Berlin* (Chapel Hill: University of North Carolina Press, 2000), 229–36.

50. Coper, *Failure of a Revolution*, 232.

51. Allan Mitchell, *Revolution in Bavaria, 1918–1919: The Eisner Regime and the Soviet Republic* (Princeton, NJ: Princeton University Press, 1965), 307, 322, 329–31.

52. Mitchell, *Revolution in Bavaria*, 256, 271, 332. Thanks to John Flora for his insights on the Bavarian Revolution and its importance to the rise of National Socialism.

53. Mitchell, *Revolution in Bavaria*, 322. Bavarian units were also mobilized, so the total number of forces of order probably was in the range of thirty-five thousand men.

54. MacGregor Knox, *To the Threshold of Power, 1922/33: Origins and Dynamics of the Fascist and National Socialist Dictatorships,* volume 1 (Cambridge: Cambridge University Press, 2007), 244.

55. While Germany had to deal with immediate demobilization of its troops and destruction of its plans for the postwar period, France and Britain, for instance, could better manage the problems of unemployment and return of soldiers by staging their demobilizations, providing temporary financial assistance, and planning for emergencies. For more information, see Joshua Cole, "The Transition to Peace, 1918–19," in *Capital Cities at War: Paris, London, Berlin, 1914–1919,* eds. Jay Winter and Jean-Louis Robert (Cambridge: Cambridge University Press, 1997), 196–226.

56. Tim Stapleton, "The Impact of the First World War on African People," in *Daily Lives of Civilians in Wartime Africa: From Slavery Days to Rwandan Genocide,* ed. John Laband (Westport, CT: Greenwood Press, 2007), 119.

57. Edward Dennis Sokol, *The Revolt of 1916 in Russian Central Asia* (Baltimore, MD: Johns Hopkins University Press, 1954), 15–16, 72–73, 87, 129, 159. See also Gatrell, *Russia's First World War*, 188–90.

58. Stapleton, "The Impact of the First World War on African People," 122.

59. Stapleton, "The Impact of the First World War on African People," 119–21.

60. Gregory Mann, *Native Sons: West African Veterans and France in the Twentieth Century* (Durham, NC: Duke University Press, 2006), 68.

61. Myron Echenberg, *Colonial Conscripts: The Tirailleurs Sénégalais in French West Africa, 1857–1960* (Portsmouth, NH: Heinemann, 1991), 71.

62. Joan Beaumont, "Australia's War," in *Australia's War, 1914–1918*, ed. Beaumont (St. Leonard's, Australia: Allen & Unwin, 1995), 45–50, 52.

63. Lord Wimbourne letter to Lloyd George, as quoted in Alan J. Ward, "Lloyd George and the 1918 Irish Conscription Crisis," *Historical Journal* 17:1 (March 1974): 108.

64. Alan J. Ward, *The Easter Rising: Revolution and Irish Nationalism*, 2nd edition (Wheeling, IL: Harlan Davidson, 2003), 110–11.

65. Beckett, *The Great War, 1914–1918*, 362.

66. Sarah Benton, "Women Disarmed: The Militarization of Politics in Ireland, 1913–1923," *Feminist Review* 50 (1995): 158; Ward, *The Easter Rising*, 147.

67. Peter Hart, *The IRA at War, 1916–1923* (Oxford: Oxford University Press, 2003), 30, 194, 197.

68. Ian Copland, *The Princes of India in the Endgame of Empire, 1917–1947* (Cambridge: Cambridge University Press, 2002), 37–38; Derek Sayer, "British Reaction to the Amritsar Massacre, 1919–1920," *Past and Present* 131 (May 1991): 134–35.

69. For a fuller account of the event, see Alfred Draper, *Amritsar: The Massacre That Ended the Raj* (London: Cassell, 1981).

70. Nasser Hussain, "Towards a Jurisprudence of Emergency: Colonialism and the Rule of Law," *Law and Critique* 10 (1999): 93.

71. Quoted in Hussain, "Towards a Jurisprudence of Emergency," 95.

72. Sayer, "British Reaction to the Amritsar Massacre, 1919–1920," 130–31, 141–43.

73. Ashutosh Varshney, "Nationalism, Ethnic Conflict, and Rationality," *Perspectives on Politics* 1:1 (2003): 93.

74. Percival Spear, "Mahatma Gandhi," *Modern Asian Studies* 3:4 (1969): 296.

75. Ellis Goldberg, "Peasants in Revolt: Egypt 1919," *International Journal of Middle East Studies* 24:2 (May 1992): 261–63, 274; Joel Beinin and Zachary Lockman, "1919: Labor Upsurge and National Revolution," in *The Modern Middle East: A Reader*, 2nd edition, eds. Albert Hourani, Philip Khoury, and Mary C. Wilson (London: Tauris, 2004), 395–97, 401–2.

76. Stapleton, "The Impact of the First World War on African People," 123–24.

77. Gregory Maddox, "Mtunya: Famine in Central Tanzania," *Journal of African History* 31:2 (1990): 194, 197.

78. Melvin E. Page, *The Chiwaya War: Malawians and the First World War* (Boulder, CO: Westview Press, 2000), 164–87.

79. Quoted in Beckett, *The Great War, 1914–1918*, 404.

80. Beckett, *The Great War, 1914–1918*, 405.

81. Joseph T. Chen, "The May Fourth Movement Redefined," *Modern Asian Studies* 4:1 (1970): 63.

82. Xu Guoqi, *China and the Great War: China's Pursuit of a New National Identity and Internationalism* (Cambridge: Cambridge University Press, 2005), 245. The journalist that Guoqi quotes is Hollington Tong, writing in *Millard's Review*.

83. Chen, "The May Fourth Movement Redefined," 63. Japan returned control of Shandong Province to China as a result of the Washington Naval Conference in 1921–1922.

84. Guoqi, *China and the Great War*, 274–75.

85. Mary Martin Diary, MS34256A, National Library of Ireland (NLI).

86. Aviel Roshwald, *Ethnic Nationalism and the Fall of Empires: Central Europe, Russia, and the Middle East, 1914–1923* (London: Routledge, 2001), 157.

CONCLUSION

1. Susan Griffin, *A Chorus of Stones: The Private Life of War* (New York: Anchor Books, 1992), 316.

2. Käthe Kollwitz to Hans Kollwitz, 18 February 1917, in *The Diary and Letters of Kaethe Kollwitz*, ed. Hans Kollwitz (Evanston, IL: Northwestern University Press, 1988), 155–56.

3. G. Kurt Piehler, "The War Dead and the Gold Star: American Commemoration of the First World War," in *Commemorations: The Politics of National Identity*, ed. John R. Gillis (Princeton, NJ: Princeton University Press, 1994), 168.

4. Michael Amara, *Des Belges à l'épreuve de l'Exil: Les réfugiés de la Première Guerre mondiale* (Brussels: Editions de l'Université de Bruxelles, 2008), 373–76; Michael Amara, "Ever Onward They Went: The Story of a Unique Belgian Odyssey," in *Strangers in a Strange Land: Belgian Refugees, 1914–1918* (Leuven, Belgium: Davidsfonds, 2004), 34–35.

5. Quoted in Maria Bucur, "Women's Stories as Sites of Memory: Gender and Remembering Romania's World Wars," in *Gender and War in Twentieth-Century Eastern Europe*, eds. Nancy M. Wingfield and Maria Bucur (Bloomington: Indiana University Press, 2006), 174–80.

6. Erez Manela, *The Wilsonian Moment: Self-Determination and the International Origins of Anticolonial Nationalism* (Oxford: Oxford University Press, 2007), 11.

7. Marina Larsson, *Shattered Anzacs: Living with the Scars of War* (Sydney: University of New South Wales Press, 2009), 18–19.

8. Leo van Bergen, *Before My Helpless Sight: Suffering, Dying, and Military Medicine on the Western Front, 1914–1918*, trans. Liz Waters (Farnham, England: Ashgate, 2009), 493.

9. Bruce Clark, *Twice a Stranger: The Mass Expulsions That Forged Modern Greece and Turkey* (Cambridge, MA: Harvard University Press, 2006), 11.

10. Clark, *Twice a Stranger*, 12–14.

11. Clark, *Twice a Stranger*, xiii.

12. Omer Bartov, *Murder in Our Midst: The Holocaust, Industrial Killing, and Representation* (New York: Oxford University Press, 1996), 26–27.

Bibliography

ARCHIVES

Archives Générale du Royaume/Algemeen Rijksarchief (AGR). Brussels, Belgium.
Records of the Service Patriotique (1914–1918), Corps d'Observation Anglais, P-212
Australian War Memorial (AWM). Canberra, ACT, Australia.
Ethel Campbell collection
Wendy M. Fisher thesis
Gilbert Graham papers
J. C. Harrop papers
Sister Edith Mackay papers
Official Records
Records of the Australian Comforts Fund
Cartoon Research Library (CRLOSU). The Ohio State University. Columbus, Ohio, USA.
La Baïonnette [Special Issue on Marraines]
Churchill College Archives (CCAC). Cambridge, United Kingdom.
Sir James Wycliffe Headlam Morley papers
Documentariecentrum Ieper, In Flanders Fields Museum (DI). Ypres, Belgium.
Mary Thorp diary and papers

MEMOIRS AND ORAL HISTORY
TRANSCRIPTIONS (PUBLISHED)

Herbert Hoover Presidential Library (HHPL). West Branch, Iowa, USA.
Belgian Relief (Commission for Relief in Belgium) correspondence 1916–17
Prentiss Gray papers
Lou Henry Hoover subject collection
Edward Eyre Hunt collection
Irwin Laughlin papers

Maurice Pate papers
John L. Simpson folders
U.S. Food Administration files

Hoover Institution (HI). Stanford. Palo Alto, California, USA.
Mildred Aldrich collection
Nancy Babb collection
Graf Adam Pavlovich Bennigsen collection
Hannah Campbell collection
Frank Chapman collection
Commission for Relief in Belgium collection
Joseph C. Green papers
Robert A. Jackson collection
Katrine Rushton Fairclough Kimball collection
Margaret W. Netherwood Mills collection
Hope Cox Pope collection
World War I Subject collection

Houghton Library (HL), Harvard University, Cambridge, Massachusetts, USA.
Joseph Grew papers

Imperial War Museum Manuscripts Collection (IWM). London, UK.
George and Eric Butling correspondence
Letters of Mrs. E. Fernside
Capt. H. S. Gulston diary
Letter from K. M. Gwynn
Sir Ivone Kirkpatrick memoirs
Miss R. A. Neal manuscript
P. C. Sarell papers
R. H. Sauter collection
Lt. Col. H. A. Strachan papers
Rev. J. T. Williams papers

Library of Congress (LC). Washington, DC, USA.
Brand Whitlock papers

Manx National Library (MNL). Douglas, Isle of Man.
James T. Baily personal papers
Government Office papers, Aliens/Internees 1914–1918
Journal of H. W. Madoc

Mitchell Library (MLS). Sydney, NSW, Australia.
Papers of Enemy Aliens, MLMSS261

National Archives (PRO). Kew Gardens, UK.
AIR 1/657/17/122
FO 141/466

FO 383/30
HO 45/10724/251861/63
HO 45/10835/329066/32
HO 45/10946-10947
MEPO 2/1657
WO32/5251-5253
WO 32/5597
WO 32/11345
WO 95/83
WO 106/33

National Archives of Australia (NAA). Canberra, ACT, Australia.
The Acts of the Parliament of the Commonwealth of Australia Passed During the
  Years 1914 and 1915
Governor-General's Office War files CA 1/A11803
Prisoners of War 1917/89/413

**National Archives and Records Administration (NARA). College Park,
Maryland, USA.**
WWI Medical Department Records, RG120

National Library of Ireland Manuscript Collection (NLI). Dublin, Ireland.
John Patrick Bradshaw, "An Innocent Abroad"
Mary Martin diary
Sheehy-Skeffington papers

National World War I Archives (LMM). Kansas City, Missouri, USA.
Ephemera from the American Committee for Relief in the Near East Collection
Ephemera from German Home Front Collection
Lena Hitchcock unpublished manuscript
Liberty Theaters correspondence
Miscellaneous Ephemera collections
Walter Arthur Richter collection
Dr. P. A. Smythe papers

**Oriental and India Office [Asia, Pacific, and Africa Collection], British Library
(OIO-BL). London, UK.**
Charles Godfrey Chenevix Trench papers
Indian Soldiers' Fund records
Shanghai Report by H. Phillips, Consul
Henry Shortt papers
Charles Augustus Tegart papers

Scout Association Archive (SA). Gilwell Park, Chingford, UK.
Headquarters Gazette
Roland House file, TC/168

Roland Philipps correspondence, TC/248
Society of Friends Library (SFL). London, UK.
Conscientious Objectors' papers
Friends' Emergency & War Victims Relief Committee (1914–1923) papers
Stadsarchief Leuven (SL). Leuven, Belgium.
Office Central Belge pour les prisonniers de guerre files
Oorlogsaffiches Collection (Verzameling), 1914–1918
Universiteit Gent, Manuscript Collection (UGMC). Ghent, Belgium.
Paul Fredericq diary and papers

NEWSPAPERS

Daily News (London)
Daily Sketch (London)
New York Times
New York World
Times (London)

PUBLISHED SOURCES

Aaronsohn, Alex. "The NILI or 'A' Organisation." In *Agents of Empire: Anglo-Zionist Intelligence Operations, 1915–1919: Brigadier Walter Gribbon, Aaron Aaronsohn, and the NILI Ring*, edited by Anthony Verrier. London: Brassey's, 1995.

Ablovatski, Eliza. "Between Red Army and White Guard: Women in Budapest, 1919." In *Gender and War in Twentieth-Century Eastern Europe*, edited by Nancy M. Wingfield and Maria Bucur. Bloomington: Indiana University Press, 2006.

Ahmad, Feroz. "War and Society under the Young Turks, 1908–1918." In *The Modern Middle East: A Reader*, edited by Albert Hourani, Philip Khoury, and Mary C. Wilson. London: Tauris, 2004.

Albert, Bill. *South America and the First World War*. Cambridge: Cambridge University Press, 1988.

Aldrich, Mildred. *A Hilltop on the Marne*. Boston: Houghton Mifflin, 1915.

Alexander, Hebert Maitland. *On Two Fronts: Being the Adventures of an Indian Mule Corps in France and Gallipoli*. London: Heinemann, 1917.

Allen, Keith. "Sharing Scarcity: Bread Rationing and the First World War in Berlin, 1914–1923." *Journal of Social History* 32:2 (Winter 1998): 371–93.

Amara, Michael. *Des Belges à l'épreuve de l'Exil: Les Réfugies de la Première Guerre mondiale, France, Grande-Bretagne, Pays-Bass, 1914–1918*. Brussels: Editions de l'Université de Bruxelles, 2008.

———. "Ever Onward They Went: The Story of a Unique Belgian Exodus." In *Strangers in a Strange Land: Belgian Refugees, 1914–1918*. Leuven, Belgium: Davidsfonds, 2004.

Anderson, Ross. *The Forgotten Front: The East African Campaign, 1914–1918*. Stroud, UK: Tempus, 2004.

Andréadès, André. *Les effets economiques et sociaux de la guerre en Grèce*. New Haven, CT: Yale University Press, 1929.

Antipa, Grigore. *L'Occupation ennemie de la Roumanie et ses conséquences économiques et sociales*. New Haven, CT: Yale University Press, [1929].

Ashe, Elizabeth H. *Intimate Letters from France during America's First Year of War*. San Francisco: Philopolis Press, 1918.

Aston, John, and L. M. Duggan. *The History of the 12ᵗʰ (Bermondsey) Battalion East Surrey Regiment*. Finsbury, UK: Union Press, 1936.

Audoin-Rouzeau, Stéphane. "Children and the Primary Schools of France, 1914–1918." In *State, Society, and Mobilization in Europe during the First World War*, edited by John Horne. Cambridge: Cambridge University Press, 1997.

———. *L'Enfant de l'Ennemi (1914–1918): Viol, avortement, infanticide pendant la Grande Guerre*. Paris: Aubier, 1995.

Audoin-Rouzeau, Stéphane, and Annette Becker. *14–18: Understanding the Great War*. Translated by Catherine Temerson. New York: Hill and Wang, 2002.

Audoin-Rouzeau, Stéphane, and Jean-Jacques Becker, eds. *Encyclopédie de la Grande Guerre 1914–1918: Histoire et culture*. Paris: Bayard, 2004.

Auger, Martin F. "On the Brink of Civil War: The Canadian Government and the Suppression of the 1918 Quebec Easter Riots." *Canadian Historical Review* 89:4 (December 2008): 503–40.

Bade, James N. *Von Luckner: A Reassessment; Count Felix von Luckner in New Zealand and the South Pacific, 1917–1919 and 1938*. Frankfurt: Peter Lang, 2004.

Baily, Leslie. *Craftsman and Quaker: The Story of James T. Baily, 1876–1957*. London: Allen & Unwin, 1959.

Barbeau, Arthur E., and Florette Henri. *The Unknown Soldiers: African American Troops in World War I*. New York: Da Capo Press, 1996.

Barry, John. *The Great Influenza: The Epic Story of the Deadliest Plague in History*. New York: Viking, 2004.

Bartov, Omer. *Murder in our Midst: The Holocaust, Industrial Killing, and Representation*. New York: Oxford University Press, 1996.

Barua, Pradeep. "Inventing Race: The British and India's Martial Races." *Historian* 58 (1995): 107–16.

Beaumont, Joan. "Australia's War." In *Australia's War, 1914–1918*, edited by Joan Beaumont. St. Leonard's, Australia: Allen & Unwin, 1995.

Becker, Annette. *Oubliés de la Grande Guerre*. Paris: Éditions Noêsies, 1998.

Becker, Jean-Jacques. *The Great War and the French People*. Translated by Arnold Pomerans. New York: St. Martin's Press, 1986.

Beckett, Ian F. W. *The Great War, 1914–1918*. Harlow, Essex: Pearson Education, 2001.

Beinin, Joel, and Zachary Lockman. "1919: Labor Upsurge and National Revolution." In *The Modern Middle East: A Reader*, 2nd edition, edited by Albert Hourani, Philip Khoury, and Mary C. Wilson. London: Tauris, 2004.

Benton, Sarah. "Women Disarmed: The Militarization of Politics in Ireland, 1913–1923." *Feminist Review* 50 (1995): 148–72.

Berov, Ljuben. "The Bulgarian Economy during World War I." In *War and Society in East Central Europe*, edited by Béla Király and Nándor F. Dreisziger. New York: Columbia University Press, 1985.

Bessel, Richard. *Germany after the First World War*. Oxford: Clarendon Press, 1993.

———. "Mobilization and Demobilization in Germany, 1916–1919." In *State, Society, and Mobilization in Europe during the First World War*, edited by John Horne. Cambridge: Cambridge University Press, 1997.

Best, Geoffrey. *Humanity in Warfare*. New York: Columbia University Press, 1980.

Bird, J. C. *Control of Enemy Alien Civilians in Great Britain, 1914–1918*. New York: Garland, 1986.

Black, Jeremy. *The Age of Total War, 1860–1945*. Westport, CT: Praeger Security International, 2006.

Bloch, I. S. *The Future of War*. Translated by R. C. Long. New York: Doubleday & McClure, 1899.

Blücher, Evelyn. *An English Wife in Berlin*. New York: Dutton, 1920.

Blüdnikow, Bent. "Denmark during the First World War." *Journal of Contemporary History* 24:4 (October 1989): 683–703.

Bonzon, Thierry. "The Labour Market and Industrial Mobilization, 1915–1917." In *Capital Cities at War: Paris, London, Berlin, 1914–1919*, volume 1, edited by Jay Winter and Jean-Louis Robert. Cambridge: Cambridge University Press, 1997.

Bonzon, Thierry, and Belinda Davis. "Feeding the Cities." In *Capital Cities at War: Paris, London, Berlin, 1914–1919*, volume 1, edited by Jay Winter and Jean-Louis Robert. Cambridge: Cambridge University Press, 1997.

Bourke, Joanna. *An Intimate History of Killing: Face-to-Face Killing in Twentieth-Century Warfare*. New York: Basic Books, 1999.

———, ed. *The Misfit Soldier: Edward Casey's War Story, 1914–1918*. Cork: Cork University Press, 1999.

Bradley, Amy Owen. *Back of the Front in France*. Boston: Butterfield, 1918.

Braeman, John. "World War One and the Crisis of American Liberty." *American Quarterly* 16:1 (Spring 1964): 104–12.

Brändström, Elsa. *Among Prisoners of War in Russia and Siberia*. Translated by C. Mabel Rickmers. London: Hutchinson, 1929.

Bristow, Nancy K. *Making Men Moral: Social Engineering during the Great War*. New York: New York University Press, 1997.

Brittain, Vera. *Testament of Youth*. New York: Penguin, 1989.

Broadberry, Stephen, and Peter Howlett. "The United Kingdom during World War I." In *The Economics of World War I*, edited by Stephen Broadberry and Mark Harrison. Cambridge: Cambridge University Press, 2005.

Brown, Michael, Owen R. Coté Jr., Sean M. Lynn-Jones, and Steven E. Miller, eds. *Offense, Defense, and War: An International Security Reader*. Cambridge: MIT Press, 2004.

Brown, Percy. "My Three Years in Rat-Infested Ruhleben." In *The Great War: I Was There*, edited by Sir John Hammerton. London: Amalgamated Press, 1938.

Bucur, Maria. "Women's Stories as Sites of Memory: Gender and Remembering Romania's World Wars." In *Gender and War in Twentieth-Century Eastern Europe*, edited by Nancy M. Wingfield and Maria Bucur. Bloomington: Indiana University Press, 2006.

Burdick, Charles B. *The Japanese Siege of Tsingtau*. Hamden, CT: Archon Books, 1976.

Cahalan, Peter. *Belgian Refugee Relief in England during the Great War*. New York: Garland, 1982.

Capozzola, Christopher. "The Only Badge Needed Is Your Patriotic Fervor: Vigilance, Coercion, and the Law in World War I America." *Journal of American History* 88:4 (2002): 1354–82.

———. *Uncle Sam Wants You: World War I and the Making of the Modern American Citizen*. Oxford: Oxford University Press, 2008.

Chakravorty, U. N. *Indian Nationalism and the First World War, 1914–1918: Recent Political and Economic History of India*. Calcutta: Progressive Publishers, 1997.

Chatelle, Albert. *Calais pendant la Guerre (1914–1918)*. Paris: Librairie Aristide Quillet, 1927.

Chen, Joseph T. "The May Fourth Movement Redefined." *Modern Asian Studies* 4:1 (1970): 63–81.

Chickering, Roger. *The Great War and Urban Life in Germany: Freiburg, 1914–1918*. Cambridge: Cambridge University Press, 2007.

Chickering, Roger, and Stig Förster, eds. *Great War, Total War: Combat and Mobilization on the Western Front, 1914–1918*. Cambridge: Cambridge University Press, 2000.

Clark, Bruce. *Twice a Stranger: The Mass Expulsions That Forged Modern Greece and Turkey*. Cambridge, MA: Harvard University Press, 2006.

Clothier, Norman. *Black Valour: The South African Native Labour Contingent, 1916–1918, and the Sinking of the Mendi.* Pietermaritzburg, South Africa: University of Natal Press, 1987.

Cohen, Eliot A. *Citizens and Soldiers: The Dilemmas of Military Service.* Ithaca, NY: Cornell University Press, 1985.

Cohen, Israel. *The Ruhleben Prison Camp: A Record of Nineteen Months' Internment.* London: Methuen, 1917.

Cohen-Porthcim, Paul. *Time Stood Still: My Internment in England, 1914–1918.* New York: Dutton, 1932.

Cole, Joshua. "The Transition to Peace, 1918–19." In *Capital Cities at War: Paris, London, Berlin, 1914–1919,* volume 1, edited by Jay Winter and Jean-Louis Robert. Cambridge: Cambridge University Press, 1997.

Comité International de la Croix-Rouge. L'Agence Internationale des Prisonniers de Guerre, Genève 1914–1918. Geneva, 1919.

Constantine, Stephen, Maurice W. Kirby, and Mary B. Rose, eds. *The First World War in British History.* London: Edward Arnold, 1995.

Cooter, Roger, Mark Harrison, and Steve Sturdy, eds. *War, Medicine, and Modernity.* Stroud, UK: Sutton, 1998.

Cooter, Roger, and Steve Sturdy. "Of War, Medicine, and Modernity: Introduction." In *War, Medicine and Modernity,* edited by Roger Cooter, Mark Harrison, and Steve Sturdy. Stroud, UK: Sutton, 1998.

Coper, Rudolf. *Failure of a Revolution: Germany in 1918–1919.* Cambridge: Cambridge University Press, 1955.

Copland, Ian. *The Princes of India in the Endgame of Empire, 1917–1947.* Cambridge: Cambridge University Press, 2002.

Coppens, E. C. *Paul Fredericq.* Ghent, Belgium: Gent Liberal Archief, 1990.

Corner, Paul, and Giovanna Procacci, "The Italian Experience of 'Total' Mobilization, 1915–1920." In *State, Society, and Mobilization in Europe during the First World War,* edited by John Horne. Cambridge: Cambridge University Press, 1997.

Crangle, John V., and Joseph O. Baylen. "Emily Hobhouse's Peace Mission, 1916." *Journal of Contemporary History* 14:4 (October 1979): 731–44.

Cresswell, Yvonne M., ed. *Living with the Wire: Civilian Internment in the Isle of Man during the Two World Wars.* Douglas, Isle of Man: Manx National Heritage, 1994.

Crossley, Robert, ed. *Talking across the World: The Love Letters of Olaf Stapledon and Agnes Miller, 1913–1919.* Hanover, NH: University Press of New England, 1987.

Crossthwait, Elizabeth. "'The Girl behind the Man behind the Gun': The Women's Army Auxiliary Corps, 1914–18." In *Our Work, Our Lives, Our Words,* edited by Leonore Davidoff and Belinda Westover. Basingstoke, UK: Macmillan Education, 1986.

Cuff, Robert D. "Herbert Hoover, the Ideology of Voluntarism, and War Organisation during the Great War." *Journal of American History* 64:2 (September 1977): 358–72.

Culleton, Clair A. *Working-Class Culture, Women, and Britain, 1914–1921.* New York: St. Martin's Press, 1999.

Curie, Marie. *Autobiographical Notes.* Translated by Charlotte and Vernon Kellogg. New York: Macmillan, 1923.

Daniel, Ute. *Arbeiterfrauen in der Kriegsgesellschaft: Beruf, Familie, und Politik im Ersten Weltkrieg.* Göttingen, Germany: Vandenhoeck & Ruprecht, 1989.

———. *The War from Within: German Working-Class Women in the First World War.* Translated by Margaret Ries. Oxford: Berg, 1997.

Darrow, Margaret. *French Women and the First World War: War Stories of the Home Front.* Oxford: Berg, 2000.

Davidoff, Leonore, and Belinda Westover, eds. *Our Work, Our Lives, Our Words.* Basingstoke, UK: Macmillan Education, 1986.

Davis, Belinda J. *Home Fires Burning: Food, Politics, and Everyday Life in World War I Berlin.* Chapel Hill: University of North Carolina Press, 2000.

———. "Homefront: Food, Politics, and Women's Everyday Life during the First World War." In *Home/Front: The Military, War, and Gender in Twentieth-Century Germany,* edited by Karen Hagemann and Stefanie Schüler-Springorum. Oxford: Berg, 2002.

Davis, Gerald H. "National Red Cross Societies and Prisoners of War in Russia, 1914–1918." *Journal of Contemporary History* 28:1 (January 1993): 31–52.

———. "Orgelsdorf: A World War I Internment Camp in America." *Yearbook of German-American Studies* 26 (1991): 249–66.

———. "Prisoners of War in Twentieth-Century War Economies." *Journal of Contemporary History* 12:4 (October 1977): 623–34.

Deak, Istvan. "Budapest and the Hungarian Revolutions of 1918–1919." *Slavonic and East European Review* 46:106 (January 1968): 129–40.

Dearmer, Mabel. *Letters from a Field Hospital.* London: Macmillan, 1915.

Debaeke, Siegfried. *Ik was 20 in '14.* Kortrijk, Belgium: De Klaproos, 1999.

Debruyne, Emmanuel. "Les services de renseignements alliés en Belgique occupée." In *14–18 Une Guerre Totale? La Belgique dans la Première Guerre mondiale,* edited by Serge Jaumain, Michaël Amara, Benoit Majerus, and Antoon Vrints. Brussels: Algemeen Rijksarchief, 2005.

DeGroot, Gerard J. *Blighty: British Society in the Era of the Great War.* London: Longman, 1996.

De Lannoy, Charles. *L'Alimentation de la Belgique par le Comité National (Novembre 1914 à November 1918).* Brussels: Office de Publicité, 1922.

Demm, Eberhard. "Propaganda and Caricature in the First World War." *Journal of Contemporary History* 28:1 (1993): 163–92.

Dendooven, Dominiek. "The British Dominions and Colonies at the Front in Flanders" and "The European Armies: No Ethno-Cultural Monoliths." In *World War I: Five Continents in Flanders*, edited by Dominiek Dendooven and Piet Chielens. Tielt, Belgium: Lannoo, 2008.

―――. "The Multicultural War in Flanders." In *Une Guerre Totale? La Belgique dans la Première Guerre Mondiale*, edited by Serge Jaumain, Michaël Amara, Benoit Majerus, and Antoon Vrints. Brussels: Algemeen Rijksarchief, 2005.

Denholm, Decie, ed. *Behind the Lines: One Woman's War, 1914–18; The Letters of Caroline Ethel Cooper*. London: Jill Norman & Hobhouse, 1982.

Deruyk, René. *1914–1918, Lille dans les Serres Allemandes*. Lille, France: La Voix du Nord, 1992.

De Schaepdrijver, Sophie. *La Belgique et la Première Guerre mondiale*. Translated by Claudine Spitaels and Vincent Marnix. Brussels: Peter Lang, 2005.

De Weerdt, Denise. *De Vrowen van de Eerste Wereldoorlog*. Ghent, Belgium: Stichting Mens en Kultuur, 1993.

Dickinson, Frederick R. *War and National Reinvention: Japan in the Great War, 1914–1919*. Cambridge, MA: Harvard University Press, 1999.

Dobson, Sean. *Authority and Upheaval in Leipzig, 1910–1920: The Story of a Relationship*. New York: Columbia University Press, 2001.

Downes, W. D. *With the Nigerians in German East Africa*. London: Methuen, 1919.

Downs, Laura Lee. *Manufacturing Inequality: Gender Division in the French and British Metalworking Industries, 1914–1939*. Ithaca, NY: Cornell University Press, 1995.

Draper, Alfred. *Amritsar: The Massacre that Ended the Raj*. London: Cassell, 1981.

Duclert, Vincent. "La Destruction des Arméniens." In *Encyclopédie de la Grande Guerre 1914–1918: Histoire et culture*, edited by Stéphane Audoin-Rouzeau and Jean-Jacques Becker. Paris: Bayard, 2004.

Dumoulin, Koenraad, Steven Vansteenkiste, and Jan Verdoodt. *Getuigen van de Grote Oorlog: Getuigenissen uit de frontstreek*. Koksijde, Belgium: De Klaproos, 2001.

Dyer, Geoff. *The Missing of the Somme*. London: Phoenix, 1994.

Earle, Rebecca, ed. *Epistolary Selves: Letters and Letter-Writers, 1600–1945*. Aldershot, UK: Ashgate, 1999.

Echenberg, Myron. *Colonial Conscripts: The Tirailleurs Sénégalais in French West Africa, 1857–1960*. Portsmouth, NH: Heinemann, 1991.

Eckart, Wolfgang U. "'The Most Extensive Experiment That the Imagination Can Conceive': War, Emotional Stress, and German Medicine, 1914–1918." In *Great War, Total War: Combat and Mobilization on the Western Front, 1914–1918*, edited by Roger Chickering and Stig Förster. Cambridge: Cambridge University Press, 2000.

Ellis, Mark. "German-Americans in World War I." In *Enemy Images in American History*, edited by Ragnhil Fiebig-von Hase and Ursula Lehnkuhl. Providence, RI: Berghahn, 1997.

Engel, Barbara Alpern. "Not by Bread Alone: Subsistence Riots in Russia during World War I." *The Journal of Modern History* 69:4 (December 1997): 696–721.

Enloe, Cynthia. *Does Khaki Become You? The Militarisation of Women's Lives.* London: South End Press, 1983.

Farcy, Jean-Claude. *Les Camps Concentration Français de la première guerre mondiale 1914–1920.* Paris: Anthropos-Economica, 1995.

Fawcett, Brian C. "The Chinese Labour Corps in France 1917–1921." *Journal of the Hong Kong Branch of the Royal Asiatic Society* 40 (2000): 33–111.

Ferguson, Niall. *The Pity of War.* New York: Basic, 1999.

Fiebig-von Hase, Ragnhil, and Ursula Lehnkuhl, eds. *Enemy Images in American History.* Providence, RI: Berghahn, 1997.

Fink, Carol. *Defending the Rights of Others: The Great Powers, the Jews, and International Minority Protection, 1878–1938.* Cambridge: Cambridge University Press, 2004.

Fischer, Gerhard. *Enemy Aliens: Internment and the Homefront Experience in Australia, 1914–1920.* St. Lucia, Australia: University of Queensland, 1989.

Fitzpatrick, Sheila. *The Russian Revolution, 1917–1932.* Oxford: Oxford University Press, 1982.

Fogarty, Richard S. *Race and War in France: Colonial Subjects in the French Army, 1914–1918.* Baltimore, MD: Johns Hopkins University Press, 2008.

Fordham, Elizabeth. "Universities." In *Capital Cities at War: Paris, London, Berlin, 1914–1919,* volume 2, edited by Jay Winter and Jean-Louis Robert. Cambridge: Cambridge University Press, 2007.

French, David. "Spy Fever in Britain, 1900–1915." *Historical Journal* 21:2 (1978): 355–70.

Frevert, Ute. *A Nation in Barracks: Modern Germany, Military Conscription, and Civil Society.* Translated by Andrew Boreham with Daniel Brückenhaus. Oxford: Berg, 2004.

Fuglister, Albert. *Louvain Ville Martyre.* Paris: Editions Delandre, 1916.

Fyson, Robert. "The Douglas Camp Shootings of 1914." *Proceedings of the Isle of Man Natural History and Antiquarian Society* 11:1 (April 1997–March 1999): 116–21.

Gatrell, Peter. "Poor Russia, Poor Show: Mobilising a Backward Economy for War, 1914–1917." In *The Economics of World War I,* edited by Stephen Broadberry and Mark Harrison. Cambridge: Cambridge University Press, 2005.

———. *Russia's First World War: A Social and Economic History.* Harlow, Essex: Pearson/Longman, 2005.

———. *A Whole Empire Walking: Refugees in Russia during World War I.* Bloomington: Indiana University Press, 1999.

Gatrell, Peter, and Mark Harrison. "The Russian and Soviet Economies in Two World Wars: A Comparative View." *Economic History Review* 46:3 (August 1993): 425–52.

Geinitz, Christian. "The First Air War against Noncombatants: Strategic Bombing of German Cities in World War I." In *Great War, Total War: Combat and Mobilization on the Western Front, 1914–1918,* edited by Roger Chickering and Stig Förster. Cambridge: Cambridge University Press, 2000.

Gerard, James W. *My Four Years in Germany.* New York: Doran, 1917.

Gibson, Hugh. *A Journal from Our Legation in Belgium.* New York: Doubleday, Page, 1917.

Gille, Louis, Alphonse Ooms, and Paul Delandsheere. *Cinquante Mois d'Occupation Allemande, 1916,* volume 2. Brussels: Librairie Albert Dewit, 1919.

Gillis, John R., ed. *Commemorations: The Politics of National Identity.* Princeton, NJ: Princeton University Press, 1994.

Gleeson, Ian. *The Unknown Force: Black, Indian, and Coloured Soldiers through Two World Wars.* Rivonia, South Africa: Ashanti, 1994.

Glidden, William B. "Internment Camps in America, 1917–1920." *Military Affairs* 37:4 (December 1973): 137–41.

Goldberg, Ellis. "Peasants in Revolt: Egypt 1919." *International Journal of Middle Eastern Studies* 24:2 (May 1992): 261–80.

Goldman, Nancy Loring, and Richard Stites. "Great Britain and the World Wars." In *Female Soldiers: Combatants or Noncombatants? Historical and Contemporary Perspectives,* edited by Nancy Loring Goldman. Westport, CT: Greenwood Press, 1982.

Graham, Mark. *British Censorship of the Civil Mails during World War I, 1914–1919.* Bristol, UK: Stuart Rossiter Trust Fund, 2000.

Graham, Robert A. "Universal Military Training in Modern History." *Annals of the American Academy of Political and Social Science* 241 (September 1945): 8–14.

Grayzel, Susan R. "The Enemy Within: The Problem of British Women's Sexuality during the First World War." In *Women and War in the Twentieth Century: Enlisted with or without Consent,* edited by Nicole Ann Dombrowski. New York: Garland, 1999.

———. "'The Souls of Soldiers': Civilians under Fire in First World War France." *Journal of Modern History* 78 (September 2006): 588–622.

———. *Women and the First World War.* London: Pearson Education, 2002.

———. *Women's Identities at War: Gender, Motherhood, and Politics in Britain and France during the First World War.* Chapel Hill: University of North Carolina Press, 1999.

Greenhut, Jeffrey. "Sahib and Sepoy: An Inquiry into the Relationship between the British Officers and Native Soldiers of the British Army." *Military Affairs* 48:1 (January 1984): 15–18.

Greenwald, Maurine Weiner. *Women, War, and Work: The Impact of World War I on Women Workers in the United States.* Westport, CT: Greenwood Press, 1980.

Gregory, Adrian. *The Last Great War: British Society and the First World War*. Cambridge: Cambridge University Press, 2008.

Griffin, Nicholas J. "Britain's Chinese Labor Corps in World War I." *Military Affairs* 40:3 (October 1976): 102–8.

———. "Scientific Management in the Direction of Britain's Military Labour Establishment during World War I." *Military Affairs* 42:4 (December 1978): 197–201.

Griffin, Susan. *A Chorus of Stones: The Private Life of War*. New York: Anchor Books, 1992.

Grundlingh, Albert. *Fighting Their Own War: South African Blacks and the First World War*. Johannesburg: Ravan Press, 1987.

Gullace, Nicoletta. *"The Blood of Our Sons": Men, Women, and the Renegotiation of British Citizenship during the Great War*. New York: Palgrave Macmillan, 2002.

———. "Friends, Aliens, and Enemies: Fictive Communities and the Lusitania Riots of 1915." *Journal of Social History* 39:2 (December 2005): 345–67.

———. "Sexual Violence and Family Honor: British Propaganda and International Law during the First World War." *American Historical Review* 102:3 (1997): 714–47.

Gumbrecht, Hans Ulrich. "I redentori della vittoria: On Fiume's Place in the Genealogy of Fascism." *Journal of Contemporary History* 31:2 (April 1996): 253–72.

Guoqi, Xu. *China and the Great War: China's Pursuit of a New National Identity and Internationalization*. Cambridge: Cambridge University Press, 2005.

Hacker, Barton. "Women and Military Institutions in Early Modern Europe: A Reconnaissance." *Signs: Journal of Women in Culture and Society* 6:4 (1981): 643–71.

Hagemann, Karen, and Stefanie Schüler-Springorum, eds. *Home/Front: The Military, War, and Gender in Twentieth-Century Germany*. Oxford: Berg, 2002.

Hagen, Gwynnie. "Eenen Dwazen Glimlach aan het Front: Chinese koelies aan het westers front in de Eerste Wereldoorlog." Licentiate thesis, Katholieke Universiteit Leuven, Belgium, 1996.

Hagood, Johnson. *The Services of Supply: A Memoir of the Great War*. Boston: Houghton Mifflin, 1927.

Hajdu, Tibor. "Army and Society in Hungary in the Era of World War I." In *War and Society in East Central Europe*, edited by Béla Király and Nándor F. Dreisziger. New York: Columbia University Press, 1985.

Hake, Sabine. "Chaplin Reception in Weimar Germany." *New German Critique* 51 (Autumn 1990): 87–111.

Hämmerle, Christa. "'You Let a Weeping Woman Call You Home?': Private Correspondences during the First World War in Austria and Germany." In *Epistolary Selves: Letters and Letter-Writers, 1600–1945*, edited by Rebecca Earle. Aldershot, UK: Ashgate, 1999.

Hanna, Martha. *The Mobilization of Intellect: French Scholars and Writers during the Great War*. Cambridge, MA: Harvard University Press, 1996.

———.*Your Death Would Be Mine: Paul and Marie Pireaud in the Great War*. Cambridge, MA: Harvard University Press, 2006.

Harris, Ruth. "The 'Child of the Barbarian': Rape, Race, and Nationalism in France during the First World War." *Past and Present* 141 (November 1993): 170–206.

Hart, Peter. *The IRA at War, 1916–1923*. Oxford: Oxford University Press, 2003.

Healy, Maureen. *Vienna and the Fall of the Habsburg Empire: Total War and Everyday Life in World War I*. Cambridge: Cambridge University Press, 2004.

Hendrix, Scott N. "In the Army: Women, Camp Followers, and Gender Roles in the British Army in the French and Indian Wars, 1755–1765." In *A Soldier and a Woman: Sexual Integration in the Military*, edited by Gerard J. DeGroot and Corinna Peniston-Bird. Harlow, Essex: Pearson Education Limited, 2000.

Hiery, Hermann Joseph. *The Neglected War: The German South Pacific and the Influence of World War I*. Honolulu: University of Hawaii Press, 1995.

Higonnet, Margaret, ed. *Lines of Fire: Women Writers of World War I*. New York: Penguin, 1999.

——, ed. *Nurses at the Front: Writing the Wounds of the Great War*. Boston: Northeastern University Press, 2001.

Hiley, Nicholas. "Counter-espionage and Security in Great Britain during the First World War." *English Historical Review* 101:400 (July 1986): 635–70.

Hodges, Geoffrey. *The Carrier Corps: Military Labor in the East African Campaign, 1914–1918*. New York: Greenwood Press, 1986.

Hoffman, Conrad. *In the Prison Camps of Germany: A Narrative of "Y" Service among Prisoners of War*. New York: Association Press, 1920.

Holquist, Peter. *Making War, Forging Revolution: Russia's Continuum of Crisis, 1914–1921*. Cambridge, MA: Harvard University Press, 2002.

Horne, John. "Immigrant Workers in France during World War I." *French Historical Studies* 14:1 (1985): 57–88.

———, ed. *State, Society, and Mobilization in Europe during the First World War*. Cambridge: Cambridge University Press, 1997.

Horne, John, and Alan Kramer. *German Atrocities, 1914: A History of Denial*. New Haven, CT: Yale University Press, 2001.

Hornung, E. W. *Notes of a Camp-Follower on the Western Front*. New York: Dutton, 1919.

Hourani, Albert, Philip Khoury, and Mary C. Wilson, eds. *The Modern Middle East: A Reader*. London: Tauris, 2004.

Hull, Isabel V. *Absolute Destruction: Military Culture and the Practices of War in Imperial Germany*. Ithaca, NY: Cornell University Press, 2005.

Hunton, Addie W., and Kathryn M. Johnson. *Two Colored Women with the American Expeditionary Forces*. Brooklyn: Brooklyn Eagle Press, 1920.

Hussain, Nasser. "Towards a Jurisprudence of Emergency: Colonialism and the Rule of Law." *Law and Critique* 10 (1999): 93–115.

Inglis, Elsie. "The Tragedy of Serbia." In *Women's Writing of the First World War: An Anthology*, edited by Angela K. Smith. Manchester, UK: Manchester University Press, 2000.

Jahn, Hubertus F. *Patriotic Culture in Russia during World War I*. Ithaca, NY: Cornell University Press, 1995.

Jensen, Joan M. *The Price of Vigilance*. Chicago: Rand McNally, 1968.

Jensen, Kimberly. "Physicians and Citizens: U.S. Medical Women and Military Service in the First World War." In *War, Medicine, and Modernity*, edited by Roger Cooter, Mark Harrison, and Steve Sturdy. Stroud, UK: Sutton, 1998.

Jesse, F. Tennyson. *The Sword of Deborah: First-Hand Impressions of the British Women's Army in France*. New York: Doran, 1919.

Johnson, Katherine Burger. "Allied Medical Personnel in World War I." In *Personal Perspectives: World War I*, edited by Timothy C. Dowling. Santa Barbara, CA: ABC-CLIO, 2006.

Jones, Heather. "Encountering the 'Enemy': Prisoner of War Transport and the Development of War Cultures in 1914." In *Warfare and Belligerence: Perspectives in First World War Studies*, edited by Pierre Purseigle. Leiden, Netherlands: Brill, 2005.

———. "A Missing Paradigm? Military Captivity and the Prisoner of War, 1914–18." *Immigrants and Minorities* 26:1/2 (March/July 2008): 19–48.

Kater, Michael H. "Professionalization and Socialization of Physicians in Wilhelmine and Weimar Germany." *Journal of Contemporary History* 20:4 (October 1985): 677–701.

Kennedy, Thomas C. *The Hound of Conscience: A History of the No-Conscription Fellowship, 1914–1919*. Fayetteville: University of Arkansas Press, 1981.

Kerr, Rose. *The Story of a Million Girls*. London: Girl Guides Association, 1937.

Killingray, David. "Gender Issues and African Colonial Armies." In *Guardians of Empire: The Armed Forces of the Colonial Powers c. 1700–1964*, edited by David Killingray and David Omissi. Manchester, UK: Manchester University Press, 1999.

———. "Labour Exploitation for Military Campaigns in British Colonial Africa, 1870–1945." *Journal of Contemporary History* 24:3 (July 1989): 483–501.

Killingray, David, and David Omissi, eds. *Guardians of Empire: The Armed Forces of the Colonial Powers c. 1700–1964*. Manchester. UK: Manchester University Press, 1999.

Kingsley Kent, Susan. "The Politics of Sexual Difference: World War I and the Demise of British Feminism." *Journal of British Studies* 27 (July 1988): 232–53.

Király, Béla, and Nándor F. Dreisziger, eds. *War and Society in East Central Europe*, volume 19. New York: Columbia University Press, 1985.

Klein, Daryl. *With the Chinks*. London: John Lane Bodley Head, 1918.

Knox, MacGregor. *To the Threshold of Power, 1922/33: Origins and Dynamics of the Fascist and National Socialist Dictatorships*, volume 1. Cambridge: Cambridge University Press, 2007.

Kollwitz, Hans, ed. *The Diary and Letters of Kaethe Kollwitz*. Evanston, IL: Northwestern University Press, 1988.

Kordan, Bohdan. *Enemy Aliens, Prisoners of War: Internment in Canada during the Great War*. Montreal: McGill-Queen's University Press, 2002.

Kramer, Alan. *Dynamic of Destruction: Culture and Mass Killing in the First World War*. Oxford: Oxford University Press, 2008.

Krippner, Monica. *The Quality of Mercy: Women at War, Serbia, 1915–1918*. London: David and Charles, 1980.

Kuhr, Piete. *There We'll Meet Again*. Translated by Walter Wright. Gloucester, UK: Walter Wright, 1998.

Laband, John, ed. *Daily Lives of Civilians in Wartime Africa: From Slavery Days to Rwandan Genocide*. Westport, CT: Greenwood Press, 2007.

Lampe, John R. *Balkans into Southeastern Europe: A Century of War and Transition*. London: Palgrave, 2006.

Lane, W. B. *A Summary of the History, with Suggestions, and Recommendations of the Seven Jail Labour and Porter Corps, Employed in Mesopotamia from October 1916 to July 1919*. Baghdad: Government Press, 1920.

Larsson, Marina. *Shattered Anzacs: Living with the Scars of War*. Sydney: University of New South Wales Press, 2009.

Lavine, A. Lincoln. *Circuits of Victory*. Garden City, NY: Doubleday, Page, 1921.

Lawrence, Jon. "The Transition to War in 1914." *Capital Cities at War: Paris, London, Berlin, 1914–1919*, volume 1, edited by Jay Winter and Jean-Louis Robert. Cambridge: Cambridge University Press, 1997.

Lee, J. Fitzgerald. *Blacklead and Whitewash: A Side-show of the Great War*. Karachi, Pakistan: G. A. Holdaway, [1923].

Leigh, M. S. *The Punjab and the War*. Lahore, Pakistan: Government Printing, 1922.

Leiser, Gary, trans. and ed. *Vetluga Memoir: A Turkish Prisoner of War in Russia, 1916–1918*. Gainesville: University Press of Florida, 1995.

Levi, Margaret. "The Institution of Conscription." *Social Science History* 20:1 (Spring 1996): 133–67.

Levine, Philippa. *Prostitution, Race, and Politics: Policing Venereal Disease in the British Empire*. New York: Routledge, 2003.

Liulevicius, Vejas Gabriel. *War Land on the Eastern Front: Culture, National Identity, and German Occupation in World War I*. Cambridge: Cambridge University Press, 2000.

Lohr, Eric. *Nationalizing the Russian Empire: The Campaign against Enemy Aliens during World War I*. Cambridge, MA: Harvard University Press, 2003.

———. "The Russian Army and the Jews: Mass Deportation, Hostages, and Violence during World War I." *Russian Review* 60 (July 2001): 404–19.

Lowe, Rodney. "Government." In *The First World War in British History*, edited by Stephen Constantine, Maurice W. Kirby, and Mary B. Rose. London: Edward Arnold, 1995.

Lucassen, Jan, and Erik Jan Zürcher. "Conscription as Military Labour: The Historical Context." *International Review of Social History* 43 (1998): 405–19.

Luebke, Frederick. *Germans in Brazil*. Baton Rouge: Louisiana State University Press, 1987.

Lyon, Bryce. *Henri Pirenne: A Biographical and Intellectual Study*. Ghent, Belgium: E. Story-Scientia, 1974.

Lyon, Bryce, and Mary Lyon, eds. *The Journal de Guerre of Henri Pirenne*. Amsterdam: North-Holland, 1976.

Macintyre, Ben. *The Englishman's Daughter: A True Story of Love and Betrayal in World War I*. New York: Farrar, Straus, Giroux, 2001.

Mackenzie, John, ed. *Popular Imperialism and the Military*. Manchester, UK: Manchester University Press, 1992.

Maclean, Pam. "War and Australian Society." In *Australia's War, 1914–1918*, edited by Joan Beaumont. St. Leonard's, Australia: Allen & Unwin, 1995.

Maddox, Gregory. "Mtunya: Famine in Central Tanzania, 1917–20." *Journal of African History* 31:2 (1990): 181–97.

Maeterlinck, Maurice. *The Wrack of the Storm*. New York: Dodd, Mead, 1916.

Majd, Mohammad Gholi. *The Great Famine and Genocide in Persia, 1917–1919*. Lanham, MD: University Press of America, 2003.

———. *Iraq in World War I: From Ottoman Rule to British Conquest*. Lanham, MD: University Press of America, 2006.

Mamatey, Victor S. "The Czech Wartime Dilemma: The Habsburgs or the Entente." In *War and Society in East Central Europe*, edited by Béla Király and Nándor F Dreisziger. New York: Columbia University Press, 1985.

Manela, Erez. *The Wilsonian Moment: Self-Determination and the International Origins of Anticolonial Nationalism*. Oxford: Oxford University Press, 2007.

Manifeste signé par 93 Savants allemands aux Nations civilisées [and Responses]. Paris: Imprimerie Descamps, 1915.

Manley, Robert N., and Elaine Manley McKee, eds. *The World War I Letters of Private Milford N. Manley*. Gardner, KS: Dageforde, 1995.

Mann, Gregory. *Native Sons: West African Veterans and France in the Twentieth Century*. Durham, NC: Duke University Press, 2006.

Marcus, Jane. "Afterword: Corpus/Corps/Corpses: Writing the Body in/at War." In *Helen Zenna Smith, Not So Quiet... Stepdaughters of War*. New York: Feminist Press, 1989.

Massart, Jean. *La Presse Clandestine dans la Belgique Occupée*. Paris: Berger-Levrault, 1917.

Maurer, Maurer. "The Court-Martialing of Camp Followers, World War I." *American Journal of Legal History* 9:3 (1965): 203–15.

Mayer, Holly A. *Belonging to the Army: Camp Followers and Community during the American Revolution*. Columbia: University of South Carolina Press, 1996.

McAuley, Mary. *Bread and Justice: State and Society in Petrograd, 1917–1922*. Oxford: Clarendon Press, 1991.

McCartney, Helen B. *Citizen Soldiers: The Liverpool Territorials in the First World War*. Cambridge: Cambridge University Press, 2005.

McEwen, Yvonne. *"It's a Long Way to Tipperary": British and Irish Nurses in the Great War*. Dunfermline, Scotland: Cualann Press, 2006.

McGill, David. *Island of Secrets: Matiu/Somes Island in Wellington Harbour*. Wellington, New Zealand: Steele Roberts & Silver Owl Press, 2001.

Melnycky, Peter. "Badly Treated in Every Way: The Internment of Ukrainians in Quebec during the First World War." In *The Ukrainian Experience in Quebec*, edited by Myroslaw Diakowsky. Toronto: Basilian Press, 1994.

Merritt, Elaine. "War Lace: Commemorating Victory and Determination." *Piecework* 7:4 (July/August 1999): 24–29.

Meyer, Ernest Louis. *Hey! Yellowbacks! The War Diary of a Conscientious Objector*. New York: John Day, 1930.

Michl, Susanne. *Im Dienste des "Volkskörpers": Deutsche und französische Artze im Ersten Weltkrieg*. Göttingen, Germany: Vandenhoeck & Ruprecht, 2007.

Mitchell, Allan. *Revolution in Bavaria, 1918–1919: The Eisner Regime and the Soviet Republic*. Princeton, NJ: Princeton University Press, 1965.

Mitchinson, K. W. *Pioneer Battalions in the Great War: Organized and Intelligent Labour*. London: Leo Cooper, 1997.

Mitrany, David. *The Effect of the War in Southeastern Europe*. New Haven, CT: Yale University Press, 1936.

Monod, Francois. "Food for France and Its Public Control." *Annals of the American Academy of Political and Social Science* 74 (November 1917): 84–91.

Moorehead, Caroline. *Dunant's Dream: War, Switzerland, and the History of the Red Cross*. London: HarperCollins, 1998.

Moran, Daniel. "Arms and the Concert: The Nation in Arms and the Dilemmas of German Liberalism." In *The People in Arms: Military Myth and National Mobilization since the French Revolution*, edited by Daniel Moran and Arthur Waldron. Cambridge: Cambridge University Press, 2003.

Moran, Daniel, and Arthur Waldron, eds. *The People in Arms: Military Myth and National Mobilization since the French Revolution.* Cambridge: Cambridge University Press, 2003.

Morgan, Janet. *The Secrets of Rue St. Roch: Hope and Heroism behind Enemy Lines in the First World War.* London: Penguin, 2005.

Morris, A. J. A. *The Scaremongers: The Advocacy of War and Rearmament, 1986–1914.* London: Routledge and Kegan Paul, 1984.

Mussolini, Benito. *My Diary, 1915–17.* Boston: Small, Maynard, 1925.

Nabulsi, Karma. *Traditions of War: Occupation, Resistance, and the Law.* Oxford: Oxford University Press, 1999.

Nasson, Bill. *Springboks on the Somme: South Africa in the Great War.* Johannesburg: Penguin, 2007.

Nivet, Philippe. "Réfugiés." In *Encyclopédie de la Grande Guerre, 1914–1918: Histoire et culture,* edited by Stéphane Audoin-Rouzeau and Jean-Jacques Becker. Paris: Bayard, 2004.

Nordvall, Axel Robert. "Sweden's Food Supply." *Annals of the American Academy of Political and Social Science* 74 (November 1917): 57–65.

Notre Labeur: La Région de Louvain pendant la Guerre. Brussels: De Bruycker, n.d.

Nym Mayhall, Laura E. *The Militant Suffrage Movement: Citizenship and Resistance in Britain, 1860–1930.* Oxford: Oxford University Press, 2003.

Offer, Avner. *The First World War: An Agrarian Interpretation.* Oxford: Clarendon Press, 1989.

Omissi, David. *Indian Voices of the Great War: Soldiers' Letters, 1914–1918.* New York: St. Martin's Press, 1999.

O'Shaughnessy, Edith. *My Lorraine Journal.* New York: Harper & Brothers, 1918.

Otter, W. D. *Internment Operations, 1914–1920.* Ottawa: T. Mulvey, 1921.

Page, Melvin E. *The Chiwaya War: Malawians and the First World War.* Boulder, CO: Westview Press, 2000.

Page, Thomas Nelson. *Italy and the World War.* New York: Scribner's, 1920.

Palmer, Svetlana, and Sarah Wallis, eds. *Intimate Voices from the First World War.* New York: Morrow, 2003.

Pamuk, Şevket. "The Ottoman Economy in World War I." In *The Economics of World War I,* edited by Stephen Broadberry and Mark Harrison. Cambridge: Cambridge University Press, 2005.

Parsons, Timothy. *The African Rank-and-File: Social Implications of Colonial Military Service in the King's African Rifles, 1902–1964.* Portsmouth, NH: Heinemann, 1999.

———. "'All Askaris Are Family Men': Sex, Domesticity, and Discipline in the King's African Rifles, 1902–1964." In *Guardians of Empire: The Armed Forces of the Colonial Powers c. 1700–1964,* edited by David Killingray and David Omissi. Manchester, UK: Manchester University Press, 1999.

————. "'Wakamba Warriors Are Soldiers of the Queen': The Evolution of the Kamba as a Martial Race, 1890–1970." *Ethnohistory* 46:4 (Autumn 1999): 671–701.

Pastor, Peter. "The Home Front in Hungary, 1914–1918." In *War and Society in East Central Europe*, edited by Béla Király and Nándor F. Dreisziger. New York: Columbia University Press, 1985.

Pickles, Katie. *Transnational Outrage: The Death and Commemoration of Edith Cavell*. New York: Palgrave Macmillan, 2007.

Piehler, G. Kurt. "The War Dead and the Gold Star: American Commemoration of the First World War." In *Commemorations: The Politics of National Identity*, edited by John R. Gillis. Princeton, NJ: Princeton University Press, 1994.

Pirenne, Henri. *Souvenirs de Captivité en Allemagne, Mars 1916–Novembre 1918*. Brussels: Maurice Lamertin, 1920.

Porch, Douglas. *The French Secret Service: From the Dreyfus Affair to the Gulf War*. New York: Farrar, Straus, Giroux, 1995.

Porter, Patrick. "New Jerusalems: Sacrifice and Redemption in the War Experiences of English and German Military Chaplains." In *Warfare and Belligerence: Perspectives in First World War Studies*, edited by Pierre Purseigle. Leiden, Netherlands: Brill, 2005.

Pourcher, Yves. "La fouille des champs d'honneur." *Terrain* 20: *La mort* (March 1993). Available at http://terrain.revues.org/document3057.html. Last accessed Oct. 28, 2009.

Prochasson, Christophe. "Les intellectuels." In *Encyclopédie de la Grande Guerre, 1914–1918: Histoire et culture*, edited by Stéphane Audoin-Rouzeau and Jean-Jacques Becker. Paris: Bayard, 2004.

Proctor, Tammy M. *Female Intelligence: Women and Espionage in the First World* War. New York: New York University Press, 2003.

————. *On My Honour: Guiding and Scouting in Interwar Britain*. Philadelphia: American Philosophical Society, 2002.

Prusin, Alexander Victor. *Nationalizing a Borderland: War, Ethnicity, and Anti-Jewish Violence in East Galicia, 1914–1920*. Tuscaloosa: University of Alabama Press, 2005.

Pugsley, Christopher. *Te Hokowhitu a Tu: The Maori Pioneer Battalion in the First World War*. Auckland, New Zealand: Reed, 1995.

Purseigle, Pierre. "Warfare and Belligerence: Approaches to the First World War." In *Warfare and Belligerence: Perspectives in First World War Studies*, edited by Pierre Purseigle. Leiden, Netherlands: Brill, 2005.

Pyke, Geoffrey. *To Ruhleben and Back: A Great Adventure in Three Phases*. Boston: Houghton Mifflin, 1916.

Quataert, Jean H. "Women's Wartime Services under the Cross." In *Great War, Total War: Combat and Mobilization on the Western Front, 1914–1918*, edited by Roger Chickering and Stig Förster. Cambridge: Cambridge University Press, 2000.

Rachamimov, Alon. "The Disruptive Comforts of Drag: (Trans)Gender Performances among Prisoners of War in Russia, 1914–1920." *American Historical Review* 111:2 (April 2006): 362–82.

———. "'Female Generals' and 'Siberian Angels': Aristocratic Nurses and the Austro-Hungarian POW Relief." In *Gender and War in Twentieth-Century Eastern Europe*, edited by Nancy M. Wingfield and Maria Bucur. Bloomington: Indiana University Press, 2006.

———. *POWs and the Great War: Captivity on the Eastern Front*. Oxford: Berg, 2002.

Rawe, Kai. ". . . *wir werden sie schon zur Arbeit bringen": Ausländerbeschäftigung und Zwangsarbeit im Ruhrkohlenbergbau während des Ersten Weltkrieges*. Essen, Germany: Klartext, 2005.

———. "Working in the Coal Mine: Belgians in the German War Industry of the Ruhr Area during World War I." In *Une Guerre Totale? La Belgique dans la Première Guerre Mondiale*, edited by Serge Jaumain, Michaël Amara, Benoit Majerus, and Antoon Vrints. Brussels: Algemeen Rijksarchief, 2005.

Reports on British Prison-Camps in India and Burma. New York: Doran, 1918.

Reports on the Treatment by the Germans of British Prisoners and Natives in German East Africa. London: HMSO, 1917.

Robert, Krisztina. "Gender, Class, and Patriotism: Women's Paramilitary Units in First World War Britain." *International History Review* 19:1 (February 1997): 52–65.

Rollet, Catherine. "The 'Other War' I: Protecting Public Health" and "The 'Other War' II: Setbacks in Public Health." In *Capital Cities at War: Paris, London, Berlin, 1914–1919*, volume 1, edited by Jay Winter and Jean-Louis Robert. Cambridge: Cambridge University Press, 1997.

Roper, Michael. *The Secret Battle: Emotional Survival in the Great War*. Manchester, UK: Manchester University Press, 2009.

Rosenberg, Scott P. "Promises of Moshoeshoe: Culture, Nationalism, and Identity in Lesotho, 1902–1966." Ph.D. diss., Indiana University, 1998.

Rosenne, Shabtai, ed. *The Hague Peace Conferences of 1899 and 1907 and International Arbitration: Reports and Documents*. The Hague: Asser Press, 2001.

Roshwald, Aviel. *Ethnic Nationalism and the Fall of Empires: Central Europe, Russia, and the Middle East, 1914–1923*. London: Routledge, 2001.

Salvadó, Francisco J. Romero. *Spain, 1914–1918: Between War and Revolution*. London: Routledge, 1999.

Samuels, Edmond. *An Illustrated Diary of Australian Internment Camps*. Goulburn: Argyle Press, 1983.

Sanborn, Josh. "The Mobilization of 1914 and the Question of the Russian Nation: A Reexamination." *Slavic Review* 59:2 (2000): 267–89.

Sanborn, Joshua A. *Drafting the Russian Nation: Military Conscription, Total War, and Mass Politics, 1905–1925*. Dekalb: Northern Illinois University Press, 2003.

Sargeaunt, B. E. *The Isle of Man and the Great War*. Douglas: Brown and Sons, 1920.

Sauerteig, Lutz D. H. "Sex, Medicine, and Morality during the First World War." In *War, Medicine, and Modernity*, edited by Roger Cooter, Mark Harrison, and Steve Sturdy. Stroud, UK: Sutton, 1998.

Savage, Donald C., and J. Forbes Munro. "Carrier Corps Recruitment in the British East Africa Protectorate, 1914–1918." *Journal of African History* 7:2 (1966): 313–42.

Sayer, Derek. "British Reaction to the Amritsar Massacre, 1919–1920." *Past and Present* 131 (May 1991): 130–64.

Scannell, Dorothy. *Mother Knew Best: Memoir of a London Girlhood*. New York: Pantheon, 1974.

Schönberger, Bianca. "Motherly Heroines and Adventurous Girls: Red Cross Nurses and Women Army Auxiliaries in the First World War." In *Home/Front: The Military, War, and Gender in Twentieth-Century Germany*, edited by Karen Hagemann and Stefanie Schüler-Springorum. Oxford: Berg, 2002.

Schulte, Regina. "Käthe Kollwitz's Sacrifice." *History Workshop Journal* 41 (Spring 1996): 193–221.

Schultheiss, Katrin. *Bodies and Souls: Politics and Professionalization of Nursing in France, 1880–1922*. Cambridge, MA: Harvard, 2001.

Seregny, Scott J. "Zemstvos, Peasants, and Citizenship: The Russian Adult Education Movement and World War I." *Slavic Review* 59:2 (Summer 2000): 290–315.

Service with Fighting Men: An Account of the Work of the American Young Men's Christian Associations in the World War, volume 2. New York: Association Press, 1922.

Showalter, Dennis. "'It All Goes Wrong!': German, French, and British Approaches to Mastering the Western Front." In *Warfare and Belligerence: Perspectives in First World War Studies*, edited by Pierre Purseigle. Leiden, Netherlands: Brill, 2005.

Sime, Ruth Lewin. *Lise Meitner: A Life in Physics*. Berkeley: University of California Press, 1996.

Simons, John. *Prisoners in Arcady: German Mariners in Berrima, 1915–1919*. Bowral, New South Wales: Berrima District Historical and Family History Society, 1999.

Singer, Peter. *Pushing Time Away*. Sydney: Fourth Estate, 2003.

Slim, Hugo. *Killing Civilians: Method, Madness, and Morality in War*. New York: Columbia University Press, 2008.

Snively, Harry Hamilton. *The Battle of the Non-Combatants*. New York: Business Bourse Publishers, 1933.

Snyder, Jack. "Civil-Military Relations and the Cult of the Offensive, 1914 and 1984." In *Offense, Defense, and War: An International Security Reader,* edited by Michael Brown, Owen R. Coté Jr., Sean M. Lynn-Jones, and Steven E. Miller. Cambridge: MIT Press, 2004.

Sokol, Edward Dennis. *The Revolt of 1916 in Russian Central Asia.* Baltimore, MD: Johns Hopkins Press, 1954.

Spear, Percival. "Mahatma Gandhi." *Modern Asian Studies* 3:4 (1969): 291–304.

Speed, Richard B. *Prisoners, Diplomats, and the Great War: A Study in the Diplomacy of Captivity.* New York: Greenwood Press, 1990.

Spiers, Edward M. *The Late Victorian Army, 1868–1902.* Manchester, UK: Manchester University Press, 1992.

Spinks, Charles Nelson. "Japan's Entrance into the World War." *Pacific Historical Review* 5:4 (1936): 297–311.

Stapleton, Tim. "The Impact of the First World War on African People." In *Daily Lives of Civilians in Wartime Africa: From Slavery Days to Rwandan Genocide,* edited by John Laband. Westport, CT: Greenwood Press, 2007.

Stibbe, Matthew. *British Civilian Internees in Germany: The Ruhleben Camp, 1914–18.* Manchester, UK: Manchester University Press, 2008.

———. "A Community at War: British Civilian Internees at the Ruhleben Camp in Germany, 1914–1918." In *Uncovered Fields: Perspectives in First World War Studies,* edited by Jenny Macleod and Pierre Purseigle. Leiden, Netherlands: Brill, 2004.

———. "The Internment of Civilians by Belligerent States during the First World War and the Response of the International Committee of the Red Cross." *Journal of Contemporary History* 41:1 (2006): 5–19.

St. John, Noel T. *Judy O'Grady and the Colonel's Lady: The Army Wife and Camp Follower since 1660.* London: Brassey's Defence Publishers, 1988.

Stockdale, Melissa. "'My Death for the Motherland Is Happiness': Women, Patriotism, and Soldiering in Russia's Great War, 1914–1917." *American Historical Review* 109:1 (February 2004): 78–116.

Stoff, Laurie. *They Fought for the Motherland: Russia's Women Soldiers in World War I and the Revolution.* Lawrence: University Press of Kansas, 2006.

———. "They Fought for Russia: Female Soldiers of the First World War." In *A Soldier and a Woman: Sexual Integration in the Military,* edited by Gerard J. DeGroot and Corinna Peniston-Bird. Harlow, Essex: Pearson Education, 2000.

Stovall, Tyler. "The Color Line behind the Lines: Racial Violence in France during the Great War." *American Historical Review* 103:3 (June 1998): 737–69.

Strachan, Hew. *The First World War.* Volume 1, *To Arms.* Oxford: Oxford University Press, 2001.

Strangers in a Strange Land: Belgian Refugees, 1914–1918. Leuven, Belgium: Davidsfonds, 2004.

Sturdy, Steve. "War as Experiment: Physiology, Innovation, and Administration in Britain, 1914–1918; The Case of Chemical Warfare." In *War, Medicine, and Morality*, edited by Roger Cooter, Mark Harrison, and Steve Sturdy. Stroud, UK: Sutton, 1998.

Stynen, Ludo, and Sylvia Van Peteghem, eds. *In Oorlogsnood: Virginie Lovelings Dagboek, 1914–1918*. Ghent, Belgium: Koninklijke Academie voor Nederlandse Taal- en Letterkunde, 1999.

Summers, Anne. *Angels and Citizens: British Women as Military Nurses*. London: Routledge and Kegan Paul, 1988.

Summerskill, Michael. *China on the Western Front: Britain's Chinese Work Force in the First World War*. London: Michael Summerskill, 1982.

Surkis, Judith, *Sexing the Citizen: Morality and Masculinity in France, 1870–1920*. Ithaca, NY: Cornell University Press, 2006.

Swart, Sandra. "'A Boer and His Gun and His Wife Are Three Things Always Together': Republican Masculinity and the 1914 Rebellion." *Journal of Southern African Studies* 24:4 (December 1998): 737–51.

Szabó, Dániel I. "The Social Basis of Opposition to the War in Hungary." In *War and Society in East Central Europe*, edited by Béla Király and Nándor F. Dreisziger. New York: Columbia University Press, 1985.

Tauber, Eliezer. "The Capture of the NILI Spies: The Turkish Version." *Intelligence and National Security* 6:4 (1991): 701–10.

Theweleit, Klaus. *Male Fantasies*, volume 1. Translated by Stephen Conway. Minneapolis: University of Minnesota Press, 1989.

Thiel, Jens. "Forced Labour, Deportation, and Recruitment: The German Reich and Belgian Labourers during the First World War." In *Une Guerre Totale? La Belgique dans la Première Guerre Mondiale*, edited by Serge Jaumain, Michaël Amara, Benoit Majerus, and Antoon Vrints. Brussels: Algemeen Rijksarchief, 2005.

———. *"Menschenbassin Belgien": Anwerbung, Deportation, und Zwangsarbeit im Ersten Weltkrieg*. Essen, Germany: Klartext, 2007.

Thompson, Mark. *The White War: Life and Death on the Italian Front, 1915–1919*. New York: Basic Books, 2008.

Tolerton, Jane. "Rout, Ettie Annie, 1877–1936." *Dictionary of New Zealand Biography*. Available at http://www.dnzb.govt.nz/.

Toma, Peter A. "The Slovak Soviet Republic of 1919." *American Slavic and East European Review* 17:2 (April 1958): 203–15.

Trausch, Gilbert. *Le Luxembourg entre la France et la Belgique, 1914–1922*. Luxembourg: Imprimerie Saint-Paul, 1975.

Trefoil around the World. London: World Association of Girl Guides and Girl Scouts, 2003.

Trustram, Myna. *Women of the Regiment: Marriage and the Victorian Army*. Cambridge: Cambridge University Press, 1984.

Turner, John. "State Purchase of the Liquor Trade in the First World War." *Historical Journal* 23:3 (September 1980): 589–615.

Valéry, Paul. *On the European Mind* [1922]. Internet History Sourcebook. Available at http://www.fordham.edu/halsall/mod/valery.html. Last accessed 14 January 2009.

Van Bergen, Leo. *Before My Helpless Sight: Suffering, Dying, and Military Medicine on the Western Front, 1914–1918*. Translated by Liz Waters. Farnham, UK: Ashgate, 2009.

Van Creveld, Martin. *Supplying War: Logistics from Wallenstein to Patton*, 2nd edition. Cambridge: Cambridge University Press, 2004.

Van Eelde, A. G. A. "The Case for Holland." *Annals of the American Academy of Political and Social Science* 74 (November 1917): 74–78.

Van Langenhove, Fernand. *Hoe een Cyclus van Legenden Ontstaat: Franc-Tireurs en Gruweldaden in België*. Leiden, Netherlands: De Flaamsche Boekenhalle, 1916.

Van Vollenhoven, M. W. R. *Memoires: Beschouwingen, Belevenissen, Reizen en Anecdoten*. Amsterdam: Elsevier, 1948.

Varshney, Ashutosh. "Nationalism, Ethnic Conflict, and Rationality." *Perspectives on Politics* 1:1 (2003): 85–99.

Verrier, Anthony, ed. *Agents of Empire: Anglo-Zionist Intelligence Operations, 1915–1919; Brigadier Walter Gribbon, Aaron Aaronsohn, and the NILI Ring*. London: Brassey's, 1995.

Vincent, C. Paul. *The Politics of Hunger: The Allied Blockade of Germany, 1915–1919*. Athens: Ohio University Press, 1985.

Von Lettow-Vorbeck, [Paul]. *My Reminiscences of East Africa*. London: Hurst and Blackett, 1920.

Vos, Luc De, J. Du Chau, W. Steurbaut, and G. Van Huffel. *Leuven: Ook een Garnizoensstad*. Leuven, Belgium: Peeters, 1989.

Waiser, Bill. *Park Prisoners: The Untold Story of Western Canada's National Parks, 1915–1946*. Saskatoon, Canada: Fifth House Publishers, 1995.

Walker, George. *Venereal Disease in the American Expeditionary Forces*. Baltimore, MD: Medical Standard, 1922.

Walzer, Michael. *Just and Unjust Wars: A Moral Argument with Historical Illustrations*. New York: Basic Books, 1977.

A War Nurse's Diary: Sketches from a Belgian Field Hospital. New York: Macmillan, 1918.

Ward, Alan J. *The Easter Rising: Revolution and Irish Nationalism*, 2nd edition. Wheeling, IL: Harlan Davidson, 2003.

———. "Lloyd George and the 1918 Irish Conscription Crisis." *Historical Journal* 17:1 (March 1974): 107–29.

Watenpaugh, Keith. *Being Modern in the Middle East: Revolution, Nationalism, Colonialism, and the Arab Middle Class*. Princeton, NJ: Princeton University Press, 2006.

Watson, Janet S. K. "Wars in the Wards: The Social Construction of Medical Work in First World War Britain." *Journal of British Studies* 41 (October 2002): 484–510.

Wesseling, H. L. *The European Colonial Empires, 1815–1919*. Translated by Diane Webb. Harlow, Essex: Pearson Longman, 2004.

White, James D. "National Communism and World Revolution: The Political Consequences of German Military Withdrawal from the Baltic Area in 1918–19." *Europe-Asia Studies* 46:8 (1994): 1349–69.

Whitlock, Brand. *Belgium: A Personal Narrative*, volume 2. Toronto: McClelland & Stewart, 1919.

Wiesinger, Otto. *Als Kriegsfreiwilliger in Tsingtau*. Shanghai: Max Nössler, 1915.

Willan, B. P. "The South African Native Labour Contingent, 1916–1918." *Journal of African History* 19:1 (1978): 61–86.

Williams, Nate. "German-Americans in World War I." Western Front Association–Phi Alpha Theta Essay Prize 2001. Available at http://www.wfa-usa.org/new/germanamer.htm.

Wingfield, Nancy M., and Maria Bucur, eds. *Gender and War in Twentieth-Century Eastern Europe*. Bloomington: Indiana University Press, 2006.

Wood, Molly. "Diplomatic Wives: The Politics of Domesticity and the 'Social Game' in the U.S. Foreign Service, 1905–1941." *Journal of Women's History* 17:2 (2005): 142–65.

Woodward, David R. *Hell in the Holy Land: World War I in the Middle East*. Lexington: University Press of Kentucky, 2006.

Woollacott, Angela. *On Her Their Lives Depend: Munition Workers in the Great War*. Berkeley: University of California Press, 1994.

Wyatt, R. J. *Death from the Skies: The Zeppelin Raids over Norfolk*. Norwich: Gliddon Books, 1990.

Yanikdag, Yucel. "Ottoman Prisoners of War in Russia, 1914–22." *Journal of Contemporary History* 34:1 (January 1999): 69–85.

Yockelson, Mitchell A. *Borrowed Soldiers: Americans under British Command*. Norman: University of Oklahoma Press, 2008.

Yovanovitch, Dragolioub. *Les effets économiques et sociaux de la guerre en Serbie*. New Haven, CT: Yale University Press, 1930.

Zeiger, Susan. *In Uncle Sam's Service: Women Workers with the American Expeditionary Force, 1917–1919*. Ithaca, NY: Cornell University Press, 1999.

Ziemann, Benjamin. *War Experiences in Rural Germany, 1914–1923*. Translated by Alex Skinner. Oxford: Berg, 2007.

Živojinović, Dragan. "Serbia and Montenegro: The Home Front, 1914–1918." *War and Society in East Central Europe*, edited by Béla Király and Nándor F. Dreisziger. New York: Columbia University Press, 1985.

Zuckerman, Larry. *The Rape of Belgium: The Untold Story of World War I*. New York: New York University Press, 2004.

Index

About the Author

TAMMY M. PROCTOR is Professor of History at Wittenberg University and author of *Female Intelligence: Women and Espionage in the First World War,* also published by NYU Press, and *Scouting for Girls: A Century of Girl Guides and Girl Scouts* (2009).